The Macintosh
iLife '06

by Jim Heid

**Peachpit
Press**

Avondale
MEDIA

The Macintosh iLife '06
Jim Heid

Peachpit Press
1249 Eighth Street
Berkeley, CA 94710
800/283-9444
510/524-2178
510/524-2221 (fax)
Find us on the Web at: www.peachpit.com
To report errors, please send a note to errata@peachpit.com

Peachpit Press is a division of Pearson Education

Published by Peachpit Press in association with Avondale Media.

Editor: Barbara Assadi, BayCreative
Book Design and Illustration: Arne Hurty, BayCreative
Compositor and Layout Design: Jonathan Woolson, thinkplaydesign
Production Coordinator: Myrna Vladic, Silver Mesa Press
Indexer: FireCrystal Communications
Cover design: Arne Hurty, BayCreative

Portions originally appeared in *Macworld* magazine, © Mac Publishing LLC.

ISBN 0-321-42654-1
9 8 7 6 5 4 3 2
Printed and bound in the United States of America.

For Maryellen,
for my mother,
and in loving memory
of George Heid, my dad.
A master of the analog
hub, he would have
loved this stuff.

George Heid (right), recording direct to disc
on a moving train, in the early 1950s.

About the Author

Jim Heid describes himself as a poster child for iLife: he has been taking photos, making movies, and playing music since he was a kid.

He began writing about personal computers in 1980, when he computerized his home-built ham radio station with a Radio Shack TRS-80 Model I. As Senior Technical Editor of one of the first computer magazines, *Kilobaud Microcomputing*, he began working with Mac prototypes in 1983. He began writing for *Macworld* magazine in 1984, and has been a Contributing Editor ever since. He has also written for *PC World, Internet World,* and *Newsweek* magazines, and wrote a weekly, nationally syndicated technology column for the *Los Angeles Times.*

Jim is a frequent speaker at user groups, conferences, and other events. He has taught at the Kodak Center for Creative Imaging in Camden, Maine, at the University of Hawaii, and at dozens of technology conferences in between.

To satisfy his craving for the latest digital cameras, Jim is a frequent seller on eBay. His interest in eBay led to a book, *Sell it On eBay*, which he coauthored with Toby Malina. *Sell it On eBay* is now in its second edition; to learn more, see www.ebaymatters.com.

Jim lives with his standard poodle and mascot, Sophie, on a windswept headland near Mendocino, California. On most Wednesday evenings, he co-hosts "Point & Click Radio," a weekly computer radio show, which you can listen to at www.kzyx.org/pc.

Acknowledgements

This book wouldn't exist if it weren't for Arne Hurty and Barbara Assadi of San Francisco's BayCreative. You two are a constant inspiration, and I am so happy we are working together.

Jonathan Woolson, principal of thinkplaydesign, crafted the layouts in Adobe InDesign. Your attention to detail staggers. You've done more than make this book gorgeous; you've made it better.

Jeff Carlson, a veteran Mac journalist and managing editor of the legendary TidBITS (www.tidbits.com), sprinted out of the bullpen in the late innings to assist with revisions of the iMovie HD and iDVD chapters. You have a fierce fastball, my friend, and I thank you. And I thank you, Emily Glossbrenner, for the meticulous index.

At Peachpit Press, my thanks to Cliff Colby, Myrna Vladic, Scott Cowlin, Kim Lombardi, Sara Todd, Damon Hampson, Mimi Heft, Marjorie Baer, Nancy Ruenzel, and indeed, to everyone who labors on Eighth Street. You're the best.

My thanks and respect go to the Apple engineers and product managers behind iLife '06. Thanks to Louise Ping, Xander Soren, Greg Scallon, Paul Towner, Grace Kvamme, Josh Fagans, Marc Dubresson, Peter Lowe, and Steve Jobs.

Then there's the home front. Maryellen, I will cherish our love forever. Toby and Judy, thank you for hugs, love, and listening when I've needed them the most. Terry, thank you for forcing me to remember: AABA. I'm honored to play in The Retsyns. Robin and Bruce: I miss you! Bob, my radio buddy: let's do Libby's. And Mimi, Violet, Coco: you're my four-pawed pals.

Another group of friends has provided support and immeasurable amounts of inspiration this past year. Cate, Rita, Sharon, Deborah, Stuart, Laurie, Amy, Karen, Karin, Caitlin, Bruno, Elin, Laura, Shawn, Ken, Chris, Christy, Kelli Craig, Gina, Art, John, Jan, Jinx, Victoria, and Von, among many more. You mean the world to me.

Thanks also to BV and to Laura Ingram; to Keri Walker and Derrick Mains; to Mitch and everyone at MCN; to Pierre, Laura, Chuck, Rennie, and Hope; and to Sophie, my sweet iPoodle.

And to Karmen. Thank you for leaving laughter behind.

Jim Heid

Table of

Contents

Preface to the iLife '06 Edition

The Macintosh iLife '06 is the fifth edition of a book that was originally called *The Macintosh Digital Hub*. The original edition contained about 120 pages and debuted in 2002—before Apple brought iTunes, iPhoto, iMovie, and iDVD under the iLife umbrella. When that happened, in January 2003, the second edition, renamed *The Macintosh iLife*, appeared.

Since then, a new version of iLife—and a new edition of this book—have become an annual adventure. The book has grown to over 400 pages and is the best-selling book on iLife.

It seems that iLife has taken over my life.

And I couldn't be happier. Apple and the Mac are on a roll, thanks in part to the iLife programs. More to the point, I get to spend a healthy (okay, sometimes unhealthy) part of each day listening to music, playing music, taking photos, and making movies: vocations and avocations I've loved since I was a kid.

If you've bought previous editions of this book, thank you and welcome back. If this is your first time here, welcome to a different kind of computer book—a book that uses beautiful design to teach programs that are also beautifully designed.

Welcome to *The Macintosh iLife '06*.

What's New in iLife '06?

Here's a quick recap of the enhancements that Apple added to iLife '06. If you're new to iLife and are unfamiliar with its jargon, don't worry—you'll find everything you need to know in the pages that follow.

iTunes and iPod. Apple's digital music jukebox is better than ever, with more options for buying and playing not only music, but TV shows and other videos, too. And the iPod has evolved to encompass video as well.

iPhoto. iPhoto 6 adds improvements across the board, including the ability to manage far larger photo libraries, and new editing features. You can now design and produce beautiful photo calendars and greeting cards, and if you subscribe to Apple's .Mac service, you can share photos using cutting-edge photocasts.

iMovie HD. Macs are always getting faster, and iMovie HD 6 takes advantage of this to display real-time previews of effects and transitions. For adding visual sizzle to your movies, iMovie HD includes motion-graphics themes that you can customize. Other enhancements include the ability to work in multiple projects at once and new audio filters and effects.

iDVD. iDVD 6 brings new menu design themes, a streamlined user interface, and support for widescreen video. And the new Magic iDVD feature lets you assemble a DVD faster than ever.

GarageBand. iLife's digital recording studio is now a radio studio, too, with features that make producing podcasts easier than ever. You can also bring QuickTime movies into GarageBand to add music soundtracks and audio enhancements.

iWeb. A new addition to iLife, iWeb lets you create Web sites, complete with blogs and podcasts. A set of design templates gives you a head start; customize them as needed.

How the Book Works

This book devotes a separate section to each of the iLife '06 programs: iTunes and iPod for listening to music; iPhoto for photography; iMovie HD for video editing; iDVD for creating DVD-Video discs, GarageBand for making music, and iWeb for creating Web sites. Each section is a series of two-page spreads, and each spread is a self-contained reference that covers one topic.

Most spreads begin with an introduction that sets the stage with an overview of the topic.

Many spreads refer to this book's companion Web site, where you can get updates and more information.

The Book, the Web Site

There's just one thing this book doesn't cover: tomorrow. The iLife scene is always evolving as new programs and new developments change the way we work with digital media.

That's why this book also has a companion Web site: www. macilife.com. At this site, you'll find links to the products discussed in the book as well as tips and news items, updates, and reviews of iLife-related products.

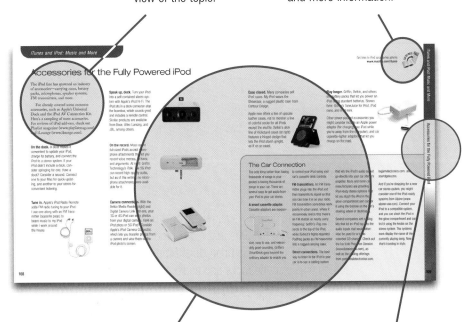

Here's the main course of each spread, where you'll find instructions, background information, and tips.

The section and spread names appear on the edges of the pages to allow you to quickly flip to specific topics.

Personal Computers Get Personal

Music, photographs, and movies can inspire, amuse, persuade, and entertain. They're time machines that recall people and places. They're vehicles that carry messages into the future. They're ingrained in infancy and become intensely personal parts of our lives. And they've all gone digital.

It's now possible to carry a music library in your pocket, to take photos without film, and to edit video in your den—or on a cross-country flight. It's easier than ever to combine music, images, and video. And it's easy to share your finished product, whether with loved ones in the living room, clients in a conference room, or a global audience on the Internet.

Behind this digital age are breakthroughs in storage technologies, processor speed, chip design, and even in the types of connectors and interfaces used to attach external gear. In the past, personal computers weren't powerful enough to manage the billions of bits that make up digital media. Today, they are.

You might say that personal computers have finally become powerful enough to become truly personal.

Audio

1972	1979	1982	1988	1989
Nippon Columbia Company begins digitally recording master tapes.	Sony's Walkman is the first portable music player.	Billy Joel's *52nd Street* is the first album released on CD.	CDs outsell vinyl albums for the first time.	MP3 audio compression scheme is patented.

Imaging

1969	1991	1992	1994	1997
Bell Labs researchers invent the charge-coupled device (CCD).	Kodak adapts Nikon F-3 camera with 1.3-megapixel CCD.	Kodak's Photo-CD system puts scanned images on CDs.	Apple's QuickTake 100 camera debuts at $699.	The Associated Press switches to digital photography.

Video

1956	1967	1975	1983	1991
First videotaped TV program is broadcast.	Sony delivers first portable videotape recorder.	Bell Labs demonstrates CCD TV camera. Sony Betamax debuts.	Sony's Betamovie is the first one-piece camcorder.	Apple's QuickTime 1.0 brings digital video to the Macintosh.

Storage

1956	1973	1980	1984	1992
IBM disk system holds 5 megabytes and uses disks two feet wide.	First hard disk: 30MB on an 8-inch disk platter.	Philips and Sony develop the compact disc standard.	First Mac hard disks store 5MB and cost over $2500.	Apple includes CD-ROM drives with Macs.

1996
Fraunhofer releases MP3 encoder and player for Windows PCs.

1999
Napster and other Internet services enable swapping of MP3 files.

2001
Apple introduces iPod. First copy-protected audio CDs appear amid controversy.

2003
iTunes Music Store debuts for Macs and Windows.

2004
Internet radio shows called podcasts begin to proliferate.

2005
iTunes Music Store ranks among the top ten music retailers for the first time.

2006
Apple adds podcast-production features to GarageBand 3.

Truly Personal Computing

1998
1-megapixel cameras proliferate. Online photo sites offer prints and other services.

1999
2-megapixel cameras, led by Nikon's $999 Coolpix 950, are the rage.

2000
3-megapixel cameras add movie modes. Digital cameras represent 18 percent of camera sales.

2001
Consumer cameras hit 4 megapixels. Digital cameras comprise 21 percent of camera market.

2002
Apple introduces iPhoto. Consumer cameras reach 5 megapixels.

2004
8-megapixel cameras appear as digital cameras outsell film cameras for the first time.

2006
Consumer cameras reach 10 megapixels. Nikon discontinues most of its film cameras and lenses.

1994
miniDV format debuts: digital audio and video on 6.3 mm wide tape.

1995
FireWire, invented by Apple in the early 90s, is adopted as industry standard.

1999
Apple builds FireWire into Macs and releases iMovie 1.0.

2001
Apple wins Primetime Emmy Engineering Award for FireWire.

2003
Sony, Canon, and others announce HDV high-definition standard.

2005
iPod gains video playback. Apple sells videos through iTunes.

2006
HD cameras begin to drop in price.

1993
A 1.4GB hard drive costs $4559.

1995
DVD standard is announced.

1999
IBM MicroDrive puts 340MB on a coin-sized platter.

2001
5GB Toshiba hard drive uses 1.8-inch platter; Apple builds it into the new iPod.

2001
Apple begins building SuperDrive DVD burners into Macs.

2005
Some Macs include dual-layer SuperDrives capable of burning over 8GB.

2006
Apple introduces 1GB iPod nano.

A Sampling of the Possibilities

This technological march of progress is exciting because it enables us to do new things with age-old media. I've already hinted at some of them: carrying a music library with you on a portable player, shooting photographs with a digital camera, and editing digital movies.

But the digital age isn't about simply replacing vinyl records, Instamatic cameras, and Super 8 movies. What makes digital technology significant is that it lets you combine various media into messages that are uniquely yours. You can tell stories, sell products, educate, or entertain.

And when you combine these various elements, the whole becomes greater than the sum of its parts.

Go Digital

Pictures That Move

The latest digital video formats have transformed video for amateurs and professionals alike. Shoot sparkling video with stereo sound using a camcorder that fits in the palm of your hand. Transfer your footage to the Mac, then edit to tell your story.

Forget Film

Use a digital camera just once, and you'll never want to go back to film. Review your shots instantly. Delete the ones you don't want. Transfer the keepers to your Mac, and then share them—through the Internet, through CDs and DVDs, and much more.

Bring It All Together

Create for the future.
Produce a book that commemorates a baby's first year.

Preserve the past.
Relive a vacation with pictures, video, and sound.

Become a digital DJ.
Assemble a music library and create music mixes that play back your favorites. Then take it all on the road.

Start a show.
Create an audio or video podcast containing rants, raves, business tips— you name it.

Tell a story.
Interview relatives and create a multimedia family history.

Promote yourself.
Create a DVD or Web portfolio of your design work or photography.

Educate.
Create a training video that teaches a new skill or lets people see your product in action.

Create a journal.
Publish a blog containing ongoing opinions, tips, or vacation dispatches.

Compose yourself.
Record your own original music, then use it in your video and DVD productions.

Tell the world.
Create a Web site about your family, company, vacation, or favorite cause.

Where the Mac Fits In

All of today's personal computers have fast processors, fat hard drives, and the other trappings of power. But powerful hardware is only a foundation. Software is what turns that box of chips into a jukebox, a digital darkroom, a movie studio, a recording studio, and a soapbox with a global audience.

Software is what really makes the Macintosh digital hub go around. Each of Apple's iLife programs—iTunes for music, iPhoto for photography, iMovie HD for video editing, iDVD for creating DVDs, GarageBand for recording music, iWeb for creating Web sites—greatly simplifies working with, creating, and combining digital media.

Similar programs are available for PCs running Microsoft Windows. But they aren't included with every PC, and they lack the design elegance and simplicity of Apple's offerings. It's simple: Apple's iLife has made the Mac the best personal computer for digital media.

iWeb

· Create Web sites and publish them on Apple's .Mac service

· Publish photo albums from iPhoto

· Publish movies from iMovie HD

· Create and maintain Web journals (blogs)

· Publish podcasts from GarageBand

iMovie HD

· Capture video from camcorders

· Edit video and create titles and effects

· Add music soundtracks from iTunes

· Add photographs from iPhoto

· Share video through tapes, DVDs, or the Web

iDVD

· Create slide shows from iPhoto images

· Add music soundtracks from iTunes

· Present video created in iMovie HD

· Distribute files in DVD-ROM format

GarageBand

- Create songs by assembling loops
- Connect a keyboard to play and record software instruments
- Record vocals, acoustic instruments, and electric guitars
- Create podcasts and add soundtracks to movies
- Transfer your productions to iTunes or iWeb

iTunes

- Convert music CDs into digital music files
- Organize songs into playlists, and burn CDs
- Shop for music, videos, and audiobooks at the iTunes Music Store
- Transfer music to portable players
- Listen to Internet radio, podcasts, and audiobooks

iPod Family

- Carry your favorite songs with you
- Synchronize with your iTunes music library
- Connect to stereo system or car audio adapter
- Store contacts, calendars, photos, video, and more

iPhoto

- Import photos from digital cameras
- Organize photos into albums
- Crop, modify, and print photos
- Share photos via photocasts
- Order prints, calendars, cards, and books

No Medium is an Island

Combining multiple media is a key part of audio-visual storytelling—even silent films had soundtracks played on mighty Wurlitzer theater organs.

Combining media is easy with the iLife programs. There's no need to plod through export and import chores to move, say, a photograph from iPhoto into iMovie HD. That's because the iLife programs have media browsers that make it easy to access your music, photos, and movies. The media browsers also have Search boxes to help you find the music track, photo, or movie you want.

You can also move items between programs by simply dragging them. Drag a photo from iPhoto into iMovie HD, iWeb, GarageBand, or iDVD. Drag a music track from iTunes into iPhoto, iMovie HD, or iDVD. And when you've finished a hot tune in GarageBand, add it to your iTunes music library with a click of the mouse.

These lines of communication extend beyond iLife, too. For example, Apple's iWork programs also provide media browsers that make it easy to add photos, music, and movies to documents and presentations.

The iLife programs work together in other ways, which I'll describe as we go. In the meantime, think about ways to marry your media and tell a stronger story.

Feel free to browse.
With the media browser (iWeb's is shown here), it's easy to access—and combine—audio, photos, and movies.

Global delivery. Use iWeb and a .Mac subscription to share your iLife creations on the World Wide Web.

Now playing: you. Use iDVD to burn your creations to DVD discs that you can watch on TV.

iLife Keeps You Connected

It's no secret that the Internet is a great way to stay current—with news, family, and anything else you find interesting.

A relatively new Internet technology makes it even easier to stay current with subjects of interest. It's called *RSS*, and it allows you to *subscribe* to information, called *feeds*, from Web sites and other Internet sources.

Say your hometown newspaper is called *The Banner*, and you're interested in keeping tabs on it. If the newspaper provides an RSS feed, you can subscribe to the feed using the latest versions of Apple's Safari browser or a separate *newsreader* program, such as NetNewsWire (www.ranchero.com).

After you've subscribed to a feed, it's updated at regular intervals—for example, every 30 minutes in Safari. Want to see what's new in the hometown? There's no need to go *The Banner*'s home page. Simply check your RSS feed in Safari. RSS brings the news to you.

What does all this have to do with iLife? Apple has built RSS into several of the iLife programs. As a result, you can subscribe to audio content, you can publish and subscribe to photos, and you can create Web journals (called *blogs*) to which others can subscribe.

I'll cover the details behind RSS and how it relates to iLife '06 throughout this book. Here's an overview of how iLife '06 and RSS work together to keep you current.

Subscribe to Podcasts

A new kind of Internet radio program, the *podcast*, is all the rage. iTunes is your gateway to thousands of podcasts. When you subscribe to a favorite podcast, iTunes downloads new episodes for you whenever they become available.

Use Safari RSS or a newsreader program? Don't forget to subscribe to the feed for this book's companion site at **www.macilife.com**

Publish and Subscribe to Photocasts

Keep friends and family current with your favorite photos by publishing photocasts of your favorite iPhoto albums. Use an optional password to keep your photos private if you like.

Know someone who's published a photocast? Use iPhoto to subscribe to it. The remote photos appear as though they were stored on your Mac, and when the photocast is updated, the latest photos appear in your iPhoto. It can be a lot more fun than emailing photos back and forth.

Publish Audio and Video Podcasts

Use GarageBand and iMovie HD to create audio or video podcasts, then use iWeb to publish them via Apple's .Mac service so that others can subscribe to them.

Create Your Own Blog

Create an online journal: a vacation travelogue, a diary, or daily tips for your business clients. Create it in iWeb, then publish it via Apple's .Mac Internet service. iWeb automatically creates an RSS feed for you, enabling others to subscribe to your blog.

What Does RSS Stand For?

RSS is YACA: yet another computer acronym. Some say it stands for *really simple syndication* while others maintain it stands for *rich site summary*. It doesn't matter. Just as you don't need to know what DVD stands for in order to create or play one, you don't need to know what RSS stands for to enjoy its benefits.

Putting the Pieces Together

Software is important, but so is hardware. Several aspects of the Mac's hardware make it ideally suited to digital media work. All Macs contain fast processors and copious hard drives—essential ingredients for storing and manipulating digital media.

Another factor in the hardware equation is ports: the connection schemes used to attach external devices, such as portable music players, digital cameras, camcorders, printers, and speakers. Every Mac contains all the ports necessary for connecting these and other add-ons.

And finally, the Mac's hardware and software work together smoothly and reliably. This lets you concentrate on your creations, not on your connections.

Here's a quick reference to the ports and connectors you'll use in your journey through iLife.

Audio Line Out

Standard 3.5 mm stereo minijack connects to headphones, amplifiers, and other audio equipment.

On the iMac shown here, this connector also provides optical digital audio output for connection to home theater and stereo systems (see page 72). Power Mac G5 systems provide a separate digital audio output.

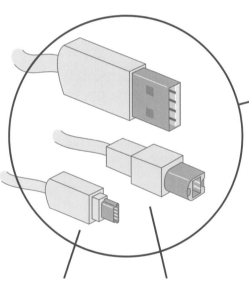

Universal Serial Bus (USB)

Connects to digital cameras, scanners, some speaker systems, microphones, printers, some music keyboards and interfaces, and other add-ons.

Many digital cameras use this miniature USB connector.

Many printers, scanners, and USB hard drives use this type of connector.

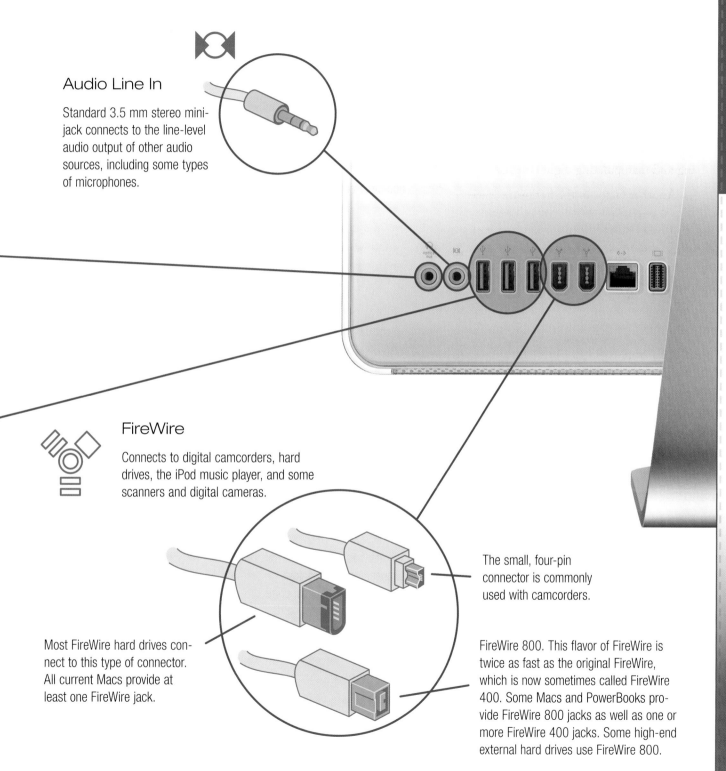

Audio Line In

Standard 3.5 mm stereo mini-jack connects to the line-level audio output of other audio sources, including some types of microphones.

FireWire

Connects to digital camcorders, hard drives, the iPod music player, and some scanners and digital cameras.

The small, four-pin connector is commonly used with camcorders.

Most FireWire hard drives connect to this type of connector. All current Macs provide at least one FireWire jack.

FireWire 800. This flavor of FireWire is twice as fast as the original FireWire, which is now sometimes called FireWire 400. Some Macs and PowerBooks provide FireWire 800 jacks as well as one or more FireWire 400 jacks. Some high-end external hard drives use FireWire 800.

Outfitting Your Mac for Digital Media

The digital lifestyle is many things, but inexpensive is not one of them. iPods, cameras, camcorders, music keyboards, microphones, accessories of all kinds—spending opportunities abound. Just ask my credit cards.

I explore many of these buying opportunities throughout this book. But first, it's important to ensure that your Mac is well equipped for your iLife endeavors.

With their built-in USB and FireWire ports, today's Macs are able to connect to cameras, portable music players, camcorders, and other digital devices.

But there's always room to grow, especially where digital media are concerned. To get the most out of iLife, consider upgrading several key components of your Mac. At right is a shopping list.

And if you're outfitting an older Mac for iLife '06, consider throwing in a copy of the latest version of Mac OS X. The iLife '06 programs run on Mac OS X 10.3.9, but some iPhoto, iMovie HD, GarageBand features require a more recent flavor—10.4.4 or a later version.

To learn more about the latest version of Mac OS X, see www.apple.com/macosx.

Storage in Two Flavors

Digital media takes up space—lots of it. Upgrading your Mac's storage capacity is an essential first step in outfitting it for digital media.

Memory Upgrade. Adding memory is a great way to boost any Mac's overall performance. On a Mac with insufficient memory, programs run slowly, particularly if you're trying to run several at once. Each of the iLife programs can benefit from plenty of memory, but GarageBand in particular will appreciate it.

With all current Mac models, you can install a memory upgrade yourself. If you have a Mac mini, Apple recommends having memory installed by a qualified technician. But if you have dexterous hands and a modicum of bravery, you can do the job yourself.

How much memory should you add? As much as you can afford. I consider 512 megabytes (MB) to be a bare minimum for the iLife programs; a gigabyte (1GB) or more is better. Memory is relatively inexpensive, especially compared to the performance benefits it provides—aim high and upgrade to a total of at least 1GB.

Hard Drive. All digital media eat up disk space—except for video, which utterly devours it. If you're serious about digital media, you'll want to expand your Mac's storage.

It's easy to do. If you have a tower-style Mac, you can install a second hard drive inside the Mac's case. For iMacs, Mac minis, and laptops, you can connect an external FireWire hard drive—or several of them, if you like.

External FireWire hard drives are available in a wide range of capacities and case sizes. Portable drives are particularly convenient: they fit in a shirt pocket and can draw power from a Mac's FireWire jack—no separate power supply needed. On the downside, though, portable drives cost more than conventional external drives, and they tend to be slower—a big drawback for GarageBand, which greatly benefits from a fast hard drive.

Digital Hubs

The Mac's FireWire connectors are durable, but they aren't indestructible. All that plugging and unplugging of camcorders, hard drives, and other doodads can take its toll. What's more, some Macs have just one FireWire connector, limiting the number of devices you can connect directly to the Mac.

A FireWire hub is an inexpensive add-on that addresses both issues. A hub is to FireWire what a power strip is to a wall outlet: it provides more jacks for your devices. After connecting the hub to your Mac, you can connect several devices to the hub.

You can also buy USB hubs that provide the same expansion benefits for USB devices. Belkin (www.belkin.com) is a major supplier of hubs and accessories of all kinds.

The Right Accounts

In order to buy music from the iTunes Music Store and order prints and more with iPhoto, you'll want an Apple Account. It's easy to set up; see page 30.

If you're serious about living the iLife, take the next step and subscribe to Apple's .Mac service. Currently $99 per year, .Mac enables you to create photocasts with iPhoto as well as Web sites with iWeb. You'll also be able to access Apple's iDisk remote storage service, where you'll find lots of software downloads.

To sign up for .Mac, go to www.mac.com. Unsure whether .Mac is for you? Sign up for a free trial membership.

Sounding Better: Speaker Options

Alfred Hitchcock once said, "In radio, sound is a rather important element." That understatement also applies to iLife. Whether listening to music or creating a narration for a movie, you'll want to hear more sound than your Mac's built-in speaker can reproduce.

You have options aplenty. If your Mac and stereo system are close to each other, you can connect them with a cable and listen through your speakers. You can also use Apple's AirPort Express Base Station to wirelessly beam audio to your stereo. For details on these options, see page 72.

When working at your Mac, you'll want speakers that are directly adjacent to your display. This delivers the most realistic stereo field—and that's essential whether you're mixing a song in GarageBand or just wanting to enjoy your favorite tunes while you type.

Several companies sell speaker systems designed for use with computers. Harman Multimedia (www.harman-multimedia.com) sells a large selection under the venerable Harman/Kardon and JBL names. Another highly regarded audio brand, Bose (www.bose.com), also sells speaker systems designed for computers and portable music players. Most systems include a *subwoofer* that sits under your desk and provides a deep, gut-punching bass.

If you're a GarageBand musician, you might prefer a set of *monitor* speakers, whose frequency response is superior to that of typical computer speakers. For my GarageBand setup, I use a pair of Yamaha MSP5 monitors. At about $500 a pair, they're pricey by computer speaker standards, but inexpensive by studio monitor standards. And they sound great—beefier and truer than a pair of inexpensive computer speakers and a subwoofer. For reviews of numerous monitor speakers, see www.emusician.com/speakers.

iTunes and iPod:
Music and More

The Macintosh
iLife '06

iTunes at a Glance

iTunes is your gateway to music, audio-books, Internet radio programs, TV shows, and much more.

With iTunes, you can create digital music files from your favorite audio CDs. You can buy and download music, videos, and more from the iTunes Music Store. You can create your own music mixes by creating playlists. And you can listen to your playlists on your Mac, burn them onto CDs, or transfer them to an iPod portable music player.

When iTunes debuted in 2001, it was a relatively simple digital music jukebox. Since then, iTunes has evolved into the computer industry's leading gateway to digital media. Indeed, in 2005, the iTunes Music Store was the seventh-ranked music retailer in the United States—ahead of giants such as Tower Records and Sam Goody—and it was the first time an online music service ever appeared among the top ten.

With the runaway success of the iPod family and with Apple continuing to add new forms of media to the iTunes Music Store, iTunes seems poised to remain the dominant digital jukebox.

Anybody have a quarter?

The arrow buttons skip to the previous or next song in a playlist.

Play/Pause (keyboard shortcut: spacebar).

Adjusts the volume (keyboard shortcut: ⌘-up arrow and ⌘-down arrow).

The iTunes library holds all your music, podcasts, and videos.

Manage podcasts to which you've subscribed (page 36).

Access videos that you've bought or added to your library (page 34).

Use the Party Shuffle playlist to have iTunes quickly create a mix for you (page 76).

Listen to Internet radio stations (page 66).

Shop at the iTunes Music Store (page 30).

Add songs to playlists to control their playback order and create your own music mixes. Use smart playlists (⚙) to have iTunes create playlists for you.

Learn the latest. Of the six iLife programs, iTunes is updated most frequently. That's where the Web comes in—you'll find updates to this section at www.macilife.com/itunes.

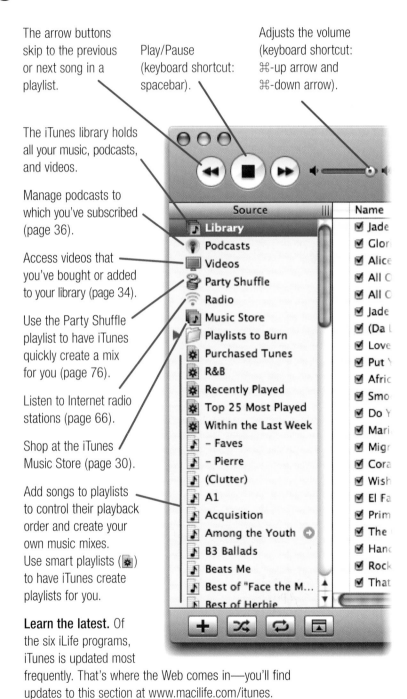

Click this tiny button to switch between song information and a flashy animation.

Share your playlists with iMix playlist publishing (page 48).

To view the song's album, click the artist name.

Drag the diamond left or right to scan through a song.

Display related songs in the iTunes Music Store (page 32) or your library (page 55).

To quickly locate the currently playing song, click the SnapBack button (page 75).

Use the Browse button to view your music by artist and album (page 55).

Use the Search box to quickly locate songs (page 54).

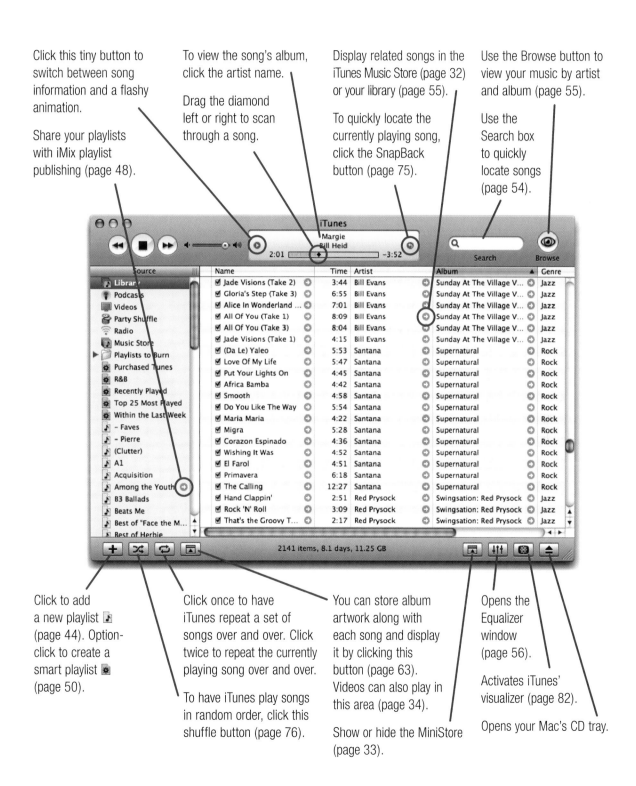

Click to add a new playlist (page 44). Option-click to create a smart playlist (page 50).

Click once to have iTunes repeat a set of songs over and over. Click twice to repeat the currently playing song over and over.

To have iTunes play songs in random order, click this shuffle button (page 76).

You can store album artwork along with each song and display it by clicking this button (page 63). Videos can also play in this area (page 34).

Show or hide the MiniStore (page 33).

Opens the Equalizer window (page 56).

Activates iTunes' visualizer (page 82).

Opens your Mac's CD tray.

19

Importing Music from CDs

The first step in stocking your digital juke-box will probably involve bringing in music from your audio CDs. Apple calls this process *importing*, but most digital music fans refer to it as *ripping* (from the Latin, meaning "to rip off").

Whatever you call this process, iTunes is good at it. Insert a compact disc into your Mac's CD drive, and iTunes launches, connects to the Internet, and retrieves the name of the CD and its tracks. Click the Import CD button, and iTunes converts the CD's contents into digital music files that are stored on your Mac's hard drive.

That's the big picture. You can create a vast digital music library with iTunes without having to know any more than that. But iTunes has several features that give you more control over the ripping process. You can, for example, specify that iTunes import only certain songs—no need to waste disk space by storing songs you don't like.

And as I describe on the following pages, you can choose to store your digital music library in a variety of formats, each with its own advantages and drawbacks. But don't feel obligated to delve into those details if you don't want to. Feel free to skip on to page 30 after you've mastered the ripping two-step: insert CD, click Import CD.

Just want to play a CD instead of ripping it? Click the play button or double-click on any track.

Indicates which songs to rip. Don't like some songs? Uncheck their boxes, and iTunes will not import them.

Tip: To uncheck all tracks, press ⌘ while clicking on a track's check box (☑).

Rips all tracks with check marks before their names.

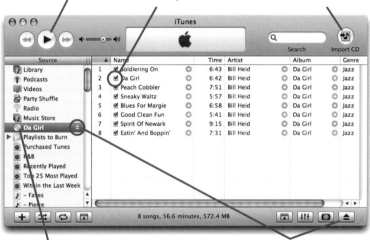

Shows the currently inserted CD.

Ejects the CD.

Joining Tracks to Eliminate Gaps

In some cases, you might not want a gap of silence between songs. For example, the songs on a CD might be composed so that one flows seamlessly into the next.

iTunes indicates joined tracks with a bracket.

You can prevent gaps between two or more songs by importing the songs as joined tracks. Select the tracks, then choose Join CD Tracks from the Advanced menu. iTunes will import the tracks as one file. If you decide to not join the tracks after all, choose Unjoin CD Tracks from the Advanced menu.

Note that you can't join tracks that you've already imported.

How iTunes Retrieves Track Names

Back in the late 1970s, when the compact disc standard was being developed, no one foresaw the iLife era. As a result, the developers of the CD standard didn't create a way for CDs to store artist, album, and track names.

So how can iTunes retrieve this information? The answer lies in the fact that no two audio CDs are the exact same length. A CD is comprised of a specific number of blocks, each of which is one seventy-fifth of a second long. You might say that every CD has its own unique digital fingerprint.

In 1996, some clever programmers in Berkeley, California, realized they could create a database that would link these fingerprints to specific information. The compact disc database, or CDDB, was born. Soon, CDDB spawned a company, Gracenote, which provides disc-lookup features to Apple and other companies that have digital music products.

When you insert a CD, iTunes calculates its digital fingerprint and then sends it over the Internet to Gracenote's server. If Gracenote finds a match, it transmits the corresponding information back to iTunes, which displays it.

Just how big is Gracenote's database? As of 2006, it contained more than 4 million CDs, representing over 55 million songs. That's even bigger than my iTunes library.

Incidentally, the audio CD specification now contains provisions for storing track information on a CD. It's called "CD-Text," but its support in the music industry is spotty. Sony has been including CD-Text information on its releases for several years, but many record labels don't support it.

Power Ripping: Changing CD Insert Preferences

Doing some binge ripping? Save yourself time and set up iTunes to automatically begin importing as soon as you insert a CD. Choose Preferences from the iTunes menu, then click the Advanced button. Next, click the Importing button. Finally, jump down to the On CD Insert pop-up menu and choose Import Songs or, better yet, Import Songs and Eject.

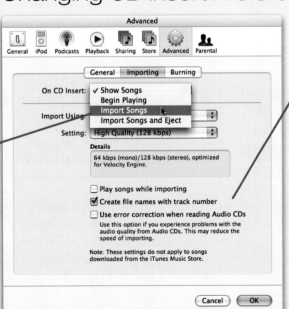

Customize the way iTunes imports CDs (see the following pages).

Choosing an Audio Format

The factory settings that iTunes uses for importing music are perfectly fine for most music lovers and listening scenarios. So if you'd rather explore some of the more musical and less technical aspects of iTunes, feel free to skip to page 30. But if you're an audiophile or are just curious, read on for a look at how audio compression works—and at how you can adjust the way iTunes applies it.

CD-quality stereo sound requires about 10MB of disk space per minute. By using *compression*, iTunes can lower audio's appetite for storage by a factor of 10 or more. Most audio-compression schemes use something called *perceptual encoding*, which eliminates those portions of an audio signal that our ears don't hear well anyway. Because some information is lost in the process, this form of compression is called *lossy*.

iTunes supports two lossy compression schemes: MP3, the format that helped fuel the Internet music revolution; and a newer method called AAC (short for *Advanced Audio Coding*). Each scheme has advantages and drawbacks.

iTunes also offers a lossless compression scheme called *Apple Lossless* encoding. It doesn't provide nearly as much compression as MP3 or AAC—files are only about half the size of the original. But true to its name, Apple Lossless imposes no quality loss. If you're a golden-eared audiophile with plenty of hard-drive space, you might prefer to rip your CDs using the Apple Lossless encoder.

Changing Importing Settings

From the factory, iTunes is set up to encode in AAC format. By adjusting the Importing options in the Preferences dialog box, you can change the encoding settings to arrive at your own ideal balance between sound quality, storage requirements, and listening plans.

Step 1. Choose Preferences from the iTunes menu.

Step 2. Click the Advanced button.

Step 3. In the Advanced preferences area, click the Importing button.

Encoder Options at a Glance

Encoder	Comments
AAC	Best balance between sound quality and small file size.
MP3	Not as efficient as AAC, but broadly compatible with non-Apple portable players and computer systems.
Apple Lossless	Creates much larger files than the MP3 or AAC encoders, but with no audio quality loss. Files won't play on iPod shuffle or older iPods.
WAV and AIFF	Create uncompressed files that use 10MB of disk space per minute. (AIFF, which stands for Audio Interchange File Format, is a standard audio format on the Mac; WAV is its equivalent on Windows. Both formats are broadly supported on Macs and Windows computers.)

Step 4. Adjust importing settings as shown below.

Fine-tune compression settings (page 24).

If you plan to burn MP3-format CDs, consider checking this box (page 60).

If a song that you've imported has audible pops or clicks, consider checking this box and then importing the song again.

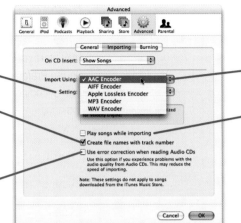

Specify how you'd like iTunes to rip your CDs.

Want to listen while you rip? Check this box.

AAC: More Bang for the Byte

You want the storage efficiency that a lossy encoder provides. Should you rip your CDs using the AAC encoder or the MP3 encoder? If you'll always use iTunes, an iPod, and the other iLife programs to play music, by all means use AAC—I do. But if you anticipate transferring tunes between computers or non-Apple portable players, use MP3.

Here's why. Audio compression is measured in terms of *bit rate*, the average number of bits required for one second of sound. To obtain near CD-quality audio, MP3 requires a bit rate in the range of 128 to 192 kilobits

per second (kbps). Higher bit rates mean less compression and better sound quality.

AAC is more efficient than MP3—it does a smarter job of encoding music, which means you can use lower bit rates and still get great sound quality. Audiophiles love to argue the fine points, but to most ears, a 128 kbps AAC file sounds at least as good as an MP3 file encoded at 160 kbps.

What does this mean to you? If you use AAC when importing CDs, you'll use disk space more efficiently. This can help you

shoehorn a mammoth music library onto an iPod.

The downside to AAC? Your music files will be less compatible with other music software and hardware. MP3 is supported by every music program, personal computer, and portable music player; AAC isn't.

There's one more reason you might consider using MP3 instead of AAC. If you plan to burn CDs in MP3 format as described on page 60, you should rip your music in MP3 format.

Any Mac with version 6.4 or later of QuickTime can play AAC

audio. For best compatibility with all of the iLife '06 programs, use QuickTime 7.0.4 or a later version, if available. You can also play AAC audio on a Windows computer after installing QuickTime for Windows, which is included with iTunes for Windows.

One more thing. As page 30 describes, the iTunes Music Store delivers its tracks in AAC format. The AAC music you buy contains some copying restrictions. But AAC files that you rip from your own CDs contain no such restrictions.

Fine-Tuning Compression Settings

Adjusting MP3 Settings

iTunes is set up to encode MP3 at a bit rate of 160 kbps. To change the bit rate and other MP3 settings, choose Custom from the Setting pop-up menu.

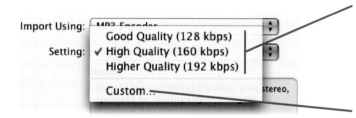

128 kbps is closer to FM-radio quality than to CD quality—you may notice a swirling quality to instruments that produce high frequencies, such as strings and cymbals. 192 kbps delivers better quality than 160 kbps, although my ears have trouble detecting the difference.

To explore the kinds of adjustments MP3 allows for, choose Custom to display the dialog box shown below. See below for custom setting choices.

Variable bit rate (VBR) encoding varies a song's bit rate according to the complexity of the sound. For example, a quiet passage with a narrow range of frequencies is less "demanding" than a loud passage with a broad range of frequencies. VBR uses disk space more efficiently and, according to many MP3 fans, sounds better, too. Many MP3 users turn on VBR and then lower the bit rate—for example, encoding at 128 kbps with VBR instead of at 160 kbps without VBR.

Restores iTunes' original settings.

iTunes will filter out inaudible, low frequencies. Leave this one checked.

Specify the bit rate here.

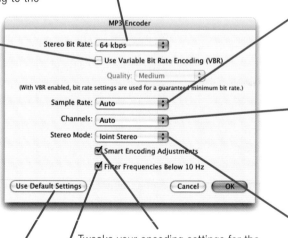

Tweaks your encoding settings for the best quality given the bit rate settings you've specified. You can usually leave this box checked, but if you're a control freak who doesn't want iTunes making adjustments for you, uncheck it.

For most uses, leave this menu set to Auto. If you're encoding a voice recording, however, you can save disk space by lowering the sample rate to 22.050 KHz or even 11.025 KHz.

In the Auto setting, iTunes detects whether the original recording is in stereo or mono. To force iTunes to encode in mono—for example, to save disk space—choose Mono.

Our ears have trouble discerning where high frequencies are coming from. Joint Stereo encoding exploits this phenomenon by combining high frequencies into a single channel, saving disk space. Careful listeners say they can sometimes hear a difference in the spatial qualities of a recording.

Adjusting AAC Settings

iTunes is set up to encode AAC at a bit rate of 128 kbps. To change the bit rate, choose Custom from the Setting pop-up menu, then choose the desired bit rate.

Some audiophiles say VBR improves audio quality. Let your ears be the judge. (For an overview of VBR, see the opposite page.)

Filters the audio to enhance voice recordings. Avoid this option for music.

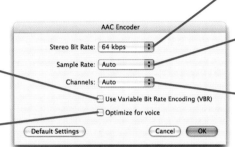

Choose the desired bit rate. Lower bit rates yield smaller files and poorer sound quality.

You can choose a 44.1 KHz or 48 KHz sample rate. Use the Auto setting: iTunes encodes to match the original recording.

You can choose to encode in mono or stereo. Use the Auto setting: iTunes detects whether the original recording is monophonic or stereophonic, and encodes to match.

Converting from MP3 to AAC and Apple Lossless

iTunes can convert existing MP3s to AAC, but you'll lose quality in the process. That's because both AAC and MP3 are lossy formats: each discards audio information in order to save disk space. Thus, when an MP3 file is compressed with AAC, the lossiness is compounded.

Bottom line: to take advantage of AAC's space savings, re-rip your original CDs instead of recompressing existing MP3s.

This re-ripping requirement also applies if you want to take advantage of the Apple Lossless encoder. You can't convert an MP3 (or an AAC) file into Apple Lossless and gain the quality benefits of the latter—the sonic damage has already been done.

iTunes has some smarts that make re-ripping less laborious: if you re-rip a CD that iTunes already has in its library, iTunes tells you that the songs have already been imported and asks if you want to import them again. Thus, you're spared from having to rebuild your playlists, retype any song information, or manually delete your old MP3s.

Note: If you've edited a song's information—changed its name or that of the artist or album as described on page 28 —iTunes won't recognize that you're importing it again, and you'll end up with two copies of the same song.

To avoid this, make the same edits before you import the CD, or edit the song information of the existing MP3s to match that of the audio CD. Or just make a mental note to delete the old MP3 files after re-ripping.

To replace the existing MP3 version, click Replace Existing.

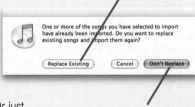

To import the CD without replacing the MP3 versions, click Don't Replace. You'll end up with two versions of each song.

How Audio Compression Works

You don't have to understand how audio compression works in order to use iTunes, but you might wonder how an MP3 or AAC file can be roughly one-tenth the size of an uncompressed audio file and still sound nearly the same.

MP3's origins go back to the 1980s, when researchers began exploring ways to reduce the storage requirements of digital audio. One of the standards that came from these efforts was MPEG (Moving Picture Experts Group) Audio Layer III—MP3 for short.

AAC is a newer kid on the block. Conceptually, AAC and MP3 are very similar: both reduce the storage requirements of sound by "shaving off" audio information that our ears have trouble hearing. But scientists have learned a lot about audio compression and human hearing in the decades since MP3 was created, and AAC takes advantage of these breakthroughs to provide better sound quality at smaller file sizes.

As for the Apple Lossless encoder, it doesn't "shave off" any audio information. Instead, it uses compression techniques that are similar to those of a file archiving program such as StuffIt. You don't save nearly as much space, but there's no loss in sound quality either.

Will your ears be able to tell the difference? Do some tests and find out. One thing is certain: your hard drive and your iPod will know the difference. Apple Lossless files require dramatically more storage space than AAC or MP3 files.

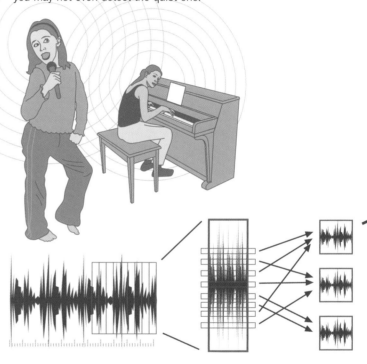

The uncompressed audio on a CD contains more information than our ears can detect. For example, if a loud sound and a quiet one reach your ears simultaneously, you may not even detect the quiet one.

An encoder's first step is to break the original audio into a series of *frames*, each a fraction of a second in length.

The encoder further breaks down each frame into *sub-bands* in order to determine how bits will need to be allocated to best represent the audio signal.

The encoder compares the sub-bands to *psychoacoustics tables*, which mathematically describe the characteristics of human hearing. This comparison process, along with the bit rate that you've chosen for encoding, determines what portion of the original audio signal will be cut and what portion will survive.

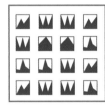

Finally, the encoded data is further compressed by about 20 percent using *Huffman* compression, which replaces redundant pieces of data with shorter codes. You do the same thing every time you say "a dozen eggs" instead of saying "egg" twelve times.

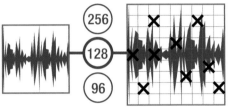

Where iTunes Stores Your Tunes

iTunes stores your music library in your Music folder. The fastest way to locate the Music folder is to choose Home from the Finder's Go menu.

You don't have to venture inside the Music folder—indeed, you should always add and remove songs to and from your music library by using iTunes itself, not by dragging files into and out of the Music folder.

iTunes Library

If you're curious, here's how the Music folder is organized. The Music folder contains another folder named iTunes, and inside *this* folder is a file named iTunes Library. This file contains a database of all the songs you've added to iTunes, as well as all the playlists you've created. But it doesn't contain the song files themselves; those files live in the folder named iTunes Music.

Note that you don't have to store your music in the Music folder. You might want to store

it elsewhere—on a portable FireWire hard drive, for example. To specify a different location for your music library, choose Preferences from the iTunes menu, click the Advanced button, and then specify the desired location. (For more iTunes library tips, see page 80.)

To tell iTunes where to store your music, click Change.

To restore the default location, click Reset.

Note: If you've been using iTunes for a while, you may find older music library files in your iTunes folder. These files will be stashed in a folder named Previous iTunes Libraries. It's safe to delete these older library files.

Editing Song Information

A digital music file holds more than just music. It also holds information about the music: the song's name, the name of the artist who recorded it, the year it was recorded, and more.

There may be times when you'll want to edit this information. Maybe the song is from an obscure CD that isn't in Gracenote's CDDB, and iTunes has given its tracks generic names like *Track 5*. (This will also happen if you rip a CD when not connected to the Internet.) Or maybe CDDB stored the song names in all-lowercase or all-capital letters, and you'd like to correct that.

Or maybe a particular artist is listed in slightly different ways on different CDs—for example *Bill Evans* and *Bill Evans Trio*. When you transfer those songs to your iPod, you'll have two separate listings in the Artist view—even though both listings refer to the same artist.

For situations like these, you can use iTunes' Get Info command to edit the information of one or more songs. First, select the song whose attributes you want to edit, and then choose Get Info from the File menu, or press ⌘-I.

You can also edit song information directly within the iTunes window: simply select the song and then click on the item you want to edit.

To edit a song's information, click Info (see opposite page).

Change equalization, volume, and other playback settings here (see pages 56 and 75).

The latest iPods can store and display lyrics (see page 103). Store those words here.

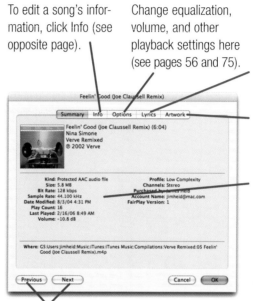

Add and remove album artwork here (see page 63).

Information about how the song is encoded appears here.

Keyboard control. Editing a lot of information? Don't reach for the mouse. Press ⌘-P and ⌘-N to "click" the Previous and Next buttons, and ⌘-[and ⌘-] to move between each pane of the dialog box.

Need to edit information for multiple songs? Rather than repeatedly choosing Get Info, just click Previous to display information for the previous song (the one above the current song in iTunes' window) or Next to get info for the next song.

Fixing "Anonymous" Music Tracks

You've ripped a few audio CDs while on a cross-country flight. Since you didn't have Internet access, iTunes wasn't able to retrieve album and song information, and now you have songs named Track 01, Track 02, and so on.

Must you venture into the Song Information dialog box to manually enter album, song, and artist information? Of course not. Simply connect to the Internet, select those "anonymous" tracks, and then choose Get CD Track Names from the Advanced menu. iTunes connects to CDDB and retrieves the information you crave.

Tips for Editing Song Information

To edit information for a song, click the Info button in the song information dialog box. While many of the items in the Info area are self-explanatory, some aren't. Let's take a look.

As you delve into this dialog box, keep in mind that you don't have to play by the rules. For example, you can store *any* piece of text in the Composer field—iTunes won't complain. Feel free to use the more obscure items in this dialog box to describe and categorize your music library as you see fit. Your efforts will pay off when you start creating smart playlists (described on page 44).

Edit the most important song information here.

On many CDs, some tracks may be related to each other. For example, a classical CD may contain two Mozart symphonies, with tracks 1 through 4 representing one work and tracks 5 through 8 representing the second work. You can use the Grouping box to store this kind of information: in the Mozart example, you might select tracks 1 through 4, choose Get Info, and then type the name of the work here. But the fact is, you can store whatever information you like here—the names of soloists who play on a given track, or even a sub-genre, such as *smooth jazz* or *Euro techno*.

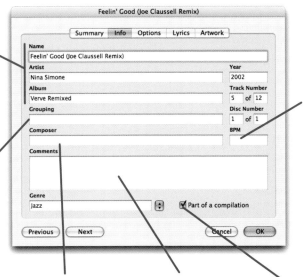

BPM stands for *beats per minute*—this field is designed to hold a numeric value that corresponds to how many beats per minute are in a song. DJs can use this information when compiling smart playlists. Don't know the exact tempo of a song? Some iTunes users create codes that represent a song's tempo: 1 for a ballad, 2 for a medium-tempo song, 3 for an up-tempo song, and so on. If you use a scheme like this, you can use smart playlists to gather and play songs in a similar tempo range.

With some genres—particularly classical—a work's composer is at least as important as the name of the artist who performed it. You can use the Composer field to hold any information, but it's intended for storing the name of the person who composed a given piece. On the iPod, you can browse by composer.

Use the Comments box to hold anything you like: a list of musicians, the record label's name, the city where it was recorded, the name of its recording engineer—or just comments such as *This song rocks!* When creating smart playlists, you can search for part or all of a comment.

Indicates that the song is part of a compilation; when browsing, you can have iTunes display a Compilations category to make it easy to find albums featuring multiple artists (see page 80).

Shopping at the iTunes Music Store

At the iTunes Music Store, you can search for, browse, audition, and buy music, music videos, TV shows, and more. Wander the store's virtual aisles or search for specific items. Check out 30-second clips of your finds. Buy entire albums, or just the songs you want. iTunes downloads your purchases into your music library, from which you can add them to playlists, burn them to CDs, and transfer them to an iPod.

If you've experimented with music-swapping services, you'll find the iTunes Music Store easier to use and much more reliable. And you'll be able to take off that eye patch, since you won't be pirating from your favorite artists.

You can use the music store with any kind of Internet connection, but a high-speed connection—for example, a cable modem or DSL line—works best. Music takes a long time to download over a slow modem connection—and videos take even longer.

Before you can buy music, you must set up an account by providing billing information and creating a password. Once that's done, you can buy songs and albums with a couple of mouse clicks.

The music you buy is stored in AAC format and is tied to your account in ways that guard against the piracy that pervades the MP3 scene. And yet you still have plenty of freedom to burn CDs and move your music between computers.

Let's go shopping.

Getting Set Up: Signing In

Step 1:
Step into the Store

Be sure you're connected to the Internet, then click the Music Store item in the iTunes Source list. iTunes connects to the music store. You can browse and search at this point, but you can't buy music until you sign in.

Step 2: Sign In

To sign in, click the Sign In button in the upper-right corner of the store, then complete the dialog box below.

If you don't have an Apple account, click Create New Account and then supply your billing information.

If you're an America Online subscriber, you can charge your purchases to your AOL account. Click AOL, specify your screen name and password, then click Sign In.

If you're a .Mac member, have purchased from the Apple online store in the past, or have ordered prints or books through iPhoto, you already have an Apple account. Specify your ID and password here, then click Sign In.

The Music Store at a Glance

Navigate within the store (see below).

Each genre has its own area of the store; choose a genre to display its area.

Publish your favorite playlists for others to see and rate (page 48).

Featured items appear in these virtual aisles. To move within an aisle, click the blue arrows at the edges of the aisle.

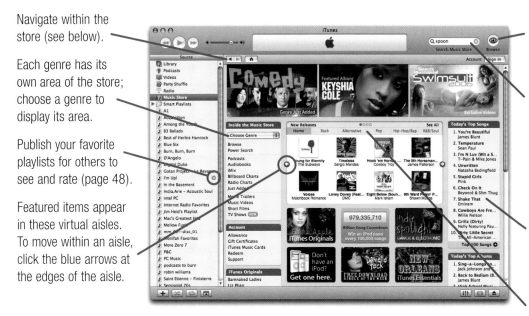

Browse by genre, artist, and album (page 33).

Search the store. For example, type the name of a song, artist, or album, then press the Return key. (For more searching tips, see page 33.)

What's everyone else buying? Top song and album downloads appear here.

To view new releases in a specific genre, click the genre. To see all recent new releases, click See All.

Getting Around in the Store

The navigation bar changes as you move within the store; click the buttons to jump to areas that relate to what's on your screen.

Go back or forward one screen (keyboard shortcuts: ⌘-[and ⌘-]).

Go to the front of the music store.

The current genre appears here; click it to go to that genre's main screen.

To go to the current artist's discography, click the artist's name. Some discographies have photos, videos, and links to artist Web sites.

The album you're currently viewing.

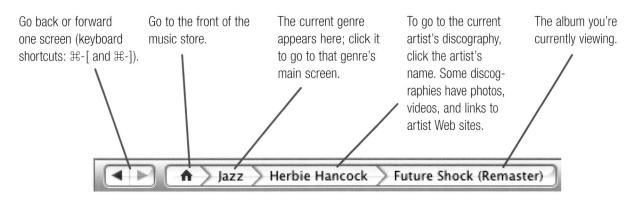

From Browsing to Buying

Once you've created an account and signed in, you're ready to shop at the iTunes Music Store. You might start by browsing the store's virtual aisles, clicking on the little album thumbnail images or the text links around them. (The links are underlined when you point to them.)

You might jump to a genre by using the Choose Genre pop-up menu. You might use the Browse button to quickly navigate genres, artists, and albums. Or you might use the Power Search option to home in on exactly what you're looking for.

The end result of any searching or browsing session is a list of songs. Here's where you can play 30-second song previews, locate additional songs from an artist or album, and most important, buy songs and albums. You can also burn your purchases to audio CDs and transfer them to an iPod.

Working with a Song List

You've searched or browsed your way to a list of songs. What happens next is up to you.

If you arrived at this song list by doing a search, you can narrow down the search results using the search bar; see page 54.

Go elsewhere: Click an album name or photo to display its songs. Click an artist name for a discography. Click the genre name to go to that genre.

Play a preview: Double-click a song to hear a sample.

See more: In the Artist column, click the arrow for the artist's discography.

Drill down: In the Album column, click the arrow to show the entire album.

Who cares? The Relevance column isn't very useful. To hide it, Control-click on its heading and uncheck Relevance. (You can show and hide other columns, too.)

Buy: To buy a song, click its Buy Song button.

To Shop Faster, Browse

If you're the type who heads for a mall directory instead of wandering around, try the music store's browse mode, where you can quickly home in on genres, sub-genres, artists, and albums. Browsing is efficient, and because it discards graphics in favor of all-text displays, it's fast, even over slow Internet connections.

Step 1. With the music store displayed, click the Browse button in the upper-right corner of the iTunes window.

Step 2. Choose a genre, then a sub-genre (if appropriate), then an artist.

Tip: You can navigate the browse boxes with the keyboard. Use the arrow keys to move up and down, or type the first few letters of a word to jump to it. To jump between boxes, press Tab or Shift-Tab.

Power Searching

With the music store's Power Search feature, you can specify multiple search criteria at once—for example, to search for only those versions of *Giant Steps* performed by John Coltrane.

Step 1. Click the music store's Power Search option, or choose Power Search from the search box's pop-up menu.

Step 2. Specify your search criteria and click Search.

Buying and Watching Videos

The iTunes Music Store is about more than music. You can also buy video: music videos, TV shows, short films, comedy performances, and more.

Buying videos is a lot like buying music. Browse your way to a video or do a search for a specific video. Watch a preview if you like; it appears right within the iTunes window. Like what you see? Click the Buy button, and iTunes downloads your video and adds it to your library. At this writing, most videos cost $1.99 each. Some TV shows are available on a $9.99 per month subscription basis called a *multi-pass*.

You can use iTunes to watch your videos. Normally, videos play back in a small corner of the iTunes window, but you can also display them in a larger window—or full-screen, if you like. If you have the latest full-sized iPod, you can transfer your videos to it and watch them in the palm of your hand (page 96).

Video files are many times larger than music files, so you'll need a fast Internet connection for your video-buying endeavors. What's more, the videos on the iTunes Music Store aren't exactly high-definition quality; they're heavily compressed in order to download within a reasonable amount of time and not use all your disk space.

Still, it's hard to beat the ability to watch some favorite shows on your next cross-country flight—or cross-town bus commute.

Let's go channel surfing.

Finding Videos

You can locate videos in a few ways.

Wander. Click the links on the music store's home screen.

Browse. You can also use the Browse mode described on the previous pages. As with music, browsing is a fast, efficient way to quickly get a glimpse of everything that's available.

Search. You can use the Search box to search for a specific show or video. If your search results contain too many songs and other non-video items, click the Video button in the search bar to narrow down the list of results to only video items.

You can also use the Power Search feature to home in on video content. In the Power

Search window, choose a video-related option from the Genre pop-up menu—for example, Music Videos or TV Shows.

Previewing What You Find

As with music, you can check out a short preview of a video by double-clicking the video's name. The preview appears in the lower-left corner of the iTunes window in an area called the *video viewer*.

Tips for Watching Videos

Resizing the video viewer. As shown on the opposite page, iTunes plays video within a small corner of its window. You can make this video viewer larger: drag the size control near the top of the Source list.

Watching in a separate window. You can also have iTunes play a video in a separate window: simply click on the video in the video viewer, and a new window opens.

The window provides some convenient controls that the video viewer lacks.

Filling the screen. To have a video fill the screen, click the ▣ button near the lower-left corner of the iTunes window.

Note: Videos from the iTunes Music Store have a resolution of 320 pixels wide by 240 pixels high. When you view them at larger sizes, particularly in full-screen mode, you'll probably notice some fuzziness and other digital artifacts. Sit back! These flaws are less apparent at greater viewing distances.

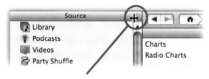

Drag left or right to resize the video viewer.

To quickly jump around within the video, drag the scrubber left and right.

Pause and resume playback.

Step backwards and forwards one frame at a time.

To resize the playback window, drag the lower-right corner.

More iTunes Video Tips

Setting playback preferences. If you always like to watch video in a separate window (or in full-screen view), use the Playback portion of the Preferences dialog box to specify your tastes.

Viewing your video library. To quickly see all the movies in your iTunes library, click the Video entry in the Source list. If you have many videos, you can narrow down the list to specific types (for example, music videos) by clicking the buttons in the search bar.

Adding your own movies. iTunes can also store your own QuickTime movies, such as ones you've downloaded from the Internet or created in iMovie HD or iPhoto. Simply drag a movie file into the iTunes window. (For details on preparing your iMovie efforts for iTunes, see page 268.)

Next, consider using the Get Info command to tweak a few settings. You can have iTunes set a "bookmark" when you stop playback, enabling you to resume from that point. In the Options portion of the Info dialog box,

click the Remember Playback Position box. And to prevent iTunes from playing a movie when in shuffle-playback mode (page 76), click the Skip When Shuffling box. (Both of these boxes are checked for videos that you buy.)

Finally, you can specify what kind of video you've stored—a movie, music video, or TV show—by using the Video Kind pop-up menu. Your setting here affects how iTunes categorizes the video when you click the buttons in the Search bar.

With add-on products such as Elgato's EyeTV, you can record TV shows and save them in a format compatible with iTunes and the iPod (page 79).

The iPod angle. iTunes can store just about any kind of QuickTime-compatible video clip, but that doesn't mean the clip will play back on an iPod with video features. The iPod requires video to be in a specific format; for details on converting video for iPod playback, see page 96.

Tuning In to Podcasts

Podcasts bring you radio and more whenever you want it. A *podcast* is typically an audio recording of a radio program—either an actual radio show that has been archived for Internet distribution, or an Internet-only program. Thousands of free podcasts await your ears, and they range from mainstream programs from the likes of National Public Radio to amateur productions that only a mother's ears could love.

Internet radio isn't new, but podcasts sweeten the pot with a couple of innovations. Foremost among them is that you don't have to remember to download podcasts. Instead, you use iTunes to *subscribe* to your favorite podcasts. When you subscribe to a podcast, iTunes automatically checks for new episodes at regular intervals. If iTunes finds a new episode, it downloads it.

At the iTunes Music Store, you'll find thousands of podcasts in over 20 categories, from technology to politics to talk radio and public radio.

Podcasts also come in several flavors. Video podcasts add the dimension of video, while *enhanced* podcasts provide extra goodies, such as photos, Web links, and chapter markers for convenient navigation. (See page 41).

And if you're curious, the term *podcast* was coined by former MTV veejay Adam Curry. A major force behind the development and popularization of podcasting, he's referred to by many in the podcasting community as the "podfather."

Radio (and more) in every imaginable category, retrieved for you automatically: now that's an offer you can't refuse.

Finding Podcasts

As with music and videos, you can find podcasts in a few ways. To wander the podcast aisles of the iTunes Music Store, click the Podcasts link on the iTunes Music Store's home screen. The podcasts page appears.

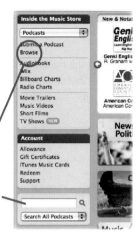

To quickly scan what's available in each podcast category, click Browse.

To search for podcasts, use the Search box. You can use the pop-up menu to refine your search to specific podcast titles or authors.

Previewing and Subscribing

Once you've made your way to a specific podcast, you can preview episodes, download them, and subscribe to the podcast.

To subscribe to the podcast, click Subscribe. iTunes subscribes to the podcast and begins downloading the most recent episode.

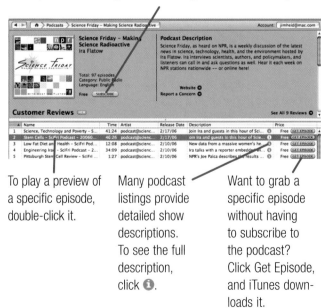

To play a preview of a specific episode, double-click it.

Many podcast listings provide detailed show descriptions. To see the full description, click ❶.

Want to grab a specific episode without having to subscribe to the podcast? Click Get Episode, and iTunes downloads it.

Tune in to my podcast, "The Digital Hub," and get links to more podcast tips.
www.macilife.com/podcast

Managing Your Podcasts

The Podcasts Playlist

Podcasts to which you've subscribed appear in the Podcasts playlist. To display this playlist, click Podcasts in the Source list.

To show or hide the episodes for a particular podcast, click the triangle.

Episodes that you haven't downloaded appear dimmed.

This episode is currently downloading. To cancel a download, click the X.

Specify various podcast preferences (below).

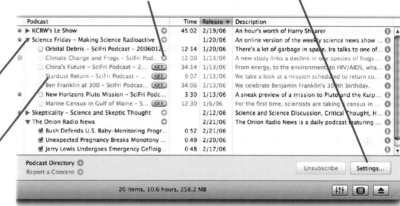

Setting Podcasts Preferences

You can control how often iTunes checks your podcast subscriptions, what happens to podcasts you've played, and more. Click the Settings button in the Podcasts playlist, or choose Preferences from the iTunes menu, then click the Podcasts button.

How often should iTunes check for new episodes? If you've subscribed to podcasts that update often (such as National Public Radio's hourly news), you might choose Hourly.

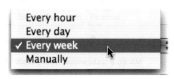

Specify which podcasts are copied to your iPod (see page 98).

Then what? Specify what you'd like iTunes to do when it finds a new episode. If you prefer to read each episode's description and then download only those episodes that sound interesting, choose Do Nothing. Then download the episodes you want by clicking their Get buttons.

And when you're done? Specify how many episodes iTunes should keep. To save disk space, you might want to keep two or three previous episodes—or only those episodes you haven't yet played.

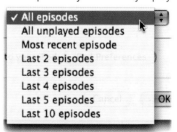

Tip: You can override this preference setting on a per-podcast basis. For example, to keep iTunes from deleting a particular episode of a podcast, locate the episode in the Podcast playlist, then Control-click on it and choose Do Not Auto Delete from the shortcut menu.

Tips for the Music Store

More Shopping Avenues

Looking for more ways to discover new music? Here are a few shopping avenues to explore. You can access all of the following options from the music store's home screen.

iTunes Essentials. In the iTunes Essentials area of the store, you'll find meticulously categorized lists of tunes selected by the staff of the music store. Categories run the gamut from "Motorcycle Music" to "Romantic Moods," and each category is divided into several subcategories that let you drill ever deeper into the groove at hand.

Celebrity Playlists. If you're interested in what your favorite musicians listen to, check out Celebrity Playlists, where top artists share their favorites.

iMixes. As page 48 describes, you can publish your own playlists for other music store customers to check out and rate. To check out and rate other shoppers' iMixes, click the iMix link.

iTunes Originals. In the iTunes Originals area of the store, you'll find exclusive tracks, song compilations, and artist interviews.

Just for You. This area of the music store's home screen lists songs that Apple thinks you'll like based on previous purchases you've made.

Radio Charts. You can get a list of top songs from more than 1,000 radio stations in over 100 cities. First, click Radio Charts in the Choose Genre area (or in Browse mode). A list of cities appears. Click a city name, and an often-diverse list of stations appears. Click a station to see its top tunes. It's a fun way to see what people are listening to in your home town, in a popular college town, or just someplace far away.

Billboard Charts. Similarly, the Billboard Charts category lists the top tunes from Billboard magazine. You can get lists of top tunes going back to the 1940s, as well as current country and R&B favorites.

Free Downloads. Apple offers a free download (of its choosing) every week, and occasionally offers a free compilation album, too.

Parental Controls

Concerned about your kids buying music and sapping your credit card? Or about them buying music or downloading podcasts that contain explicit content?

By using the Parental option of the Preferences dialog box, you can control what the munchkins can access. Choose Preferences from the iTunes menu, then click the Parental button.

Next, choose the options you want. For example, to prevent access to music store content labeled as explicit, click Restrict Explicit Content. Finally, click the lock icon and enter your password.

To remove restrictions, click the lock icon again, enter your password, and then uncheck options as desired.

Stopping Stutters

Saddled with a slow connection? Improve song previewing by tweaking iTunes' preferences.

Choose Preferences from the iTunes menu, click the Store button, and then check the box labeled Load Complete Preview Before Playing. From now on, iTunes will load the entire preview before playing it. You'll wait longer to hear the preview, but at least it won't be interrupted.

This option also works with podcast and video previews.

Authorizing and Deauthorizing

Unlike the music files that iTunes creates when you rip a CD, the music tracks you buy contain some playback and copying restrictions designed to prevent music thieves from sharing the songs through Internet file-swapping services.

When you buy a song, the iTunes Music Store embeds your Apple ID in the music file that downloads to your hard drive. To play the song, you must authorize your Mac, a one-time process that simply involves typing your Apple ID and password. You can authorize up to five Macs (or Windows PCs) per Apple ID.

If you've already authorized five computers to play your purchases and you want to play them on a sixth computer, you'll have to deauthorize one of the other five. Choose Deauthorize Computer from the Advanced menu, choose Apple Account in the subsequent dialog box, and then type your Apple ID and password. You must be connected to the Internet to deauthorize a computer.

Parting with your computer? If you're parting with your Mac for any reason—selling it, giving it away, or even just sending it off for repairs—be sure to deauthorize it first.

Deauthorizing everything. You forgot to deauthorize a computer that you no longer have—and you've reached your five-computer limit and thus can't authorize your newest Mac. What do to? Wipe the slate clean.

You can deauthorize all the computers that are tied to your music store account. To do so, go to your account information screen by signing into the music store and clicking the account button in the upper-right corner. On the Account Information screen, click the Deauthorize All button.

Important: You can deauthorize all your computers only once a year, so don't use this option unless you really need to.

Burning What You Buy

You can burn purchased songs to audio CDs, but iTunes imposes a minor restriction on your burning endeavors. If a playlist contains purchased music, you can burn a maximum of seven CDs containing that playlist.

Chris Breen, editor-in-chief of *Playlist* magazine, has done some interesting research on how iTunes tracks the number of times you've burned a playlist—and on steps you can take to work around the seven-CD limit. I've linked to the articles at www.macilife.com/itunes.

And incidentally, you can't burn DVDs containing videos that you've purchased from the music store. You can burn backups of the video files themselves (and you should), but you can't, for example, use iDVD to create a DVD that contains some episodes of *Lost* that you've bought.

Binge Buying? Get a Cart

When you go into a store, chances are you don't just buy one thing. Most of the time, you grab a shopping cart so you can haul all of your purchases to the cashier at once.

iTunes provides a shopping cart, and using it is a better way to shop when you're picking up several songs.

When the shopping cart is active, iTunes doesn't download each purchased song immediately. Instead, it slings the songs into a shopping cart. When you're ready to check out, a couple of clicks buys the songs and begins their download.

Shopping for multiple tunes is more convenient in shopping-cart mode. Navigating the music store is faster, too, since iTunes isn't downloading a song in the background while you shop.

To use the shopping-cart mode, choose Preferences from the iTunes menu, click Store, and then click the option labeled Buy Using a Shopping Cart. The Buy Song button that appears next to each song now reads Add Song: click it to add a song to your cart.

To buy the songs in your cart, click the Shopping Cart item in the Source list, then click the Buy Now button near the lower-right corner of the iTunes window.

More Tips for the Music Store

Creating Playlists from Collections

A huge number of song compilations are available at the iTunes Music Store—just a few examples include the iMixes that your fellow music lovers create; the iTunes Essentials mixes that Apple creates; the celebrity playlists that, well, celebrities create; and the iTunes Originals compilations described on page 38.

When you buy a song compilation, you'll probably want to create a playlist containing its tunes. That way, you'll be able to easily listen to (and burn) the entire compilation instead of simply having its songs scattered throughout your music library.

iTunes has a feature that automatically creates playlists for you when you buy a compilation. Choose Preferences from the iTunes menu, click the Store button, and be sure that the box labeled Automatically Create Playlists When Buying Song Collections is checked.

For details on playlists, see page 44.

When Downloads Go Awry

If your Internet connection is interrupted during a download, you haven't lost your money. Simply reconnect and choose Check for Purchases from the Advanced menu. iTunes will resume any incomplete downloads.

Keep Informed

If you use iCal (page 106), you can subscribe to daily calendar updates of top songs, albums, and new releases by going to Apple's iCal site, www.apple.com/ical.

And if you use a newsreader program, such as NetNewsWire or the latest versions of Apple's Safari Web browser, you can create RSS newsfeeds that contain this information by going to www.apple.com/rss.

PDF Liner Notes

One of the drawbacks of the digital music era is that you don't get a booklet of lyrics and other liner notes with your purchases. That's slowly changing: Apple now offers liner notes in PDF form for some albums. Many iTunes Originals collections also include PDF booklets.

The PDFs are downloaded automatically with your purchase, and appear right in your iTunes music library. Double-click the PDF, and your Mac launches Preview (or Adobe Acrobat Reader, if installed) and opens the PDF.

To learn more about working with PDFs in iTunes, see page 70.

Get that Song's Address

Every item—song, album, video, podcast—in the music store has its own Internet address. You can copy this address and include it in an email, or link to it from your personal Web site.

Using this address is a fun way to let other people know about the stuff you've found.

To copy an item's Web address, point to the item, press the Control key (that's Control, not ⌘), and choose Copy iTunes Music Store URL from the shortcut menu that appears.

Next, switch to your email program, create a blank email, then paste the address into the body of the email.

You can also drag a song to the desktop; this creates an icon that, when double-clicked, takes iTunes to the appropriate song or album. If you've stumbled onto an interesting-sounding album but you want to wait and explore it later, use this technique to put a temporary bookmark on your desktop.

Hiding the Link Buttons

The music store provides link arrows (⊙) that let you jump to a page for an artist, album, or song. These buttons also appear when you're viewing your music library or a playlist. The buttons are Apple's way of letting you search for (and buy) songs related to ones you already have.

If you'd rather not see these buttons—maybe so you don't accidentally click one and beam yourself into the music store—you can turn them off. Choose Preferences, click the General button, then uncheck the box labeled Show Links to the Music Store.

The Enhanced Podcast Difference

Enhanced podcasts can contain artwork, such as photos, that play back along with the audio. The artwork can even be synchronized so that, for example, different photos appear as a narrator talks about them.

Enhanced podcasts can also contain Web links that appear in the iTunes video viewer. You can click on the link to go to a Web site.

And enhanced podcasts can contain chapter markers that make it easy for the listener (or viewer) to jump from one part of the podcast to another. When an enhanced podcast contains chapter markers, iTunes displays a chapter menu that lets you jump to specific spots.

You can also navigate from one chapter to the next by using the click wheel on an iPod (see page 103).

Tips for Working with Podcasts

Subscribing Manually

The iTunes Music Store has a vast podcast directory, but you may sometimes encounter a podcast on the Web that isn't listed in the music store. You can still use iTunes to subscribe to such a podcast.

On the Web site hosting the podcast, locate the link for the podcast's feed. Copy that link by Control-clicking on it and choosing Copy Link from the shortcut menu. Next, switch back to

iTunes and choose Subscribe to Podcast from the Advanced menu. Paste the link you copied, and click OK or press Return.

Adding Downloaded Podcasts

If you have podcasts that you've already downloaded with a Web browser, you can add them to your iTunes library by simply dragging their icons to the Library item in the iTunes Source list. Note that such podcasts will not appear in the

Podcasts playlist, however. That playlist shows only podcasts that you've downloaded with iTunes.

Send to a Friend

You've subscribed to a great podcast and want to let a friend know about it. It's easy. In the Podcasts playlist, choose the title of the podcast, then drag it to the desktop. iTunes creates an address file whose name ends with .pcast.

You can email this file to your friends, who can drag it into

their copies of iTunes to subscribe to the podcast.

The Blue Dot

You've probably noticed that podcast subscriptions and individual episodes often have a blue dot (●) next to them. A blue dot next to a podcast episode indicates that you haven't started listening to that episode. A blue dot next to a podcast subscription indicates that there's at least one episode of that podcast you haven't started listening to yet.

Giving the Gift of Music

Thinking of buying a music CD for someone? That's *so* twentieth century. If the music lovers in your life use iTunes, treat them to some music at the iTunes Music Store.

The iTunes Music Store offers a few options for giving music. If you want to give a specific album, song, or video to someone, you can. Don't have anything specific in mind? You can also buy prepaid music cards and gift certificates that let your lucky recipients pick and choose exactly what they want. You can even set up a monthly music allowance that keeps on giving.

To access most of these options, use the links in the Account area of the music store's main screen—it's located along the left edge of the screen.

Allowance: Music Monthly

Want to give all year long? Set up an allowance to give a monthly music stipend. You can give as little as $10 per month—about one album's worth—or as much as, gulp, $200.

You aren't giving cash, of course, but rather the ability to buy a given amount of music each month. And if your recipient ends up being a bad boy or girl, you can cancel the allowance at any time during the subsequent year. Try *that* with a music CD.

Your recipient must have an Apple account. If he or she doesn't have one, you can set up an account when creating an allowance.

Note: If you know your recipient has an Apple account but you don't know what the account name is, *don't* set up a separate account for the allowance. That would complicate your recipient's life, since music store purchases are locked to a specific account. Instead, either find out what the recipient's Apple account is, or, if you want to maintain the element of surprise, buy a gift certificate or prepaid card instead.

Gift Certificate

If you don't know your recipient's Apple account name—or you aren't feeling generous enough for a monthly allowance—consider a gift certificate. You can give between $10 and $200. Apple emails the gift certificate to the recipient, who can redeem it by simply clicking a link.

For an analog touch, you can also have the gift certificate printed and mailed to the recipient. Or print it yourself and tuck it into a card.

Prepaid Cards

Prepaid iTunes Music Cards are available in various denominations from Amazon.com, Target, CompUSA, Circuit City, and the Apple online and retail stores.

To redeem the card, your recipient clicks the Redeem link on the music store's home screen, then types the card's serial number (it's printed on the back of the card, beneath a scratch-off coating). After the card is redeemed, the recipient's copy of iTunes will show that he or she has an additional credit.

Giving Specific Items

You can give any item that's sold at the iTunes Music Store. Make your way to the main page for an album or TV series, then click the Gift link. (For albums, the link reads Gift This Album; for shows, it reads Gift This TV Show.)

A new screen appears that enables you to give the entire album (or season, for TV shows) or only certain songs or episodes.

You can also give something that you already have in your music library; see page 48.

More Musical Gift Ideas

Don't want to give music? Consider a gift that enhances a music collection.

An iPod. If your music lover doesn't have an iPod, he or she is missing out on one of the best parts of the digital music era.

Headphones. My favorite earwear is a pair of Bose QuietComfort II headphones, whose noise-cancelling circuitry does an amazing job of removing annoying background noise. They're ideal for long plane flights, not to mention vacuuming sessions.

Portable speakers. Does your music lover travel? A pair of portable speakers makes listening in a hotel room a lot more fun. Bose, JBL, Altec Lansing, and other companies sell portable speakers designed for the iPod; check out iLounge (www.ilounge.com) and Playlist magazine (www.playlistmag.com) for reviews.

I frequently travel with Sony's SRS-T77 speakers, which, unlike iPod-specific speakers, also connect to the headphone jack on my PowerBook.

iPod accessories. Carrying cases, radio adapters, micro-phones, and car chargers are among the accessories competing for your dollars. Check out iLounge and Playlist for some ideas.

Before you buy, remember that many accessories are designed for specific iPod models. Be sure that the item you're considering works with your recipient's specific iPod model.

Sequencing Songs with Playlists

Once you've created a digital music library, you'll want to create playlists: collections of songs sequenced in whatever order you like.

You might create playlists whose songs set a mood: Workout Tunes, Road Trip Songs, Romantic Getaway Music.

You might create playlists that play all your favorite tunes from specific artists: The Best of U2, John Coltrane Favorites, The Artistry of Britney Spears. (That last one is pretty small.)

With playlists, you can mix and match songs in any way you see fit. You can add a song to as many playlists as you like, or even create a playlist that plays one song five times in a row.

Once you've created playlists, you can, of course, play them. But you can also transfer them to an iPod (page 86) and burn them to create your own compilation CDs (page 58).

This section describes how to create playlists "by hand." You can also use iTunes' smart playlists feature to have the program create playlists for you. For details on smart playlists, see page 50.

Once you've created some playlists, share them with the rest of us. As page 48 describes, you can publish your playlists on the iTunes Music Store for everyone to see—and rate.

Step 1.
Create a New Playlist

To create a new playlist, click the plus sign or choose New Playlist from the File menu.

Step 2.
Rename the New Playlist

Type a name for the new playlist.

Step 3.
Drag Songs to the Playlist

You can drag songs into the playlist one at a time or select a series of songs and drag them all at once. To select a range of songs that are adjacent to each other, use the Shift key: click on the first song, then Shift-click on the last one. To select songs that aren't adjacent to one another, press ⌘ while clicking on each song.

Viewing and Fine-Tuning a Playlist

To view a playlist's contents, simply click on its name. To change the playlist's name, click again and then edit the name. To delete a playlist, select it and press Delete. (Deleting a playlist *doesn't* delete its songs from your Library.)

To omit a song from a playlist, select the song and press the Delete key. To omit the song without deleting it—for example, if you want to keep it in the playlist but not burn it or play it back this time—uncheck the box next to the song's name.

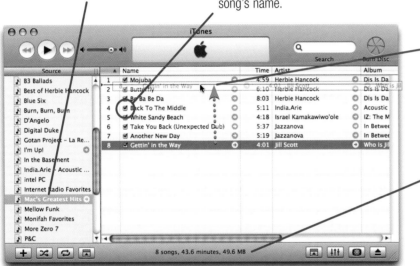

To change the playback order of the songs in the playlist, drag songs up or down. Here, the last song in the playlist is being moved to between songs 1 and 2.

iTunes displays the playlist's statistics, including its duration, here.

Important: If you plan to burn this playlist to an audio CD, keep the playlist's duration under 74 minutes.

Organizing Playlists with Folders

As your collection of playlists grows, consider organizing them by stashing related playlists in folders. To create a new folder, choose File > New Folder. Then, drag playlists into that folder.

To open or close a folder, click the triangle.

How you use folders is up to you. You might create one for all your jazz playlists and another for your classical playlists. If you have a lot of playlists for various artists, consider stashing each artist's playlists in a folder. If a few members of your household use iTunes, create a folder for each person's playlists. You get the idea.

Tip: Folders are also a great way to assemble "playlists of playlists." If you select a folder in the Source list, iTunes displays (and will play) all the tracks in each of the playlists contained in the folder.

You can also use folders as criteria in smart playlists, described on page 50.

Playlist Tips

Designing Playlists

A well-crafted playlist is more than a slew of songs slung into one place.

Consider the setting. A good playlist complements an event. For example, say you're creating a playlist for a dinner party, and you expect that guests will be mingling for an hour or so before sitting down to dinner. Start your playlist with about 15 minutes of fairly mellow tunes, then build up to some more energetic ones for the next 30 minutes or so. Then start to wind down again, and lead into a solid block of fairly unobtrusive music that won't overwhelm the dinner conversation.

Similarly, for a workout playlist, you might start and end with slower songs to accommodate warm-up and cool-down times, and put the pulse-pounding tunes in the middle. You get the idea: if your playlist will be accompanying an event, assemble tunes that complement the event's "story arc."

Mix artists. To make a playlist that's more interesting to the ears, mix and match artists.

Consider the transitions. Think about how the songs in your playlist flow from one to the next. You might follow a barn-burner with a slower ballad, for example, or put an instrumental after a vocal. To assess the transitions between songs, start playing one song and then fast-forward by dragging the little playback diamond to near the end on the

song (see page 19). Then listen as the songs change. If the transition sounds jarring, consider reorganizing the songs to create a more pleasing segue.

Opening a Playlist in a Separate Window

To open a playlist in its own window, double-click the playlist's name. iTunes opens the playlist in a new window, and switches its main window to the Library view.

You can open as many playlist windows as you like and drag songs between them, as shown here. It's a handy way to work, since it lets you see the contents of your Library and your playlist at the same time.

Previews in Playlists

You can drag a song preview from the music store into a playlist. This can be a handy way to put together a temporary shopping list—drag previews into a playlist, then go back and review them again before deciding what to buy.

You can also publish a wish list of tunes: drag previews into a playlist, then publish the playlist as described on page 48. Who

knows? Maybe someone will buy the tunes for you.

To help you tell a preview from a full-length song, iTunes displays a little badge (⟨30⟩) adjacent to a preview song's name.

Creating a Playlist From a Selection

Here's a shortcut for creating a playlist: in the Library view, select the songs you want to include in a playlist, and then choose New Playlist From Selection from the File menu. iTunes adds the songs to a new playlist, which you can then rename.

Naming Playlists with iPod in Mind

If you plan to transfer your playlists to an iPod, there's a trick you can use to ensure that a given playlist will appear at the top of the iPod's Playlists menu. This cuts down on the time and scrolling required to find a specific playlist.

To have a playlist appear at the top of the iPod's Playlists menu, precede the playlist's name with a hyphen (-) character, as in - *Mac's Greatest Hits*.

A few other punctuation characters, including period (.), will also send a playlist to the top of the heap.

Adding One Playlist to Another

You can add the entire contents of one playlist to other playlists. In the Source area of the iTunes window, simply drag one playlist to another.

Playlist Shortcuts

Curious about which playlists contain a particular song? Hold down the Control key, click on the song, and a shortcut menu appears. Open the Show in Playlist submenu to see which playlists contain the song. To jump to a specific playlist, choose its name.

You can also add a song to an existing playlist using this shortcut menu: choose the playlist's name from the Add to Playlist submenu.

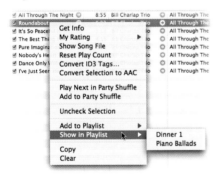

From CD to Playlist in One Drag

You're about to rip an audio CD and you're planning to add some of its tracks to a playlist. Here's a shortcut: simply drag the tracks from the CD list to the playlist. iTunes will import the tracks and add them to the playlist for you.

Exporting and Importing Playlists

You've crafted the perfect playlist and now want to move it over to a different Mac, or email it to a friend. Here's how: select the playlist, then choose Export Song List from the File menu. In the Save dialog box, choose XML from the Format pop-up menu, then click Save.

Next, move the playlist over to a different computer. On that computer, choose Import from the File menu. Locate the playlist and double-click its name. You're done.

Note that iTunes exports and imports only *information* about the songs in a playlist—it doesn't copy the songs' music files themselves. If any of the songs are missing on the importing computer, iTunes displays a warning and removes those songs from the imported playlist.

To export all of your playlists (an ideal prelude to backing them up), choose Export Library from the File menu.

Export Playlists as Plain Text

By choosing the Plain Text format in the Export Playlist dialog box, you can export a playlist in text format—perhaps to bring it into a database manager or spreadsheet program. (Hey, some iTunes users are very obsessive audio librarians.)

When you export a playlist in this way, iTunes creates a text file containing all the information about each song, from

its name to its bit rate. You can open this text file using a word processor, or you can import it into a spreadsheet or database program. The items—artist, song name, album name, and so on—in an exported playlist are separated by tab characters. (In geek speak, this command creates a *tab-delimited* text file.) Most spreadsheet and database programs can read these tabs and use them to put each piece of information in its own spreadsheet cell or database field.

Some programmers have created free AppleScripts that provide more control over playlist exporting. (To learn about expanding iTunes with AppleScript, see page 48.)

Printing to PDF

Another way to publish a song list is to use the Print command in iTunes. With Mac OS X's ability to "print" to a PDF file, you can create a PDF listing of songs, then email it or post it on a Web site.

In the Print dialog box, click the Song Listing or Album Listing option, pick a theme, then click Print. Click Save As PDF in the next dialog box, and give the PDF a name. Now share the PDF as you see fit. You can even drag the PDF into the iTunes window and store it as part of your iTunes library. (For more details on working with PDFs in iTunes, see page 78).

Tip: Looking for yet another way to get information from iTunes into another program? Print to a PDF, then open the PDF, copy its text, and paste it elsewhere.

iMix: Publishing Your Playlists

You've crafted the perfect playlist? Share it with the rest of us by publishing it at the iTunes Music Store. (You must have an account at the music store or with America Online before you can publish a playlist.)

A published playlist is called an *iMix*, and it appears in its own screen, much like an artist or album page. Each iMix is available for one year. After you create one, you can tell your friends by sending them e-cards or by publishing your iMix's address on a Web site.

Giving a Playlist

Want to buy the songs in a playlist for a friend? In the dialog box that appears after you click the arrow to the right of the playlist's name, click the Give Playlist button.

iTunes displays a list of the songs that are available in the music store, along with options that let you notify the recipient via email or print a note that you can tuck into a card.

For more music-giving options, see page 42.

Creating an iMix

Step 1. Select the playlist you want to publish, and click the arrow next to its name.

iTunes asks if you'd like to give the playlist as a gift or publish it as an iMix. For details on giving the playlist as a gift, see the tip at lower left. Otherwise, click Create iMix.

If iTunes displays its sign-in screen, supply your account name and password.

Step 2. Describe your iMix.

iTunes creates a collage based on the artwork for the songs in the playlist.

Type a description of your iMix and change its name, if you like.

To publish the iMix, click Publish. If your playlist includes songs that are *not* available at the iTunes Music Store, those songs don't appear in your iMix.

Step 3 (optional). Tell the world, or at least a friend.

To let someone know about your iMix, click the Tell a Friend button that appears after you publish the iMix.

After your iMix is published, you'll receive an email containing a summary of its tunes as well as a link that you can include in an email or on a Web page.

iMix Tips

Exploring iMixes. To explore the iMixes that other people have created, click the iMix item in the Genre area of the music store's home screen.

You can view mixes chronologically or in order of their rating. On the iMix page, you can also search for songs, artists, and albums that others have included in their iMixes. Highly rated iMixes also appear in relevant artist and album pages.

What else? If you like someone's iMix, you might want to explore other iMixes that he or she has created. In an iMix window, click the link that reads *See all iMixes by this user.*

Linking to an iMix. Want to grab the Internet address for an iMix? Control-click on the iMix's name or artwork, and

choose Copy iTunes Music Store URL from the shortcut menu. Paste the resulting link into an email or the Web tool of your choice.

As with individual songs, you can also create a desktop icon for an iMix—just drag its title or artwork icon to the desktop.

Updating an iMix. To make changes to an iMix, edit the original playlist, then publish it again. When you've published a playlist, a link arrow appears next to it, even when the playlist isn't selected.

A Piece of the Action: iTunes Affiliates

Now that you're recommending songs to people, you might as well get a piece of the action. It's easy: if you have a Web site of your own, you can join the iTunes Affiliate Program and receive commissions when you send customers to the iTunes Music Store.

Start by signing up for the iTunes Affiliate Program at Apple's Web site (www.apple.com/itunes/affiliates). Be prepared to provide some information, such as the Web address, a brief description of your site, and a Social Security number. Then wait a few days for your acceptance email to arrive.

Once you're enrolled in the program, you can build links to specific songs, albums, artists, iMixes, or audiobooks. You can also embellish your site with banner ads and other graphics that shuttle visitors off to the music store.

What's in it for you? A commission (at this writing, five percent) of any purchases made through your links. If you have an obscure, infrequently visited blog, don't expect any instant riches. But if you have a heavily visited site—maybe one that deals with music—the commissions can add up.

Smart Playlists: iTunes as DJ

iTunes can create playlists for you based on criteria that you specify. When you're in a hurry—or if you're just curious to see what iTunes comes up with—use iTunes' *smart playlists* feature to quickly assemble playlists. Smart playlists take advantage of all that information that's stored along with your music—its genre, artist, year, and more—to enable you to enjoy and present your music library in some fun ways.

Creating a smart playlist involves specifying the criteria for the songs you want included in the playlist—for example, songs whose genre is jazz and whose year is in the range of 1960 to 1969. You can choose to limit the size of the playlist using various criteria, including playing time (don't create a playlist longer than 74 minutes); disk space (don't create a playlist larger than 2 GB); number of songs (limit this playlist to 20 songs); and much more. You'll find some smart playlist ideas on page 52.

The smart playlists feature is really just a sophisticated search command. But remember, a good playlist is more than a series of songs that meet certain rules— it also presents those songs in a musically and emotionally pleasing way. A ballad may segue into an up-tempo tune, for example, or a laid-back instrumental may follow a dramatic vocal.

So go ahead and use iTunes' smart playlist feature to quickly throw together playlists. But to really do justice to your music, fine-tune the order of the songs in the smart playlists that iTunes creates. Or build your playlists by hand.

Creating a Smart Playlist

To create a smart playlist, choose New Smart Playlist from the File menu or press the Option key while clicking the playlist button (⚙) in the lower-left corner of the iTunes window.

What are you interested in? Choose options from the pop-up menus and type text in the box. Here, I'm building a smart playlist of all my Herbie Hancock tunes.

iTunes normally organizes the songs in a smart playlist in random order, but you can choose to organize them by artist name, song name, and other criteria.

Want to be more specific? Click ⊕ to add another criterion (see opposite page).

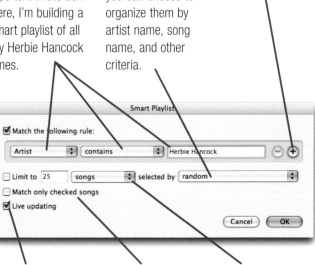

iTunes updates a smart playlist's contents as you add songs to (or remove them from) your music library.

To turn a smart playlist into a static one, uncheck Live Updating.

To have iTunes search only those songs that have a checkmark next to them in your library, click this box.

You can limit the size of the smart playlist to a maximum number of songs, minutes, hours, megabytes (MB), or gigabytes (GB).

Be More Specific:
Adding Criteria

When you want to be more specific, use more than one rule in your smart playlist. In this example, my smart playlist will contain all George Duke songs from the 1970s that are under five minutes long.

To add another rule, click the plus button (⊕).
To remove a rule, click the minus button (⊖) .

To have iTunes apply all of your criteria as it searches and compiles the playlist, choose All. If you choose Any, iTunes adds a song if it matches any of your criteria.

You can choose from and combine rules in more than twenty categories. For some inspiration, see the following pages.

Smart Playlist Tips

Changing a Smart Playlist

To modify a smart playlist's criteria or update settings, select the smart playlist and choose Edit Smart Playlist from the File menu (or press ⌘-I).

Create a Purchased Music Playlist

iTunes lists items you've purchased from the iTunes Music Store in a special playlist named Purchased. However, the Purchased playlist lists only songs you've purchased using

that particular computer. If you move those purchased songs to a different computer, they won't show up in its Purchased playlist. And that can complicate backup sessions.

The solution? Create a smart playlist containing only music you've purchased. Set up the Smart Playlist window to read

Kind contains *protected AAC*. Keep the Live Updating box checked, and you'll always have a full list of your purchases, no matter which Mac you use to do your buying.

A Cookbook of Smart Playlists

Some smart playlist ideas are obvious: a playlist containing songs from your favorite artist, a playlist of dance tunes, and so on.

But smart playlists aren't just a quick way to create playlists; they're also a great way to rediscover your music and explore your library in ways you might not think of otherwise. In short, don't restrict yourself to the obvious.

As you can see, the Smart Playlist dialog box lets you search on more than 20 criteria. Here are some smart playlist ideas to get your creative juices flowing.

Album ✓
Artist
BPM
Bit Rate
Category
Comment
Compilation
Composer
Date Added
Date Modified
Description
Disc Number
Genre
Grouping
Kind
Last Played
My Rating
Name
Play Count
Playlist
Podcast
Sample Rate
Size
Time
Track Number
Year

Smart Playlist Suggestions

For a Compilation of	Specify These Criteria
Short dance tunes	Genre is *Dance* and Time is less than 5:00 minutes
The same song performed by various artists	Song Name is equal to *name*
Songs added to your library recently	Date Added is in the last 1 week (adjust date value as desired)
Songs from a particular artist and era	Artist is *name* and Year is in the range *years here*.
Songs you haven't listened to recently	Last Played is not in the last *x* days (adjust date value as desired)
Songs by any of a few favorite artists	Artist is *name* or Artist is *name* (add a rule for each artist and choose Any from the Match pop-up menu)
Audio files that are not in MP3 format	Kind is not *MPEG audio file*
Songs you've added but never listened to	Play Count is 0 (zero)
Songs you've created in GarageBand and exported to iTunes	Kind contains *AIFF audio file*
Audiobooks downloaded from Audible.com	Kind contains *audible*
PDF documents in your music library	Kind contains *PDF*
Songs that ask a question	Song Name contains *?*
Songs from your high-school days (assuming that you've reached them)	Year is in the range 1975 to 1978 (for example)
Songs you've purchased from the iTunes Music Store	Kind contains *protected AAC*
Videos you've purchased	Kind contains *protected MPEG-4 video*
Podcasts	Podcast is true

More Smart Playlist Tips

A Smart Playlist for Small iPods

Do you have an iPod with a relatively limited capacity—an iPod shuffle or mini, for example? Instead of letting iTunes decide what to copy to the iPod as described on page 101, you might want to set up a smart playlist that selects only songs you like and omits ones in space-consuming audio formats.

The smart playlist below, based on one originally developed by *Playlist* magazine's Chris Breen, does exactly that.

You might want to fine-tune the *Limit to* value to accommodate your specific iPod. The 3500MB value (roughly 3.5GB) is ideal for a 4GB iPod mini.

After creating this playlist, set up your iPod preferences to update only that playlist (see page 98).

Including or Excluding Existing Playlists

You can have iTunes include or exclude specific playlists when putting together a smart playlist. Choose the Playlist item from the leftmost pop-up menu, choose "is" or "is not" from the middle pop-up menu, then choose a playlist name from the rightmost pop-up menu.

This gives you more control over which songs iTunes selects. For example, to put together a playlist of all the jazz you've bought from the iTunes Music Store, create two criteria: Genre is jazz, and Playlist is Purchased Music.

Or, assemble a playlist of the highest rated songs in a favorite playlist: My Rating is greater than three stars, and Playlist is My Favorites (for example).

You can also use this feature to create more sophisticated search rules. For example, say you want to assemble a smart playlist of your R&B and jazz tunes from the 1960s. First, create a smart playlist that locates all your R&B and jazz. Create two criteria: Genre is R&B *and* Genre is Jazz, then choose Any from the Match pop-up menu. Name this playlist something like "R&B and Jazz."

Next, create another smart playlist with the following two criteria: Playlist is R&B and Jazz and Year is in the range 1960 to 1969.

Don't Forget Comments

As described on page 28, you can assign comments and other tidbits of information to your songs. These tidbits pair up beautifully with smart playlists. For example, if you're a jazz buff, you might use the Comments field to store the sidemen who appear on a given song—Ron Carter on bass, Freddie Hubbard on trumpet. You could then create a smart playlist containing songs in which Freddie Hubbard appears: Comment contains *Freddie Hubbard*.

Something Completely Different

Want to explore your music library in a completely different way? Try making a smart playlist built around the Track Number field. For example, to create a smart playlist containing the first song in all of your albums, specify Track Number is 1. If one of your favorite artists always starts his or her albums with a particularly cool track, add the artist's name: Artist is George Duke and Track Number is 1.

Want More?

Looking for even more smart playlists? Believe it or not, there's a Web site devoted to them: www.smartplaylists.com. Check it out for smart playlist ideas and iTunes tips of all kinds.

Find that Tune: Searching and Browsing

As your music library grows, you'll want to take advantage of the features iTunes provides for locating songs, artists, videos, podcasts, and albums.

With the iTunes Search box, you can quickly narrow down the list of songs displayed to only those songs that match the criterion you typed. You can narrow your searches to specific items—for example, podcasts, albums, or videos—by using the search bar.

With the Browse button, you can quickly scan your music library by artist, album name, or genre.

And with the Show Song File command in the File menu, you can quickly display the actual disk file that corresponds to a given song in your library or in a playlist.

Finding a Song's Disk File

There may be times when you want to locate a song's disk file on your hard drive—to back it up, for example, to move it to another drive, or to simply determine where it's stored.

To locate a song's disk file, select the song and choose Show Song File from the File menu (or press ⌘-R). iTunes switches you to the Finder, opens the folder containing the song, and highlights the song file.

Searching

To search your entire music library, be sure the Library item is selected in the Source list. To search a specific playlist, select that playlist's name. Then click within the Search box and begin typing.

As you type in the Search box, iTunes narrows down the list of items displayed. iTunes searches the album title, artist, genre, composer, and song title items. To see all the songs in your library or the selected playlist, select the text in the Search box and press Delete, or simply click the ⊗ in the Search box.

Be More Specific: The Search Bar

When you perform a search, iTunes displays the Search bar, which lets you narrow down your search results.

To show only specific kinds of media, click a button.

To apply your search text to only an artist, album, or track name, click a button. For example, to display all songs by Jennifer Love Hewitt without also displaying all songs with "love" in their names, click Artist.

Tip: Normally, the Search bar disappears when you remove the text from the Search box. But if you'd like to display the Search bar all the time, choose Show Search Bar from the Edit menu.

Browsing

The Artist pane lists all the artists in your library. Select an artist name, and iTunes displays that artist's albums in the Album pane.

Use the link arrows to quickly browse your library: press the Option key while clicking on the link arrow for an artist, song, or album. (To customize this feature, see page 78.)

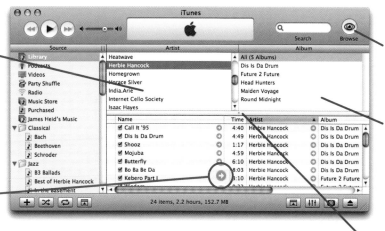

To browse your music library by artist and album name, click the Browse button.

The Album pane lists all the albums in your library or those from a selected artist. Select an album name, and iTunes displays the songs from that album.

Drag the separator up or down to resize the window panes.

Browsing by Genre

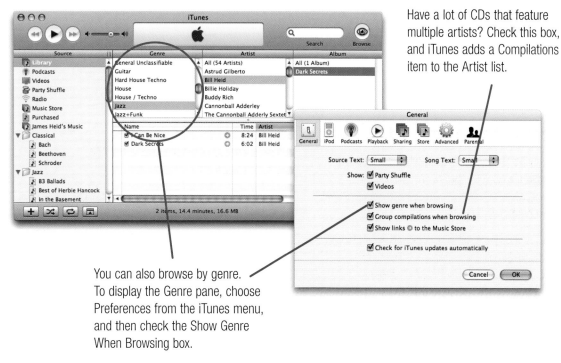

Have a lot of CDs that feature multiple artists? Check this box, and iTunes adds a Compilations item to the Artist list.

You can also browse by genre. To display the Genre pane, choose Preferences from the iTunes menu, and then check the Show Genre When Browsing box.

Improving Sound Quality with the Equalizer

The iTunes *equalizer* lets you boost and attenuate various frequency ranges; think of it as a very sophisticated set of bass and treble controls. You might pump up the bass to make up for small speakers. You might boost the high frequencies to make up for aging ears. Or you might just prefer a little extra sonic seasoning on your music.

The iTunes equalizer (EQ) divides the audio spectrum into ten *bands*, and provides a slider that lets you boost or attenuate frequencies in each band. The bands start at 32 hertz (Hz), a deeper bass than most of us can hear, and go all the way up to 16 kilohertz (KHz), which, while short of dog-whistle territory, approaches the upper limits of human hearing. (If you've been around for more than several decades or have listened to a lot of loud music, 16 KHz is probably out of your hearing range.)

iTunes provides more than 20 equalization presets from which to choose. You can listen to all your music with one setting applied, or you can assign separate settings to individual songs. You can also adjust EQ settings by hand and create your own presets.

Your iPod will also grant your EQ wishes. If you assign an EQ setting to a song and then copy the song to an iPod, the iPod plays the song with that setting.

To display the equalizer, click the Equalizer button (▥) near the lower-right corner of the iTunes window, or choose Equalizer from the Window menu (⌘-2).

Finding Your Way Around the Equalizer

Drag a slider up to boost the frequencies in that range; drag it down to attenuate them.

Click to turn on the equalizer.

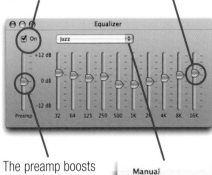

The preamp boosts or attenuates the volume for all frequencies equally. For example, If you create a custom EQ setting for your quiet classical guitar recordings, you might boost the preamp volume as well.

Choose a preset, create a new preset, or manage your list of presets.

Creating Your Own Preset

1. To save a customized preset, choose Make Preset from the preset pop-up menu.

2. Type a name for the preset and click OK.

The new preset appears in the pop-up menu.

Assigning Presets to Individual Songs

If you've turned on the equalizer, iTunes applies the current EQ setting to any song you play back. However, you can also assign EQ settings on a song-by-song basis.

First, choose View Options from the Edit menu and verify that the Equalizer box is checked.

Next, choose the desired preset from the pop-up menu in the Equalizer column.

To change the EQ settings for several songs at once, select the songs and choose Get Info from the File menu. Then choose the desired EQ setting.

Presets that Make You Smile

You may have noticed that many of iTunes' presets have a smile-like appearance: the low- and high-frequency ranges are boosted to a greater degree than the mid-range frequencies.

Audio gurus call this shape the *Fletcher-Munson curve.* It reflects the fact that, at most listening levels, our ears are less sensitive to low and high frequencies than they are to mid-range frequencies.

Chances are your stereo system has a Loudness button. When you turn it on, the stereo applies a similar curve to make the music sound more natural at lower volume levels.

Classical

Jazz

Rock

Latin

"That Song Needs a Bit More 250"

Being able to control the volume of 10 different frequency ranges is great, but how do you know which ranges to adjust? Here's a guide to how frequency ranges correlate with those of some common musical instruments and the human voice. Note that these ranges don't take into account harmonics, which are the tonal complexities that help us discern between instruments. Harmonics can easily exceed 20 KHz.

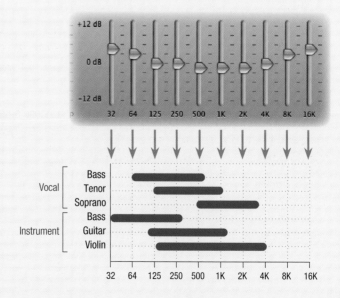

57

Burning Audio CDs

It may be on life support, but the compact disc player isn't dead yet. If your Mac contains a CD burner (all current models do), you can create your own audio CDs— to play in the car, in the living room, on a boombox, or at a friend's house.

To burn some songs onto a CD, you must first add them to a playlist. Once you've done that, burning a CD is a two-click proposition.

iTunes also has some advanced burning features that enable you to burn other types of discs; for details on them and for tips for all your burning endeavors, see page 60.

Chances are you'll be burning using the CD or DVD burner built into your Mac. But iTunes also works with many external burners sold by La Cie, Formac, EZQuest, and others. These drives typically connect to the Mac's USB or FireWire connector.

Step 1.
Select the Playlist You Want to Burn

If the playlist contains a song that you don't want to burn, uncheck the box next to the song's name.

iTunes displays the playlist's total duration here.

Important: If you're burning an audio CD, keep the playlist's duration under 74 minutes. If your entire playlist won't fit on one audio CD, iTunes will offer to burn additional discs.

Step 2.
Click the Burn Disc Button

When you click Burn Disc, iTunes opens your Mac's CD tray and instructs you to insert a blank CD.

Note: As an alternative to clicking the Burn Disc button, you can choose Burn Playlist to Disc from the File menu.

To cancel the burn, click here.

Step 3.
Insert a Blank Disc

As the CD burns, iTunes displays a status message. You can cancel a burn in progress by clicking the ⊗ button, but you'll end up with a *coaster*—a damaged CD blank whose only useful purpose is to sit beneath a cold drink.

What You Can't Burn

iTunes lets you burn audio CDs containing just about anything—just about.

Here are some items that are *not* flammable.

Purchased videos. You can't burn audio CDs or DVD-Video discs containing videos purchased from the iTunes Music Store. You can, however, burn backups of the videos by burning a data CD as described on the following pages.

Unauthorized purchased music. You can't burn a song purchased from the iTunes Music Store unless your Mac is authorized for the same account as the one used to buy the tune. If you try, a dialog box appears asking for the account and

password for the account used to buy the song.

The pesky eighth copy. As noted on page 38, you can't burn more than seven copies of a playlist that contains purchased music.

Tips for Your Burning Endeavors

By adjusting burning preferences, you can control the pause between songs, volume levels, and even the format of your final CD. Choose Preferences from the iTunes menu, click the Advanced button, then click Burning.

Gap Control

When iTunes burns an audio CD, it uses a two-second gap to separate songs. Depending on what you're burning, you may want to omit, or at least change, that gap. On many albums, one song flows seamlessly into the next. When burning these kinds of tracks, close the gap: choose None from the Gap Between Songs pop-up menu.

Unfortunately, because of the nature of audio compression, you may still hear a tiny gap between songs. If you can't bear even the smallest pause, rip the songs from an audio CD using the Join Tracks option (page 20).

Volume Control

Not all albums are mastered at the same volume level, and if you mix and match tracks from a few CDs, some songs may sound much quieter than others. Don't reach for the volume knob—click the Sound Check box before burning, and iTunes adjusts each track to make the final CD's levels consistent.

You can also apply Sound Check when playing music in iTunes; see page 74 for details.

Burning MP3 CDs

Normally, iTunes burns CDs in standard audio CD format. But you can also burn tracks as MP3 files; this lets you take advantage of MP3's compression so you can squeeze more music onto a CD— roughly ten times the number of songs that an audio CD will hold.

But there are a couple of catches. Catch Number One: Most audio CD players can't play MP3-format CDs. If you're shopping for a CD or DVD player, you may want to look for one that supports MP3 playback.

Catch Number Two: When you burn a playlist in MP3 format, iTunes skips over any songs that are stored in AAC format. If you're taking advantage of AAC's superior efficiency—or if you've built a library of purchases from the iTunes Music Store—the MP3 CD format won't be of much use to you.

To have iTunes burn in MP3 format, click the MP3 CD button in the Burning preferences dialog box.

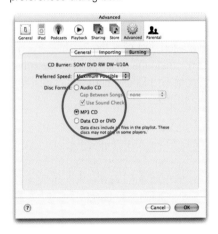

When ripping CDs that you'll subsequently be burning in MP3 format, you might find it useful to activate the iTunes track numbering option: in the Preferences dialog box, click Importing and then check the box labeled Create file names with track number.

Track numbering is useful because many players play the songs on MP3 CDs in alphanumeric order—activating track numbering will enable the tracks to play back in the correct order.

Back Up What You Buy

You've bought some music—and then your hard drive dies. The songs and videos you bought are gone, and the only way to download them again is to buy them again.

Clearly, backing up is good to do. iTunes can help.

Choose Preferences from the iTunes menu, click Burning, then choose the Data CD option. Next, create a playlist of the songs you want to back up. (If you want to back up only the items you've purchased, just click the Purchased playlist or create the smart playlist I describe on page 51.) Finally, burn that playlist to a CD or DVD.

If you have more music than will fit on a single CD or DVD, iTunes displays a message letting you know. Verify that you have a few blank discs available, then click the Data Discs button.

Another way to back up a huge music library is to drag it to a second hard drive. An external FireWire hard drive is inexpensive and makes great backup media for music and photos alike. Go to your Home directory (choose Home from the Finder's Go menu), then locate and double-click your Music folder. Locate the folder named iTunes and drag it to the other hard drive. Unlike the burning approach, this technique also backs up all of your playlists.

Tip: If you've copied your entire music library to an iPod, you can use an iPod utility to recover your songs; see page 100.

Blank Advice

Many brands of CD-R media are available, and some people swear by a given brand. Some users even claim that certain colors of CD-R blanks are better than others.

My advice: don't sweat it—just buy name-brand CD-R blanks. And don't fret about their colors. Color varies depending on the organic dyes used by the CD-R's manufacturer, and different manufacturers use different dye formulations. Color isn't a useful indicator of CD-R quality anyway.

How long will your burned CDs last? Manufacturers toss out figures ranging from 75 to 200 years, but these are only estimates based on accelerated aging tests that attempt to simulate the effects of time.

One thing is certain: a CD-R will last longer when kept away from heat and bright light. Avoid scratching either side of a CD-R—use a felt-tipped pen to label it, and don't write any more than you need to. (The solvents in the ink can damage the CD over time.)

Also, think twice about applying a peel-and-stick label to the CD. The label's adhesive can damage the CD over time, and if you don't center the label perfectly, the CD will be out of balance as it spins, which could cause playback problems.

To learn more about CD-R media, visit the CD-Recordable FAQ at www.cdrfaq.org.

Burning to CD-RW Media

For broadest compatibility with CD players, you'll want to burn using CD-R blanks, which can't be erased and reused. But the CD burners in all current Macs can also use CD-RW media—rewritable media, which costs more but can be erased and reused again and again.

A growing number of CD players can play back rewritable media, and if yours is among them, you might consider using rewritable media for some burning jobs—such as burning some podcasts for car listening. This media is also ideal for backing up your iTunes music library.

Note that iTunes can't erase a CD-RW disc. To do that, use Mac OS X's Disk Utility program; it's located in the Utilities folder, inside the Applications folder.

Finishing Touches: Printing Case Inserts and More

After you've burned a CD, you might want to print an insert that you can slide into the disc's jewel case. With the printing features in iTunes, you can do this and more.

When printing a case insert, you can choose from a variety of insert designs, called *themes*. Some themes take advantage of the album artwork feature described on the opposite page. If your playlist's songs have corresponding album art, iTunes uses the art for the front and back of the case insert. With a few mouse clicks, you can even put your own artwork on a jewel case insert.

You can also print several types of song and album lists. They're a great way to produce a hard-copy reference of your music library and favorite playlists.

If your playlist contains songs from multiple albums, you can use the Mosaic themes to produce a collage of album art.

Want to use just one album's art for the cover? Before you choose Print, select the song containing that art.

To Print a Jewel Case Insert

Step 1. In the Source area, select the playlist for which you want a case insert.

Step 2. Choose Print from the File menu and choose a theme.

Step 3. Adjust Page Setup options as needed, then click Print or press Return.

Step 4. Trim the case insert, using the crop marks as a guide.

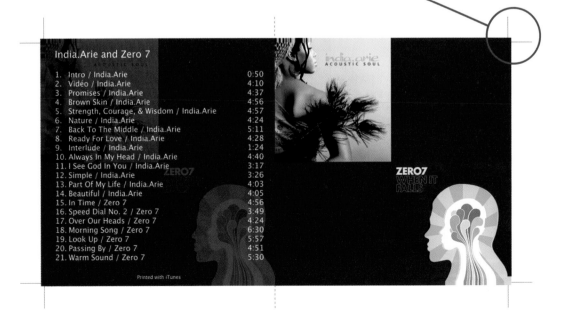

India.Arie and Zero 7

1.	Intro / India.Arie	0:50
2.	Vidéo / India.Arie	4:10
3.	Promises / India.Arie	4:37
4.	Brown Skin / India.Arie	4:56
5.	Strength, Courage, & Wisdom / India.Arie	4:57
6.	Nature / India.Arie	4:24
7.	Back To The Middle / India.Arie	5:11
8.	Ready For Love / India.Arie	4:28
9.	Interlude / India.Arie	1:24
10.	Always In My Head / India.Arie	4:40
11.	I See God In You / India.Arie	3:17
12.	Simple / India.Arie	3:26
13.	Part Of My Life / India.Arie	4:03
14.	Beautiful / India.Arie	4:05
15.	In Time / Zero 7	4:56
16.	Speed Dial No. 2 / Zero 7	3:49
17.	Over Our Heads / Zero 7	4:24
18.	Morning Song / Zero 7	6:30
19.	Look Up / Zero 7	5:57
20.	Passing By / Zero 7	4:51
21.	Warm Sound / Zero 7	5:30

Printed with iTunes

More About Artwork

iTunes can store album artwork— for example, an image of a CD cover— along with your music. The artwork is embedded into a music file itself, so if you move the file to another Mac, the art moves along with it. The artwork also displays on an iPod's screen as a song plays (see page 103).

Music that you buy from the iTunes Music Store usually has artwork. To display it, click the Show/Hide Artwork button.

To switch between the currently playing song and the currently selected song, click here. A song can contain multiple images; click the little arrows to display other images.

To hide (or show) the art-work, click this button.

Adding Artwork to Songs

What about all the songs in your library that don't have artwork? If you'd like to add art to them, you have several options. Some free utilities will search for, and retrieve, artwork over the Internet; I use a program called Fetch Art, by Yoel Inbar. Like other artwork utilities, it looks up the name of an album on Amazon.com, then retrieves the artwork from Amazon's site.

For more artwork-related utilities, see macilife.com/itunes.

To rearrange the images, drag them left and right. To use a specific image in a jewel case insert, drag it so that it's the first image in the list.

To add another image, click Add. To delete an image, select it and then click Delete.

To display the artwork in a larger window, click here. To add an image to the currently selected song, drag an image here. To copy the art into another program, drag it from here to the program.

More Artwork Tips

You can also view and modify a song's artwork by using the Song Information dialog box. Select a song, choose Get Info from File menu, and click the Artwork option. In the example below, the song contains four images. You can store even more, but keep in mind that each image increases the size of your music file, thus leaving less free space on your hard drive and iPod.

To make the thumbnail images smaller or larger, drag the slider.

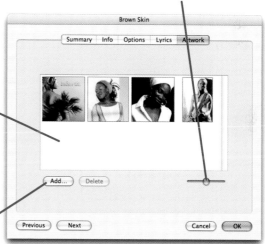

Print your own artwork. You can print your own artwork—including a photo from your iPhoto library—on a jewel case insert. First, add the image to a song. (For a photo, simply drag it from the iPhoto window to the artwork area.) Drag the image so it's the first image in the list, then print. To reduce the size of the song file, delete the image after printing.

Sharing Music on a Network

If you have multiple Macs or Windows PCs on a network, you can use iTunes' sharing feature to turn them into jukeboxes whose music other computers can play. (You'll need to install iTunes for Windows on the PCs.)

Sharing enables all manner of music networking options. You might keep all of your music on one Mac—no wasting disk space by storing a music library on each Mac or PC on your network. Conversely, you might prefer to segregate your music—put your kids' music on their iMac and your music on yours—while still giving each Mac access to every song. You might want to set up a jukebox Mac to dish out tunes to the office. Or use AirPort wireless networking to listen at poolside using your PowerBook.

If you use a Mac that supports Apple's FrontRow software, you can also access shared music libraries using FrontRow's Music mode.

The sharing feature relies on streaming: when you listen to another Mac's music, the song files are streamed across your network. The files are never actually copied from one Mac to another.

Activating Sharing

To share your music library with other Macs on your network, choose Preferences from the iTunes menu, then click the Sharing button.

To have your Mac automatically connect to shared libraries on your network, check this box.

To share your music, check this box.

You can share your entire library or only selected playlists. To share a specific playlist, click its check box.

When other users connect to your shared music, this name will appear in their copies of iTunes.

Don't want your kids (or parents) to access your shared library? Check this box, then specify a password.

When sharing is on, the Status area also shows how many users are connected.

Note: Be sure you're using the same version of iTunes on each computer on the network. Apple has changed the iTunes sharing feature a couple of times, and as a result, different versions of iTunes aren't always able to share libraries. If a shared library appears grey and an error message appears when you select it, it's probably because the shared library is coming from an older version of iTunes.

Accessing Shared Music

If you've checked the Look for Shared Music box in the Sharing portion of the Preferences dialog box, iTunes automatically scans your network and finds shared libraries.

To view a shared library, click its name in the Source list. If the library requires a password, a dialog box appears.

To view playlists in a shared library, click the little triangle next to the library's name.

Tips for Sharing

Shared Songs Are Play-Only

Because shared songs don't reside on your hard drive, you can't add them to playlists, delete them, burn them to a CD, or modify their information.

Up to Five a Day

Up to five computers can connect to a shared library on a given day. If a sixth user tries to connect, he or she sees an error message along these lines: *The shared music library "Jim's Music" accepts only five different users each day. Please try again later.*

There is but one solution to this restriction: wait until tomorrow.

Disconnecting

To disconnect from a shared library click the Disconnect button (⬛) in the lower-right corner of the iTunes window, or Control-click on the library in the Source list and choose Disconnect from the pop-up shortcut menu. Or, click on the eject button that appears next to the music library's name in the Source list.

Authorization

If you want to play a purchased song from a shared library, you'll have to authorize your Mac by supplying your account name and password. As noted on page 38, you can authorize up to five computers per account.

Tuning In to Internet Radio

The Internet is transforming a lot of things, and broadcasting is one of them. You can tune in to thousands of streaming Internet radio stations using iTunes and other programs.

Many of these stations are commercial or public broadcasters that are also making their audio available on the 'net. But most stations are Internet-only affairs, often set up by music lovers who simply want to share their tastes with the rest of us. You can join them—create your own radio station using a service such as Live365 (www.live365.com) or a streaming server program such as Rogue Amoeba's NiceCast (www.rogueamoeba.com).

If part of streaming audio's appeal is its diversity, the other part is its immediacy. Streaming playback begins just a few seconds after you click on a link—there's no waiting for huge sound files to download before you hear a single note.

Several formats for streaming audio exist, and MP3 is one of them. Using the iTunes Radio tuner, you can listen to Internet radio stations that stream in MP3 format.

Turn on the Tuner

The first step in using iTunes to listen to Internet radio is to activate the iTunes radio tuner.

Click Radio to switch the iTunes view to the radio tuner. To display the tuner in its own window, double-click.

Note: If you don't see the Radio item, choose Preferences from the iTunes menu, click General, and be sure the Radio check box is selected.

iTunes retrieves its list of Internet radio categories and stations from the Internet. Click Refresh to have iTunes contact the tuning service and update its list of categories and stations.

iTunes groups Internet radio stations by genre; to display the stations in a genre, double-click the genre name or click on the triangle to its left.

Bandwidth:
Internet Radio's Antenna

The quality of your Internet radio "reception" depends in part on the speed of your Internet connection.

With Internet radio, information listed in the Bit Rate column is particularly important. It reflects not only how much the audio has been compressed, but also how fast a connection you'll need in order to listen without interruption. For example, if you have a 56 kbps modem connection, you won't be able to listen to a stream whose bit rate is higher than 56 kbps. (Indeed, even a 56 kbps stream may hiccup occasionally.)

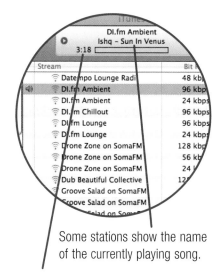

Some stations show the name of the currently playing song.

iTunes shows how long you've been listening to a stream. Notice that when you're listening to a live stream, there is no control for skipping forward and backward within a song.

To listen to a station, double-click the station's name.

How Streaming Works

When you begin playing back an Internet radio stream, iTunes connects to a streaming server, which downloads several seconds' worth of audio into an area of memory called a *buffer*. When the buffer is full, playback begins. The player then continues downloading audio into the buffer while simultaneously playing back the audio that it has already buffered. It's this just-in-time downloading that gives streaming its near-immediate gratification—most of the time, anyway.

If Internet congestion or connection problems interrupt the incoming stream, the buffer may empty completely, stalling playback while the buffer refills.

Recording Internet Radio and More

Internet radio is a fleeting affair—just as your radio doesn't store programs, iTunes and other streaming players don't store Internet audio on your hard drive. That means you can't add your favorite streaming radio programming to your iTunes library or listen to it on your iPod.

At least not without a little help. Several inexpensive programs can record streaming audio on your hard drive. In fact, they can record any sound your Mac can play. Thus, you can also record audio from DVDs: record some tunes from a favorite concert movie—or some dialog from your favorite Cheech and Chong romp—and burn an audio CD to play in the car.

You can also use one of these programs to record real-time performance effects in GarageBand. You can even record the soundtrack and explosions of a favorite video game, if that's your idea of easy listening.

Incidentally, if you have favorite AM or FM radio broadcasts that you'd like to record and add to your iTunes library (and iPod), check out Griffin Technology's RadioShark. It turns your Mac into a TiVo for radio, enabling you to schedule and record radio broadcasts.

Hijacking in Three Easy Steps

The top tool for recording the unrecordable is Rogue Amoeba Software's Audio Hijack (see opposite page for a look at other tools). Here's how to use it.

Step 1. Hijack.

Create a preset for the program whose audio you want to record. If you like, set a timer to start or stop recording at specific times. You can also specify that Audio Hijack run an AppleScript after recording (see page 82 for an introduc-

tion to AppleScripts). Audio Hijack includes scripts that use iTunes to encode a recording into AAC or MP3 format.

Step 2. Click the Record button and start playback.

Click Audio Hijack's Record button and then begin playing back the audio. Audio Hijack starts recording when playback begins.

Step 3. Add to iTunes and tweak track info.

Add the recording to iTunes if necessary (if you run either of the encoding scripts after recording, this happens automatically). Then, locate the track in your iTunes library, choose Get Info from the File menu, and edit the song information.

For more information about adding audio files to iTunes "by hand," see page 80.

Link to audio-recording programs and more.
www.macilife.com/itunes

GO TO WEB

Getting the Best Sound

When recording Internet audio, you'll often have to make audio-quality decisions.

The right rate. Internet audio is often heavily compressed to allow streaming over slow modem connections. To avoid degrading the sound quality even more, encode at a relatively high bit rate, such as 96 kbps for spoken-word programming, and 128 or 160 kbps for music.

If you're recording talk radio, record in mono rather than stereo.

As for format decisions, as I've mentioned elsewhere, AAC provides better sound quality at a given bit rate than does MP3.

Before or after? With some programs, including Audio Hijack Pro, you can choose these settings before you record. With most of the other tools, you must use iTunes to encode after you record.

Being able to encode as you record is a timesaving convenience that uses disk space more efficiently. On the downside, you don't have the opportunity to experiment with different encoding settings. If you're recording music and want to get the best sound quality, record in uncompressed AIFF format first, then use iTunes to encode, experimenting with different bit rates and formats until you arrive at the combination that sounds best to your ears.

Which Program to Use?

Several stream recorders are available, and each fills a useful niche.

The casual recorder. You want to record the unrecordable only occasionally. You don't want or need complicated features, and heaven forbid that you should have to pay a dime.

For you, there's Ambrosia Software's free WireTap. WireTap couldn't be simpler: start the audio playing and click WireTap's Record button. The only other control WireTap provides is a button for pausing and resuming recording—great for cutting out talk radio commercials.

When you click WireTap's Stop button, you have an audio file

that you can immediately play back in Apple's QuickTime Player or in iTunes.

For more control, consider Ambrosia's WireTap Pro. It taps into Apple's iCal software to let you schedule recordings, and save recordings in several audio formats.

Serious sound. The premiere programs for recording the unrecordable are Rogue Amoeba Software's Audio Hijack and Audio Hijack Pro; unlike the WireTap family, both can snag the sound from specific programs. And if you don't want to hear the audio as you're recording it, one click of the Mute button silences the stream even as it's being recorded.

Both Audio Hijack programs have VCR-like timers that let you start and stop recording at specific times. Both programs also allow you to make bass and treble adjustments as you record, and both provide a feature that removes some of the muddiness associated with Internet audio. Audio Hijack Pro goes much further, providing a broad selection of audio-processing effects: apply the reverberation effect, and you can make Howard Stern sound like he's in a cathedral—at least from an acoustical standpoint.

For the radio lover. Bitcartel's RadioLover specializes in recording MP3 stations, such as those that iTunes can tune in. Many MP3-based stations send artist

and song information along with their streams, and RadioLover can use this information to create separate song files as it records. Set up RadioLover to record for a few hours, and you'll return to find dozens of separate MP3 tracks, already named and ready to add to your iTunes library. It's the kind of feature that makes recording executives reach for antacid, but it's a fabulous way to discover new music. It's also imperfect: the beginning or end of a song is almost always cut off. (You can sometimes fix the problem by adjusting the program's recording preferences.)

Converting Old Tapes and Albums

If you're like me, you're desperate to recapture the past: you want to create digital audio files from audio cassettes and vinyl albums.

Bridging the gap between the analog and digital worlds requires some software and hardware. The process involves connecting your Mac to an audio source, such as a cassette deck or stereo system, and then using recording software to save the audio on your hard drive as it plays back. You can encode the resulting files into AAC or MP3 format and add them to your iTunes music library.

Most current Mac models contain audio-input jacks to that you can connect to a sound source, such as a cassette deck or stereo system. If your Mac doesn't have an audio-input jack, you'll need an adapter such as Griffin Technology's iMic (below), which is inexpensive and includes Final Vinyl, a cutely named recording program. Griffin, M-Audio, and other companies also sell more sophisticated (and better-sounding) audio hardware that you might prefer if you're an audiophile or you plan to record acoustic instruments using GarageBand.

Step 1.
Make the Connections

Recording analog sources is easiest when you connect the Mac to the audio output of a stereo system. This will enable you to record anything your stereo can play, from vinyl albums to cassettes to FM radio.

Most stereo receivers have auxiliary output jacks on their back panels. To make the connection, use a cable with two RCA phono plugs on one end and a ⅛-inch stereo miniplug on the other. Connect the phono plugs to the receiver's output jacks, and the miniplug to the input jack on your Mac or audio adapter.

Step 2.
Prepare to Record

Before you record, set your audio levels properly: you want the audio signal to be as loud as possible without distorting the sound.

Fire up your audio recording software (Roxio's CD Spin Doctor is shown here), and adjust its recording levels so that the loudest passages of music fully illuminate the volume meters.

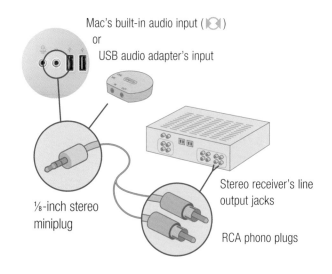

Mac's built-in audio input ( ) or USB audio adapter's input

⅛-inch stereo miniplug

Stereo receiver's line output jacks

RCA phono plugs

Step 3. Record

First, do a test recording. Activate your software's Record mode and begin playing back the original audio, preferably a loud passage. After a minute or two, stop and play back the recorded audio to verify that the recording levels you set are correct. Listen for distortion in loud passages; if you hear any, decrease the levels slightly.

Once you've arrived at the correct setting for recording levels, record the original audio in its entirety.

Step 4. Encode and Edit Song Information

Your completed recording will almost certainly be stored in uncompressed AIFF format—the format used by Mac recording programs.

To save disk space, you'll probably want to encode the recording into AAC or MP3 format. Naturally, you can use iTunes to do this.

Before encoding your recordings, use the Preferences command to choose your preferred encoding settings as described on page 22. Next, hold down the Option key and check out the Advanced menu—you'll see a command that reads Convert to AAC. (If you specified the MP3 encoder in the Preferences dialog box, the command reads Convert to MP3.)

Choose the Convert to AAC (or Convert to MP3) command, and then locate and double-click on the recording you just made. iTunes will encode the track and store the resulting digital audio file in your iTunes library.

iTunes can also encode multiple recordings in one operation. After choosing Convert to AAC (or Convert to MP3), simply ⌘-click on each file you want to import.

After you've encoded your recordings, edit their song information as described on pages 28 and 29. By adding song, artist, album, and genre information, you'll be able to conveniently browse your converted recordings on an iPod and include them in smart playlists.

Choosing a Recording Program

The spectrum of audio-recording software ranges from free (Audacity) to inexpensive (SoundStudio and Amadeus II) to pricey (Bias Peak) and beyond.

One of my favorites is CD Spin Doctor, included with Roxio's Toast Titanium CD burning software. CD Spin Doctor creates AIFF files, which you can encode into AAC or MP3

format using iTunes, as described above.

A few features make CD Spin Doctor ideal for converting analog recordings into digital form. One is the Auto-Define Tracks command: choose it, and CD Spin Doctor scans a recording, detects the silence between each song, and then divides the recording into

multiple tracks. This makes it easy to record one side of an album and then divvy it up into separate tracks.

CD Spin Doctor also has noise and pop filters that can clean up abused records, as well as an "exciter" filter that enhances old recordings by beefing up bass and improving the sense of stereo separation. (Bias'

SoundSoap provides even more noise-cleanup features.)

For detailed audio editing, try Amadeus II or SoundStudio. Get links to these and other audio programs at the iTunes page on macilife.com.

iTunes and Your Stereo

Once you've assembled a digital music library, you're going to want to listen to it using your stereo system. One option is, of course, an iPod: copy your music library to one, then connect the iPod to your stereo (or anyone else's) as shown on page 108.

But you can also connect your Mac to an audio system, and there are some good reasons to do so. You can play music with DJ-like crossfades: one song fades out even as the next song fades in (see page 74). You can play Internet radio—another trick no iPod can perform. You can play audio from other sources, from games to DVDs, and from streaming players to GarageBand. And if your Mac supports Apple's FrontRow software and includes a remote control, you can control your music playback without having to leave your recliner.

The journey from Mac to stereo system has several possible paths; the best one for you depends on the distance between your computer and your audio system, the specific Mac model you have, and your listening goals. Here's a roadmap of some popular routes.

Three Ways to Connect

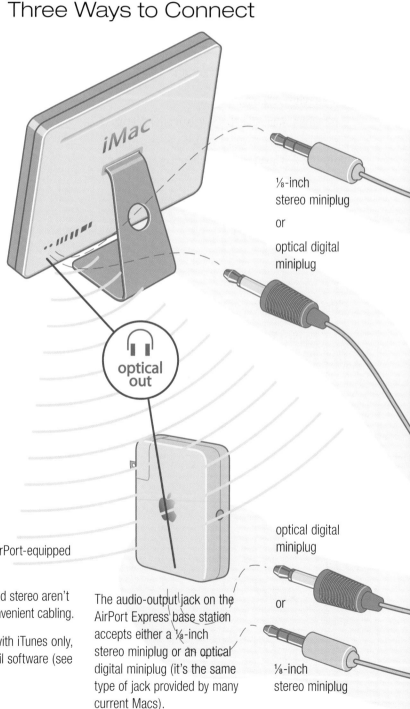

⅛-inch stereo miniplug

or

optical digital miniplug

optical out

optical digital miniplug

or

⅛-inch stereo miniplug

AirPort Express

Connect an AirPort Express base station to your stereo, and you can transmit music from any AirPort-equipped Mac within range. In iTunes, simply select the base station from the pop-up menu.

Works with: Any AirPort-equipped Mac.

Best when: Mac and stereo aren't close enough for convenient cabling.

Downside: Works with iTunes only, unless you use Airfoil software (see page 83).

The audio-output jack on the AirPort Express base station accepts either a ⅛-inch stereo miniplug or an optical digital miniplug (it's the same type of jack provided by many current Macs).

Analog Direct Connection

You can connect any Mac to a stereo system by plugging a cable into the Mac's headphone jack.

Works with: Any Mac.

Best when: Mac and audio system are relatively close together.

Downside: Audio is less pristine than with digital connections, although most ears will never notice.

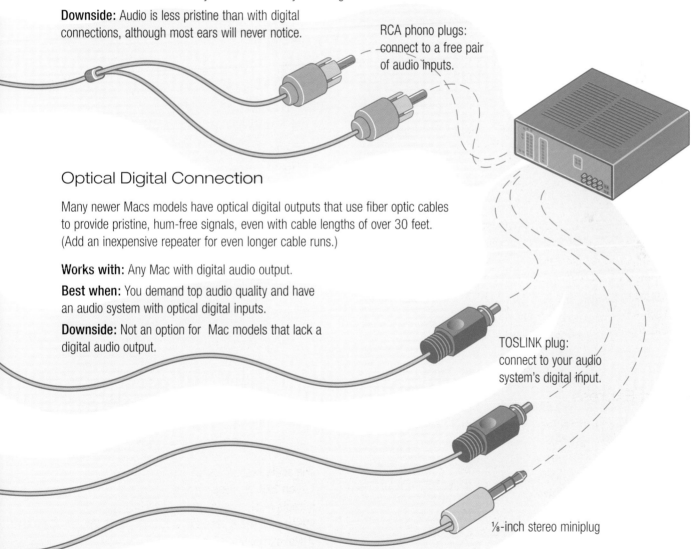

RCA phono plugs: connect to a free pair of audio inputs.

Optical Digital Connection

Many newer Macs models have optical digital outputs that use fiber optic cables to provide pristine, hum-free signals, even with cable lengths of over 30 feet. (Add an inexpensive repeater for even longer cable runs.)

Works with: Any Mac with digital audio output.

Best when: You demand top audio quality and have an audio system with optical digital inputs.

Downside: Not an option for Mac models that lack a digital audio output.

TOSLINK plug: connect to your audio system's digital input.

⅛-inch stereo miniplug

Tips for Playing Music

Crossfading Songs

You hear it on the radio all the time: as one song nears its end, it begins to fade as the next song starts to play. You can recreate this effect in iTunes. First, choose Preferences from the iTunes menu, click the Playback button, and then check the Crossfade Playback box.

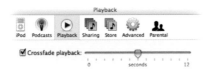

With crossfading, one song fades out...

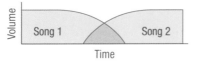

...as the next song fades in.

Dock Control

When iTunes is running, you can start and stop playback and perform other tasks using the iTunes icon in your dock. Point to the icon and hold down the mouse button (or simply Control-click on the icon), then choose the desired command from the shortcut menu. For even more control over iTunes, check out Synergy, described on page 83.

Making iTunes Tiny

To instantly miniaturize the iTunes window, click the green button in its upper-left corner.

To make the window even smaller, drag the size control in the lower-right corner.

Stash this micro-iTunes window in a corner of your screen for convenient access. And if you always want it to be visible, even when you're working in other programs, choose Preferences from the iTunes menu, click Advanced, click General, and then check the box labeled *Keep Mini Player on top of all other windows*.

To restore the full iTunes window, click the green button again.

Optimizing Levels

When you create a playlist containing songs from numerous albums, you may notice that some songs are louder than others. One way to compensate for this is by adjusting the playback volume for specific songs. First, Control-click on

a song and then choose Get Info from the contextual pop-up menu.

In the Options tab of the Song Information dialog box, drag the Volume Adjustment slider to decrease or increase the song's playback volume.

A faster alternative to adjusting playback levels for individual songs is to use the Sound Check option, which optimizes playback volumes so that all songs play back with similar volume levels. To turn Sound Check on, choose Preferences from the iTunes menu, click the Playback button, then check the Sound Check box.

The Sound Enhancer

You can add aural punch by improving what audio gurus call *presence*, the perception that the instruments are right in the room with you. To do this, use the Sound Enhancer option in the Playback tab of the Preferences dialog box. Drag the slider toward the High setting, and you may notice brighter-sounding high frequencies and an enhanced sense of stereo separation. Experiment with the setting that sounds best for your ears—and your audio equipment.

Skipping to the Next or Previous Album

As I noted on page 19, you can skip to the next song by clicking ▶▶ and to the previous song by clicking ◀◀. To skip to the next or previous album, press the Option key while clicking these buttons.

You can also skip to the next and previous album using the keyboard: press Option along with the right-arrow or left-arrow key.

Adjusting Volume with a Scroll Wheel Mouse

Apple's Mighty Mouse and many third-party mice have a scroll wheel. If your rodent is so equipped, you can use the scroll wheel to adjust the volume when iTunes is in its tiny-window mode—just point to the volume slider and roll the wheel.

Showing the Current Song

Here's a common scenario: As you listen to a tune, you begin browsing your music library or maybe even shopping at the iTunes Music Store. Then you decide to add the currently playing song to a playlist.

How can you quickly find it? Easy: choose Show Current Song from the File menu (⌘-L). Choose this command, and iTunes displays and highlights the song that's currently playing.

You can also click the SnapBack button, which appears near the right-hand side of the iTunes LCD—that wide area at the top of the iTunes window.

How to "Crop" Songs

Scenario #1: You have an album that was recorded live, and each song starts with a long, rambling introduction by the recording artist. You'd like to cut out that intro and just start with the music.

Scenario #2: There's a song you really want to like but, two thirds of the way through, it degenerates into an ear-bleeding cacophony of noise.

iTunes has a little-used feature that beautifully addresses both of these scenarios: you can "crop" a song—lop off part of the beginning, part of the end, or both—to hear only the part you want to hear. This cropping is even retained when you transfer the song to an iPod. And best of all, it's easy.

First, listen to the song you want to crop, and use the iTunes time display to note where the offensive portion ends or begins. Now select the song, choose Get Info from the File menu, and click the Options button.

Next, configure the Start Time and/or Stop Time boxes as needed. In the

example below, I'm skipping over the first 34 seconds of the song.

Click OK when you've finished, and you're done.

And if you ever do want to hear that cropped-out portion, you can do so by simply dragging the little playback diamond that appears near the top of the iTunes window. Or, return to the Get Info dialog box and uncheck the Start Time and/or Stop Time boxes.

Marking Your Place

iTunes has the ability to remember the point where you stopped listening to or watching an item, and then resume at that point the next time you play it back. Audiobooks and videos work this way automatically, but you can add the "bookmarking" capability to any song, podcast, or video. Select the item, choose Get Info from the File menu, click the Options button, then check the Remember Playback Position box.

As page 85 describes, bookmarking extends to the iPod, too: when you play an item that you've already started, the iPod resumes where you left off.

Surprise Me: Shuffle Playback Options

When long-playing albums appeared in the 1940s, recording artists gained the ability to present more than one song at a time. LPs enabled artists to present songs in a sequence of their choosing. And for the next forty years or so, music lovers would be locked into their choices.

Then compact discs appeared. Unlike phonographs, CD players could instantly access any part of an album. To take advantage of this, player manufacturers added *shuffle* features: press a button, and the player skipped around within a CD, playing tracks at random. One comedian even worked the concept into his routine: "I ran into a famous musician on the street and I told him, 'I'm familiar with your latest CD—but not in the order you want me to be.'"

iTunes takes the shuffle concept to the next level. Sure, you can play tracks or albums at random, but with the Party Shuffle playlist, you can combine the serendipity of shuffle mode with the forethought of a well-crafted playlist.

Some music lovers want full control over playback; others love the game of chance that shuffle modes provide. One thing is certain: random-playback features are a great way to rediscover songs you haven't listened to in a while.

Here's how turn your music jukebox into a slot machine.

Using Shuffle Mode

The simplest form of random playback is shuffle mode. To play random songs from your library, select the Library item, then click the shuffle button (⤭).

Shuffling a playlist. To simply hear a playlist in random order, select the playlist, then click the shuffle button.

If you'd like to *see* what kind of random order iTunes comes up with, click the playlist's leftmost column heading to sort it in numeric order, *then* click the shuffle button.

Keeping a shuffle. Sometimes a random pick is perfect—just ask any lottery winner. If you like the way iTunes has shuffled a playlist, you can tell iTunes to reorder the songs so that they always play back in that order. Simply Control-click on the playlist's name and then choose Copy to Play Order from the shortcut menu.

Album and grouping shuffle. Normally, shuffle mode plays back songs in random order. You can, however, also choose to shuffle by album or by grouping. In album-shuffle mode, iTunes plays back an entire album in its original song order, then randomly chooses another album and plays all of it.

To use these modes, use the Playback pane of the iTunes Preferences dialog box. While you're there, you can also drag the Smart Shuffle slider to fine-tune how likely you are to hear multiple songs in a row by the same artist or from the same album.

Tip: To ensure that a particular item—for example, a podcast—never plays in shuffle mode, select that item and choose File > Get Info. Next, click Options and check the Skip When Shuffling box.

Read some articles about the joys of shuffle.
www.macilife.com/itunes

Mix it Up: Party Shuffle

The Party Shuffle playlist is a hybrid of random shuffle mode, smart playlists, and conventional playlists.

To use Party Shuffle, click it in the Source list of the iTunes window (🎵). iTunes instantly assembles a list of songs.

The blue bar separates songs that have been played from upcoming songs (see related tip, right).

Another good reason to rate your music (page 78): you can have iTunes weight its selection toward higher-rated songs.

Don't like what iTunes has come up with? Click Refresh, and iTunes rolls the dice and chooses another batch of songs.

You can tell iTunes to narrow its pool of eligible songs to specific playlists. **Tip:** To create a party shuffle mix based on a specific genre, create a smart playlist for that genre (for example, genre is Rock), then specify that smart playlist here (see "Freeze the mix," below).

You can have iTunes display the last songs it played from the shuffle, and up to 100 upcoming songs.

Party Shuffle Tips

Customizing the mix. As with other types of playlists, you can change the Party Shuffle playlist on a song-by-song basis: drag songs up or down to change their playback order, delete songs you don't want to hear, and manually add songs from your iTunes library by dragging them into the playlist.

Adding a song. You can add a song to the Party Shuffle playlist by simply dragging it, but there's a shortcut. Control-click on a song, then, from the shortcut menu, choose either Play Next in

Party Shuffle (to hear the song next) or Add to Party Shuffle (to add the song to the end of the Party Shuffle playlist).

Selecting from multiple playlists. To base a party shuffle mix on more than one playlist, create a smart playlist that selects those playlists (for example, Playlist is *My Favorites* and Playlist is *Jazz Hits*), then specify that smart playlist.

Freeze the mix. If you like what Party Shuffle comes up with, you can save the mix as a conven-

tional playlist: choose Select All (⌘-A), then choose New Playlist from Selection (Option-⌘-N).

Drag the blue bar. As described above, the blue bar separates songs that have played from upcoming songs— when a song finishes playing, it moves above the bar.

You can also use the blue bar in another way. If you like some, but not all, of the songs that iTunes has chosen, you can retain the songs you like, then have iTunes choose more at random.

First, choose 0 (zero) from the Recently Played Songs pop-up menu. Now drag the songs you want to keep in the playlist to the top of the list. Next, tell iTunes to display some recently played songs—choose 5 or 10 or any other value from the pop-up menu. Finally, drag the blue bar so that it's just below the last song you want to keep.

Now click Refresh. iTunes whips up a fresh batch of random selections, but retains the songs that appear above the blue bar.

Tips for Customizing and More

Customizing Columns

You can specify which columns of information iTunes displays in its windows—to remove columns you never use, or to add ones that iTunes normally doesn't display.

One way to customize columns is to use the Edit menu's View Options command. Here's an easier way: Control-click on any column heading, and uncheck or check columns in the shortcut menu.

You can also use the shortcut menu to automatically resize columns to fit the longest item in each one. And you can change the order of the columns themselves, moving them left and right to suit your tastes. To move a column, click on its heading and then drag left or right.

It's worth mentioning that you can customize columns on a playlist-by-playlist basis. For example, if you want to see the Composer column when viewing a favorite classical music playlist, click on the playlist's name in the Source list, then display the Composer column using the techniques described here.

Customizing Link Arrows

As described on page 39, link arrows appear next to all the songs in your library. Click a link arrow, and iTunes beams you to the music store and displays relevant songs. Option-click an arrow, and iTunes switches into browse mode and displays relevant songs in your library.

By using an AppleScript that you can download from this book's companion Web site, you can reverse this behavior so that a simple click switches you to browse mode and an Option-click takes you to the music store.

To download the script and instructions, go to www.macilife.com/itunes.

Rating Your Songs

iTunes lets you express your inner music critic by assigning a rating of between one and five stars to songs. You don't have to assign ratings, but if you do, you can use the Ratings category as a criterion when creating smart playlists. You can also have iTunes take ratings into account when compiling Party Shuffle playlists (page 77).

The fastest way to rate a song is to Control-click on it and then choose the desired rating from the My Rating popup menu.

You can also rate songs by clicking within the My Ratings column in the iTunes window or by opening the Options portion of the Song Info dialog box. And finally, you can rate the song that is currently playing by using the iTunes icon in your dock. Control-click on the iTunes icon, and a pop-up menu appears. Use the My Ratings submenu to assign a rating.

Your Own PDFs

On page 39, I mentioned that some songs on the iTunes Music Store include liner notes in PDF form. You can add your own PDFs to your iTunes music library. Scan a CD booklet, and then save it as a PDF. Find some lyrics on a Web site? Save them as a PDF. (Mac OS X makes it easy to create a PDF: just choose a program's Print command and then use the PDF options in the Print dialog box.) Then, drag the PDF into your iTunes window to add it to your library.

Doug Adams has created an AppleScript that associates a PDF with a specific artist or album. The script is called PDF Adder, and you can get it at Doug's site (www.dougscripts.com).

Watch Me Listen

While you're listening, iTunes is watching: the program keeps track of how many times you listen to a song and when you last listened to it.

iTunes displays this audio odometer in its Play Count and Last Played columns. This means you can sort your music library or a playlist according to how many times you listened to a song (click the Play Count column heading) or when you last listened to it (click the Last Played column heading). Note that you'll probably have to scroll the iTunes window to the right to see these columns.

You can also use these data as criteria when creating a smart playlist (see pages 50–53)—have iTunes create a playlist of your favorite songs or of those you haven't listened to lately.

iTunes uses its play-count records for other tasks. Play count can factor into whether a song is included in the Party Shuffle playlist (page 77). Play count also comes into play if you've told iTunes to create an iPod Selection playlist (page 101).

Customizing the Source List

I've mentioned it elsewhere, but it's worth repeating: you can customize the Source list by using the Preferences dialog box. Most of your customizing opportunities lurk within the General pane: that's where you can change the font size iTunes displays; show or hide Party Shuffle and Videos; and show link arrows.

To control whether the Music Store and Radio items appear in the Source list, use the Parental portion of the Preferences dialog box. Note that if you disable the music store, you'll also lose link arrows and, therefore, the ability to jump to related songs in your local library.

Tip: When the Preferences dialog box is open, you can use keyboard shortcuts to access specific panes. Press ⌘-1 for General, ⌘-2 for iPod, ⌘-3 for Podcasts, and so on.

More iTunes Food: Free Music and More

I've already mentioned that Apple offers a free weekly song download. Many Web sites also publish links to freebies; see iLounge (www.ilounge.com) and Playlist magazine (www.playlistmag.com/downloads).

Peer-to-peer networks. Although record industry executives wouldn't want me to say so, you can also download music using utilities such as Acquisition (www.acquisitionx.com) and LimeWire (www.limewire.com), both of which access peer-to-peer file-sharing networks. Put on your eye patch first—most of the songs available through file-swapping networks have been shared

without the permission of their copyright holders.

The Internet Archive. Another bottomless repository of free music—and video—is the Internet Archive (www.archive.org). Here you'll find tens of thousands of public-domain or otherwise free recordings, live concert and club recordings, cartoons, films, and more.

Most the audio files are available in MP3 format, and the video files are often provided in multiple formats. (As described on page 97, you can use iTunes and other tools to convert video into formats playable on an iPod.)

Podiobooks. Check out www.podiobooks.com, where you can download free audiobooks in podcast form.

RadioLovers. Like old-time radio? At www.radiolovers.com, you can download thousands of old shows, from Gunsmoke to Buck Rodgers and beyond.

Democracy. This innovative "software tuner" software brings Internet TV to your desktop and makes finding interesting video easier than ever. You can learn more and download the free software at www.getdemocracy.com.

You. With products such as El Gato's EyeTV, you can record favorite TV shows and then add them to your iTunes library—and your iPod. And, of course, you can create your own music and movies in GarageBand and iMovie HD and add your efforts to your iTunes library.

Regardless of where your other items come from, you can add them to your iTunes music library by simply dragging them into the iTunes window or by using the File menu's Add to Library command.

For details on adding items to your iTunes library, see the following pages.

Tips for the iTunes Library

Adding Items to Your Library

When you import music from a CD or buy items from the iTunes Music Store, iTunes stashes the audio or video files in your iTunes library for you. And as described in the following tip, iTunes is set up to manage the items in your library for you.

But what about items that you get from other sources—for example, audio files downloaded from Web sites or from file-sharing networks, or video files created with a product such as El Gato's EyeTV? How do you get those items to show up in your iTunes library?

Easy: simply drag their icons into the iTunes window. When you do, iTunes copies the item to your iTunes folder and adds it to your library. To add the item and put it in a specific playlist, simply drag its icon to the playlist in the Source list.

As an alternative to dragging icons into the iTunes window, you can also use the Add to Library command in the File menu. Choose the command, then locate and double-click the item you want to add.

Keeping Your Music Library Organized

iTunes normally stores your music in the Music folder, as described on page 27. If you download an MP3 file from the Internet and drag it into the iTunes window, you'll actually have two copies of the MP3 file on your hard drive.

If you don't want iTunes to copy files to its Music folder—if you'd prefer to have your music files scattered throughout your hard drive—choose Preferences from the iTunes menu, click the Advanced button, and then uncheck the box labeled Copy Files to iTunes Music Folder When Adding to Library. You can also temporarily override the copying feature: press Option while dragging a file into the iTunes window. Note, though, that having music scattered across your hard drive makes backing up your music library much more cumbersome. I don't recommend it.

Tip: If you already have files scattered across your hard drive and you want to move them all to the Music folder, choose Consolidate Library from the Advanced menu.

The How and Why Behind Specifying Compilations

Chances are you have some compilation CDs in your music collection: *Solid Gold 70s, The Best of Bartok, Tuvanese Throat Singing Mania*, and so on. You can have iTunes store the music files for compilations in a separate folder within your iTunes Music folder. This helps reduce folder clutter and makes it easier to locate and manage your music files.

For example, say you have a compilation CD that contains tracks from a dozen different artists. Normally, iTunes creates a separate folder for each artist—even though that folder might contain just one music file. But if you designate those songs as being part of a compilation, iTunes will store all of those tracks together in their own folder.

To tell iTunes that a song is part of a compilation, select the song and choose Get Info from the File menu or press ⌘-I. In the Info area of the Song Information window, check the Part of a Compilation box. As with other tag-editing tasks, you can do this for multiple songs at once by selecting them all before choosing Get Info.

iTunes stores compilations within a folder whose name is, you guessed it, Compilations. Within this folder, iTunes creates a separate folder for each compilation you've specified.

Keep Your Music Library Healthy

I've already mentioned the importance of backing up your iTunes playlists and your music (page 60). This message bears repeating. Make a habit of backing up your playlists by using the Export Library command in the File menu, and of backing up your music files by burning them to CDs or DVDs. Or simply drag your entire iTunes folder to an external hard drive every now and then.

Recreating a Damaged Music Library

Sometimes the worst happens—a power failure or other glitch may damage your iTunes Library file, that all-important music database that I described on page 27. If this file becomes corrupted, you may see an error message when you start iTunes—something along the lines of "The iTunes Music Library file cannot be read because it does not appear to be a valid library file."

Don't despair. Okay, go ahead and despair, but don't lose hope. Your entire music library is almost certainly still intact; it's just that the librarian has lost its mind. Here's how to restore some sanity to the situation.

Got backup? If you have a current backup of the files named iTunes Library and iTunes Music Library.xml, you'll be up and running again in seconds. Quit iTunes, then open your iTunes folder (unless you've moved it elsewhere, it's inside the Music folder of your home directory). Next, locate the files named "iTunes Library" and "iTunes Music Library.xml" and drag them to the Trash. Finally, copy the backups of these files to your iTunes folder. You're done.

No backup? If you don't have current backups of your iTunes Library and iTunes Music Library.xml files, you have more work to do. First, locate the corrupted versions of these files and drag them to the Trash. If you also find older Music Library files there (for example, one named iTunes 4 Music Library), drag them to the Trash—these files are left over from older versions of iTunes that you had installed on your computer, and you don't need them anymore. Do not delete anything inside the iTunes Music folder—as you'll recall from page 27, this folder contains your digital music files.

Next, start up iTunes. When you do, you'll notice its library window is completely empty. Let's fix that. Choose Add to Library from the File menu, navigate to your iTunes Music folder, and click Choose. iTunes will read all your music files and recreate your library.

Alas, performing these steps will cause you to lose the playlists you've created. To avoid this heartache, back up your iTunes Music Library.xml file now and then—by dragging it to another drive, by burning it to a CD, or by using the File menu's Export Library command.

Merging Two Music Libraries

It's a frequently asked question: how do you merge two iTunes libraries into one? Maybe you've been maintaining separate libraries on your PowerBook and desktop Macs, and you'd like to unite them into a single, unified library.

To synchronize two libraries or merge one library's contents into another, try out a free program called syncOtunes; it's available at VersionTracker and other download sites. syncOtunes will open two iTunes music libraries, compare the two, and then let you know which songs are present in one library but not the other.

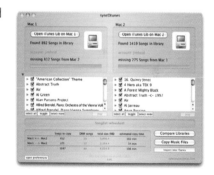

From there, you can have the program synchronize the two libraries or just copy songs from one library to another.

The one thing syncOtunes won't do is also synchronize your playlists. To copy a playlist from one Mac's library to another, you'll need to export it from that Mac's copy of iTunes, then move the resulting XML file over to the other Mac and import it. (For more details on this process, see page 47.)

Adding On: Scripts and Beyond

I've already mentioned that you can enhance the capabilities of iTunes through AppleScripts that automate iTunes in various ways.

You can also enhance the iTunes visualizer—the feature that displays those psychedelic patterns as your music plays back—by adding plug-ins. Visualizer plug-ins may not be as practical as AppleScripts, but on-screen psychedelics can often be more fun than practicalities.

Here's how to download and install iTunes AppleScripts and visualizer plug-ins, as well as information on some other programs that can round out the audio spoke of your digital hub.

Visualize Cool Graphics

If you're a fan of the iTunes visualizer, try out some of the free visualizer plug-ins available on the Web. My favorite is Andy O'Meara's free G-Force, which goes well beyond the built-in iTunes visualizer. For example, you can "play" G-Force—controlling its patterns and colors—by pressing keys on your keyboard as a song plays back.

You can find G-Force and other visualizer plug-ins by going to www.macilife.com/itunes.

Most visualizers include installation programs that tuck the plug-ins into the appropriate spot. But, just for the record, iTunes visualizer plug-ins are generally located within the iTunes folder of your Library folder.

Automating with AppleScript

AppleScript is a powerful automation technology that is part of the Mac OS and many Mac programs, including iTunes. AppleScript puts your Mac on autopilot: when you run a script, its commands can control one or more programs and make them perform a series of steps.

Dozens of useful scripts are available for iTunes. You might start by downloading the set of scripts created by Apple (www.apple.com/applescript/itunes). After you've experimented with them, sprint to Doug's AppleScripts for iTunes (www.dougscripts.com), where you'll find the best collection of iTunes AppleScripts.

Installing scripts. After you've acquired an iTunes AppleScript, you need to move it to a specific place in order for iTunes to recognize it. First, quit iTunes. Then, click the Home button or choose Home from the Finder's Go menu. Next, locate and open the Library folder, and then locate and open the iTunes folder within that Library folder. Create a folder named Scripts inside this iTunes folder and stash your scripts here.

Completing Your Audio Arsenal

Dozens of programs are available that enhance or complement iTunes. Here's a quick look at a few of my favorite audio things. For links to these and many more iTunes companions, see the Web address above.

Synergy This inexpensive program lets you control iTunes without having to switch into iTunes. Synergy provides keyboard shortcuts that let you play, pause, change volume, and even assign ratings to songs—no matter which program you're using at the moment. Synergy also adds a menu to your Mac's menu bar that lets you start and stop playback, skip to a particular playlist, and much more. When a song begins playing, Synergy displays a cool-looking "floater" that lists the song and artist name, album cover art, and other information.

Toast Titanium Roxio's Toast Titanium is a burning program for serious CD arsonists. Toast can burn DVDs as well as audio and data CDs, and provides more control over the burning process. Just one example: while iTunes puts the same amount of time between each song on a CD, Toast Titanium lets you specify a different interval for each song. Toast Titanium also includes the CD Spin Doctor audio-recording program discussed on page 71.

For even more burning power, spring for Toast with Jam. A companion program to Toast, Jam adds advanced burning features, including the ability to create DJ-like crossfades between music tracks: you can have one track fade out while the next track fades in.

Volume Logic This inexpensive plug-in from Octiv installs within iTunes and essentially remasters your music as it's playing back. Technically, Volume Logic performs five-band dynamics processing and look-head peak limiting. Oversimplified, it's a set of volume, bass, and treble knobs that adjust themselves thousands of times per second. FM radio stations have long used this kind of audio processing to add punch to their signals; now it's available for iTunes.

The results are amazing. A cheap set of computer speakers suddenly sounds better, and a good set of speakers suddenly sounds superb. Volume Logic excels at enhancing dance, electronic, and R&B tracks, but it also adds sparkle and punch to subtler genres, such as jazz and classical.

Airfoil On page 72, I lamented that the AirPort Express base station supports wireless streaming from iTunes only. With Rogue Amoeba's Airfoil, you can work around this limitation. Airfoil hijacks any program's audio output and routes it through AirPort Express, making it possible to pump RealAudio and Windows Media sound to your AirPort Express.

Salling Clicker If you have a Bluetooth-equipped Mac and a Bluetooth-equipped Palm handheld, you can turn the handheld into a powerful remote control for iTunes (and many other Mac programs, including iPhoto). A version of Salling Clicker is also available for many popular Bluetooth-quipped cell phones. Combine Salling Clicker with an AirPort Express base station, and you've got a wireless audio system with a remote control.

Clutter The freeware Clutter program puts the iTunes album-artwork feature to work in a genuinely fun way. Clutter displays a CD's artwork in a Now Playing window and in the Mac OS X dock. Here's the fun part: drag the artwork from the Now Playing window to your desktop, and Clutter creates a small button containing the artwork image. Double-click that button, and the CD begins playing back.

Having a party? Create a few on-screen stacks of your favorite CDs and let folks riffle through them. Have a few favorite discs? Stack them on your desktop, where they're just a couple of clicks away. When you're tired of the clutter, just quit the program, and the buttons disappear.

Books on Bytes: Listening to Audiobooks

iTunes isn't just about tunes. You can also use it to listen to recorded *audiobooks* that you can buy and download from the iTunes Music Store or from Audible.com (www.audible.com). Listen to a novel on your next flight, burn it to a CD so you can listen to it in the car, or transfer it to your iPod and listen while you jog. You can buy audio versions of novels, magazines, newspapers, comedy shows, and much more. With the latest iPods, you can even speed up or slow down the reading speed (see page 101).

The easiest way to shop for audiobooks is to use the iTunes Music Store. Simply go to the Music Store's main screen and choose the Audiobooks option from the Choose Genre pop-up menu.

If you want a larger selection, shop at Audible.com's Web site. Buying audiobooks through Audible.com is a bit trickier than buying them through the iTunes Music Store. You'll also have to perform an extra couple of steps to add your purchased audiobooks to your iTunes library. These steps are outlined at right.

And to ensure that your Mac handles audiobooks correctly, be that sure iTunes is set up to handle Internet playback. Quit your Web browser and email program, then choose Preferences from the iTunes menu. Click the Advanced button at the top of the Preferences window, then click the General button. Finally, click the Set button that appears next to the label Use iTunes for Internet Music Playback.

Now your Mac is ready to read aloud.

Working with Audiobooks

If you already have an Apple account, you're ready to buy audiobooks from the iTunes Music Store. If you're interested in the broader selection available from Audible.com's site, visit www.audible.com and create an account. Then read on for details on working with Audible.com files.

Step 1. Purchase and Download

When buying an audiobook from Audible.com's Web site, you typically have a choice of formats, which are numbered 1 through 4. The iPod supports formats 2, 3, and 4. Which should you use? If you're using a modem connection, you might choose format 2—its files are smaller and thus download faster. If you have a fast connection, you might lean toward formats 3 or 4. They sound better, but they'll take longer to download and use more disk space on your Mac and iPod. (Audiobooks that you buy from the iTunes Music Store are available in AAC format only.)

Step 2. Add the Audiobook to Your iTunes Library

When you download an audiobook from Audible.com's site, the audiobook should be added to your iTunes library automatically. If it if isn't, you'll need to do the job yourself. Locate the audiobook on your desktop (its name ends with the file extension .aa), then drag its icon into the iTunes window.

Step 3.
Specify Account Information

The first time you add an audiobook to iTunes, you must specify the user name and password you created when signing up at Audible.com. iTunes contacts Audible.com to verify your account information.

Step 4.
Listen

An audiobook appears in your iTunes library, just like any other song. You can listen to it, apply equalization to it, and burn it to a CD.

Audiobooks Tips

One Account

You can use one Audible.com account with up to three computers. If you try to add an account to a fourth computer, an error message appears. If you want to add the account to that computer, you must deauthorize one of the other three. Choose Deauthorize Computer from the Advanced menu, choose the Audible account button, and click OK.

To remove an account, choose Deauthorize Computer from the Advanced menu.

Audiobookmarks

The audiobook format provides bookmarks: when you pause or stop an audiobook, iTunes creates a bookmark at the point where you stopped. When you resume playing the audiobook, playback resumes at the bookmark's position.

It gets better. The iPod also supports audiobookmarks, and it synchronizes them with iTunes when you synchronize your music library. This synchronization process works in both directions: if you pause an audiobook on your iPod, the bookmark is transferred to your Mac when you sync. Thus, you can use your iPod to start listening to an audiobook on your evening commute, then use your iMac to pick up where you left off when you get home.

Chapter Markers

On the latest iPods and the iPod mini family, audiobooks can have chapter markers that allow for convenient navigation between chapters or other sections. To jump from one chapter to the next, press the iPod's Select button while the audiobook is playing. If the audiobook has section markers, they appear as vertical bars in the iPod's on-screen navigation bar. Use the Rewind and Fast Forward buttons to jump between chapters.

Burning a Book

To burn an audiobook to a CD, create a playlist and drag the audiobook to the playlist. Next, select the playlist and click the Burn Disc button.

If your audiobook is longer than roughly one hour, it won't fit on a standard audio CD. No problem. iTunes will burn as much as will fit on one CD, and will then prompt you to insert additional blank discs until you've burned the entire book.

iPod: Portable Music and More

It's hard to appreciate the significance of the iPod until you load it up with hundreds of songs and begin carrying it around with you.

Then it hits you: all of your favorite songs are right there with you, ready to play—in the car, on a walk, in the living room, on a plane. There's no finding and fumbling with CDs, and every song is only a couple of button presses away.

Several factors work together to make the iPod the best portable music player, starting with its integration with the iTunes Music Store: no other portable music player can tap into the store's vast selection of music, videos, podcasts, and more.

Another factor is the iPod's integration with iTunes: connect the iPod to your Mac, and iTunes automatically synchronizes your music library and playlists.

And finally, there's the iPod's versatility. Its ability to store videos, photos, contact information, your calendar, appointment schedule, and other files make the iPod more than a portable music player.

Life with an iPod

Step 1.
Build a Music Library

Use the techniques described earlier in this section to import songs from audio CDs, buy music and videos from the iTunes Music Store, subscribe to podcasts, assign equalization settings (optional), edit song information (if necessary), and create playlists.

Step 2.
Transfer to the iPod

Connect the iPod to your Mac's USB port (older iPods connect to the FireWire port instead). You can also buy a dock that makes connecting to the Mac even faster and more convenient (see page 108). Whether you use the dock or just a cable, when you connect the iPod to a Mac, iTunes copies your music library and playlists to the iPod.

While the iPod is connected, its battery charges. The battery charges to 80 percent of its capacity in an hour or two, and charges fully in about three to four hours.

The iPod's battery gauge is located in the top right corner of its screen.

You can adjust settings for updating the contents of your iPod by using the iPod Preferences dialog box, described on pages 98 and 99.

The iPod is more than a music player—it's a cultural phenomenon. There's even a service, podapic.com, that will turn a photo you supply into a mock iPod ad. Here's Sophie modeling the latest earwear.

Step 3. Listen and Repeat

Disconnect the iPod and start listening. When you modify your iTunes music library or playlists, you can update the iPod's contents to match by simply connecting the iPod again.

If you don't have a dock, you can use the headphones jack to connect the iPod to a stereo system or other audio hardware, such as an FM transmitter. To connect to a stereo system, use a cable with a ⅛-inch miniplug on one end and two RCA phono plugs on the other. Connect the cable as described on page 72.

To the right of the iPod's audio-output jack is the Hold button. Slide it to the left to disable the iPod's buttons. This is useful when you're transporting the iPod in a briefcase or purse, where its buttons could get pressed, causing the battery to drain.

The battery gauge shows how much power remains.

The iPod's menu system uses a "drill-down" scheme: select an option and press the Select button to drill down one level to another menu or list of choices.

To back up to the previous list of choices, press Menu.

To choose an item in a menu, press the Select button.

To pause and resume playback, press Play/Pause. To turn off the iPod, press and hold this button for a few seconds.

To skip to the previous or next song, press Previous or Next.

Use the click wheel to move the menu highlight up and down, and to adjust the playback volume.

The Full-Sized iPods

The iPod has changed since its debut in 2001, and it continues to evolve. Sometimes the changes are simple: bigger hard drives to store even more songs. Sometimes the changes bring significant new capabilities, such as the ability to store photographs and play video.

Each new generation brings improvements and enhancements to the software inside the iPod. Apple often makes these enhancements available as software updates for older iPods, although the oldest models have been left behind by some upgrades. For example, older iPods (specifically, ones that do not have dock connectors) can't play back songs compressed using the Apple Lossless encoder, nor do they provide as many menu-customizing options.

But every iPod, from the latest nano to the original 5GB granddaddy, can play back purchases from the iTunes Music Store. (With the oldest iPods, you must download and install a software update that teaches them about the AAC format.)

The features change, but the iPod's name remains the same. Because of this, the iPod family is often categorized according to "generations." Here's a look at each generation of full-sized iPod and the features and capabilities that are common across the iPod line. We'll take a closer look at the littlest iPods—the mini, the nano, and the shuffle—on later pages.

iPod Common Ground

All current iPods that have display screens (as opposed to the tiny, screenless iPod shuffle) provide a common set of features and capabilities—starting with the obvious ability to play audio files. All iPods support iTunes playlists and provide shuffle modes for random-listening fun. And they all provide sound-enhancing equalizer settings similar to those provided by iTunes itself (page 56).

Beyond these basics, all current iPods also have some non-musical talents, which are covered in the following pages.

Video Playback

All current full-sized iPods (but not the iPod nano) can store and play videos that you buy from the iTunes Music Store (page 34) or convert for iPod playback yourself (page 96). You can watch the videos on the iPod's screen or connect the iPod to a TV set.

Photo Display

Use iTunes to transfer photos from your iPhoto library, then view them on the iPod's screen or on a connected TV set (page 94).

Address Book

If you store addresses in Mac OS X's Address Book, Microsoft's Entourage, or other programs, you can transfer that information to your iPod and carry your contacts with you (page 104).

Calendar

Similarly, you can stash calendar events in Mac OS X's iCal software and transfer them to your Mac. You can even have the iPod sound an audible alarm when a calendar event arrives.

Extras

All current iPods also provide some fun and practical (and sometimes both) extras: a stopwatch function, an alarm clock mode, and some games.

Dock Connector

An iPod's dock connector is the gateway to a world of accessories and expansion opportunities, from radio receivers to radio transmitters to external speaker systems (page 108).

On a more basic level, if you buy an optional dock (below), you can connect the dock to your stereo and a power outlet and have a convenient way to charge your iPod and play it through your stereo system.

An iPod Timeline

First Generation
2001–2002

5GB and 10GB capacities; mechanical scroll wheel.

Second Generation
2002

10GB and 20GB capacities; non-moving *touch* wheel.

Third Generation
2003

10GB–40GB capacities; backlit buttons; dock support.

Fourth Generation
2004

20GB–40GB capacities; color screen and photo-display capabilities (iPod photo only); elegant *click wheel* controller.

Fifth Generation
2005

30GB–60GB capacities; large color screen; video display capabilities.

The Compact iPods: mini and nano

Honey, I shrunk the iPod—that about sums up the iPod mini and iPod nano. Both have most of the talents of their bigger brethren, but are much more compact—or, in the case of the nano, much, much more compact.

The iPod mini was the first of Apple's petite iPods. It's no longer made, but if you crave a pink iPod, a visit to eBay will probably turn up plenty. Like full-sized iPods, the mini contained a hard drive. Functionally, its features match those of the 4G iPods. The mini can't store photos or videos.

As for the iPod nano, it makes the mini look maxi. Its compact size is due in part to its use of flash memory—the same type of memory used by your digital camera—instead of a hard drive. And while the nano may be a fraction of the size and half the weight of the mini, it does more—you can store photos on it and view them on its tiny screen. (Alas, you can't connect the nano to a TV set for photo display.)

All of the general iPod techniques described in this section apply to the mini and the nano. Here's a look at what's different about these compact iPods.

iPod Model	Weight (ounces)	
60GB iPod 5G	5.50	▰▰▰▰▰▰▰
iPod mini	3.60	▰▰▰▰
iPod nano	1.50	▰▰
iPod shuffle	.78	▰

iPod mini

About the height and width of a business card, the iPod mini debuted in January 2004 with a 4GB capacity. In February 2005, Apple added a 6GB model and changed the available colors.

Like the latest full-sized iPods, the iPod mini provides a customizable main menu, editable on-the-go playlists, and the ability to speed-shift audiobooks (page 101). Many of these capabilities arrived with a November 2004 software update; if you have an older mini, download the latest iPod updater from Apple's Web site.

On top are a hold switch and jacks for earphones and an optional remote control.

The 1.6-inch display is bright and crisp but smaller than that of other iPods.

The click wheel, now standard across the full-sized iPod line, debuted on the mini.

Made of anodized aluminum, the mini's case was available in several colors.

A mini-specific dock is optional. The iPod mini's dock connector works with many iPod accessories, but not Belkin's Media Reader or Voice Recorder.

iPod nano

Introduced in September 2005, the iPod nano packs most of the features of the full-sized iPods into a package that Apple accurately describes as "impossibly small."

At this writing, the nano is available in 1GB, 2GB, and 4GB capacities. You can expect roughly 14 hours of continuous play on a single battery charge. (Caffeine not included.)

A dock connector on the bottom means the nano will work with most accessories that use the iPod dock connector. (Some accessories are incompatible, however; for example, you can't use the Apple Digital Camera connector with the nano.) The nano includes a Universal Dock Adaptor (see the sidebar on this page). Apple also sells a dock specific to the iPod nano, but if you anticipate expanding your iPod collection, you're better off buying a Universal Dock, which is large enough to accommodate full-sized iPods, too.

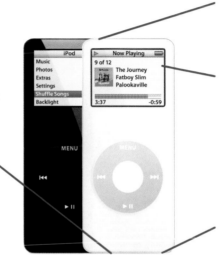

The Hold switch is the only occupant of the nano's top floor.

The nano's 1.5-inch color screen may be tiny, but it's bright and eminently readable.

The nano's audio-output jack is on the bottom, next to the dock connector.

The One-Size-Fits-All Dock

Remember that chorus of primal screams you heard a couple of years ago? It came from the many companies that build iPod docking accessories, and the reason for it was the Apple kept rendering their products obsolete. The problem was that companies were basing their dock dimensions around one specific iPod model, but new models would often be slightly thicker or thinner.

To quiet the screams, Apple standardized on one size of docking socket, and most iPod docking accessories now use this size. (Look for products that say "Made for iPod.") Each iPod now includes a dock adapter, a small piece of plastic that sits inside a dock and accommodates a specific iPod model.

As a result, you can buy an Apple Universal Dock—or an accessory from another company—and know that it will work with all iPods that include a dock adapter.

For more on iPod dock and accessory options, see page 108.

The Littlest iPod: shuffle

iPod shuffle is something completely different. It lacks a display and click wheel. You can navigate to the next and previous song, but you can't skip around within songs or jump to a specific song in a playlist or album. And forget about storing photos, contacts, and calendar information.

But where iPod shuffle shines is in your pocket—and pocketbook. This is a truly tiny music player—you've carried bigger packs of chewing gum. It's also the least expensive iPod, starting at $69.

And true to its name and marketing campaign, iPod shuffle embraces the random world of shuffle discussed on page 76. iTunes has a special Autofill feature that will pack your iPod shuffle with a random selection of tunes. You can, of course, also take the reins yourself and manually copy specific songs, albums, and playlists.

iPod shuffle at a Glance

iPod shuffle debuted in January 2005 in two capacities: 512MB (about 120 songs) and 1GB (about 240 songs). You can connect an iPod shuffle to any USB port that provides sufficient power. For much faster music transfers, use a USB 2.0 port, if your Mac provides one (all current Macs do).

You can't see them here, but colored lights indicate charging status and other information.

Atop iPod shuffle is a standard ⅛-inch output jack.

Play/Pause. To activate hold mode (disabling other buttons), press and hold for three seconds. Repeat to exit hold mode.

Power switch positions: Off, play-in-order mode, shuffle mode.

Battery status button and light (green: charged; amber: running low; red: charge soon).

Clockwise from top: volume up, next track, volume down, previous track.

A removable, easy-to-lose cap protects iPod shuffle's USB connector. Replace the cap with the included lanyard to hang the iPod around your neck.

Filling your iPod shuffle

Unless you have a ridiculously small iTunes library, you won't be able to fit all your music into an iPod shuffle. That's where the Autofill feature comes in: it lets you easily corral a collection of songs into your shuffle.

Normally, the Autofill feature chooses songs from your entire music library. To have Autofill choose songs from a specific playlist, choose its name.

If you uncheck this box, iTunes transfers songs in the order they appear in the library or selected playlist.

Click Autofill to have iTunes roll the dice, choose some songs, and then transfer them.

To add to iPod shuffle's contents instead of replacing them, uncheck this box.

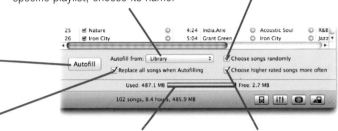

The gauge shows how much of iPod shuffle's capacity you've used.

If you've rated your songs, you can increase the chances of their being chosen for Autofill transfer by checking this box.

iPod shuffle Tips

Keeping the fill. Like what Autofill has come up with? You can save it as a standard playlist: select any song in the Autofill list, and then choose Select All from the Edit menu (⌘-A). Finally, choose New Playlist from Selection from the File menu.

Autofill based on playlists. When you simply Autofill your shuffle from your main library, you're likely to end up with a lot of songs you might not have chosen otherwise. When you want more control over Autofill, choose a specific playlist from the Autofill From pop-up menu.

Indeed, you might want to create some smart playlists that allow you to Autofill based on genre—classical, jazz, rock, and so on—or on other key criteria, such as an artist's or composer's name. (For details on smart playlists, see pages 50–53.)

Self-serve fill-up. Autofill is an easy way to sling some songs onto a shuffle, but you might prefer more control over what gets copied. No problem—fill your shuffle yourself. You can copy songs directly to the shuffle by simply dragging them from your iTunes library to the iPod shuffle in the Source list. Drag

songs one at a time, or use the selection techniques described on page 44. You can also copy an entire playlist by simply dragging it to the shuffle.

Middle ground. You can combine the convenience of Autofill with the control of manual management. If you like most of what Autofill has come up with, just delete the tunes you don't want on your shuffle: be sure that your shuffle is selected in the Source list, then select tunes

you don't want on the shuffle and press the Delete key on your keyboard. Then, add some additional tunes if you like.

Or take the opposite approach: start off by manually adding the songs and playlists that you want, and then click Autofill to finish the job.

Take it from the top. When your iPod shuffle is in play-in-order mode, you can jump to the first song in the shuffle's playlist by pressing the Play/Pause button three times.

For more iPod shuffle tips, see page 102.

Viewing Photos on Your iPod

Talented musicians often branch out into other arts after a while. All current full-sized iPods, as well as the iPod nano family, are able to store and display photos. Stash some favorite shots on your iPod, then show them to friends, family, or the person sitting next to you on the plane.

Scroll through photos one at a time at your own pace, or have your iPod display a slide show, complete with a music from your iTunes library. You can even play the game of chance and view a slide show in shuffle mode—which photo will appear next?

Just as iTunes is the conduit between your music library and your iPod, it's also the bridge between your photos and your iPod. Using the iPod Preferences dialog box, you can tell iTunes to copy photos from your iPhoto library to the iPod. You can copy all photos and albums, or only the ones you want to carry with you.

Because large photos devour space and take more time to display, iTunes creates a small, iPod-friendly version of each shot before transferring it to the iPod. You can also choose to transfer the full-resolution photos. This can be a handy way to back up photos or take them to a friend's house for sharing.

The full-sized iPods can also connect to a TV set. Just add Apple's iPod AV Cable or, better yet, Apple's iPod AV Connection Kit, which also includes a remote control and a dock with video-output jacks. The little iPod nano can't connect to a TV.

Here's how to turn your iPod into a pocket slide projector.

Step 1. Create Albums

There are several ways to transfer photos to iPod photo. For example, you can transfer your entire photo library or just the albums you want to carry along with you.

For the latter approach, use iPhoto to create an album containing the photos you want to show. If you want to create slide shows for several different events—your summer vacation, the Halloween party, your family reunion—create a separate album for each event. (For tips on creating albums, see pages 130–133.)

Don't forget music. The iPod can play music while displaying a slide show. If you want a particular song or playlist to play during a slide show, assign that song or playlist to the album, as described on page 164.

The New Slide Projector

When you use the iPod's menus to select an album or roll, the iPod displays thumbnail versions of your photos. To scroll the thumbnails, use the click wheel.

To see a full-screen version of the highlighted photo, press the Select button.

To display the next and previous screen of thumbnails, press Next or Previous.

To begin a slide show, press the Play/Pause button.

Step 2. Update Your iPod

Connect your iPod to your Mac. Choose Preferences from the iTunes menu, then click the iPod button.

To transfer photos stored in a folder that isn't part of your iPhoto library, use the pop-up menu.

To transfer only some albums, choose this option and then check the albums you want to transfer.

Check this box to include full-resolution photos, which are stored on iPod photo's hard drive in a folder named Photos. To access the originals, activate the iPod's disk mode as described on page 98.

To access photo-updating options, click Photos.

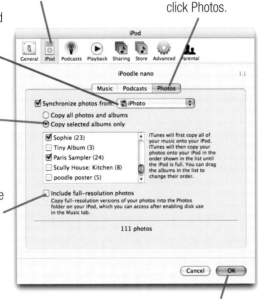

Click OK to have iTunes prepare and transfer the photos.

Step 4. Start the Show

Navigate to the album that holds the photos you want to display, and press the Play/Pause button on the clickwheel. The Start Slideshow screen appears. To display the slide show on your TV, choose TV On, then press the Select button.

As the slide show plays, small versions of the previous and next photos appear on iPod photo's screen. To jump to the previous or next photo, press the Rewind or Forward buttons.

To pause the slide show, press Play/Pause. To end the show, press Menu.

You can also adjust several slide show settings by using the Slideshow Settings screen (right). To access these settings, choose the Slideshow Settings command at the top of the Slideshow menu.

Step 3 (optional). Connect to TV

If you have the iPod AV Cable, use it to connect the iPod to your TV and stereo. Connect the yellow phono plug to your TV's video-input jack, and the red and white plugs to some spare audio inputs on your TV or stereo system.

The S-video option. If you have the iPod AV Connection Kit and a TV with an S-video input, here's how to get better image quality. Pick up a male-to-male S-video cable at your local Radio Shack (ask for catalog number 15-2404). Connect one end of the cable to the S-video jack on the iPod's dock, and the other end to your TV's S-video input. You may have to use your TV's setup menus to switch to its S-video input.

Note that S-video carries video signals only. To have music play with your slide show, connect the iPod photo to your stereo system's or TV's audio inputs. If you're using the iPod AV Cable, just let its yellow connector dangle behind your TV or stereo. Or use any standard stereo cable that has a ⅛-inch miniplug on one end and two RCA phono plugs on the other.

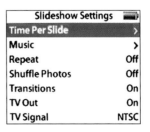

Video and Your iPod

The latest full-sized iPods can play videos that you purchase from the iTunes Music Store (page 34) or that you prepare for the iPod yourself.

Watching video on an iPod isn't all that different from listening to music. Use the Videos menu to navigate to the type of video you want: movies, music videos, TV shows, video podcasts. Locate the video, press the iPod's Select button, and watch, hopefully not while also driving.

Video that you buy from the iTunes Music Store is in a format that's ready for iPod playback. But what about movies you find on the Web? Or that friends or family email to you? Or that you create yourself? Although iTunes can store nearly any type of movie, the iPod is a more finicky eater. To play on an iPod, a movie must be compressed in a specific way.

And as with audio compression (page 26), video compression comes in various formats. I delve into this glamorous topic in further detail on page 224 and elsewhere in the iMovie HD chapter but, for now, the names to drop when you're talking iPod compression are *MPEG-4* and *H.264*. And the virtue to practice is called *patience*—compressing video can take a long time.

iTunes can compress video for the iPod, as can other programs, some of which are free. Here's an overview of the options you have for preparing movies for their small-screen debut, as well as a collection of video-related iPod tips.

A Handful of Video Tips

The TV connection. All video-capable iPods can connect to TV sets, the vast majority of which provide larger screens than an iPod's. Better still, a growing number of TVs, including many in hotels, provide front-panel input jacks that allow you to make connections without groping around the back of the cabinet.

To connect your iPod to a TV, use Apple's iPod AV Cable. Better still, spring for the iPod AV Connection Kit, which includes the cable as well as a dock and remote control. The dock also lets you use an S-Video cable for better picture quality, as described on the previous page.

Once you connect the cable, you need to tell your iPod to display video on the TV set. On the iPod, go to Videos > Video Settings > TV Out, then choose On. (If you'd rather switch this setting each time you play a video, choose Ask.)

Other video devices. You can also connect the iPod to video-recording devices, such as a VCR, camcorder, or set-top DVD recorder. This lets you record videos you've purchased from the iTunes store, not to mention slide shows displayed with the iPod's photo display features.

Got juice? When playing video, an iPod's battery charge will drain much more quickly—partly because the hard drive will spin more often, but largely because the screen's backlight is on the entire time. For the fifth-generation iPod, Apple estimates about two hours of playback time for video, compared to roughly 14 hours of music playback.

Video playlists. You can add videos to playlists and smart playlists. You can even mix and match videos and music in the same playlist. If you frequently buy music videos from the iTunes Music Store, you may want to listen to their soundtracks along with tunes from your music library.

Video bookmarking. As with audiobooks, videos that you buy from the iTunes Music Store provide bookmarking: if you stop playback partway through, playback continues at that point when you resume. As described on the opposite page, you can use the Info dialog box to add bookmarking to videos you prepare yourself.

Get more tips and tools for playing video on your iPod.
www.macilife.com/itunes

Converting Movies for iPod Playback

Converting with iTunes. First, add the movie to your iTunes library (page 80). Then, select the movie in iTunes and choose Convert Selection for iPod from the Advanced menu.

Converting with QuickTime Pro. Apple's $29 QuickTime Pro adds the ability to export movies using the QuickTime Player that you already have. QuickTime Pro provides a Movie to iPod setting that delivers fine results, albeit with long encoding times. You can also take the reins yourself and specify encoding settings.

Converting with Podner. Splasm Software's Podner is an inexpensive and elegantly designed conversion program.

Handbrake and Handbrake Lite. Video on a DVD-Video disc is compressed in MPEG-2 format (page 307). Video on a commercial DVD, such as a Hollywood movie, is also shackled by encryption to thwart copying.

Neither of these issues bothers either of these programs. Eric Petit's HandBrake is a power tool that gives you precise control over the conversion process, including the ability to tweak compression settings and even choose which chapters you want to extract.

HandBrake Lite can also suck video from a DVD, but doesn't let you tweak settings or choose specific chapters.

Video Conversion at a Glance

Source	Best Option(s)
A DVD	Use Handbrake or Handbrake Light.
A QuickTime movie that a friend emailed to you	Use iTunes, Podner, or QuickTime Pro.
A movie in Windows Media format	Install free Flip4Mac WMV (www.flip4mac.com), then use a conversion program.
An MPEG-format movie taken by a Sony digital camera	Use Podner.
A movie you've created in iMovie HD	Use iMovie HD's Share command (page 268).
A Final Cut Express or Final Cut Pro project	Choose File > Export > Using QuickTime Conversion, then choose iPod (320x240) from the Format pop-up menu.

El Gato's EyeTV. Got a TiVo's worth of shows you'd like to pod? Connect El Gato's EyeTV box to your TiVo, then record the shows on your Mac's hard drive. Then, use the EyeTV software to export a version encoded for the iPod.

What quality settings? Podner, QuickTime Pro, and other programs provide several encoding settings that let you balance compression time, image quality, and file size. I recommend sticking with the default settings. iPod video is all about portability, not high-definition quality.

But if you want to sweat the details, here are a few guidelines: the H.264 setting often gives better quality and smaller file sizes, though encoding can take much longer than MPEG-4. For maximum quality, specify two-pass H.264.

If you'll be connecting your iPod to a TV and viewing on the big screen, consider using MPEG-4 and choosing the 480- by 480-pixel frame size. This larger frame size appears more crisp on a TV than the standard iPod video size of 240 by 480 pixels.

What kind of video? After preparing some video for the iPod and adding it to your iTunes library, consider using the Get Info command to specify a category for the movie. This allows the video to appear in the right category on the iPod's Videos menu. In iTunes, select the video, choose File > Get Info, click Options, then choose an option from the Video Kind pop-up menu. While you're there, check the Remember Playback Position box to add bookmarking. To avoid the chance of the video being played when the iPod is in shuffle mode, check Skip When Shuffling, too.

Setting iPod Preferences

Normally, iTunes will synchronize all your playlists and your entire music library, or at least as much of it as will fit on the iPod.

But there may be times when you want to manually control which playlists and songs iTunes copies to the iPod. Maybe your iTunes music library is larger than will fit on the iPod, and you'd like to specify what you want to copy. Or maybe you listen to some podcasts on your Mac but not on your iPod, and you don't want to waste iPod disk space by copying those podcasts.

Whatever the reason, you can use the iPod Preferences dialog box to specify updating preferences.

You can also use this dialog box to activate *disk mode*, in which the iPod appears on your desktop just like a hard drive (which, for a full-sized iPod, it is). In disk mode, you can use the Mac's Finder to copy files to and from the iPod's hard drive. This is a handy way to shuttle documents to and from work, to back up your iPhoto library, or to carry backups of important programs or files with you on the road.

To display the iPod Preferences dialog box, choose Preferences from the iTunes menu and then click the iPod button. As the opposite page shows, the specific options available in the dialog box can depend on which iPod model you have.

iPoodle Photo

Opening iPod Preferences

When you connect the iPod to the Mac and start iTunes, the iPod appears in the Source pane of the iTunes window, and an iPod preferences icon appears next to the Equalizer button.

If iTunes is configured to update automatically (above), the iPod's contents appear dimmed (below) and you can't manually change them.

To rename the iPod, click its name and then type a new name. The name appears in iTunes, as shown above, and in the Finder (below left) when the iPod is in disk mode. It also appears in the iPod's Info screen. To disconnect the iPod, click the eject symbol next to its name or click the Eject button (⏏) in the lower-right corner of the iTunes window.

The graph shows how much iPod storage space you've used and how much remains.

You can also specify iPod preferences by clicking the Options button (⊟).

Choosing Preferences Settings

You can specify which podcasts episodes get copied—only the most recent, only those you haven't played, and so on.

The Photos button appears only if you've connected an iPod that can display photos. For details on photo preferences, see page 95.

You can choose how the iPod syncs with your Address Book and iCal data (pages 104 and 106).

Normally, iTunes copies everything when you connect the iPod.

To copy only some playlists, click this option and check the box next to each playlist you want to copy.

To update songs and playlists by hand, click this option. See "Manual Management" on page 100.

If you've chosen automatic updating but don't want to copy all new songs to the iPod, check this box and then, in the Library, uncheck any new songs that you do not want copied. When you next update the iPod, only the new songs that are checked will be copied to it.

To display album artwork on the iPod's screen, check this box. For more details, see page 103.

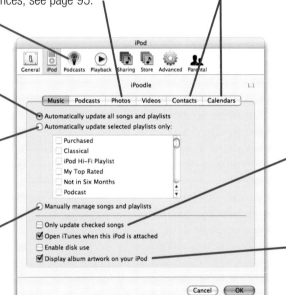

Setting iPod shuffle Preferences

The iPod shuffle provides different preferences options.

Toy iPoodle

Normally, an iPod's name disappears from the Source list when you disconnect the iPod. But you can tell iTunes to keep the iPod shuffle in the source list. This lets you do "virtual updates"—you can add and remove songs to and from the list, and iTunes applies your changes the next time you connect your iPod shuffle.

Digital dieting: this option lets you play Apple Lossless and AIFF files, formats that iPod shuffle doesn't otherwise support (see page 102).

When using iPod shuffle in disk mode, you can specify how much space to set aside for both songs and data.

iPod Tips

Here are some tips for getting more out of your iPod and appreciating its finer points.

Not So Loud!

Do you love music? Then turn it down. At the risk of sounding like a nagging parent, I'm telling you that you shouldn't listen to music at high volume levels, especially when you're wearing headphones or earbuds. Your brain can acclimate to loud volume levels, but your ears can't—they'll be damaged.

When you're wearing headphones or earbuds, set the iPod's volume so that it's *just* loud enough. When you start playing back a tune, you should be thinking to yourself, "I wish that was a just a little bit louder."

Pay attention, kids. In a couple of decades, a lot of iPod users are going to be cupping their ears and saying, "Pardon me?" Don't be one of them. Just remember: your hearing is the only sense you can damage with too much of a good thing.

Apple has released a software update that enables you to specify a maximum volume for the fifth-generation iPod and iPod nano. For details and more background on the importance of safe listening, see www.apple.com/sound.

Scrubbing within a Song

You can quickly move around, or scrub, within a song while it plays. Press the Select button, and the elapsed-time gauge on the iPod's screen is replaced with a little diamond—just like the one iTunes displays during playback. Using the scroll wheel, move the diamond left and right to scrub within the song. You can zip around within podcasts and videos using the same technique.

Extending Battery Life

To get the longest playing time, turn off the screen's backlighting, avoid jumping between songs frequently (the hard drive is one of the iPod's biggest power consumers), and use the Settings menu to turn off the iPod's equalizer. And remember, you can play songs when the iPod is plugged in. If you put the iPod in manual-updating mode or use one of the iPod utilities discussed here, you can even play songs while the iPod is connected to (and charging from) the Mac.

When the Music Dies

The iPod's battery doesn't last forever, and many iPod users were incensed when their batteries began dying and Apple seemed to turn a deaf ear.

The good news is, Apple has launched a $59 iPod battery-replacement program. Some companies also sell replacement batteries that you can install yourself—if you dare to crack open the iPod's case and venture inside. One source is www.ipodbattery.com.

For details on replacement batteries and on iPod batteries in general, see www.ipodbatteryfaq.com.

Accessing Your Music Directly

Apple built a simple anti-piracy system into the iPod: its music files are stored in an invisible folder on the iPod's hard drive. Thus, you can't use the Finder to copy music files from the iPod to your hard drive. Music transfer is a one-way street: from the Mac to the iPod.

However, several free or inexpensive utilities let you directly access the music files on an iPod. This can be a great way to restore your music library should something happen to the copy on your Mac.

I'm fond of Findley Designs' iPod Access, which lets you access and play music on an iPod as well as copy it to your Mac's hard drive. Another popular iPod utility is CrispSofties' iPod.iTunes. You can find these and other iPod utilities at software download sites.

Manual Management

If you use the iPod Preferences dialog box to specify manual updating, you can manage the iPod's contents by hand using iTunes. (The iPod shuffle is always in manual-update mode.)

To delete songs from the iPod, be sure that the iPod is selected in the Source list, then select the songs and press the Delete key. To copy songs and playlists to the iPod, drag them from the iTunes library to the iPod's name in the Source list.

When you have the iPod set up for manual updating, you can use iTunes to create playlists that exist only on the iPod. In the Source area of the iTunes window, select the iPod and then create the new playlist.

When manual updating is active, you must manually unmount the iPod when you're done with it. You can do this in iTunes (select the iPod in the Source list and then click the Eject button) or by using the Finder (drag the iPod's icon to the Trash or select it and press ⌘-E).

If you ever decide to switch back to iTunes' automatic updating mode, iTunes will replace the iPod's contents with the current music library and playlists.

Playing While Charging

When the iPod is connected to the Mac, its menus aren't available, preventing you from playing music located on the iPod. One way to work around this is to put the iPod in manual-updating mode, as described previously. You can then play tunes on the iPod by using iTunes. The other technique is to use a direct-access utility, such as iPod Access.

Library Too Big?

The time may come when your music library is larger than will fit on your full-sized iPod, iPod mini, or iPod nano. One solution is to use the iPod Preferences dialog box to switch into manual-management mode.

There's also an automatic alternative. iTunes can create a playlist containing only songs that will fit on your iPod. This playlist is called the iPod Selection playlist, and iTunes will offer to create it for you if it determines that your library won't fit on your iPod.

The iPod Selection playlist uses a five-step process to determine which songs will be copied to your iPod.

1. iTunes groups all tracks into albums.

2. iTunes calculates an average play count and average user rating for each album.

3. iTunes begins filling the iPod with albums that have non-zero average play counts and non-zero ratings, in descending order. In other words, albums with higher play counts and higher ratings get higher priority.

4. If Step 3 completes and there's still some free space, iTunes starts copying albums that were recently played or recently added to your library.

5. If there's *still* some free space after Step 4 completes, iTunes adds random albums until the iPod is filled to the gills and loosening its belt.

If there's a lesson here, it's this: rate your music. Ratings clearly play an important role in the iPod Selection playlist, so if you rate your songs, you'll stand a better chance of shoehorning your favorites into your iPod.

Of course, in the end, there's no substitute for your own smarts: you can probably do a better job of budgeting iPod disk space by manually managing your iPod's library.

Audiobook Speed Control

You love listening to audiobooks, but sometimes you wish the narrator spoke a bit faster or slower. With most recent iPods, you can get your wish. Go to Settings > Audiobooks, and then choose Slower or Faster.

The iPod adjusts its playback speed without changing the pitch (a trick it may have learned from GarageBand). To restore the normal playback speed, go to Settings > Audiobooks and choose Normal.

Time for the iPod

The iPod's alarm clock feature lets you wake up to music (or to a beep). You can also have the iPod always display the current time in the title bar area at the top of its screen. Choose Settings > Date & Time > Time in Title. Now you'll always know what time it is.

The iPod syncs its clock with your Mac's, and if you use the Network Time option in Mac OS X's Date & Time system preference, your iPod's clock will always be accurate.

More iPod Tips

Customizing the iPod's Main Menu

You can add items to and remove them from the iPod's main menu. For example, if you frequently browse your library by artist, add an Artist menu to the main menu. Go to Settings > Main Menu, then scroll to Artists and press Select. While you're there, check out the other customizing options and tweak your iPod's main menu to contain the commands you use most.

Menu customizing is not available on 1G and 2G iPod models.

The On-The-Go Playlist

You have a sudden hankering to hear some songs from six different albums, but you're on the road and thus can't build a new playlist using iTunes. Solution: the On-The-Go playlist, a special, temporary playlist that lives within the iPod.

To add a song to this playlist, scroll to the song and then press and hold the Select button until the song flashes a few times. Repeat for the next song.

You can even add entire albums, artists, genres, and playlists to the On-The-Go playlist. Simply scroll to the item you want and hold down Select.

To clear the On-The-Go playlist, navigate to it, scroll to the bottom of the song list, and choose Clear Playlist. The playlist is also cleared when you connect the iPod to your Mac, but if you've set up iTunes to automatically update the iPod when you

connect it, the On-The-Go playlist will be copied to iTunes so you can use it again.

Current iPods (as well as 4G and mini models) provide two more On-The-Go playlist features: the ability to delete a song from the playlist and to save the playlist.

To delete a song from the playlist, highlight the song and hold down Select until the highlight flashes. To save the On-The-Go playlist, navigate to it, scroll to the bottom of the song list, and choose Save Playlist. The saved playlist will have the name *New Playlist* followed by a numeral. When you sync up your iPod, the saved playlist will be transferred to iTunes, where you can rename it.

The On-The-Go playlist is not available on the 1G and 2G iPod models.

iPod shuffle: Converting to AAC

The iPod shuffle can play all formats supported by larger iPods, with two exceptions: Apple Lossless and AIFF. What if you've been ripping your CDs in Apple Lossless format and want to play those tunes with your shuffle? Or what if you've exported some GarageBand songs and want to shuffle around with your music dangling from your neck?

As page 99 showed, the iPod shuffle has a preference setting that lets you accomplish both tasks: it's the check box labeled *Convert higher bit rate songs to*

128 kbps AAC for this iPod. That's a mouthful, but it's a useful option.

When this box is checked, iTunes will create 128 kbps AAC versions of any Apple Lossless or AIFF songs that you try to copy to your iPod shuffle. The song files remain in their original format in your iTunes library; iTunes simply encodes an AAC version on the fly before transferring it to the iPod shuffle.

iPod shuffle and the Gray Dot

If you've chosen to have your iPod shuffle always appear in the Source list (page 99), you may sometimes see a circular gray dot next to a song name.

iTunes displays this dot to indicate that the song hasn't yet been copied to the iPod shuffle. When you connect the shuffle and copy the song, the dot disappears.

Extracting Photos from an iPod

You copied some photos to your iPod, but didn't include the original, high-resolution versions. Now you're at a friend's house and she'd like a copy of the photos. You connect your iPod to her Mac, put it in disk mode, and open up the Photos folder. But instead of seeing individual image files, you see only a couple of files with cryptic names such as F1023_1.ithmb.

When iTunes prepares photos for iPod storage, it stashes them in a format that isn't readable by imaging programs such as iPhoto or Photoshop. But that doesn't mean there isn't a way to get to those photos. A free utility named Keith's iPod Photo Reader can open files and reveal the images they contain. You can copy some or all of the images and save them as PICT image files.

Keith's iPod Photo Reader is available through download sites such as VersionTracker. Consider stashing it on your iPod for those times when you want to copy photos.

Navigating Podcasts

When you're listening to an enhanced podcast on your iPod, you can jump between chapters by pressing the iPod's Prev or Next buttons.

Getting Lyrical

Starting with the 5G and nano models, the iPod has the ability to display song lyrics. If you use the Song Info window to add lyrics to a song (page 28), you can display the lyrics on the iPod as the song plays. Navigate to the Now Playing screen if necessary, then press the Select button until the lyrics appear. You can retrieve song lyrics from innumerable Web sites; search for "song lyrics" using your favorite search engine.

iPod Key Sequences

To Do This	Do This
Turn off the iPod	Hold down Play/Pause.
Restart the iPod	**3G and older iPods:** Hold down Menu and Play/Pause until the Apple logo appears on the screen (five to 10 seconds). **4G and later:** Toggle the Hold switch, then hold down Menu and Select until the Apple logo appears (about six seconds).
Access the iPod's diagnostic mode	**3G and older iPods:** Restart, then immediately hold down Previous, Next, and Select. **4G and later:** Restart, then immediately hold down Previous and Select.

Rating Songs

You can use the iPod to assign star ratings (page 78) to a song while it's playing. Navigate to the Now Playing screen, then press the Select button until the rating screen appears. Use the click wheel to assign a rating. When you update your iPod, iTunes retrieves the rating and assigns it to the song in your library.

Full-Screen Artwork

Page 99 described an iPod preference setting named *Display album artwork on your iPod*. If you check this box, the iPod will display any album artwork associated with the currently playing song. To enlarge the artwork to fill the iPod screen, press the Select button while the song is playing.

Note that when album artwork is visible, scrubbing within a song (described on page 100) requires an extra button press. You need to press Select to display the artwork full-screen, then press Select again to get the little scrubber diamond. If you use the scrubbing feature a lot, you might want to uncheck the album artwork preference setting.

iPod as Address Book and More

You can store more than just music on your iPod. You can also store names and addresses and short text notes.

The iPod's address book feature is made possible by an Internet standard called vCard. All current email programs support vCard, as does the Mac OS X Address Book program. You'll also find support for vCard in Palm- and PocketPC-based handheld computers and even some cell phones.

If you use Mac OS X Tiger (10.4) or a later version, you can have iTunes automatically copy some or all of your contacts from Mac OS X's Address Book program. If you're using an earlier Mac OS X version, you must use Apple's iSync utility. If you don't have iSync, you can download version 1.5 from the Downloads area of Apple's Web site.

You can also store text notes that are accessible through the iPod's Notes menu item: simply peck your notes into a text-only file and then copy the file to the iPod's Notes folder. As the sidebar on the opposite page describes, numerous utilities are available that let you convert various types of documents into text notes that you can read on the iPod's screen.

Updating Address Book Contacts

To copy contacts from Mac OS X's Address Book program to your iPod, connect your iPod, choose Preferences from the iTunes menu, and click the Contacts button.

Begin by checking this box.

To copy all of your Address Book contacts to the iPod, select this option.

The Address Book program lets you organize your contacts into groups. To copy only certain groups to your iPod, select this button and then check the groups you want to copy.

Using an older cat? If you're using a Mac OS version prior to 10.4 Tiger, use iSync to synchronize your Address Book contacts. To download iSync 1.5, the version compatible with pre-Tiger operating systems, visit www.apple.com/downloads.

iPod and Hypertext

The Notes feature, provided by 3G and later iPods, supports hyperlinks not unlike those on Web sites. A text note can contain a link to another note or even to a song: navigating to the link and then clicking the iPod's Select button is the equivalent of clicking on a hyperlink.

If you're interested in learning more about creating hyperlinked text notes, check out the article that my *Macworld* colleague Chris Breen wrote in the September 2004 issue. The article is called "Hack the iPod's Notes," and is online at macworld.com.

Find these and other iPod utilities.
www.macilife.com/itunes

Adding Contacts from Microsoft Entourage

In order for the iPod to recognize vCards, you must store them in the iPod's Contacts folder.
To copy contacts from Microsoft Entourage to the iPod, open the Entourage address book and select the contacts you want to copy to the iPod. Next, drag those contacts to the iPod's Contacts folder.

If you frequently shuttle contacts from Entourage to your iPod, consider using Zapptek's iPDA software, described below.

iPod Scripts

Numerous programmers have created useful AppleScripts for the iPod that enable you to manage playlists, copy songs, and more. The best source for these scripts is Doug Adams' excellent Doug's AppleScripts for iTunes site (www.dougscripts.com).

Deleting Contacts

If you've added contacts to your iPod using the technique described at left, you can remove them by dragging them from the iPod's Contacts folder to the Trash. (Your iPod must be in disk mode; see page 98.)

Beyond Music: A Sampling of iPod Utilities

Dozens of free or inexpensive utilities are available that let you store all manner of information on an iPod. Here's a sampling of a few noteworthy offerings.

iSpeak It. With Michael Zapp's iSpeak It (www.zapptek.com), you can create your own audiobooks—kind of. iSpeak It turns any text file or Microsoft Word document into an MP3 or AAC audio file. Add the resulting file to your iTunes music library, and listen.

iSpeak It uses the Mac's text-to-speech technology to create its files, so your homemade audiobooks will have a decidedly robotic quality to them.

iPresent It. Also from Michael Zapp, iPresent It converts presentations created in PowerPoint or Apple's Keynote into iPod slide shows. (It also works with any PDF file.) Create a presentation and run it through iPresent It. Then connect your iPod to a projection system and pontificate—no laptop required.

iPDA. Yet another Michael Zapp creation, iPDA can export calendar events, email, notes, and contacts from Microsoft Entourage X, iCal, and the Mac OS X Mail program. It can also download news headlines and weather forecasts.

PocketMac iPod. This inexpensive utility specializes in syncing contacts, email, and notes from Microsoft Office. Try it at www.pocketmac.net.

Text2iPod. This freeware utility by Beniot Terradillos will convert any text-only file into a note file that you can read on the iPod.

PodQuest. This slick little utility from Mibasoft (www.mibasoft.dk) downloads driving directions from MapQuest and stores them in the iPod's Notes folder. Just remember to pull over to the side of the road before trying to read them.

iPod as Calendar: Using iCal

With Apple's iCal software, you can keep track of appointments, schedules, and events of all kinds. You can create multiple calendars—for example, one for personal events such as birthdays and another for work appointments.

Use iCal to display multiple calendars at once to quickly identify schedule conflicts. You can also share calendars—with friends, coworkers, or complete strangers—by *publishing* them through your .Mac account.

You can even download and use calendars that other people have created. Hundreds of free calendars are available in categories ranging from TV schedules to holidays to the phases of the moon.

You can also use appointment information from iCal calendars when creating wall calendars in iPhoto. Check a box, and iPhoto adds iCal events to your calendar. For details, see page 196.

iCal is included with Mac OS X 10.4 Tiger. If you're using an older version of the Mac OS, you can download iCal 1.5.5 from Apple's software downloads site (www.apple.com/downloads).

What does iCal have to do with the iPod? Simply this: You can copy your calendars to the iPod and view them on the road. You can also set up alarms in iCal and have your iPod beep to notify you of important appointments. Or TV shows.

Updating Calendars

To set up iTunes to update your Calendars, connect your iPod to your Mac, choose Preferences from the iTunes menu, then click the Calendars button.

Begin by checking this box.

To copy all of your calendars to the iPod, select this option.

To copy only certain calendars to your iPod, select this button and then check the calendars you want to copy.

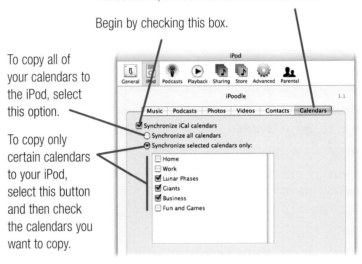

Syncing calendars from elsewhere. You may also have calendar files that originated somewhere other than in your copy of iCal—perhaps you downloaded a calendar from a Web site, or someone emailed it to you as an attachment, or you simply copied it from a different Mac. To add a calendar file to the iPod, drag its icon into the Calendars folder.

The iPod can also store calendars in the industry-standard vCal format. Files in vCal format end with the extension .vcs.

Navigating Calendars and Events

As with music and addresses, the iPod uses a drill-down menu scheme for calendars and events: the deeper you go, the more detail you get.

To display calendars, go to Extras > Calendar.

Each calendar appears as a separate menu item. To display a specific calendar, use the click wheel to highlight it, then press the iPod's Select button.

Days that have events associated with them are indicated with a small dot. To see a day's events, highlight the day, then press the iPod's Select button.

The iPod displays a summary of the event. To see event details, select the event and press the Select button again.

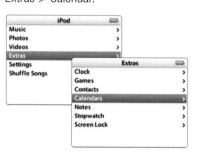

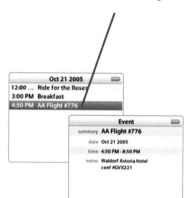

Calendar Tips

iCal Calling iTunes

Doug Adams' iCal Calling iTunes is a slick AppleScript that turns iCal and iTunes into a musical alarm clock: it enables iTunes to play a specific playlist at a time you specify.

iCal Calling iTunes is a cinch to use. Simply create an iCal event whose name is the same as one of your iTunes playlists. When the event time arrives, iTunes begins playing the playlist.

Silencing Alarms

If you've used iCal to specify that some events have alarms, your iPod will beep at the specified times. But there may be times when you don't want the iPod to beep.

To silence the iPod's alarms, go to Extras > Calendar > Alarms where you'll find three options: On (the iPod beeps and the alarm text appears on the iPod's screen); Silent (no beep but the alarm text still appears); and Off (no beep or alarm text).

Dates of All Kinds

You don't use iCal to manage your schedule? Don't let that stop you from sampling the world of calendars that other people have published on the Web. You can download hundreds of calendars in dozens of categories: sports schedules, TV schedules, lunar phases, celebrity personal appearances, holidays of all kinds, and more.

One place to find calendars is Apple's iCal Web site, but the ultimate collection of calendars lives at an independent site called iCalShare (www.icalshare. com). I downloaded the Moon Phases calendar, and now my iPod knows the phases of the moon through the year 2015.

So even if you don't use iCal to manage your appointments, you might find it a useful tool for keeping track of events that take place elsewhere in the solar system.

Accessories for the Fully Powered iPod

The iPod line has spawned an industry of accessories—carrying cases, battery packs, microphones, speaker systems, FM transmitters, and more.

I've already covered some common accessories, such as Apple's Universal Dock and the iPod AV Connection Kit. Here's a sampling of more accessories. For reviews of iPod add-ons, check out Playlist magazine (www.playlistmag.com) and iLounge (www.ilounge.com).

Speak up, dock. Turn your iPod into a self-contained stereo system with Apple's iPod Hi-Fi. The iPod sits in a dock connector atop the boombox, which sounds great and includes a remote control. Similar products are available from Bose, Altec Lansing, and JBL, among others.

On the dock. A dock makes it convenient to update your iPod, charge its battery, and connect the iPod to a stereo system. If your iPod didn't include a dock, consider springing for one. Have a dock? Consider a second. Connect one to your Mac for quick updating, and another to your stereo for convenient listening.

On the record. Most recent full-sized iPods accept microphone attachments that let you record voice memos, lectures, and arguments. At right: Griffin Technology's iTalk. The 5G iPod can record high-quality audio, but as of this writing, no microphone attachments were available for it.

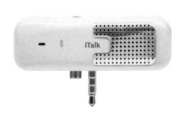

Tune in. Apple's iPod Radio Remote adds FM radio tuning to your iPod. I use one along with an FM transmitter (opposite page) to beam music to my iPod while I work around the house.

Camera connections. With the Belkin Media Reader (right) and Digital Camera Link add-ons, your 3G or 4G iPod can store photos from your digital camera. Have an iPod photo or 5G iPod? Consider Apple's iPod Camera Connector, which lets you transfer photos from a camera and view them on the iPod photo's screen.

Get links to iPod accessories aplenty.
www.macilife.com/itunes

Case closed. Many companies sell iPod cases. My iPod wears the Showcase, a rugged plastic case from Contour Design.

Apple now offers a line of upscale leather cases, not to mention a line of colorful socks for all iPods except the shuffle. Belkin's slick line of Kickstand cases (at right) features a hinged design that lets the iPod stand upright, as if on an easel.

Play longer. Griffin, Belkin, and others sell battery packs that let you power an iPod using standard batteries. Shown here: Griffin's TuneJuice for iPod, iPod nano, and iPod mini.

Other power-packed accessories you might consider include an Apple power adaptor (for charging your iPod while you're away from the computer); and car cigarette-lighter adaptors that let you charge on the road.

The Car Connection

The only thing better than having thousands of songs in your pocket is having thousands of songs in your car. There are several ways to get audio from your iPod to your car stereo.

A smart cassette adaptor. Cassette adaptors are inexpen-

sive, easy to use, and reasonably good-sounding. Griffin's SmartDeck goes beyond the ordinary adaptor to enable you

to control your iPod using your car's cassette deck controls.

FM transmitters. An FM transmitter plugs into the iPod and then transmits its signal so that you can tune it in on your radio. FM transmitters sometimes work poorly in urban areas, where it occasionally seems that there's an FM station on nearly every frequency. Griffin's iTrip connects to the top of the iPod, while Sonnet's highly regarded Podfreq packs an FM transmitter into a rugged carrying case.

Direct connections. The best way to listen to the iPod in your car is to use a cabling system

that lets the iPod's audio output go directly into your car stereo's amplifier. More and more car manufacturers are providing iPod-ready stereo systems that let you stash the iPod in the glove compartment and control it using the buttons on the car's steering wheel or dashboard.

Several companies sell cabling kits that let an iPod tap into the audio inputs that would otherwise be used for a trunk-mounted CD changer. Check out the Ice-Link Plus from Dension (www.densionusa.com), as well as the cabling offerings from peripheralelectronics.com,

logjamelectronics.com, and soundgate.com.

And if you're shopping for a new car stereo system, you might consider one of the iPod-ready systems from Alpine (www. alpine-usa.com). Connect your iPod to a compatible system, and you can stash the iPod in the glove compartment and control it using the knobs on the stereo system. The systems even display the name of the currently playing song. Now *that's* traveling in style.

iPhoto and Digital Photography

The Macintosh
iLife '06

iPhoto at a Glance

Millions of photographs lead lives of loneliness, trapped in unorganized boxes where they're never seen. Their digital brethren often share the same fate, exiled to cluttered folders on a hard drive and rarely opened.

With iPhoto, you can free your photos—and organize, print, and share them, too. iPhoto simplifies the entire process. You begin by *importing* images from a digital camera, your hard drive, a CD from a photofinisher, or other source. Then you can create *albums*, organizing the images in whatever order you want. You can even have iPhoto create the albums for you.

Along the way, you might also use iPhoto's editing features to make your photos look better. And you might use iPhoto's keyword features and search box to help you file and locate images.

When you've finished organizing and editing photos, share them. Order prints or make your own. Design gorgeous photo books, arranging photos on each page and adding captions. Design calendars and greeting cards. Create slide shows, complete with music from iTunes, and then watch them on the Mac's screen, burn them to DVDs, or transfer them to an iPod.

Prefer to share over the Internet? Email photos to friends and family. Have an Apple .Mac account? Create Web photo albums with iWeb (page 366). Or create automatically updating photo albums, called *photocasts*, that others can subscribe to.

Welcome to the Photo Liberation Society.

Beyond the Shoebox

Use the panes in the lower-left corner of the iPhoto window to view and edit information, find photos from specific dates, and assign descriptive keywords. To display a pane, click its button (circled below).

Information pane. Edit information for photos, albums, and books (page 120).

Calendar pane. Quickly view photos from specific dates, weeks, or months (page 123).

Keywords pane. Assign keywords to photos to make them easier to find and organize (pages 126–129).

The Library contains everything you import into iPhoto. Each set of items you import is called a *roll*, as in roll of film.

To quickly see photos from a recent year, click the triangle (page 122).

To see the last set of photos you imported, click Last Roll (page 122).

Use folders to organize albums and other items (page 133).

Use smart albums to have iPhoto create albums for you (page 134).

Assemble photos into albums, and then share the albums (pages 130–133).

Create books, calendars, and cards (pages 184–199).

Create and display slide shows (pages 160–165).

To resize the Source area, drag this control left or right.

Publish photocast albums via .Mac (pages 168–171).

To show or hide a roll's images, click the triangle. **Note:** If your library isn't being displayed by roll, choose Film Rolls from the View menu.

Get in the habit of giving each roll a descriptive name (page 128).

iPhoto can also store movie clips, such as those taken by a digital camera. Movie clips are labeled with a movie badge (page 117).

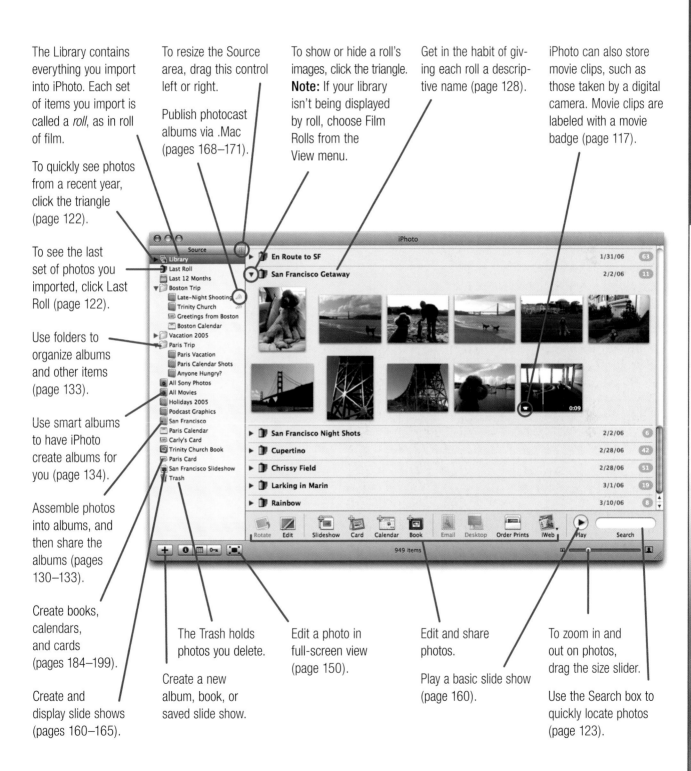

The Trash holds photos you delete.

Create a new album, book, or saved slide show.

Edit a photo in full-screen view (page 150).

Edit and share photos.

Play a basic slide show (page 160).

To zoom in and out on photos, drag the size slider.

Use the Search box to quickly locate photos (page 123).

The Essentials of Digital Imaging

Like the digital audio world and other specialized fields, digital imaging has its own jargon and technical concepts to understand. You can accomplish a lot in iPhoto without having to know these things, but a solid foundation in imaging essentials will help you get more out of iPhoto, your digital camera, and other imaging hardware.

There are two key points to take away from this little lesson. First, although iPhoto works beautifully with digital cameras, it can also accept images that you've scanned or received from a photofinisher.

Second, the concept of resolution will arise again and again in your digital imaging endeavors. You'll want big, high-resolution images for good-quality prints, and small, low-resolution images for convenient emailing to friends and family. As described on page 167, you can use iPhoto to create low-resolution versions of your images.

Where Digital Images Come From

iPhoto can work with digital images from a variety of sources.

Digital camera

Digital cameras are more plentiful and capable than ever. The key factor that differentiates cameras is *resolution*: how many *pixels* of information they store in each image. Even inexpensive digital cameras now provide resolutions of between 4 and 6 megapixels—more than enough to make large prints.

Most digital cameras connect to the Mac's USB port. Images are usually stored on removable-media cards; you can also transfer images into iPhoto by connecting a *media reader* to the Mac and inserting the memory card into the reader (page 118).

Scanner

With a scanner, you can create digital images from photographs and other hard-copy originals.

Scanners also connect via USB, although some high-end models connect via FireWire. Film scanners are a bit pricier, but can scan negatives and slides and deliver great image quality (page 206). Save your scanned images in JPEG format, and then add them to iPhoto by dragging their icons into the iPhoto window (page 119).

For tips on getting high-quality scans, visit www.scantips.com.

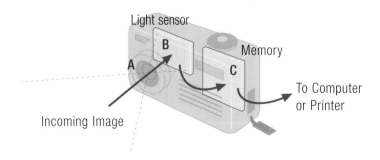

Light sensor

B

Memory

A

C

Incoming Image

To Computer
or Printer

In a digital camera, the image is focused by the lens (**A**) onto a sensor (**B**), where tiny, light-sensitive diodes called photosites convert photons into electrons. Those electrical values are converted into digital data and stored by a memory card or other medium (**C**), from which they can be transferred to a computer or printer.

Compact Disc

For an extra charge, most photofinishers will burn your images on a compact disc in Kodak Picture CD format. You get not only prints and negatives, but also a CD that you use with the Mac.

To learn more about Picture CD, go to www.kodak.com and search for *picture cd*.

Internet

Many photofinishers also provide extra-cost Internet delivery options. After processing and scanning your film, they send you an email containing a Web address where you can view and download images. After downloading images, you can drag their icons into iPhoto's window.

A Short Glossary of Imaging Terms

artifacts Visible flaws in an image, often as a result of excessive *compression* or when you try to create a large print from a low-resolution image.

CompactFlash A removable-memory storage medium commonly used by digital cameras. A CompactFlash card measures 43 by 36 by 3.3 mm. The thicker *Type 2* cards are 5.5 mm wide.

compression The process of making image files use less storage space, usually by removing information that our eyes don't detect anyway. The most common form of image compression is *JPEG*.

EXIF Pronounced *ex-if*, a standard file format used by virtually all of today's digital cameras. EXIF files use JPEG compression but also contain details about each image: the date and time it was taken, its resolution, the type of camera used, the exposure settings, and more. iPhoto retrieves and stores EXIF information when you import images. EXIF stands for *Exchangeable Image File*.

JPEG Pronounced *jay-peg*, the most common format for storing digital camera images. Like MP3, JPEG is a *lossy*

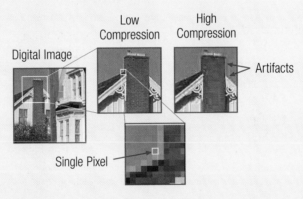

Digital Image

Low Compression

High Compression

Artifacts

Single Pixel

compression format: it shrinks files by discarding information that we can't perceive anyway. And as with MP3, there are varying degrees of JPEG compression; many imaging programs enable you to specify how heavily JPEG images are compressed. Note that a heavily compressed JPEG image can contain *artifacts*. JPEG stands for *Joint Photographic Experts Group*.

megapixel One million pixels.

pixel Short for *picture element*, the smallest building block of an image. The number of pixels that a camera or scanner captures determines the *resolution* of the image.

raw An image containing the data captured by the camera's light sensor, with no additional in-camera image processing applied (see page 154).

resolution 1. The size of an image, expressed in pixels. For example, an image whose resolution is 640 by 480 contains 480 vertical rows of pixels, each containing 640 pixels from left to right. **2.** A measure of the capabilities of a digital camera or scanner.

SmartMedia A commonly used design for removable-memory storage cards.

Importing Photos from a Camera

The first step in assembling a digital photo library is to import photos into iPhoto. There are several ways to import photos, but the most common method is to connect your camera to your Mac and transfer the photos using a USB cable. iPhoto can directly import photos from the vast majority of digital cameras. (See a list at www.apple.com/iphoto/compatibility/.)

You can have iPhoto erase the camera's contents after importing them, but I don't recommend it. It's always best to erase your memory card using the controls on your digital camera. And call me cautious, but I prefer to see that my photos imported correctly before wiping them off of my memory card.

When you get a set of prints back from a photo lab, they're stored in an envelope. When you import a set of digital photos, iPhoto stores them in a digital envelope called a *roll* (as in roll of film—get it?). And just as you can write on an envelope full of prints, you can give each roll a descriptive name that will help in your photo-filing efforts.

iPhoto can also import the movie clips that most cameras are capable of taking. If you shot some movie clips along with your photos, iPhoto will import them, too. (For more details on shooting movies with a digital camera, see page 275.)

Step 1: Connect your camera to one of your Mac's USB ports (the port on the keyboard is particularly convenient) and turn the camera on. When iPhoto recognizes your camera, it displays the Import panel.

Tip: If your camera has a battery-saving sleep mode, adjust it so that the camera won't drift into slumber while your photos are still importing.

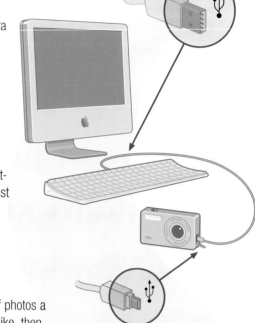

Step 2: Give your new roll of photos a name and description if you like, then click Import.

iPhoto will often display your camera's make and model here.

You don't have to type a roll name and description at this point, but you should—you'll have an easier time finding photos later.

Pretend this option isn't here—always delete photos using your camera's controls.

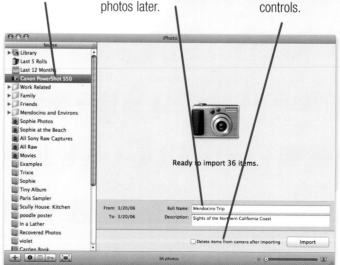

After the Import: Immediate Gratification

Once you import photos into iPhoto, the real fun begins. Your first step is obvious: check out your photos. Here are some tips for immediate photo gratification.

Eject the Camera

Some cameras display an icon on your Finder desktop. If your camera does, be sure to "eject" the icon before disconnecting the camera: click the Eject button next to the camera's name in the iPhoto

source list. (If you don't see the Eject button, you don't have to perform this step.)

View Your Shots

Here's the fastest way to review a fresh batch of photos. In the Source list, click the Last Roll item. Then, jump down to the lower right corner and use the size slider to enlarge the photo thumbnails until just one photo fills your iPhoto window. Finally, use the scroll bar or the up-arrow and down-arrow keys on your keyboard to display each photo.

Another fun way to review your shots is to use iPhoto's full-screen edit view, described on page 150. If your batch of photos included a movie clip, you can play it by double-clicking its thumbnail image. iPhoto starts the QuickTime Player

program, which loads the movie. To play the movie, press the spacebar or click the Play button.

Display an Instant Slide Show

To screen your photos with a bit more style, display a basic slide show. First, click the Last Roll item in the Source list. Next, hold down the Option key on your keyboard and click the Play button (▶) near the lower-right corner of the screen. To stop the slide show, click the mouse or press the Esc key. (To learn more about slide shows, see pages 160–165.)

Delete the Dregs

See a photo that you know you don't want to keep? Trash it. To delete a photo, select it (click it once), then press the Delete key. You can also delete a photo by dragging it to the Trash item in the Source list.

iPhoto won't actually erase the photo from your hard drive until you choose Empty Trash from the iPhoto menu. If you change your mind about deleting a photo, click the Trash item in the Source list, select the photo you want to keep, and choose Restore to Photo Library from the Photos menu.

Dealing with Duplicates

Here's a common scenario: you use iPhoto to import some photos from your camera, and you don't delete the photos from the camera after importing. Then, you shoot more photos and prepare to import them. iPhoto detects that you've already imported some of the photos, and it asks you if you want to skip those duplicates.

To not import the duplicate, click Don't Import.

To cancel the import session, click Cancel.

To have iPhoto apply your choice to all duplicates it finds during this import session, click Apply to all duplicates.

To import the duplicate displayed, click Import.

More Ways to Import Photos

Most iPhoto users import photos directly from a camera using the technique I described on the previous pages. But you have more than one way to get photos into iPhoto.

A media reader is a great way to import photos from a camera's memory card. Plug the reader into your Mac, then insert the memory card into the reader. Because you aren't using your camera to transfer photos, its battery charge will last longer.

Be sure to get a reader that supports the type of memory cards your camera uses. Or get a multi-format reader that supports several types of memory cards. And look for a reader that connects to the Mac's FireWire jack or to its USB 2.0 jack, if your Mac has one. FireWire and USB 2.0 readers transfer images much faster than a USB 1.0 connection.

You can also import images by dragging their icons into the iPhoto window. If you've scanned a batch of images, you'll use this technique to bring them into iPhoto. You can also use this technique to save photos that people email to you or that you find on Web sites.

Using a Media Reader

Here's the photo-importing technique I use most often.

Step 1. Connect the media reader to your Mac.

Step 2. Be sure your camera's power is off, then remove the memory card from the camera and insert it into the reader. iPhoto recognizes the card and displays the Import panel shown on page 116.

Step 3. Type a name and description for the photos you're about to import, then click the Import button.

Step 4. After iPhoto has imported the photos, click the Eject button next to the memory card's name in the Source list. Finally, remove the memory card from the reader, return the card to your camera, and then erase the card.

Variations

The laptop angle. You can buy a media reader that plugs into the PC Card slot of a PowerBook. If you're traveling with a PowerBook, a PC Card-based reader is a compact alternative to a FireWire or USB reader.

At this writing, media readers were starting to become available for the ExpressCard/34 slot provided by the MacBook Pro laptops, too. Unfortunately, the ExpressCard/34 slot is too small to accommodate a Compact Flash card, requiring you to use a fragile and awkward adaptor. If you use Compact Flash cards and own a MacBook Pro, you're probably better off with an external FireWire or USB 2.0 reader. Look at it this way: at least your external modem will have company in your briefcase.

The iPod angle. Belkin's Digital Camera Link for iPod is a media reader that attaches to the dock connector on a 3G or 4G iPod, enabling you to transfer photos to the iPod. When you connect an iPod containing photos to your Mac, iPhoto recognizes it and displays the Import panel. And, as described on page 108, Apple's iPod Camera Connector lets you transfer photos to an iPod photo or 5G iPod.

Importing from the Finder

To import an entire folder full of images, drag the folder to the Library item or into the photo area.

iPhoto gives the new roll the same name as the folder from which its images came. You can rename the roll using the Information pane (see page 121).

To import only some images, select their icons and then drag them to the Library item or into the iPhoto window.

Note: When you import images that are already stored on your hard drive, iPhoto makes duplicate copies of them in your iPhoto library. You can change this using the Preferences command; see page 211.

Tip: If you have a media reader, you can use the Finder to selectively import only some photos from a memory card. See page 209 for details.

Importing from Email and Web Pages

A friend has emailed some photos to you, and you want to add them to your iPhoto library. If you're using Mail, the email program included with Mac OS X, simply drag the photos from the email message into the iPhoto window. If the email message contains several photos, Shift-click on each one to select them all before dragging.

If you use Microsoft Entourage, your job is a bit more difficult. First, save the photos on your Mac's desktop. Next, drag them into the iPhoto window as shown at left. Finally, delete the photos from your desktop.

To save a photo that's on a Web page, just drag the photo from your Web browser into the iPhoto window.

Importing from Picture CDs and PhotoCDs

iPhoto can also import images saved on a Kodak PhotoCD or Picture CD. (PhotoCD is an older format that you aren't likely to see too often. Picture CD is a newer format that most photo finishers use.)

Picture CD. Choose Add to Library from iPhoto's File menu, locate the Picture CD, and then locate and double-click the folder named Pictures. Finally, click the Open button. Or, use the Finder to open the Pictures folder on the CD and then drag images into iPhoto's window.

PhotoCD. Simply insert the PhotoCD in your Mac's optical drive. iPhoto launches and displays its Import panel. Type a name and description for the photos, then click Import.

Where iPhoto Stores Your Photos

When you import photos, iPhoto stores them in a folder called iPhoto Library, located inside the Pictures folder. (If you like, you can store your iPhoto Library folder elsewhere, such as on an external hard drive. For details, see page 205.)

Get in the habit of frequently backing up the iPhoto Library folder to avoid losing your images to a hardware or software problem. You can use iPhoto's disc-burning features to back up photos, or you can copy your iPhoto Library folder to a

different hard drive—or even to your iPod. For advice on backing up your photos, see page 205.

Whatever you do, don't futz with the files inside the iPhoto Library folder—renaming or moving them could cause iPhoto to have

problems finding your photos. Never try to add photos to your library by dragging them into the iPhoto Library folder. Always add photos by dragging them into the iPhoto window itself.

After the Import: Getting Organized

iPhoto forces some organization on you by storing each set of imported images as a separate roll. Even if you never use iPhoto's other organizational features, you're still ahead of the old shoebox photo-filing system: you will always be able to view your photos in chronological order.

But don't stop there. Take the time to assign *titles* and *comments* to your favorite shots. By using the Information pane to perform these and other housekeeping tasks, you can make photos easier to find and keep your library well organized.

Titles are names or brief descriptions that you assign to photos and rolls: Party Photos, Mary at the Beach, and so on. iPhoto can use these titles as captions for its Web photo albums and books. Using the View menu, you can have iPhoto display titles below each thumbnail image. You can also search for photos by typing title or comment text in the Search box (page 123).

There's one more benefit to assigning titles to photos: when you're working in other iLife programs, you can search for a photo by typing part of its title in the photo media browser's Search box.

iPhoto also provides a feature that lets you assign titles more or less automatically. It's the Batch Change command, and you can read about it on page 125.

Take advantage of iPhoto's filing features, and you'll be able locate images in, well, a flash.

Assigning Titles and Comments

Use the Information pane to assign a title and comment to a photo. To display the Information pane, click the ⬛ button.

Step 1.

Select the photo to which you want to assign a title and/or comment.

Step 2.

Click in the Title or Comments area of the Information pane, then type the title or comment.

Keep your titles fairly short.

Think of a comment as the text you'd normally write on the back of a photo.

Tips

On a roll. Want to quickly title (or comment) one photo after another? Press ⌘-] after typing a title or comment, and iPhoto selects the next photo and highlights its title or comment field so you can immediately begin typing. To move to the previous photo, press ⌘-[. And to keep your hands on the keyboard, press Tab and Shift-Tab to jump from one field to the next in the Information pane.

Check your spelling. Want to check the spelling of your titles and comments? Select the text you want to proofread, then choose Check Spelling from the Edit menu's Spelling submenu. Or use the keyboard: select the text you want to proofread and press ⌘-;.

Information

title Blue Penstemon
date 5/18/2002
time 11:59:16 AM
rating · · · · ·
format JPEG Image
size 1600 × 1200
828 KB

A beautiful blue penstemon shares the garden with iris and roses.

Assigning Titles to Rolls

iPhoto's Import panel lets you title a roll of photos before importing them. But you don't get this opportunity when dragging photos into iPhoto from the Finder or other programs. No problem: you can use the Information panel to rename any roll.

Changing the Date

You can also edit the date of a roll or a single image. This is handy if your digital camera's built-in clock wasn't set correctly or if you want a roll's date to reflect the day you shot its images, not the day you imported them.

Rotate Verticals as Needed

Some cameras automatically rotate photos taken in vertical orientation. If yours doesn't, the job is yours. Select the photo or photos and then click the Rotate button or press ⌘-R (to rotate counterclockwise) or ⌘-Option-R (to rotate clockwise). You can also rotate photos while viewing a slide show; see page 161.

To title a roll, select it by clicking on its name, then type a title in the Title field.
Tip: To highlight the contents of any field in the Information panel, click its label.

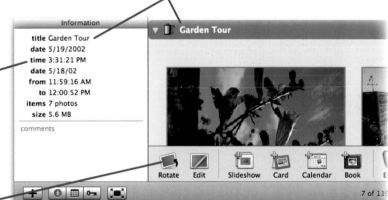

At the right edge of each roll name, iPhoto displays the roll's date and the number of photos in that roll. This ability to see how many shots are in a roll is handy when you've hidden a roll's photos as described below.

Tips for Working with Rolls

Scroll Guide

As you scroll through your photos, iPhoto displays a semi-transparent scroll guide listing roll names and dates. This can help you home in on a specific roll quickly, but if you'd rather not see this guide, choose Preferences from the iPhoto menu, click Appearance, then uncheck the Show Scrolling Information box.

Hiding Rolls You Aren't Using

To the left of each roll's name is a tiny, down-pointing triangle: click it, and iPhoto collapses the roll, hiding its images. I like to collapse every roll whose photos I don't need to see at the moment. This clears the clutter in my iPhoto window and speeds up scrolling and changing the size of thumbnails.

A related tip: press the Option key while clicking on a collapsed roll's triangle, and iPhoto expands every roll in your library. Similarly, to collapse every roll, Option-click on the down-pointing triangle of any roll.

Viewing Rolls

If iPhoto isn't displaying individual rolls, and is instead showing all the photos in your library, choose Film Rolls from the View menu. When this command has a check mark next to it, iPhoto displays your library sorted by roll.

Browsing Your Photo Library

As your photo library grows, you'll want to take advantage of the features iPhoto provides for browsing your library and locating specific photos.

Want to quickly view the last set of shots you brought in? Click the Last Roll item. Want to see all the shots you took in the last year? Click the Last 12 Months item. Better yet, use the Preferences command to customize both features to match the way you like to view your library.

You can also quickly display photos from a specific year. Instead of scrolling through your library to find those photos from 2003, for example, beam yourself back in time with a couple of clicks: click the little triangle next to the Library item, then click 2003.

When you want to travel back in time with more precision, use the Calendar pane. It lets you view your photos chronologically, clicking on specific months, weeks, or days to display photos taken during those periods.

You can also use the Search box to locate photos by typing text present in their titles, comments, roll names, file names, and keywords.

If you're just getting started with iPhoto and you have a small photo library, these browsing features may not mean much to you. But as your library grows, you'll grow to appreciate them.

Customizing Your View

To customize the organizational aids in iPhoto's Source area, choose Preferences from the iPhoto menu and click the General button.

Don't want a particular year's photos to appear as you browse your library? Uncheck its box.

To customize the Last Months album, specify the desired number of months. The maximum value is 18 months; I set mine to 1 month to put my most recent photos just a click away.

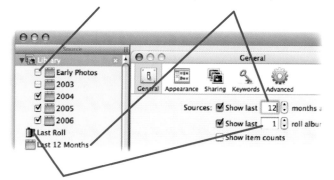

To be able to quickly peruse more than just the last set of photos you imported, customize the Last Roll item. You can specify up to 25 rolls.

Appearance Preferences

While you have the Preferences dialog box open, you might want to click its Appearance button and examine those options.

Want to see your thumbnail photos against a gray background? Drag the Background slider to the left. You can also choose to turn off the shadow effect that iPhoto puts behind each photo in Organize view, and to display a border around each thumbnail photo.

Time Machine: the Calendar Pane

With the Calendar pane, you can display photos taken during specific periods or even on specific days. Be sure that the Library item is selected in the Source list, then click the 📅 button.

The big picture. When you first display the Calendar pane, it shows the current year.

Switch between viewing the current year and a specific month.

To display the previous or next year, click the arrow buttons.

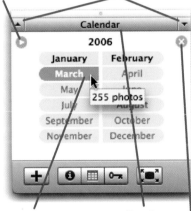

Months in which you've taken photos appear in bold. To display a specific month's photos, click that month. You can also select multiple months by dragging across them, by Shift-clicking, or by ⌘-clicking.

To return to the present, click Calendar.

To return to viewing your entire library, click the ⊗ button.

Tip: If you point to a month without clicking, iPhoto tells you how many photos you took in that month, as shown above.

Narrow your view. Want to explore a specific month? Double-click its name, and iPhoto displays a calendar for that month.

Click the arrows to display the previous or next month. **Tip:** To see several months at once, enlarge the Calendar pane by dragging the horizontal bar above it.

To select a week, click the dot to its left, or double-click any day in that week.

Days on which you took photos appear in bold. To see a day's photos, click its date. **Tip:** You can select multiple days by dragging across them, by Shift-clicking, or by ⌘-clicking.

Calendar Pane Tips

Browsing albums. You can use the Calendar pane to browse within specific albums, too. Simply select the album in the Source list before clicking on months and dates in the Calendar pane.

Not seeing all your photos? It may be because you had previously used the Calendar pane to narrow down your display. If the Calendar pane is still visible, clear the search by clicking the ⊗ button. If the Calendar pane is closed, look at its button. When a calendar search is in effect, the button has a little blue dot on it: 📅 . Click the button to reopen the pane, then clear the search.

Using the Search Box

The Search box lets you home in photos by typing text. iPhoto searches photo filenames, roll names, titles, comments, or keywords. The more librarian work you do—assigning titles and comments, for example—the better the search feature works.

Like the Calendar pane, the Search box searches whatever item is selected in the Source list. To search your entire library, be sure the Library item is selected.

To clear a search, click the ⊗ button in the Search box.

Working with Rolls

Anxious to start having fun with your photos? Go ahead and skip to page 130, where you can learn about creating photo albums and much more.

But if you're an obsessive organizer or an iPhoto veteran whose photo library has become cluttered over the years, read on. iPhoto provides features that let you combine multiple rolls into one roll, move photos from one roll to another, and more.

Why bother? Better organization. For example, say you take six shots at a party and you import them right away so that everyone can have a look. Then you fire off another 28 shots as the party progresses. When you bring that second set in, iPhoto stores its photos in their own roll, as always. But for organization's sake, you probably want both sets of photos in the same roll. No problem: just use the techniques described here to combine the two rolls into one.

To use most of the techniques described here, you need to be viewing your library by roll: choose Film Rolls from the View menu. As I've said more than once, this is the most efficient way to view and work with your iPhoto library.

Combining Several Rolls into One

A family member emails you a few photos now and then, and you add them to your iPhoto library by dragging them into iPhoto, as described on page 119. Over time, you end up with numerous rolls containing just a few photos apiece.

Here's how to consolidate multiple rolls into a single roll.

Step 1.

Select the rolls you want to consolidate by Shift-clicking on their names: click on the first roll's name, then press Shift while clicking on subsequent rolls.

Tip: As you can see here, you don't have to display a roll's photos in order to select the roll. As long as you see the blue rectangle around the roll's name, the roll and all its photos are selected.

Step 2.

Choose Create Film Roll from the File menu. iPhoto creates a new roll and moves all of the selected rolls' photos into it.

Change your mind? If you decide not to consolidate the rolls—or if you erred and selected the wrong rolls to begin with—just head up to the Edit menu and choose Undo Create Roll.

Merging Rolls by Dragging

There's another way to combine rolls: drag one roll to the other.

Step 1. Select the roll by clicking the roll's name.

Step 2. Drag until the name of the destination roll is highlighted by the bold blue bar, then release the mouse button.

Moving Just a Few Photos

Just as you can move prints from one envelope to another after getting them back from the photo lab, you can move your digital photos from one roll to another after bringing them into iPhoto.

To move just a few photos to a different roll, select them and then drag them to the destination roll. (For tips on selecting photos, see page 131.)

As this example shows, the destination roll's photos don't even have to be visible. Simply drag the photos to the destination roll's name.

Wrong roll? If you dragged too far (or not far enough) and ended up depositing some photos in the wrong roll, just choose Undo Add to Roll from the Edit menu.

In One Fell Swoop: The Batch Change Command

Since you're already wearing your photo librarian's hat, this is a good time to remind you of the power of the Batch Change command in the Photos menu. It lets you change, at once, the title, date, or comments for an entire set of photos.

Select the photos whose information you want to change, then choose Batch Change. Use the pop-up menu to choose the tidbit of information you want to modify.

Tip: If you're changing the date, it's a good idea to add an interval between photos. This helps iPhoto sort the photos.

If you're like me and are too lazy to assign titles and comments to individual photos, the Batch Change command is a good compromise: assign a phrase to a set of related photos, and you can search for that phrase when creating smart albums.

Assigning Keywords and Ratings

Chances are that many of your photos fall into specific categories: baby photos, scenic shots, and so on. By creating and assigning *keywords*, you make related images easier to find.

Keywords are labels useful for categorizing and locating all the photos of a given kind: vacation shots, baby pictures, mug shots, you name it.

iPhoto has several predefined keywords that cover common categories. But you can replace the existing ones to cover the kinds of photos you take, and you can add as many new keywords as you like.

You can assign multiple keywords to a single image. For example, if you have a Beach keyword, a Dog keyword, and a Summer keyword, you assign all three to a photo of your dog taken at the beach in July.

Keywords are one way to categorize your photos; ratings are another. You can assign a rating of from one to five stars to a photo—rank your favorites for quick searching, or mark the stinkers for future deletion.

As with many iPhoto housekeeping tasks, assigning keywords and ratings is entirely optional. But if you take the time, you can use iPhoto's search and Smart Albums features to quickly locate and collect photos that meet specific criteria.

Assigning Keywords

You can assign keywords by using the Photo Info window or by dragging photos to the Keywords pane. Using the Photo Info window tends to be more efficient.

With the Photo Info Window

Step 1. Select the photo or photos to which you want to assign keywords.

Step 2. Choose Get Info from the Photos menu (⌘-I).

Step 3. In the Photo Info window, click Keywords.

Step 4. Check each keyword you want to assign. Here, I'm assigning the keywords Sophie and San Francisco to some shots of my dog in my favorite city.

With the Keywords Pane

Step 1. Display the Keywords pane by clicking the 🔑 button.

Step 2. Select one or more photos, then drag them to the desired keyword. Here, I'm dragging an entire collapsed roll.

Tips

Displaying keywords. To have iPhoto display keywords beneath your photo thumbnails, choose Keywords from the View menu.

Removing a keyword. To remove a keyword from a photo, select the photo, return to the Photo Info window, and uncheck the keyword. Or, press the Option key while dragging the photo to the keyword in the Keywords pane.

Creating and Editing Keywords

To create, rename, and delete keywords, use the Keywords portion of the Preferences dialog box.

To rename a keyword, select it, click the Rename button, then type a new name.

To remove a keyword, select it and then click the ⊟ button.

Note: If you simply want to remove a keyword from one or more photos, use the technique described on the opposite page.

To add a keyword, click the ⊞ button and then type a name for the new keyword.

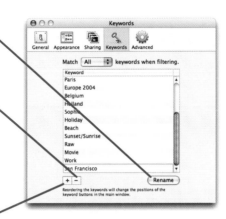

Renaming keywords: a caution. If you've already assigned a given keyword to some photos, think twice about renaming that keyword. If you do rename it, the photos to which you've assigned that keyword will inherit the new keyword.

Automatic keywords. When you import movies and raw images, iPhoto assigns them the keywords Movie and Raw, respectively. This makes it easier to locate those items (see page 128).

Art Critic: Rating Your Photos

You can assign a rating of from one to five stars to a photo.

There are several ways to rate a photo.

With the Photos menu. Choose a rating from the My Rating submenu.

With the keyboard. Press ⌘ along with 0 (zero) through 5. This shortcut pairs up nicely with the arrow keys: rate a photo, press an arrow key to move to the next photo, and repeat.

With the shortcut menu. Control-click on a photo and choose a rating from the My Rating submenu.

In one fell swoop. Want to give a bunch of photos the same rating? Select them, then use one of the previous techniques.

With the Information pane. Select a photo and then click the stars in the Information pane.

During a slide show. Move the mouse, then click the desired rating. Or just press 0 (zero)

through 5 to rate the currently displayed photo.

Viewing Ratings

To see ratings displayed beneath your photo thumbnails, choose My Rating from the View menu (Shift-⌘-R).

You can also use ratings as a search criterion when creating smart albums (page 134).

▼ 🎞 **Morning Walk, Ravens, Field Fence**

★★

★★★★

★★★★

Searching by Keywords

You've taken the time to assign keywords to your photos. I congratulate you on your organizational fortitude.

Now what? Now you can search for photos based on the keywords you've assigned.

One way to search by keyword is to use the Search box. If you have a keyword named Beach, you can quickly find beach shots by typing *beach* in the Search box.

But there's a problem: iPhoto's search feature may be too broad for your needs. If you have photos that contain *beach* in their roll names, comments, or file names, those photos will also show up in your search results.

What's more, you can't use the Search box to perform a complex keyword search— for example, to find photos with the keyword *Beach* but not the keyword *Sunset*.

When you want to conduct searches based only on keywords, forget the Search box—use the Keywords pane. When you click on keywords in the Keywords pane, iPhoto narrows down the photos displayed to only those photos that have the selected keywords.

If you suspect you'll want to conduct a specific keyword search again in the future, consider creating a smart album to automate the task for you; see page 134.

Using the Keywords Pane

Step 1.

To search your entire library, select the Library item in the Source list. To search a specific album, select its name.

Step 2.

Display the Keywords pane by clicking the [⊶] button.

Step 3.

Click on the keyword or keywords for which you want to search.

To end the search and view all photos, click Reset.

The check mark "keyword" is built into iPhoto and can't be renamed or deleted. Use it for anything you like—I use it to temporarily flag photos that I want to print.

To broaden the search and search on multiple keywords, click each keyword. Here, I'm searching for any photos of Sophie that were taken at the beach. To remove a keyword from the search, click it again so it isn't highlighted.

Tips for Keyword Searching

Being More Specific

Sometimes, you may want to search for all photos that have one keyword but not another—for example, show all photos of Sophie that *weren't* taken at the beach. To exclude a keyword, press Option while clicking on it.

Being Less Specific

At other times, you may want to broaden a search to find, for example, photos of your trip to Hawaii or your trip to Paris. Normally, iPhoto performs "and" searches—a photo must have all the keywords you click in order to be considered found.

To have iPhoto perform "or" searches instead, choose Preferences from the iPhoto menu, click Keywords, then choose Any from the pop-up menu above the keyword list. Now, iPhoto finds all photos that have *any* of the keywords you click in the Keywords pane.

A Bigger Pane

Have a lot of keywords? Make the Keywords pane larger by dragging the horizontal bar above it.

Get a Photo Count

Curious to know how many photos have a specific keyword? Point to the keyword without clicking, pause a moment, and iPhoto tells you.

EXIF Exposed: Getting Information About Photos

I mentioned earlier that digital cameras store information along with each photo—the date and time when the photo was taken, its exposure, the kind of camera used, and more. This is called the *EXIF* data.

iPhoto saves this EXIF data when you import photos. To view it, select a photo and choose Get Info from the Photos menu (⌘-I).

Much of this information may not be useful to you, but some of it might. If you have more than one digital camera, for example, you can use the window's Photo tab to see which camera you used for a given shot.

If you're interested in learning more about the nuts and bolts of photography, explore the Exposure tab to see what kinds of exposure settings your camera used.

At the very least, you might just want to explore the Photo Info window to see the kind of

information iPhoto is keeping track of for you.

Creating Albums

Getting photos back from a lab is always exciting, but what's really fun is creating a photo album that turns a collection of photos into a story.

An iPhoto album contains a series of photographs sequenced in an order that helps tell a story or document an event. Creating an album is often the first step in sharing a set of photos. For example, before creating a slide show or book, you'll usually want to create an album containing the photos you want to use.

Creating albums in iPhoto is a simple matter of dragging thumbnail images. You can add and remove photos to and from albums at any time, and you can sequence the photos in whatever order you like. You can even include the same photo in many different albums.

The photos in an album might be from one roll, or from a dozen different rolls. Just as an iTunes playlist lets you create your own music compilations, an iPhoto album lets you create your own image compilations.

And once you create albums, you can share them in a variety of ways.

Step 1. Create an Empty Album

To create a new album, choose New Album from the File menu. You can also use the ⌘-N keyboard shortcut, or click the ⊕ button and then choose Album in the subsequent dialog box.

Step 2. Name the Album

iPhoto asks you to name the new album.

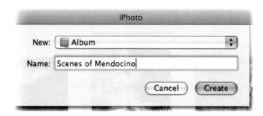

Step 3. Add Photos

After you've named the album, begin dragging photos into it. You can drag photos one at a time, or select multiple photos and drag them in all at once.

As you drag, iPhoto indicates how many photos you've selected.

Organizing an Album

The order of the photos in an album is important: when you create slide shows, books, or Web photo galleries, iPhoto presents the photos in the order in which they appear in the album.

Once you've created an album, you may want to fine-tune the order of its photos.

To edit an album's name, double-click it or use the Information pane.

To move an album to a different location in the Source area, drag it up or down. As the following pages describe, you can also create folders in the Source list to organize related albums.

To change the order of the photos, drag them. Here, the flower close-up is being moved so it will appear after the other garden shot.

Removing a photo. Don't want a photo in an album after all? Select it and press the Delete key. This removes the photo from the album, but not from your hard drive or photo library.

Tips for Selecting Photos

Selecting photos is a common activity in iPhoto: you select photos in order to delete them, add them to an album, move them around within an album, and more.

When working with multiple photos, remember the standard Mac OS selection shortcuts: To select a range of photos, click on the first one and Shift-click on the last one. To select multiple photos that aren't adjacent to each other, press ⌘ while clicking on each photo.

As the screen below shows, you can also select a series of pictures by dragging a selection rectangle around them.

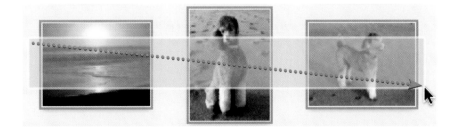

Tips for Working with Albums

Albums are Optional

You don't *have* to create an album in order to share photos: you can create slide shows, books, calendars, and Web pages by simply selecting photos in your library, and then using the appropriate button or command.

But it's better to create an album first. Albums give you the ability to change the sequence of photos. You can resequence photos while creating slide shows, books, and the like, but creating these items is easier when you start with the photos that are in roughly the final order that you plan to use.

Album Shortcuts

You can create an album and add images to it in one step. Select one or more images and choose New Album from Selection from the File menu (Shift-⌘-N).

You can also drag the images into a blank spot of the Source area (below). When you use this technique, iPhoto gives the new album a generic name, such as *untitled album*. To rename the album, double-click its name and type a new name.

If you have photos on a storage device—your hard drive, a Picture CD, or a digital camera's memory card—you can import them into iPhoto *and* create an album in one fell swoop.

Simply drag the photos from the Finder into a blank area of the Source list. iPhoto imports the photos, storing them in their own roll. iPhoto also creates an album and adds the photos to it.

Photo Count

You can have iPhoto display the number of photos in each album next to each album's name. In the Preferences dialog box, click General, then check the Show Item Counts box.

To Experiment, Duplicate

You have a photo that appears in multiple albums, but you want to edit its appearance in just one album, leaving the original version unchanged in other albums. Time for the Duplicate command: select the photo and choose Duplicate from the Photos menu (⌘-D). Now edit the duplicate.

Duplicating an album. There may be times when you'll want several versions of an album. For example, you might have one version with photos sequenced for a slide show and another version with photos organized for a book. Or you might simply want to experiment with several different photo arrangements until you find the one you like best.

iPhoto makes this kind of experimentation easy. Simply duplicate an album by selecting its name and choosing Duplicate from the Photos menu (⌘-D). iPhoto makes a duplicate of the album, which you can rename and experiment with.

You can make as many duplicates of an album as you like. You can even duplicate a smart album—perhaps as a prelude to experimenting with different search criteria. Don't worry about devouring disk space. Albums don't include your actual photos; they simply contain "pointers" to the photos in your library.

Albums and iLife

Another good reason to create albums surfaces elsewhere in iLife: iMovie HD, iDVD, GarageBand, and iWeb all display iPhoto albums in their photo media browsers.

Have a batch of photos you want to use in another iLife program? Rather than searching through your library using those programs' media browsers, first stash the photos in an album. Then, choose that album in the other iLife program.

iPhoto album support is also built into other programs, including Mac OS X's screen saver and Apple's Pages word processor. And as shown on page 94, you can choose to transfer only some albums to a photo-capable iPod.

Organize Your Source List with Folders

As you create albums, slide shows, and books, your Source list will become cluttered. Take advantage of the ability to create folders in the Source list.

Folders in the source list have the same benefit that they have on your hard drive: they let you store related items. And as with the documents on your hard drive, the definition of "related items" is up to you.

Filing strategies. You can use folders in any way you like. You might want to set up a project-based filing system: create a folder for a project, then stash albums, books, and slide shows in that folder.

Or you might prefer an object-oriented filing system: stash all

your albums in one folder, all your slide shows in another, and all your books in yet another, as shown at right.

You might want to mix and match these approaches or come up with something completely different. What's important is that you create a filing scheme that helps you quickly locate items.

Creating a folder. To create a folder, choose New Folder from the File menu. Or, Control-click

on a blank area of the Source list and choose New Folder from the shortcut menu. iPhoto names a new folder *untitled folder*, and selects its name. To rename the folder, just start typing.

Working with folders. To move an item into a folder, simply drag it to the folder until you see a black border around the folder.

To close or open a folder, click the little triangle to the left of its name.

Like folders in the Mac's Finder, iPhoto folders are "spring-loaded"—if you drag something to a closed folder and pause briefly, the folder opens.

Folders within folders. You can create folders inside of folders. You might use this scheme to store all the albums, books, and slide shows that relate to a specific event or theme.

To open a folder and all the nested folders within it, press Option while clicking on the folder's triangle.

Duplicating a folder. To duplicate a folder, select it and choose Duplicate from the Photos menu (⌘-D).

This can be handy if you've standardized on a project-based filing scheme: a project folder containing subfolders for albums, slide shows, and books. Create a hierarchical set of folders, but don't store anything in them—use the set as a template for a filing system.

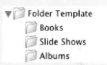

Then, when you're embarking on a new project, duplicate that set of template folders, rename the folders as necessary, and start filing.

If you duplicate a folder that already contains albums, slide shows, or books, iPhoto creates duplicates of those items, too.

Creating Smart Albums

iPhoto can assemble albums for you based on criteria that you specify. The *smart album* feature works much like the smart playlist feature in iTunes: spell out what you want, and your Mac does the work for you.

A few possibilities: Create an album containing every shot you took in the last week. Or of every photo you took in November 2002. Or of every November 2002 photo that has *Sophie* in its title. Or of every photo from 2004 that has *Paris* as a keyword, *croissant* in its title, and a rating of at least four stars.

If you've taken the time to assign titles, comments, and keywords to your photos, here's where your investment pays off. You can still use smart albums if you haven't assigned titles and other information to photos; you just won't be able to search on as broad a range of things.

You can also create smart albums that have criteria based on the EXIF information I discuss on page 129. Create one smart album that corrals all the shots you took with your Sony camera, and another that collects all your Canon shots. Or create a smart album of all your photos shot at a high ISO speed (page 212), or at a fast shutter speed.

Smart albums are a great way to quickly gather up related photos for printing, backing up, browsing, emailing—you name it.

Creating a Smart Album

Step 1. Choose New Smart Album from the File menu (Option-⌘-N).

You can also create a new smart album by pressing the Option key and clicking on the ⬛ button in the lower-left corner of the iPhoto window.

Step 2. Specify what to look for.

Type a name for the smart album.

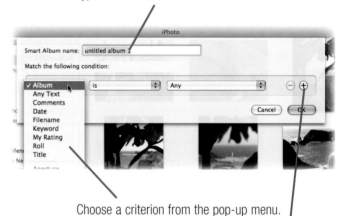

Choose a criterion from the pop-up menu.

To add another criterion, click the ⊕ button (see opposite page).

Step 3. Click OK or press Return.

In the Source area, iPhoto indicates smart albums with a special icon: ⬛ .

Changing a Smart Album

To modify a smart album, select it in the Source area and choose Edit Smart Album from the File menu or Get Info from the Photos menu (⌘-I).

Get more smart album ideas.
www.macilife.com/iphoto

Be More Specific: Specifying Multiple Criteria

By adding additional criteria, you can be very specific about what you want to find.

Normally, iPhoto locates photos that meet all the criteria you specify. To have iPhoto locate a photo that meets any of the criteria, choose any.

To delete a criterion, click the ⊖ button. To add a criterion, click the ⊕ button.

Tips for Smart Albums

They're alive. iPhoto is always watching. If you import photos that meet a smart album's criteria, iPhoto adds those photos to the album. iPhoto may also add to a smart album when you edit photo information. For example, if you change a photo's title to *Beach picnic*, iPhoto adds the photo to any smart album set up to search for *beach* in the title.

From smart to dumb. You can't turn a smart album into a static one—unlike iTunes, iPhoto doesn't provide a Live Updating check box. Here's a workaround. Click the smart album in the Source list, then select all the photos in

the album. (Click one photo, then press ⌘-A.) Next, choose New Album from Selection from the File menu. This creates an album containing the photos currently in the smart album.

Deleting photos. To delete a photo from a smart album, select it and press Option-Delete. Note that this also deletes the photo from your library and moves it to the iPhoto Trash.

Smart Album Suggestions	
For a Compilation Of	**Specify These Criteria**
All your movies	Keyword is Movie
All your raw-format photos	Keyword is Raw
Recent favorites	Date is in the last 1 month (for example) and My Rating is greater than three stars
All your Winter photos	Date is in the range 12/21/2005 to 3/20/2006
All photos that aren't in any album	Album is not Any
Photos from a specific camera	Camera is *model*
Photos from the second-to-last roll you shot	Roll is not in the last 1 roll and Roll is in the last two rolls
Photos from two weeks ago	Date is not in the last 1 week and Date is in the last 2 weeks
Photos that contain (or do not contain) any comments	Comments contains (or does not contain) ? (a single question mark)

Basic Photo Editing

Many photos can benefit from some tweaking. Maybe you'd like to crop out that huge telephone pole that distracts from your subject. Maybe the exposure is too light, too dark, or lacks contrast. Or maybe the camera's flash gave your subject's eyes the dreaded red-eye flaw.

iPhoto's edit view can fix these problems and others. And it does so in a clever way that doesn't replace your original image: if you don't like your edits, choose Revert to Original from the Photos menu.

iPhoto's editing features make it easy to fix many common image problems, but iPhoto isn't a full-fledged digital darkroom. You can't, for example, remove power lines that snake across an otherwise scenic vista, nor can you darken only a portion of an image. For tasks like these, you'll want to use Adobe Photoshop or Photoshop Elements—both of which pair up beautifully with iPhoto (see page 158).

Editing Essentials

To switch to iPhoto's edit mode, select a photo—either in the Library or in an album—and click the Edit button or press Return. Or, simply double-click the photo.

The photo browser shows adjacent photos in the library or selected album. To edit a photo, click it. To show or hide the photo browser, choose Thumbnails from the View menu.

Cropping controls; see "Cropping Photos," on the next page.

Saves any changes and opens the previous or next image for editing (keyboard shortcut: left arrow and right arrow).

Red-Eye control; see "Get the Red Out," on the next page.

Saves any changes and exits edit view.

Edit a photo in full-screen view (page 150).

Improve image quality and retouch flaws; see page 138.

Apply a variety of special effects (page 140).

Displays the Adjust panel (page 142).

Use the size slider to zoom in and out. When zoomed in, you can quickly scroll by pressing the spacebar and then dragging within the image.

Cropping Photos

You can often improve a photo's composition by cropping the photo.

Step 1. Drag to create a selection. To move the selection, drag within it. To resize it, drag any corner or edge. To start over, click on the image anywhere outside the selection.

Have a specific output dimension in mind? Choose the most appropriate option from the Constrain pop-up menu. For example, if you plan to order a 4 by 6 print, choose 4 x 6 (Postcard). iPhoto restricts the proportions of the cropping area to match the option you choose. If you're planning a vertically oriented print, choose Constrain as Portrait or press the Option key while dragging. To create a cropping selection of any size, choose None. To override the current constrain setting, press Shift while dragging.

Note: When you crop a photo, you throw away pixels, effectively lowering the photo's resolution. If you print a heavily cropped photo, you may notice ugly digital artifacts. Think twice about cropping the daylights out of a photo. And always shoot at the highest resolution your camera provides; this gives you more flexibility to crop later (see page 212).

Step 2. To apply the crop area to the image, click Crop.

Tip: Keep in mind that cropping a photo changes its appearance in all albums where it appears. If you want to crop the photo for just one album, duplicate the photo and then crop the duplicate. And if you want to adjust a photo's composition in a slide show, greeting card, calendar, or book, don't use cropping—use iPhoto's zoom controls instead. See pages 163 and 190.

Get the Red Out

Red-eye is caused by the bright light of an electronic flash reflecting off a subject's retinas and the blood vessels around them.

Step 1. Click the Red-Eye button.

Step 2. Click the center of each eye. If some red remains, click it.

Step 3. Click the Red-Eye button again to turn off the tool.

Tips: Use the size slider to zoom in for more precision. And if you prefer the red-eye removal technique provided by earlier iPhoto versions, see page 208.

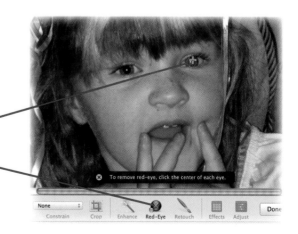

To remove red-eye, click the center of each eye.

Enhancing and Retouching Photos

Some photos need work. Old photos can appear faded, their color washed out by Father Time. They might also have scratches and creases brought on by decades of shoebox imprisonment.

New photos can often benefit from some enhancement, too. That shot you took in a dark room with the flash turned off—its color could use some punching up. That family photo you want to use as a holiday card—the clan might look better with fewer wrinkles and blemishes.

iPhoto's enhance and retouch tools are ideal for tasks like these. With the enhance tool, you can improve a photo's colors and exposure, and rescue a photo you might otherwise delete. With the retouch tool, you can remove minor scratches and blemishes, not to mention that chocolate smudge on your kid's face.

iPhoto lets you view before-and-after versions of your work: press the Control key, and iPhoto shows you what the image looked like before you began retouching and enhancing. And you can always backtrack one step by using the Undo command, or return to Square One by choosing Revert to Original from the Photos menu.

As with iPhoto's other editing features, the Enhance and Retouch buttons appear in iPhoto's edit view. If you aren't familiar with how to switch to edit view, see "Basic Photo Editing" on page 136.

Using One-Click Enhance

To apply one-click enhance, click the Enhance button at the bottom of the iPhoto window.

Before: This dimly lit shot is barely visible.

After: iPhoto has let the dogs out.

Tips

If at first you don't succeed, click, click again. Each time you click Enhance, iPhoto processes the image again. But too much enhancement can make an image appear grainy and artificial. If that happens, choose Undo Enhance Photo from the Edit menu as many times as needed to backtrack.

If the Enhance tool isn't doing the job—maybe its results are too harsh—undo your enhancements and turn to the tools in the Adjust panel (see page 142).

Using the Retouch Tool

To use the retouch tool, click the Retouch button at the bottom of the iPhoto window. If you want to edit the image in other ways after retouching, click the button again to turn off the retouch tool.

Retouch

To remove a flaw, position the crosshair pointer over the flaw and then drag away from the flaw in short strokes.

Before: Cute kid, but a little dirty.

After: We lost the dirt, but kept the freckles.

Tips

Before and after. As with the Enhance tool, you can see a "before" version of your photo by pressing and holding down the Control key.

Zoom for precision. To retouch with more precision, use the size slider to zoom in on the area of the image that you're working on. You can also zoom by pressing the 0 (zero), 1, or 2 keys.

Undo and revert. You can undo each mouse click by choosing Undo Retouch from the Edit menu. To undo all of your retouching, choose Revert to Original from the Photos menu. Note that you'll also lose any other edits, such as cropping, that you performed since switching into edit view. (For more details on the workings of the Revert to Original command, see page 153.)

Rub right. Scratches are best removed by rubbing the mouse pointer over a scratch until it disappears. That's because iPhoto learns the pattern on either side of a scratch, and rubbing makes this pattern easier to learn. Also, some scratches disappear faster if you rub at a ninety-degree angle to the scratch. Experiment and undo as needed.

Retouch before sharpening. If you plan to retouch an image, do so before applying sharpening. That way, you won't risk the sharpening process drawing attention to your retouching work. (For details on sharpening, see page 148.)

Applying Effects to Photos

With the Effects panel, you can alter a photo to give it a unique look. Evoke the colors of an old, faded tintype. Turn a color photo into a black-and-white one. Blur the edges of a scene to create a gauzy, romantic look. Juice up the colors in a photo or tone them down.

As the tips at right describe, you can apply more than one effect to a photo, and you can apply an effect more than once.

Keep in mind that applying an effect to a photo changes that photo everywhere it appears—in albums, books, slide shows, and so on. If you want to retain the previous version of a photo, be sure to duplicate it before applying an effect: select the photo and choose Duplicate from the Photos menu or use the ⌘-D keyboard shortcut.

Effective Tips

Combining effects. Good cooks don't restrict themselves to just one spice. By combining effects, you can create some striking results.

Some effects pair up particularly well. For a dream-like look, try combining Edge Blur with the B&W effect. For an old-fashioned look, pair the Sepia or Antique effects with the Vignette effect. To create an oval border around a photo, combine the Matte and Vignette effects.

Don't be afraid to try offbeat combinations, either. It might seem contradictory to follow the Boost Color effect with the Fade Color effect, but you can get some interesting results when you do.

And remember, if you paint yourself into a corner, just click the Current button in the center of the Effects panel to return to safety.

When once isn't enough. You can apply most effects more than once: simply click the desired effect's button over and over again. (The two exceptions are the B&W and Sepia effects; clicking their buttons repeatedly will only wear out your mouse.)

Alas, if you go too far and choose the Undo command, iPhoto removes the effect entirely instead of just undoing the last mouse click. I've gotten in the habit of counting how many times I click an effect button. That way, if I go too far and use Undo, I can retrace my steps—minus one.

Refining an effect. You can refine the appearance of an effect by using the controls in the Adjust panel (discussed on the following pages). In particular, you can improve the contrast and tonal range of a black-and-white conversion by adjusting the Saturation, Tint, and Temperature sliders. For details, see page 147.

A Gallery of Effects

No single photo is ideally suited to every effect, but that didn't stop me from working my dog into this example.

To remove the effects you've applied, click the Current thumbnail in the center of the Effects panel.

B&W. Convert to black and white.

Sepia. Add a warm brown cast.

Antique. Simulate the faded colors of an old photo.

Fade Color. Decrease a photo's color saturation (for more control, use the Adjust panel; page 146).

Boost Color. Increase a photo's color saturation (for more control, use the Adjust panel; page 146).

Matte. Add a soft-edged white border.

Vignette. Add a soft black border.

Edge Blur. Blur the edges of a photo. **Tip:** Try clicking this one a few times and combining it with the B&W effect.

Tip: The Matte and Vignette effects work best when a photo's subject is in the center of the image. For these examples, I cropped the photo before applying the effect, and I clicked the effect's button several times.

Advanced Editing and the Adjust Panel

Some photos need more help than others. That shot of a beach sunset would be more dramatic if the ocean didn't appear to be slanted uphill. That shot of a beautiful white gardenia would be prettier if the flower didn't have a jaundiced yellow color cast. And that scene of Paris on a rainy day would look more romantic if it didn't appear so flat and washed out.

To fix problems like these, use the Adjust panel—its controls let you straighten a crooked photo, adjust the sharpness of a photo, fine-tune exposure, tweak color balance, and more.

The basics of the Adjust panel are a cinch: after opening a photo for editing (see page 136), summon the Adjust panel by clicking the Adjust button in the edit view toolbar. Then, drag the appropriate sliders left or right until you get the desired results.

That last part—getting the desired results—isn't always a cinch. Adjusting exposure, color balance, and sharpness can be tricky, and knowing a few digital imaging concepts can help you reach your goals. You'll find a detailed look at these concepts in the following pages. Here's the big picture.

A Sampling of Adjustments

Straighten Crooked Shots

Horizon a little crooked? Use the Straighten slider to level things out (opposite page).

Fix Color Problems

Use the Saturation, Temperature, and Tint sliders to remove unwanted color casts, increase or decrease color vividness, and more (page 146).

Adjust Exposure

Use the Exposure and Levels sliders to brighten or darken photos and improve contrast (page 144).

The Adjust Panel at a Glance

The Brightness and Contrast sliders let you adjust tonality, but the Exposure and Levels sliders provide superior control.

The Exposure slider adjusts the overall brightness of the photo; use it and the Levels sliders to fix exposure and contrast problems (page 144).

The histogram is a bar graph that shows a photo's distribution of tonal values—blacks, whites, and everything in between. Knowing how to read the histogram can help you improve the brightness and contrast of a photo (see the following page).

Use the Levels sliders to adjust the image's tonal values to improve brightness and contrast.

Tip: To adjust any slider in small increments, click on the symbol to the left or right of the slider.

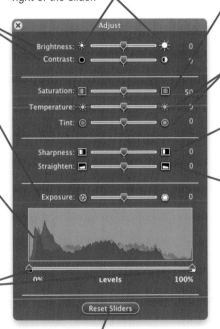

Never mind! If you've adjusted yourself into a corner, click Reset Sliders to restore all the sliders to their factory settings.

Before and after. As with all iPhoto edits, you can see a before-and-after view of your adjustments by pressing the Control key.

The Saturation slider makes the photo's colors less vivid or more vivid (page 146).

The Temperature and Tint sliders adjust the photo's color balance; use them to fix unwanted color casts and create special effects (pages 146–147).

The Sharpness slider increases or decreases sharpness; sharpening before printing can add crispness to an image (page 148).

Use the Straighten slider to fix crooked shots (below).

Straightening Crooked Photos

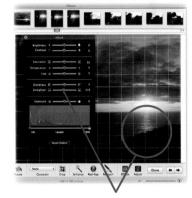

As you drag the Straighten slider, iPhoto rotates and crops the photo, displaying an alignment grid that helps you straighten up. Drag the slider left and right until the horizontal and vertical lines in your shot are in alignment with the grid.

Adjusting Exposure and Levels

iPhoto's Enhance button often does a good job of punching up a photo, but it's a "my way or the highway" feature: you either like its results or you undo.

The Adjust panel is a more accommodating place to fix brightness and contrast problems. And not by using the Brightness and Contrast sliders, either: they're blunt instruments that lack the precision you need.

For improving a photo's exposure and contrast, use the Levels sliders and the Exposure slider. By adjusting them—while keeping a close eye on the photo's histogram—you can often make dramatic improvements in a photo's appearance.

Which tools should you use? It depends on the photo. Some photos respond better to the Exposure slider, while others benefit from levels adjustments. Still other photos benefit from both approaches: do some initial tweaks with the Exposure slider, then fine-tune the levels.

Reading a Histogram

A *histogram* is a bar graph that shows how much black, white, and mid-tone data a photograph has. Pure black is on the left, pure white is on the right, and the mid-tones are in between. iPhoto displays a color histogram that breaks this information down into an image's three primary-color channels: red, green, and blue.

Reading a histogram can help you discern problems in an image. And adjusting the Levels and Exposure sliders can often fix those problems.

A Sampling of Histograms

This properly exposed shot has a good distribution of dark, bright, and mid-tone areas. Notice that the histogram shows a lot of bright blue data: the ocean and sky.

This overexposed shot has very little data in the blacks; everything is bunched up toward the right side—the white side— of the histogram.

This photo's histogram shows a similar amount of red, green, and blue data around the mid-tones—exactly what you'd expect from photo of a predominantly white flower. But the whites could be a bit whiter; notice the absence of data at the right end of the histogram.

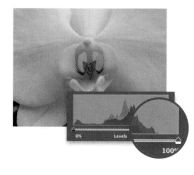

Using the Levels Sliders

Beneath the histogram display is a pair of sliders that let you change what iPhoto considers to be pure black or pure white. By dragging these sliders, you can often improve a photo's brightness and contrast.

Before

This photo of a rainy Paris lacks contrast and looks a bit flat. Its histogram tells the tale: there's little data in the darkest blacks and brightest whites.

To darken the photo, drag the *black-point* slider to the right.

After

The photo's brightness and contrast are improved, and its histogram shows a broader tonal range.

Drag until the sliders almost reach the point where the image data begins. These sloped areas are often called the *shoulders* of the histogram.

To brighten the photo, drag the *white-point* slider to the left.

How it Works

When you drag the black- or white-point sliders, you tell iPhoto to stretch the photo's existing tonal values to cover a broader tonal range. Oversimplified, when you change the black point, you tell iPhoto, "See this grayish black? I want you to treat it as a darker black and adjust everything else accordingly."

Going too far. The Levels sliders can often work wonders, but they can't work miracles. If a photo has an extremely narrow contrast range, you may see visible *banding* after adjusting levels. You're telling iPhoto to stretch a molehill into a mountain, and there may not be enough data to allow for smooth gradations in shading and color.

Avoid clipping. Similarly, if you drag the black- or white-point sliders beyond the histogram's shoulders into the image data, you'll throw away tonal detail: areas that were almost black will become pure black, and areas that were almost white will become pure white. This is called *clipping*, and unless you're looking to create a special effect, you should avoid it.

You can use a histogram to spot clipping: if the histogram has a tall bar at its leftmost or rightmost edge, its blacks (or whites) have been clipped.

Using the Exposure Slider

The Adjust panel's Exposure slider makes a photo brighter or darker.

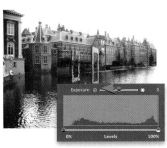

I rescued this overexposed photo by dragging the Exposure slider to the left. Notice that its histogram is much broader than the original (see opposite page). The sky is still blown out to pure white, though—iPhoto can't create image data where none existed in the original photo.

For details on how the Exposure slider works, see page 157.

Changing a Photo's Colors

The Adjust panel lets you perform several types of color-related adjustments. With the Saturation slider, you can adjust the vividness of a photo's colors. Turn down the saturation to create a muted look or to compensate for a camera's overly enthusiastic built-in color settings. Or turn up the saturation to make a photo's colors more intense.

With the Temperature and Tint sliders, you can change a photo's color balance. Fix a color cast introduced by artificial light or caused by fading film. Or create a special effect to make a photo feel warmer or colder.

How can you tell if the colors you see on your screen will accurately translate to an inkjet or photographic print? Advanced Photoshop users rely on display-calibration hardware and other tools to calibrate their systems so that displayed colors match printed colors as closely as possible.

You can apply this strategy to iPhoto. Or you can take a simpler approach. First, calibrate your screen using the Displays system preference. Second, if you'll be creating your own inkjet prints, make test prints as you work on a photo, duplicating the photo as necessary to get different versions.

Adjusting Color Saturation

To make a photo's colors more vivid, drag the Saturation slider to the right. To make colors more muted, drag the slider to the left.

Original

Increased Saturation

Decreased Saturation

Tips

Pale and pastel. To give a pastel-like quality to a photo's colors, decrease the saturation.

Going gray. If you drag the Saturation slider all the way to the left, you create a *grayscale* version of the photo. Generally, the B&W button does a better job, but experiment and see which version you like best.

Watch your gamut. If you significantly increase a photo's saturation, you probably won't be able to print a version that matches what you see on screen. Printers have a much narrower color range, or *gamut*, than does the Mac's screen.

Adjusting Color Balance

To adjust a photo's color balance, use the Temperature slider, the Tint slider, or both.

Temperature. The Temperature slider adjusts a photo's color temperature. To make a photo appear *cooler* (more bluish tones), drag the slider to the left. To make a photo appear warmer (more yellow/orange tones), drag the slider to the right.

Original

Cooler

Warmer

Tint. The Tint slider adjusts red/green color balance. If you drag the slider to the left, iPhoto adds red, making a photo appear less green. If you drag the slider to the right, you add green and lessen the amount of red. The Tint slider can help remove the greenish color cast that you may find in photos taken under fluorescent lighting.

Colorful Tips

Temperature Tips. Photos taken under incandescent light with your camera's flash turned off tend to have a yellowish cast to them. I like this warm look, but if you don't, try dragging the Temperature slider to the left to cool things off. If the corrected image looks dark, bump up the Exposure slider.

You can often simulate different lighting conditions by shifting a photo's color temperature slightly. Warm up a photo to simulate late afternoon sun, or cool it down to simulate shade or twilight.

Old color photos often take on a reddish-yellow appearance as their color dyes fade. To fix this, drag the Temperature slider to the left a bit.

Gray Balancing. If you have an off-color photo containing an object that you know should be gray, ⌘-click on the gray object. iPhoto adjusts the Temperature and Tint sliders as best it can to make the object a neutral gray.

Better Black and White

iPhoto's B&W effect does a good job of converting a color photo to black and white, but you can often improve on its efforts: after clicking B&W, adjust the Saturation, Temperature, and Tint sliders.

When you drag the color sliders after converting a photo to black and white, iPhoto blends the photo's red, green, and blue color channels in different ways. To make a black-and-white photo appear richer, bump up the saturation after clicking the B&W button. While you're experimenting, drag the Temperature and Tint sliders to see how they alter the photo's tonal values. (For you film fogies, this is the digital equivalent of exposing black-and-white film through color filters.)

After Clicking B&W Button

After Adjustments

Sharpening Strategies

First things first: iPhoto can't take a blurry photo and make it tack-sharp. No digital imaging program can, regardless of what you see on TV. If your subject is out of focus or blurred, it's going to stay out of focus or blurred.

So why have a sharpening feature? Because all digital images—whether captured by a scanner or a camera—have an inherent softness. Some softness is introduced by inexpensive lenses. Still more is introduced by imaging sensors and their fixed grid of pixels.

Digital cameras compensate for this inherent softness by applying some sharpening immediately after you take a photo. You can often adjust the amount of sharpness they apply; I like to turn down the sharpness settings on my cameras, preferring to sharpen later, if necessary. (If you shoot in raw mode, your camera applies little or no sharpening to the image; see page 154.)

Inkjet printers and offset printing presses (including the kind used to print iPhoto books, greeting cards, and calendars) also introduce some softness. The bottom line: several factors are working against your image to obscure fine details.

And *that's* where sharpening can help. By sharpening a photo just before printing it, you can often get a much better print.

Sharpening is a serious form of image surgery. There are right times and wrong times to do it, and it's easy to introduce ugly visual artifacts by sharpening at the wrong times. Here's how and when to sharpen up.

Sharpening Basics

To sharpen a photo, drag the Adjust panel's Sharpness slider to the right.

Before Sharpening

After Sharpening

How it Works

iPhoto uses a sharpening technique called *unsharp masking*. The term derives from an old photographic process. In the digital world, unsharp masking works by increasing the image contrast between light and dark pixels. iPhoto detects boundaries of light and dark, and it makes light edges a bit lighter and dark edges a bit darker. When it's done right—that is, not to excess—our eyes perceive this as increased sharpness.

Sharpening Tips

Should You Sharpen?

Just because digital images have an inherent softness doesn't mean that you should apply sharpening to every photo you take. First, consider the photo itself. A photo that lacks fine details—say, a close-up of a baby's face—won't gain much from sharpening, and may even be hurt by it. Conversely, a photo containing fine details—such as the one on the opposite page—may benefit greatly from sharpening.

Also consider how you'll be using the photo. A photo destined for an iDVD slide show or iMovie HD project probably doesn't need sharpening. A photo that you plan to print—either yourself or by ordering prints or a book—is a better candidate for sharpening, especially if the photo contains fine details.

Sharpen Last

If you remember one tip about sharpening, remember this one: sharpening should be the last step in a photo-correction session. If you crop, straighten, retouch, or otherwise modify a photo after sharpening it, you risk ugly visual artifacts.

If you're performing numerous edits in one session—for example, you open an image in edit view and then do some cropping, straightening, exposure tweaking, and sharpening—iPhoto applies some built-in smarts when you click the Done button. iPhoto applies your edits in a sequence that optimizes quality, and

that process includes applying your sharpness settings as the very last step before saving the edited photo.

But if you're like me, you sometimes perform edits in multiple passes. You might crop a photo, then save it and email it to a friend. Then, you might return to it for some exposure tweaking.

If this describes your working style, avoid applying sharpening unless you know you won't be doing any further edits. If you think you might need to edit the image again, make a duplicate (⌘-D) before sharpening, and indicate in the duplicate's title or comment that it's a pre-sharpened version.

(For more advice on developing an iPhoto editing workflow, see page 153.)

When in Doubt, Duplicate

The only way to remove sharpening from a photo is to revert to the original version—a step that also discards any other edits you've made. For this reason, it's a good idea to duplicate a photo before sharpening it.

View Right

iPhoto's edit view introduces some softness of its own when it scales a photo to whatever zoom setting you've made. To get the most accurate on-screen view possible, view your photo at 100 or 200 percent when making sharpness adjustments: press the 1 key to view at 100 percent, and the 2 key to view at 200 percent.

Printing? Sharpen Heavily

Don't be afraid to heavily sharpen a photo that you're going to print. Even if the photo looks a bit too sharp on screen, chances are it will print nicely. When I'm creating 5- by 7-inch or larger prints on my Epson inkjet printer, I'll often crank the Sharpness slider all the way up to 100 (after first duplicating the photo, of course).

Also consider the paper you're using. Premium glossy photo paper shows fine details best, so photos destined for it can benefit from sharpening. On the other hand, matte- and luster-finish photo papers have a fine texture that obscures detail a bit.

Blurring a Photo

Sharpening cuts both ways. You can also blur a photo by dragging the Sharpness slider to the left of its center point. If you have a noisy photo shot at a high ISO setting (see page 212), try introducing just a bit of softness to reduce the digital noise.

Or soften up a photo to create a special effect. You can create a lovely background for a video title or DVD menu by blurring up a photo and optionally adjusting its brightness and contrast (see page 301).

The Big Picture: Full-Screen Editing

When you're editing and enhancing a photo, it's often helpful to see the big picture—that is, to display your photo at as large a size as possible. When you go big, it's easier to perform color and exposure adjustments and to find flaws that need retouching.

iPhoto's full-screen editing view gives you a picture window into your pictures. Click the Full Screen button, and your Source list and most of iPhoto's other buttons and controls step aside to make room for your photos. You can free up even more screen space by hiding the toolbar at the bottom of the screen and the small photo thumbnails along the top.

If you prefer to use full-screen view for all your editing tasks, use iPhoto's Preferences command to always have photos open in full-screen view; see page 152.

Full-screen view teams up nicely with another iPhoto feature: the ability to compare two or more photos in order to find the best shot in a series. You can display two or more photos side-by-side and even edit them.

It's worth noting that you can also compare photos in iPhoto's standard edit view and in the editing window (see page 152). But, because full-screen view maximizes your screen space, it's the best place for your photo-comparison sessions.

Comparing Photos

It's always smart to take more than one version of an important shot—to experiment with different exposure settings or to simply increase your chances of capturing that perfect smile.

After you've imported those multiple variations into iPhoto, compare the photos to find the best one of the bunch.

To compare photos

In edit view. If you're already working in full-screen edit view (opposite page), click the Compare button (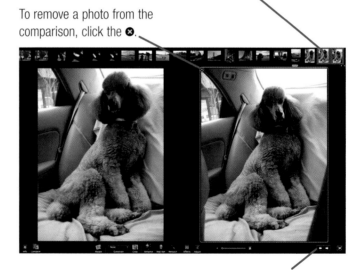). iPhoto loads the next photo and displays both side-by-side.

When you click a different thumbnail, its photo replaces the selected photo (in this example, the one on the right). To compare more than two photos, ⌘-click on their thumbnails. (If you don't see the thumbnails, choose Show Thumbnails from the View menu.)

To remove a photo from the comparison, click the ⊗.

You can also move to the next or previous photo by clicking the arrow buttons or by using the arrow keys on your keyboard.

When browsing. You can also set up a comparison *before* entering edit view. Select the photos first, then click the Full Screen button (). For a review of ways to select photos, see page 131.

Full-Screen Editing

Use full-screen view to compare photos or scrutinize a photo for editing (or just when you want to show it off).

As the sidebar below describes, you can customize the full-screen view to free up even more precious pixels for your pictures.

Switching to full-screen view

To edit a photo in full-screen view, select the photo and then click the Full Screen button (⬚).

Similarly, if you're already in the standard edit view, you can switch to full-screen view by clicking the same button.

You can view and edit photo information in full-screen view; click the Info button to display the Information panel shown here.

To display a different photo, click its thumbnail. To compare photos, ⌘-click on each thumbnail.

If you've zoomed in on a photo, the Navigation panel appears. Drag the rectangle to quickly pan around the zoomed photo.

To exit full-screen view, click the ⬚ button. **Note:** You can also exit full-screen view by pressing your keyboard's Esc key, although this discards any edits you made.

Tips for Comparing Photos and Full-screen Editing

Comparing Photos

You can compare up to eight photos. Select the photos and then click the Full Screen button, or, if you're already in edit view, ⌘-click on the thumbnail image of each photo that you want to add to the comparison.

The more photos you compare, the smaller each one appears, so you may not want to compare eight nearly identical photos on a Mac with a small screen.

To remove a photo from a comparison, deselect the photo by ⌘-clicking on its thumbnail image.

All of iPhoto's editing features are available when you're comparing photos.

Full-Screen View

To free up more screen space, hide the thumbnails that iPhoto normally displays along the top of the screen. Choose View > Hide Thumbnails or press Option-⌘-T.

To see the thumbnails again, move the mouse pointer toward the top of your screen, and they'll glide down into view. Or, restore the thumbnail display by using the View menu or Option-⌘-T.

Want to free up every bit of screen space? Hide the toolbar at the bottom of the screen, too: choose View > Hide Toolbar.

To have the toolbar pop back into view, move the mouse pointer near the bottom of your screen.

Don't forget the shortcut menu. You're in full-screen view and you've hidden the toolbar. You can still access most editing functions by using the shortcut menu: Control-click anywhere within the photo, then choose a command from the shortcut menu.

By hiding both the thumbnails and the toolbar and then using the shortcut menu, you can take full advantage of every pixel on your display.

Editing Tips

The Edit Window and Editing Preferences

Normally, iPhoto displays the image you're editing within the iPhoto window itself. But you can also open and edit a photo in a separate window that has its own editing toolbar.

You can have multiple edit windows open simultaneously, which makes it easy to compare images. For example, if you've duplicated a photo a few times and are trying out different sharpening or exposure-correction approaches, you can open each version in its own window and compare them.

The ability to have multiple edit windows also means that you can work on several photos at once. Here's a look at several photos as seen on my 23-inch Apple Cinema Display.

To open an image in a separate window, press the Option key while double-clicking on the image. You can also open a photo in a separate window by Control-clicking on it and choosing Edit in Separate Window from the shortcut menu.

Specifying editing preferences. You can also use the Preferences command to have iPhoto always use the separate window when you double-click on an image. If you *always* want to use a separate edit window, choose Preferences from the iPhoto menu, click the General button, and from the Edit Photo pop-up menu, choose In Separate Window.

Similarly, to always have a photo open in full-screen edit view, choose Using Full Screen from the pop-up menu.

Tips for the Edit Window

Here are a few tips for taking advantage of the edit window.

Showing thumbnails. Normally, the edit window doesn't display a photo browser containing thumbnails of adjacent images. If you'd like to see them, choose Thumbnails from the View menu.

Switching between windows. When you have multiple edit windows open simultaneously, use the Window menu to switch between them and the main iPhoto window. Or use the keyboard: press ⌘-~ (that's the tilde, located above the Tab key) to cycle through open windows. That key sequence works in many Mac programs.

Closing everything. You can close multiple edit windows in one fell swoop by pressing Option while clicking any window's close box.

Zooming differently. Unlike iPhoto's standard edit view, the edit window has a Size pop-up menu that lets you choose a specific zoom percentage for your photo. As I mentioned on the previous page, if you're sharpening, you'll get the most accurate preview of your work by viewing at 100 or 200 percent.

Resizing the window. Remember that you can quickly resize the edit window to fill your screen by clicking the green button in the upper-left corner of the window.

Developing an Editing Workflow

To get the best quality out of iPhoto's editing tools, do as much editing in one session as possible. By *session*, I'm referring to the time between opening a photo in edit view and saving its edited version. If you repeatedly edit and save a photo, you run the risk of introducing visible flaws in the image, particularly if you crop, straighten, or retouch the image after sharpening it.

If an image requires several types of edits—cropping, straightening, exposure and color tweaking, sharpening—try to perform them all in one pass, without closing the image and moving on to a different one while between steps. When you edit in one pass, iPhoto is able to apply your changes in a specific order that maximizes quality.

Note: Photos taken in a camera's raw mode introduce their own workflow issues, which you can read about on page 156.

Understanding the Revert to Original Command

I've mentioned a few times that you can revert to the original version of a photo by choosing Revert to Original from the Photos menu.

There's a bit more to the story. The Revert to Original command works differently depending on what you're doing when you choose the command. If you've performed some edits and are still in edit view, choosing Revert to Original restores the photo to the state it was in before you opened it in edit view. If you had changed the photo in earlier editing sessions, those changes are retained.

On the other hand, if you choose Revert to Original when browsing your library, iPhoto restores the photo to the state it was in when you imported it—discarding every edit you made. The same happens if you open a photo in edit view and then choose Revert to Original before doing any edits.

You can always tell when you're on the precipice of The Big Revert because iPhoto displays a message asking if you're sure you want to revert to the original version.

From Publisher to Editor

Most of the time, you probably enter edit view by double-clicking on a photo in your library or in an album. But you can also enter edit view while working on a book, calendar, or greeting card: just Control-click on the photo and choose Edit Photo from the shortcut menu.

From Edit Thumbnails to Elsewhere

The photo browser—that row of thumbnail images visible at the top of the edit view—is a handy tool for quickly accessing another photo in the same roll or album.

But it has another use, too: you can drag a thumbnail from the photo browser directly into an album, book, or slide show. If you're on an editing binge and suddenly realize that a certain photo would go nicely in a specific album, slide show, or book, there's no need to exit edit view. Just drag the photo from the photo browser to the album, slide show, or book.

Shooting in Raw Mode

If you're an advanced photographer, a control freak, or both, there's an image format that may change the way you shoot. The image format is called *raw*, and it's supported by many mid-range and virtually all high-end cameras.

Here's why raw matters. When you shoot in JPEG format, your camera permanently alters the photo: tweaking color balance and saturation, adjusting sharpness, and compressing the image to use less space.

Today's cameras do these jobs well, but you pay a price: you lose some control. You can still adjust the color balance, exposure, and sharpness of a JPEG image, but within a relatively narrow range. Exceed those limits, and you risk visible flaws.

When you shoot in raw mode, your camera saves the exact data recorded by its light sensors. Instead of being locked into the camera's alterations, you get the original, unprocessed image data: the raw data. Transfer this raw image to the Mac, and you can use iPhoto or other imaging software to fine-tune the image to a degree that the JPEG format doesn't permit.

Equally significant, you'll always have that original image data. If Apple builds a miraculous image-processing feature into iPhoto 7, you'll be able to apply it to your raw photos.

Shooting raw has drawbacks, and most digital photographers (myself included) prefer the convenience and efficiency of JPEG. But for those extra-special shots—and for forward-looking pixel perfectionists who want maximum control—raw is the best way to shoot.

Choosing Raw

To shoot in raw mode, venture into your camera's menus—specifically, to the menu that controls image format. In some cameras, you'll find this option in the Mode menu. With others, such as the Canon EOS-10D shown here, this option is in the Quality menu.

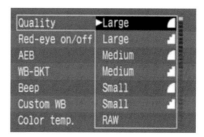

Make sure. It's a sad fact of life: each camera company has created its own raw format. Even if iPhoto supports your camera, it may not recognize its raw-format images. Before shooting raw, verify that iPhoto supports your camera's raw format. You may find that you need to update to a newer Mac OS X version—Apple often adds support for new cameras when it releases a Mac OS update. For a current list of supported cameras, go to www.macilife.com/iphoto.

Make room. Raw files are often several times larger than their JPEG equivalents. For example, an eight-megapixel JPEG might use 4MB while its raw version uses 16MB. Because you'll get fewer raw images on a memory card, you might want to buy a few extra cards.

Make time. With some cameras, raw images can take longer to save after you snap the shutter. If you're shooting a fast-changing scene, verify that your camera's raw mode is fast enough to keep up with your subject.

Those large raw files also take longer to transfer to the Mac. If your camera and Mac don't provide USB 2.0 interfaces, get a FireWire media reader and use it to transfer your shots (see page 119).

Learn more about raw-format photography.
www.macilife.com/iphoto

The Basics of Working with Raw Photos

In some ways, working with raw photos in iPhoto is no different than working with JPEG photos. You can import raw photos into your library, edit them using all of the edit-view features I've described previously, and share them using all of iPhoto's sharing features.

Behind the curtain, iPhoto performs several tasks that make this possible. To get the most out of iPhoto's raw support, it helps to understand what's going on behind that curtain.

Importing Raw Photos

Aside from making sure you have plenty of free disk space, you don't have to do anything special to import raw photos into iPhoto. If iPhoto supports your camera's raw format, it imports the raw photos and stores them in your photo library.

Invisible JPEG Companions

When you import raw photos, iPhoto creates JPEG versions of them. You don't see thumbnails for these JPEG companions in your photo library, but they're there.

iPhoto creates these JPEG versions for use by programs that don't understand the raw format. For example, when you access your iPhoto library from a different program, such as iDVD, that program uses these JPEG versions. iPhoto also uses these JPEG versions for printing.

However, when you open a raw photo in edit view, iPhoto does indeed use the original raw-format image. For details on how iPhoto handles raw images during and after the editing process, see the following pages.

Separated at Birth: Raw and JPEG

Some cameras save a JPEG version of a photo at the same time that you shoot a raw version. This is a handy convenience that gives you the best of both worlds: a compact JPEG and a *digital negative*—a phrase often used to describe raw-format images.

When you import photos from such a camera, iPhoto imports both the JPEG and the raw versions of each shot. It also *displays* both versions, and if you're planning to do some editing, you'll want to make sure you open the version you need.

To see which photo is the JPEG version and which is the raw version, open the Information pane and select one of the photos. iPhoto displays its format in the Format area of the Information pane.

Max Headroom: The 16-Bit Advantage

I've already mentioned one big benefit of shooting in raw format: you aren't locked into the color, sharpness, and exposure settings made by your camera.

Another advantage deals with something called *latitude* or *headroom*: the ability to make dramatic adjustments without risking visible flaws. Simply put, a raw image is more malleable than a JPEG.

Raw photos have more latitude because they store more image data to begin with. JPEG images are eight-bit images; each of the three primary-color channels—red, green, and blue—are represented by eight bits of data. That means that each channel can have up to 256 different tonal values, from 0 (black) through 255 (white). (Yes, things are getting a bit technical here, but such is life in the raw.)

Most cameras, however, are capable of capturing at least 12 bits of data for each color channel, for a possible 4,096 different levels. When a camera creates a JPEG, it essentially throws away at least one-third of the data it originally captured.

Most of the time, that loss of data isn't a problem. But if you need to make significant changes to an image's exposure

and color balance, the more data you have to start with, the better. Where this extra latitude really pays off is with photos that were poorly exposed or taken under tricky lighting conditions.

Think of the extra data as money in the bank: when times get tough, you'll be glad it's there.

Working with Raw Images

How iPhoto Manages Raw Photos

iPhoto works hard to insulate you from the technicalities of working with raw photos. But there are some potentially confusing aspects of the process, especially when you edit a raw photo and then want to perform additional edits later.

Here's a summary of how iPhoto works with raw captures.

iPhoto also creates a JPEG "stand-in" for printing and for use by other programs.

When you import a raw photo, iPhoto stores it in your photo library.

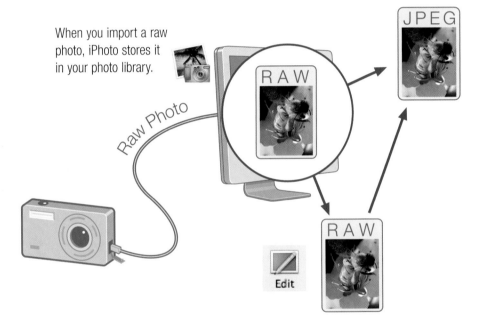

Raw Photo

Edit

Editing an Already-Edited Raw Photo

Here's where the forks in the road can become confusing. If you double-click the photo later to do additional editing, iPhoto opens the JPEG version that it created in the first editing session. iPhoto doesn't open the raw version—you don't see the RAW badge in edit view—and your edits apply to the JPEG version.

If you want to work with the original raw version instead, you'll need to revert to the original. Choose Revert to Original from the Photos menu, and iPhoto discards the JPEG version created from your previous edits and returns to the original raw data for your future edits.

Tip: To avoid losing the edits you made earlier, duplicate the photo before reverting.

When you open a raw photo in edit view, iPhoto uses the original raw data that you imported. The RAW badge shown below appears near the bottom of the iPhoto window.

When you leave edit view, iPhoto applies your edits to the raw data, then creates a JPEG photo that reflects the edits. The original raw file always remains unchanged, and you can access it in a couple of ways (see next page).

Exporting the Original Raw File

There's another way to get to your original raw data after making edits: export the original raw file from iPhoto.

First, select the JPEG version of the photo that iPhoto created after you edited the raw file. Next, choose Export from the File menu. Finally, in the Export Photos dialog box, choose Original from the Format pop-up menu. Save the file elsewhere (not in your iPhoto Library folder), such as on your desktop.

When might you use this approach? Here's one scenario. You've edited a raw photo in iPhoto, but then you decide to try editing the original raw file in Adobe Photoshop Elements. You want to keep the version you edited in iPhoto, so instead of reverting the photo or duplicating the edited version, you export a raw version for use in Photoshop.

Frankly, this scenario is a bit of a stretch. If you want to save a previous edit but re-edit the raw file, it's usually easier to duplicate the edited JPEG, then revert the edited JPEG to the original raw file, then open the raw file in Photoshop as described in the following tip.

Raw Photos and Photoshop

As I describe on the following pages, iPhoto pairs up beautifully with the Adobe Photoshop family. This marriage is particularly happy where raw images

are concerned: in my experience, Adobe's Camera Raw software does a better job than iPhoto when it comes to decoding and processing raw files. Camera Raw, even the version included with Photoshop Elements, provides more control than iPhoto's edit view—and control is what raw is all about.

I use iPhoto to import and store raw photos, but when I'm after maximum quality, I bring those photos into Photoshop. I fine-tune the photos in Photoshop, export them as JPEGs, then import those JPEGs back into iPhoto. It's more work, but the results are better.

To ensure that iPhoto supplies Photoshop with the original raw file and not the JPEG stand-in, choose Preferences from the iPhoto menu, click Advanced, and then check the box labelled Use RAW Files with External Editor. If you don't, iPhoto will hand Photoshop a JPEG when you double-click the raw file—exactly what you *don't* want.

Note that this option is available only with Mac OS X 10.4 and later. If you're using an earlier Mac OS version, open a raw file by dragging its thumbnail to the Photoshop icon in your dock.

Saving as TIFF

Given that you're obsessed enough with image quality to be shooting in raw mode to begin with, you might lament the fact that iPhoto saves your edited images in the lossy JPEG format. If you're using Mac OS X 10.4 or later, you

have a higher-quality alternative: tell iPhoto to use the TIFF format when saving edits to raw images.

To do so, choose Preferences from the iPhoto menu, click Advanced, and check the box labelled Save Edited RAW Files as 16-bit TIFFs. The resulting file will be much larger than a JPEG, but it will have that 16-bit headroom described on page 157.

Is it worth the extra storage space? Let your eyes be your guide. And if you're that quality-obsessed, consider using Photoshop or Photoshop Elements for your raw work.

Raw Differences in the Exposure Slider

The Adjust panel's Exposure slider works differently when you're editing a raw photo. When you're editing a JPEG, the Exposure slider works hard to avoid clipping blacks or whites: as data approaches the black or white limits of the histogram, it tends to bunch up before it finally spills over the brink into the abyss of clipping.

With raw photos, the Exposure slider shifts tonality in a different way, one that is more analogous to decreasing or increasing the f/stops on a camera's lens.

One side effect of this approach is that it's much easier to introduce clipping by dragging the slider too far in either direction. A little bit goes a long way.

Using iPhoto with Photoshop

The editing features in iPhoto can handle many image-tuning tasks, but at the end of the day, Adobe Photoshop Elements is a better-equipped digital darkroom. Photoshop Elements provides far more sophisticated retouching tools and more ways to improve a photo's lighting and exposure.

Elements is also a better tool for serious raw-format work. As I mentioned on the previous page, Adobe's Camera Raw software, included with Elements, often does a better job of processing raw images than does iPhoto.

And Elements has slick features that have no counterparts in iPhoto. A library of exotic visual effects lets you simulate pastels, watercolors, brush strokes, and more. With the Magic Extractor, you can cut out the subject of a photo and superimpose it over a different background. And with the Photomerge feature, you can stitch photos together into dramatic panoramas (see page 216).

Using Elements for retouching doesn't mean abandoning iPhoto. The two programs work well together: you can use iPhoto to import, organize, and share photos, and Elements to enhance and retouch them.

Here's how to put iPhoto and Elements together. Not sure if Photoshop Elements is for you? Download a free trial version from Adobe's Web site (www.adobe.com).

From iPhoto to Elements

A photo in your iPhoto library needs some help. How do you open it in Photoshop Elements? You have a few options.

Drag and drop. If you've already started Elements, its icon appears in your dock. To open a photo, simply click on the photo in your iPhoto library and drag it to the Elements icon in the dock. When the icon highlights, release the mouse button, and Elements opens the photo directly from your iPhoto library.

Direct connection. This drag-and-drop technique is handy if you use Elements only occasionally. If you end up using Elements for all your image editing, you can set up iPhoto to directly hand off photos to Elements.

Choose Preferences from the iPhoto menu and click the General button. From the Edit Photo pop-up menu, choose In Application. In the dialog box that appears, navigate to your Applications folder and double-click on the Adobe Photoshop Elements item.

From now on, when you double-click a photo in your library, iPhoto will hand that photo off to Elements.

Note: If you plan to send raw images from iPhoto to Elements, be sure to follow the instructions on the previous page.

Middle ground. Maybe you use Elements frequently, but you also use iPhoto's edit mode for cropping and other simple tasks. Head for the middle ground: specify Elements as your external image editor as described above, then return to the Preferences dialog box and choose one of the other Edit Photo options, such as In Main Window or Using Full Screen.

This restores iPhoto's factory setting: double-clicking a photo opens it in Edit mode. But iPhoto doesn't forget that you're also an Elements user. To open a photo in Elements, Control-click on the photo and choose Edit in External Editor from the pop-up shortcut menu.

A Sampling of Elements Editing Ideas

Recovering Shadow and Highlight Details

When you photograph a high-contrast scene, you may be disappointed to see little detail in the shadows. Those shadows may *look* coal-black, but they usually contain detail that Photoshop Elements can recover. In the Enhance menu, choose Shadows/Highlights from the Adjust Lighting submenu. To bring out shadow detail, drag the Lighten Shadows slider to the right.

Maybe your photo's shadows are fine, but its bright areas, or *highlights*, were washed out by the sun or your camera's flash. In this case, drag the Darken Highlights slider to the right to bring out highlight detail.

In this example, I've tweaked both the shadow and highlight settings to bring out detail in the baby's face and to tone down the highlights in his sleeves and forearm.

The Power of Layers

One of the best reasons to use Photoshop Elements is a feature called *layers*. In Elements, an image can have multiple layers, and each layer can contain imagery or image-correction information. By using layers, you can make dramatic modifications to an image without ever altering the original data. This not only gives you more editing flexibility, it helps preserves image quality.

There is more to layers than I can describe here. To learn about them, open Photoshop Elements' online help and search for *layers* and *adjustment layers*.

Retouch the Flaws Away

iPhoto's Retouch tool does a good job of removing blemishes, dust specks, and other minor flaws. But it's no plastic surgeon. When an image needs serious retouching, wheel it into Photoshop Elements' operating room.

In this photo, a pair of utility wires slice across a scenic vista. I used two retouching tools to improve the view.

Spot healing brush. Elements' *spot healing brush* works much like iPhoto's Retouch tool, only better. Click the spot healing brush tool in the tool palette,

then specify a brush size that's slightly larger than the flaw you want to remove. You can choose a brush size in the Tool Options toolbar, but it's more efficient to use the keyboard: press the right bracket key (]) for a larger brush, and the left bracket key ([) for a smaller one.

Next, simply click on the flaw you want to remove. To remove a larger flaw, such as a scratch or utility wire, click and drag to paint over it.

Clone stamp tool. The spot healing brush works best when the area surrounding the flaw is similar to the area containing the flaw. For this example, the spot healing brush did a great job of removing the wires from the areas surrounded by open sky or water, but it had trouble with areas that were surrounded by fine details, such as the offshore rocks and distant shoreline.

To fix those areas, I used the Photoshop Elements clone stamp tool, which copies pixels from one area of an image to a different area.

After activating the clone stamp tool, point to an area adjacent to the flaw you want to fix. Then, hold down the Option key and click. Option-clicking tells Elements what area to use as a guide when healing the flaw, a process Photoshop gurus refer to as "defining the *source point.*" After you've done that, paint across the flaw to copy pixels from the source point.

Slide Shows: iPhoto as Projector

With iPhoto's slide show features, you can display on-screen slide shows, complete with background music from your iTunes music library. iPhoto even displays a gorgeous transition between images. With the dissolve effect, for example, one photo fades out as the next one fades in.

And with the automatic Ken Burns effect, you can have iPhoto pan and zoom across each photo.

Better still, you can create two different types of slide shows: a *basic* slide show similar to the kind iPhoto has always provided, and a *saved* slide show that allows for much more control, including the ability to specify different durations and transitions for every photo, and to design your own Ken Burns panning and zooming moves (see page 162). Apple calls this kind of slide show a *cinematic* slide show.

Most of the time, you'll want to add photos to an album before viewing them as a basic slide show. That way, you can arrange the photos in a sequence that best tells your story. If you're in a hurry, though, just select some photos in your library and then display the slide show as described at right.

Somebody get the lights.

Viewing a Basic Slide Show

In a hurry? Select the album or photos you want to screen, press the Option key, click the ▶ button near the bottom of the iPhoto window, and sit back and watch.

Want more control? Follow these instructions to customize your slide show's music, transitions, and more.

Step 1.
Select the photos you want to show.
To show an entire album, select the album.

Step 2.
Click the ▶ button.
The Slideshow dialog box appears.

Choose a transition style.

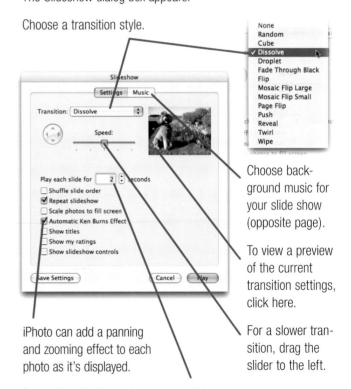

Choose background music for your slide show (opposite page).

To view a preview of the current transition settings, click here.

For a slower transition, drag the slider to the left.

iPhoto can add a panning and zooming effect to each photo as it's displayed.

Type a duration for each image, or click the up and down arrows to set a duration.

Step 2 (continued).

When this box is checked, iPhoto repeats the slide show until time itself comes to an end or until you press the Esc key or the mouse button, whichever comes first.

iPhoto can adjust the way it projects each picture to ensure that the screen is always completely filled, with no black borders. Note that vertically oriented shots and photos you've cropped may display strangely.

Display information and do some housekeeping while the slide show plays (below).

Displays the photos in random order instead of in the order they appear in the iPhoto window.

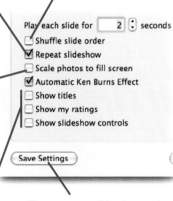

To save your slide show settings but not actually view the slide show, click Save Settings.

For a silent slide show, uncheck the box.

To assign an entire playlist to the slide show, choose the playlist's name.

Note: If you plan to export a slide show as a QuickTime movie, avoid using songs from the iTunes Music Store; see page 208.

To hear a song, double-click it or select it and click the ▶ button.

To sort the song list, click a column heading. You can also move the columns (drag their headings) and resize them (drag their boundaries).

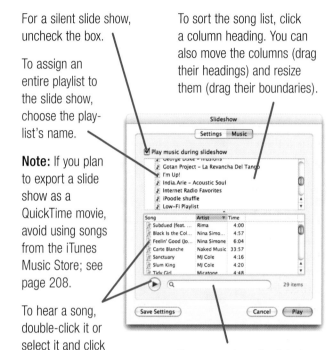

To narrow down the list of songs displayed, type part or all of a song or artist name.

Step 3.

Click (Play) to begin.

Screen Test: Reviewing Photos

If you move the mouse while a slide show plays back, a set of controls appears that lets you rotate, rate, and delete the currently displayed photo. This is a handy way to perform common housekeeping chores on a freshly imported set of photos: click Last Roll, start the slide show, and get to work.

Note: The workings of the Trash button depend on what you're viewing. If you're viewing a slide show of an album, clicking the

Trash button removes a photo from the album. If you're viewing photos directly from the Photo Library (for example, you clicked the Last Roll item), clicking the Trash button moves the photo to the iPhoto Trash.

Beyond the Basic Slide Show

iPhoto's basic slide shows are easy to create, but they have design limitations. Every photo appears on the screen for the same amount of time. All photos have the same transition between them. And you can't design your own Ken Burns pan-and-zoom moves.

iPhoto provides a second type of slide show that shatters these limitations. Depending on whom you ask, it's called a saved slide show or a *cinematic* slide show. You'll call it cool.

With a saved slide show, you can specify different durations for each shot. That opening view of the Parisian skyline? Five seconds. That montage of mouth-watering bakery shots? Just a couple of seconds apiece.

A saved slide show also lets you mix and match transitions. For example, you might want a dissolve between most shots, but when you change major themes, spice things up with a page peel.

With a saved slide show, you can also tell Ken Burns exactly what to do. Set up your own pans and zooms to highlight a photo's subject. Or simply zoom in to crop a photo—no need to change the original photo in your library.

Similarly, you can apply black-and-white and sepia effects to the photos in a saved slide show without having to edit the original photos.

When you've finished designing your slide show, you can view it on screen, export it as a QuickTime movie (page 200), or send it to iDVD (page 292).

Creating a Saved Slide Show

Step 1.

Select the photos you want to include in the slide show. To include an entire album, select its name in the Source list.

Step 2.

Click the Slideshow button.

iPhoto creates a saved slide show, adds it to your Source list, and displays the slide show editor.

Use the photo browser to jump to a specific photo. To change the sequence of photos, drag photos left or right. To delete a photo from the slide show, select it and press the Delete key. You can also select multiple photos by Shift-clicking and ⌘-clicking.

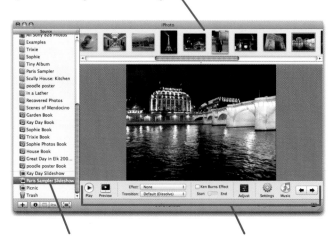

A saved slide show is a separate item in your library. If you based the slide show on an album, you can change the album without affecting the slide show. To rename a saved slide show, double-click its name or use the Information pane.

Change slide show and music settings (see opposite page).

Step 3.

Use the tools in the slide show editor to design your slide show.

Most of these tools operate on the currently selected photo—the one that appears above the tools and is selected in the photo browser. But you can also apply some settings, such as transition, to several photos at once: select the photos' thumbnails in the photo browser, then make your settings.

Preview the selected photo's Ken Burns, duration, and transition settings.

Play the slide show full-screen.

Choose an effect and transition for the selected photo or photos.

Create a custom Ken Burns move for the selected photo (see "Tips for Ken Burns," below).

Choose music for your slide show; see page 161.

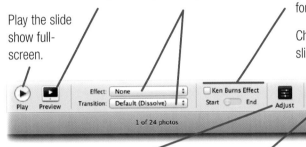

Display the Adjust panel, which lets you set a duration and transition for the selected photo or photos.

Most of these settings are identical to their counterparts on the previous page; see "More Settings Options" on the next page.

Display the previous or next photo (keyboard shortcut: left or right arrow key).

Tips for Ken Burns

By creating your own Ken Burns moves, you can better showcase and crop your photos, and more.

Creating a custom move. To create a Ken Burns move, check the Ken Burns Effect box. Then, use the size slider in the lower-right corner to specify the starting and ending zoom positions for the move. When you've zoomed

in, you can specify which part of the photo you want to see by dragging within the photo.

Zooming without moving. You want to show only part of a photo, but you don't want to crop it because that would change its appearance throughout your library. Solution: Check the Ken Burns Effect box, click

the Start position, then zoom in. Now press the Option key and click the End position.

Pressing Option tells iPhoto to copy the starting position to the ending position. I call this technique *soft cropping*—it's a great way to improve a photo's composition in a slide show without having to actually crop the photo.

Panning without zooming. This Option-key trick also lets you set up moves that pan across an image but don't zoom in or out. Set up the starting position, and drag within the photo to indicate which portion you want to see. Next, Option-click the End position and drag within the photo again.

Slide Show Tips

More Settings Options

When you're creating a saved slide show, you have some additional settings options. Use the Transition pop-up menu to specify a default transition for the slide show—that is, a transition that iPhoto will use unless you specify a different transition for a specific photo or photos.

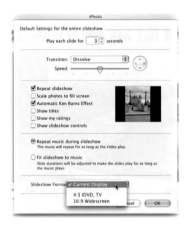

You can also have iPhoto fit the slide show's duration to match the length of its music soundtrack: click the Fit Slideshow to Music option.

And finally, you can have iPhoto create a widescreen (16:9 format) version of your slide show—ideal if you have an Apple Cinema display or want to create a widescreen-format DVD in iDVD. To create a widescreen slide show, choose 16:9 Widescreen from the Slideshow Format pop-up menu.

Adding to a Saved Slide Show

You've crafted a gorgeous slide show and decide you want to add more photos to it. It's easy: just drag the photos to the slide show's item in your Source list. You can even drag photos from the edit view's photo browser into a slide show.

Ken Burns and Transitions

Planning to use any form of a Ken Burns effect in a slide show? There's something you should know about Ken: he prefers the dissolve transition and the fade through black transition.

If you use any other type of transition in a slide show, a Ken Burns move will end right before the transition starts, and won't begin for the next photo until the transition has finished displaying. Having those smooth moves abruptly stop and start before and after each transition can appear jarring with some transitions.

Bottom line: if you're using Ken Burns, lean toward the dissolve or fade through black transitions.

When Just One Song Won't Do

Want more than one song to play back during a slide show? In iTunes, create a playlist containing the songs you want to use. Then, return to iPhoto and choose the playlist's name when assigning music to the slide show or album.

Assigning Songs to Albums

You can assign a different song to each of your albums. When you view a particular album as a basic slide show, iPhoto plays the song you've assigned to it.

To assign a song to a specific album, start iTunes and position its window so you can see it and your iPhoto albums. Then, simply drag a song to an album.

Expand the List

If you're choosing music for a saved slide show and you have a very large iTunes library, enlarge the Music dialog box by dragging its lower-right corner. You won't have do to quite as much scrolling to locate a song.

To Each Its Own

Every album can have its own basic slide show settings—and not just for music. All of the other options that you can adjust in the Slideshow dialog box—transition style, photo scaling, and so on—can also apply on an album-by-album basis. Just select the album whose settings you want to adjust, click the Play button near the bottom of the iPhoto window, make your adjustments, and click Save Settings.

Keep in mind that this tip refers to basic slide shows—the kind I described on pages 160 and 161. Saved (cinematic) slide shows can obviously have their own settings, too, but you adjust them using the slide show editor.

Videotaping a Slide Show

Many Mac models can output an S-video signal, which enables you to display their screen images on a TV set, or record them using a camcorder or videocassette recorder. You can take advantage of these TV-savvy Macs to record a slide show on tape.

First, use a cable to connect the Mac's S-video connector to a camcorder or VCR, open System Preferences, and use Displays to turn on video mirroring. Next, press your video deck's Record button, and begin playing back the slide show. To record the background music, too, connect the Mac's speaker jack to your video deck's audio-input jacks.

Creating Special Effects

You can add some interesting special effects to your slide shows by duplicating photos, modifying the duplicates, then sequencing them in the slide show. For example, you can have a photo start out in black and white and then dissolve or wipe into a color version.

Slide Show Keyboard Controls	
To Do This	**Press**
Pause the slide show	Spacebar To resume the slide show, press the spacebar again.
Adjust the speed of the slide show	The up arrow and down arrow keys
Manually move through the slide show	The left arrow and right arrow keys
Rate the currently displayed photo	0 (zero) through 5
Rotate the currently displayed photo	⌘-R (clockwise) or Option-⌘-R (counterclockwise)
Stop the slide show	Esc (or click the mouse button)

To duplicate a photo, select it, then choose Duplicate from the Photos menu (⌘-D).

Choosing Display Preferences

You can have iPhoto display additional information and other items during a slide show. For a basic slide show, use the Slideshow dialog box. For a saved slide show, use the Settings dialog box.

Display Titles. Each photo's title appears in the upper-left corner of the screen.

Display My Ratings. Each photo's rating appears centered at the bottom of the screen.

Display Slideshow Controls. The rotation, rating, and deletion tools described on page 161 appear immediately—no need to move the mouse first.

Exporting a Slide Show as a QuickTime Movie

Want to email a slide show to someone or post it on a Web site? Configure the slide show settings as desired, then use the Export command to create a QuickTime movie as described on page 200.

Note: If you plan to distribute your slide show's movie, avoid using iTunes Music Store purchases as soundtracks—the songs won't play on computers that aren't authorized for your iTunes account (for a workaround, see page 208).

Sharing Photos via Email

Email takes the immediacy of digital photography to a global scale. You can take a photo of a birthday cake and email it across the world before the candle wax solidifies. It takes just a few mouse clicks—iPhoto takes care of the often tricky chores behind creating email photo attachments.

iPhoto can also make images smaller so they transfer faster. Take advantage of this feature, and you won't bog down your recipients' email sessions with huge image attachments.

Normally, iPhoto uses the Mac OS X Mail program to email photos. If you use a different email program, you can configure iPhoto to use it, as described on the next page.

Step 1.
Select the Photos

Select the photos you want to email. Remember that you can select multiple photos by Shift-clicking and ⌘-clicking.

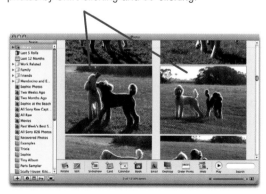

Step 2.
Click the Email Button

iPhoto displays the Mail Photo dialog box.

Step 3.
Specify the Image Size

iPhoto can make the images smaller before emailing. (This doesn't change the dimensions or file sizes of your original images, which iPhoto always stores in all their high-resolution glory.)

After you've specified mail settings, click Compose.

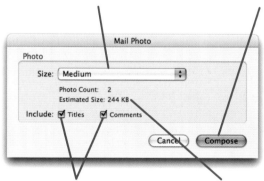

You have the option to include titles and comments along with the images—another good reason to assign this information when organizing your photos.

After iPhoto creates smaller versions, it starts Mac OS X's Mail program. Your photos are added to a new email, which you can complete and send on its way.

iPhoto estimates the size of the final attachments. If you're sending images to someone who is connecting using a modem (as opposed to a high-speed connection), try to keep the estimated size below 300KB or so. As a rule of thumb, each 100KB will take about 15 seconds to transfer over a 56 kbps modem.

Tips for Emailing Photos

Setting Email Preferences

You don't use Mac OS X's email program? Me neither—I prefer Microsoft Entourage. You can use iPhoto's Preferences command to tell iPhoto to use a program other than Mail to send your photos. Besides Mac OS X's Mail program, iPhoto can work with Microsoft Entourage, Qualcomm's Eudora, or America Online.

To change your email program preference, choose Preferences from the iPhoto menu and click the General button. Then, choose your preferred email program from the pop-up menu at the bottom of the Preferences window.

Tip: If iPhoto won't let you choose a program that you know you have, check that you haven't renamed the program's icon. For example, iPhoto expects your AOL program to be named *America Online*.

Exporting Photos By Hand

When you email a photo using iPhoto's Email button, iPhoto uses the name of the original photo's disk file as the name of the attachment. Problem is, most of your photos probably have incomprehensible filenames, such as 200203241958.jpg, that were assigned to them by your digital camera.

You might want an attachment to have a friendlier file name, such as holidays.jpg. For such cases, export the photo "by hand" and then add it to an email as an attachment. Choose Export from iPhoto's File menu, and be sure the File Export tab is active.

Export the photo as described at right. Save the exported photo in a convenient location, such as on your desktop. (You can delete it after you've emailed it.) Finally, switch to your email program, create a new email message, and add the photo to it as an attachment.

To make the images smaller and thus faster to transfer, type a dimension in the Width or Height box. You need type only one dimension; iPhoto will calculate the other dimension for you.

If your original image is stored in a format other than JPEG, consider choosing JPEG from this pop-up menu.

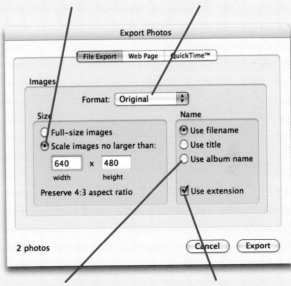

You can have iPhoto name the exported file according to its title or album name. If you're exporting just one photo, you can also type a name after clicking the Export button.

Leave this box checked to improve compatibility with Windows computers.

Sharing Photos via Photocasts

Email is a great way to share photos over the Internet, but it has its drawbacks. Frequently emailing photos to a large group of friends and family can be a chore. And your recipients end up with a collection of photos scattered throughout their email inboxes.

If you have an account with Apple's .Mac Internet service, you can take advantage of a much more automatic way to share photos over the Internet: *photocasts*. Publish an iPhoto album as a photocast, and friends and family can subscribe to the album—much as they might subscribe to a podcast in iTunes.

And like podcast subscriptions, photocast subscriptions can update automatically. Want to share a few new photos with your subscribers? Toss them into your photocast album. The next time your subscribers update their subscriptions, they'll see your latest shots.

To subscribe to your photocasts, friends and family can use iPhoto 6 or any Mac or Windows newsreader program (see page 170). But photocasting is best when your subscribers also use iPhoto 6. Then they get to do things with the photos you've published: print them; add them to slide shows, books, calendars, and greeting cards; and order prints. They can even use your published photos in the other iLife programs (page 170).

Important: To publish and subscribe to photocasts, you must be running Mac OS X 10.4.4 or a later version. If you're running an earlier Mac OS X, you can still subscribe to photocasts using a newsreader, as described on page 170.

To Publish a Photocast

Step 1. If the photos you want to publish aren't yet in an album, create a new album and add the photos to it (page 130).

Step 2. In the Source list, select the album you want to photocast, then choose Photocast from the Share menu.

To have iPhoto automatically update the photocast album whenever you add or remove a photo, check this box.

Choose a size for the photos (see page 170).

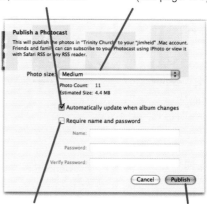

Normally, anyone who knows the address of the photocast album can access it. If you'd rather hire a security guard, check this box and then enter a name and password.

Step 3. To publish the photocast album, click Publish.

Step 4. Tell the world. After publishing the photocast, iPhoto displays a message containing its Internet address. To send an email announcement containing this address, click Announce Photocast. You can also copy the address to the Mac's Clipboard—perhaps as a prelude to pasting it into your own email message or using it as a link in iWeb—by selecting the address and choosing the Copy command.

When you've published an album as a photocast, a photocast icon appears next to its name in the Source list.

To Subscribe to a Photocast

With iPhoto. If you're using iPhoto 6 and you've received an email announcing a photocast, simply click the address in the announcement email.

iPhoto displays a dialog box asking if you're sure you want to subscribe. Click Subscribe or press the Return key. If the photocast requires a user name and password, a dialog box appears asking for it. iPhoto subscribes to the photocast album and loads its images.

Another way to subscribe to a photocast is by choosing File > Subscribe to Photocast, and then typing or pasting the photocast's address into the dialog box that appears.

Neat and tidy. When you subscribe to more than one photocast, iPhoto automatically creates a folder in your Source list for holding the photocasts. The folder is named—wait for it—Photocasts.

Updating your subscription. To have iPhoto check for and load photos that have been added to the photocast, click the 🔄 icon next to the photocast album's name (or next to your Photocasts folder).

With a newsreader program. To subscribe to the photocast with a newsreader, follow the steps at right.

Step 1. In the photocast announcement email, select the address of the photocast and choose Edit > Copy.

Step 2. Open your newsreader program and choose the appropriate subscribe command. (For example, in Ranchero Software's NetNewsWire, choose File > New Subscription.)

Step 3. Paste the photocast's address into the dialog box that appears, then click the program's OK or Subscribe button. If the photocast requires a user name and password, supply it when prompted by your newsreader program.

To Unsubscribe to a Photocast

Lose interest in a particular photocast? To cancel your subscription, simply select the photocast album in your Source list and press the Delete key.

iPhoto warns you that the photos will be moved to the iPhoto trash unless you choose to add them to your library.

To import the photos to your library before deleting the photocast album, check this box. (For more details on adding photocast photos to your iPhoto library, see the following pages.)

Make it so: delete the photocast album.

Setting Photocast Preferences

To specify photocasting preferences, choose Preferences from the iPhoto menu, then click Photocasts.

Specify how often you want iPhoto to check your photocast subscriptions for new photos. If you choose Manually, iPhoto updates photocasts only when you click the 📶 icon.

Albums you've published as photocasts appear here. To discontinue a photocast, select its name and click Stop Publishing.

Photocasting Tips

Size Concerns

On the previous pages, I mentioned that iPhoto lets you choose a size for the photos in a photocast. The smallest size is ideal if you or your subscribers are burdened with slow, dial-up Internet connections, but the larger sizes give your subscribers more creative options.

For example, iPhoto lets you order prints of the photos in a photocast album as well as add those photos to calendars or greeting cards. But for photocasts whose images are published in the smallest size, the photos lack sufficient resolution for any prints larger than wallet-sized. (For more details on resolution at it relates to print size, see page 180.) And if you try to add small photos to a calendar, book, or greeting card, you may see the dreaded warning triangle discussed on pages 190 and 196.

The size you choose when you publish a photocast should be based not only on Internet connection speeds, but also on how you see the photocast being used. Do you want its subscribers to be able to print photos or zoom in dramatically in slide shows? If so, plan to publish larger sizes.

And in case you're curious, at the Small size, a photo's longest dimension is 640 pixels. At the Medium size, it's 1280 pixels. At the Large size, it's 1920 pixels.

Get the Address of that Photocast

You published a photocast album a couple of weeks ago, and now you want to let another person know about it. Here's the easiest way to do so: display the Information pane, then click the URL entry.

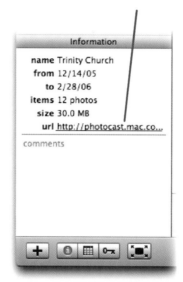

Doing so displays the Announce Photocast dialog box that appeared when you originally created the photocast. Click its Announce Photocast button, and you can send an announcement email on its way.

Elsewhere in iLife

I've already mentioned that you can do things with the photos you've subscribed to—order prints, make greeting cards and slide shows, and so on.

Your creative options don't stop in iPhoto. Photocast albums to which you've sub-

scribed appear in the other iLife programs, too. That means you can add them to iMovie HD projects, iDVD slide shows, GarageBand podcasts, and iWeb pages.

Did you subscribe to a family member's vacation photocast? Surprise her by creating an iMovie HD montage of the photos, complete with Ken Burns moves. Or create an iDVD slide show with background music.

If the creator of the photocast provided only small versions of the photos, the degree to which you can zoom in using the Ken Burns effect may be limited. But give it a try.

Flickr Meets iPhoto

When it comes to the Flickr photo sharing site (described on page 173), it's no secret that I'm a fan. Okay, I'm a rabid, obsessed zealot. One of the many things I love about Flickr is that the site provides RSS feeds for just about everything: the photos in someone's photostream, the photos in a group pool, and much more.

Some clever programmers have created Web sites that let you turn a Flickr RSS feed into a format compatible with iPhoto. Thus, you can keep an eye on the photos that specific Flickr members have posted, or on the photos in a specific group. And as I've mentioned elsewhere, this lets you do fun things with those photos, such as create slide shows.

Get links to photocasting utilities and resources.
www.macilife.com/iphoto

You'll find links for these services on my Web site's iPhoto resources page: www.macilife.com/iphoto.

Other Ways to View Photocasts

I've already mentioned that you can subscribe to and view photocasts using most RSS newsreaders, such as Ranchero Software's NetNewsWire. There are also programs designed for photocasts. If you don't want or need the complexity of a full-blown newsreader, check out Photocast Viewer (www.photocastviewer.com), which is free and available for Macs and Windows alike.

Another free program for the Windows users in your life is dmAlbums. Both Photocast Viewer and dmAlbums can also subscribe to RSS feeds from Flickr.

You can also subscribe to photocasts using Safari RSS, the version of Apple's Safari Web browser included with Mac OS X Tiger. But there's trick to it. If you've installed iPhoto 6 on the Mac, pasting the photocast's Internet address causes the Mac to switch to iPhoto—exactly what you don't want.

The trick? Paste the photocast's address into Safari RSS's address bar, then edit the beginning of the URL to read web.mac.com instead of photocast.mac.com. Then press Return, and Safari RSS loads the photos in the photocast.

Adding to the Library

You can do a lot with the photos in a photocast, but you can't edit them. If you want to edit a photocast photo, you need to add it to your iPhoto library first.

To add a photocast photo to your library, you might think that you can simply drag the photo to the Library item in the Source list. Good thinking—but it doesn't work.

Instead, you must drag the photo to any existing item—album, book, slide show, calendar, or greeting card—in your Source list. Doing so adds the photo to your library and to the item to which you dragged it.

Another way to add photocast photos to your library is to delete the photocast album to which you've subscribed. When you delete a photocast album to which you've subscribed, iPhoto reminds you that its photos aren't actually in your library and gives you the opportunity to add them.

Click the check box before clicking the Delete button, and iPhoto adds the photocast album's photos to your library before deleting the album.

Customizing the Photocast Announcement Email

The photocast-announcement email that iPhoto creates contains useful information, but maybe you'd like to augment it with some of your own. You can edit the email every time, but that's a lot of work.

My colleague Rob Griffiths has published a customizing tip for replacing the stock iPhoto photocast announcement text with some verbiage of your own. I've linked to Rob's handy tip on my site's iPhoto reference page, www.macilife.com/iphoto.

Discontinuing a Photocast

Don't want to make an album available as a photocast anymore? Select the album in the Source list and choose Photocast from the Share menu. In the dialog box that appears, click Stop Publishing.

Note: When you discontinue a photocast, you aren't deleting its photos from your iPhoto library. Subscribers to the photocast will still be able to see the photos that they loaded before you discontinued the photocast. But if subscribers try to update the photocast to see if any new photos have arrived, they'll see an error message.

More Internet Sharing Options

Chances are most of the Internet sharing you do will be through email and Home-Page albums. But when you're in the mood for something completely different, iPhoto is ready. You can also create custom Web photo albums as well as slide shows that are shared through Apple's .Mac service.

.Mac slide shows are a fun way to share photos with other Mac users. Publish some photos as .Mac slides, and other Mac OS X users can configure their Macs to use those photos as their screen savers.

You might create a custom Web album if you already have your own Web site, perhaps one that is served by your local Internet provider rather than Apple's .Mac service.

If you're a Web publisher, you can modify these pages as you see fit. You might open them in a program such as Macromedia Dreamweaver, embellish them with additional graphics or other tweaks, and then upload them to a Web site. It's a lot more work than creating Web albums with iWeb, but has the potential to give you much more control over your designs.

iPhoto's Web pages are on the bland side. To spice up iPhoto's HTML exporting, try an iPhoto add-on called BetterHTMLExport (www.geeksrus.com). BetterHTMLExport provides numerous design templates for you to choose from and modify.

Creating a .Mac Slide Show

Step 1. Select the photos you want to publish. To select an entire album, click its name.

Step 2. Choose .Mac Slides from the Share menu.

iPhoto connects to .Mac, then displays a message asking if you're sure you want to publish the slide show.

Step 3. Click the Publish button.

iPhoto transfers your images to your iDisk. When the transfer is complete, a message appears enabling you to send an announcement email. The announcement contains instructions on how users can access the slide show.

To view a .Mac slide show, use the Desktop & Screen Saver system preference.

Tip: If you frequently publish .Mac slides, you can add a button to the bottom of the iPhoto window for doing so. Choose View > Show in Toolbar > .Mac Slides.

Exporting Web Pages

You can export photos and albums as Web pages to post on Web sites or burn to CDs (opposite page). iPhoto creates small thumbnail versions of your images, as well as the HTML pages that display them. (HTML stands for *HyperText Markup Language*—it's the set of codes used to design Web pages.)

To export a Web page, select some photos or an album, choose Export from the File menu, then click the Web Page tab. Specify the page appearance and dimensions of the thumbnails and the images, then click Export. In the Export dialog box, click the New Folder button to create a new folder. If you'll be publishing the pages on a Web server, I recommend naming the new folder *index*. This causes iPhoto to create a home page named *index.html,* as required by most Web servers.

Check out my Flickr photos.
www.flickr.com/photos/jimheid/

The Flickr of Addiction

If you aren't a .Mac subscriber and you don't want to fuss with Web servers, you have other Web album options. Most online photofinishers provide free Web album features, but given that the primary focus of these sites is to sell prints and photo gifts, your albums tend to be surrounded by ads and e-commerce clutter.

A better choice is a site designed specifically for online photo sharing. I'm a huge fan of Flickr (www.flickr.com), which combines photo sharing and print-ordering services with an inspiring community of creative photographers who comment on each other's photos.

Flickr is packed with slick features you won't find elsewhere, starting with an uploading tool that lets you transfer photos directly from iPhoto's Export dialog box. Instead of the thumbnail-page albums that other sharing sites use, Flickr displays your

albums as slide shows—complete with cross-dissolve transitions between images.

You can also assign descriptive tags, such as *beach*, to your photos, and other Flickr users can search for images based on those tags. The Flickr iPhoto plug-in even supports iPhoto titles, comments, and keywords. Titles and comments are

displayed along with your photos, and keywords are converted into Flickr tags.

Best of all is Flickr's pervasive support for RSS and newsreaders. Subscribe to another user's photo stream, and small thumbnails appear in your newsreader whenever that user uploads new photos. You can also subscribe to specific tags. Subscribe to the *beach* tag, and your newsreader will display everyone's beach photos as they're uploaded.

Flickr can also automatically publish, on your blog, your recent photos. It's a happy marriage between photography and the latest geek technologies. A Flickr account is free, although if you upload many photos, you'll quickly reach the 20MB-per-month bandwidth limit of a free account. A Pro account costs $24.95 per year and boosts the upload limit to 1GB per month.

Burning HTML Albums on a CD

Even if you aren't a Web jockey, there's a good reason to consider exporting an album as a set of Web pages: you can burn the exported pages onto CDs, and then mail them to others. They can view the album on their Macs or PCs using a Web

browser—no attachment hassles, no long downloads.

After exporting the Web page, use the Mac OS X Finder to copy its folders and HTML pages to a blank CD-R disc. Burn the disc, eject it, and you have a photo Web site on a disc.

To view the site, simply double-click on the site's home page file. (If you followed my recommendation on the opposite page, this file is named *index.html*.)

And by the way, resist the urge to rename the site's home page file. If you change the name, the

links in the Web album won't work. If you want a different name for the home page file, export the Web pages anew.

Similarly, don't rename any image files or move them from their folders.

Sharing Photos on a Network

If you have more than one Mac on a network, you can share each Mac's photo library and make it accessible to the other Macs on the network.

Network photo sharing leads to all kinds of possibilities. Keep your "master" photo library on one Mac, and then access it from other Macs when you need to—no need to copy the library from one Mac to another and worry about which library is the most current.

Don't like centralization? Embrace anarchy: let everyone in the family have his or her own photo library, and then use sharing to make the libraries available to others.

Have an AirPort-equipped laptop Mac? Sit on the sofa (or at poolside) and show your photos to friends and family. Or take your laptop to their house and browse their libraries. Network sharing, a laptop Mac, and AirPort form the ultimate portable slide projector.

You can choose to share an entire photo library or only some albums. And you can require a password to keep your kids (or your parents) out of your library.

Activating Sharing

To share your photo library with other Macs on a network, choose Preferences from the iPhoto menu, then click the Sharing button.

To have the Mac automatically connect to shared libraries it finds on the network, check this box.

You can share your entire library or only selected albums. To share a specific album, click its check box.

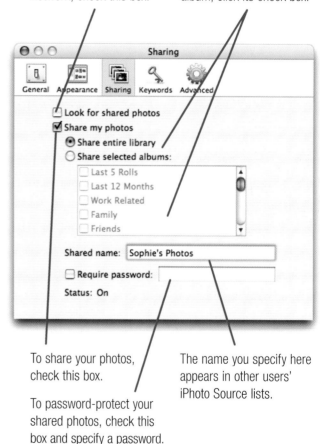

To share your photos, check this box.

To password-protect your shared photos, check this box and specify a password.

The name you specify here appears in other users' iPhoto Source lists.

Accessing Shared Photos

To access shared photos, choose Preferences from the iPhoto menu, click the Sharing button, and be sure the Look for Shared Photos box is checked. iPhoto scans your network and, if it finds any shared photo libraries, adds their names to the Source list.

To view a shared library, click its name in the Source list.

To view albums in a shared library, click the little triangle next to the library's name.

To disconnect from a shared library (perhaps to reduce traffic on your network), click the Eject button.

Working with Shared Photos

No Keywords or Info

Unfortunately, iPhoto ignores any keywords, titles, or comments that you may have assigned to the photos in a shared library, even if you copy those photos to your local photo library.

As a result, you can't use the Search box, smart albums, or keyword searches to find photos in a shared library.

If you want to copy some photos to your local library *and* preserve this information, burn the photos to a CD or DVD using the techniques described on page 202. Then, insert the CD in your Mac and copy the photos to your library.

Slide Show Music

You can view a slide show of a shared album, but if the shared album has music assigned to it, you won't hear that music. Instead, iPhoto plays its default music, unless you've assigned a different song to your library.

But here's an interesting twist: you can temporarily assign a song or playlist from *your* local iTunes library to a *shared* album. Just use the techniques described on pages 160 and 161.

When you assign local music to a shared album, iPhoto doesn't save your assignment. If you disconnect from the shared album and then reconnect, it's back to whatever your default song happens to be.

Just Looking

You can view and print shared photos. You can also email them, order prints, and display a basic slide show. But you can't edit shared photos, nor can you send them to iWeb or access them from the photo browsers in the other iLife programs.

To perform these tasks, copy the shared photos you want to your local iPhoto library: select the photos, then drag them to the Library item in the Source list or to an album.

And what about adding shared photos to saved slide shows, calendars, cards, or books? You can do it: if you drag a photo to one of these items in your Source list, iPhoto imports the photo, adds it to your local library, and then adds it to the item.

Folders and Shared Libraries

If you store albums in folders, as I recommend on page 133, you'll be in for an unpleasant surprise when you connect to your library from a different Mac. iPhoto doesn't display the individual albums within a folder. Instead, it simply displays the name of the folder containing the albums. If you select the folder's name, you'll see the photos in *all* of the albums contained in that folder.

The unfortunate moral: when you want to be able to connect to a specific album from a different Mac, don't store that album in a folder.

Printing Photos

Internet photo sharing is great, but hard copy isn't dead. You might want to share photos with people who don't have computers. Or, you might want to tack a photo to a bulletin board or hang it on your wall—you'll never see "suitable for framing" stamped on an email message.

iPhoto makes hard copy easy. If you have a photo-inkjet printer, you can use iPhoto to create beautiful color prints in a variety of sizes. This assumes, of course, that your photos are both beautiful and in color.

When printing your photos, you can choose from several formatting options, called *print styles*, by using the Style pop-up menu in the Print dialog box. For example, if you choose the Sampler style, you can print pages that contain the same photo in several different sizes. With the style named N-Up, you can print up to 16 photos per page.

Printing with iPhoto is straightforward, but to avoid wasting pricey photo paper and ink, you'll want to be aware of a couple of fine points. And to get the best results, you'll want to use images with a resolution high enough to yield sharp results at your chosen print size. You'll find more details on this aspect of printing on the following pages.

Step 1 (optional).

Crop the photo so that its proportions match that of the paper size you want to print. For details on cropping, see page 137.

You don't have to crop before printing, but if you don't crop or use the Zoom and Crop option described on the opposite page, your print will probably have wildly uneven borders. If you choose the Standard Prints print style, iPhoto may even refuse to print the photo (see "When iPhoto Balks," on page 179).

Tip: If you want to retain an uncropped version of the photo, make a duplicate before cropping: select the photo and press ⌘-D.

Step 2.

Be sure that the photo you want to print is selected or displayed in the iPhoto edit view. To print multiple photos, select the photos.

Don't Bother with Page Setup

In many Mac programs, you use the Page Setup command to specify paper size and other printing settings. Not so in iPhoto. To specify paper size and all other printing settings, you use the Print dialog box shown on the opposite page. iPhoto ignores any settings you make in the Page Setup dialog box.

Printing from Edit and Slide Show Views

If you're like me, you do most of your printing while browsing your library or an album. But you can also print while in edit or slide show view. In edit view, you can print only one photo at a time (the photo that's currently open for editing), but in slide show view, you can print multiple photos by selecting them in the photo browser at the top of the iPhoto window.

Step 3.

Choose Print from the File menu, choose the appropriate settings, then click Print or press Return.

iPhoto includes presets for many popular inkjet printers. Choose the preset that best matches the type of paper you're using.

Choose the paper size you're using.

The Full Page style is the most versatile and reliable. Other styles include Contact Sheet, Standard Prints, N-Up, Sampler, and Greeting Card (see the following pages).

iPhoto displays a preview of your first page. To see a preview of all pages, click Preview.

Be sure your printer is selected here.

When you've chosen the Full Page style, you can adjust margin dimensions here.

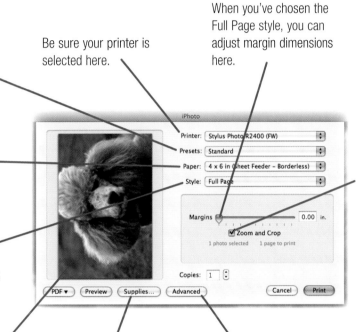

Want a borderless print without having to manually crop the photo? Check this box, and iPhoto enlarges the image just enough to fill the paper size you've specified. When you don't want to crop a photo by hand before printing it, this is the option to use.

Note: To create borderless prints, your printer must support borderless printing and you must choose a borderless paper-size option using the Paper pop-up menu.

Running low? Click this button to connect to Apple's online store, which will display available supplies for the printer you have chosen with the Printer pop-up menu.

Access additional printing options specific to your printer—for example, to fine-tune paper or print-quality settings.

Printing Tips and Troubleshooting

Other Print Styles

When you want to make more than just a simple print, investigate iPhoto's other print styles.

The Greeting Card style formats the page so you can fold it into a card.

The N-Up style prints multiple copies of a single photo on each page. You can choose to print as few as two copies per page, or as many as 16.

The Sampler style mixes and matches sizes on a single sheet—much like the combination of print sizes you might get from a portrait studio. This style provides two templates, which you can choose using the Template pop-up menu.

The Contact Sheet style, described at right, lets you print numerous shots on a single sheet—handy for reference purposes or to simply squeeze a lot of photos out of a sheet of paper.

Printing a Contact Sheet

Photographers often create *contact sheets*—quick-reference prints containing small versions of multiple photos, usually an entire roll's worth. (The term derives from the traditional technique: a contact sheet is created by sandwiching negatives between a piece of glass and photographic paper, and then exposing the sandwich to light.)

Specify how many images you want to appear on each row of the contact sheet.

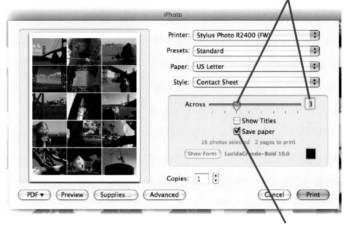

To include only certain photos on a contact sheet, select them before choosing the Print command. You can use contact sheets to provide an at-a-glance reference for a series of photos. But you can also use a contact sheet to squeeze several images onto a single sheet of paper.

Check the Save paper box to have iPhoto print vertical images in horizontal orientation, even if you rotated them. You'll have to turn the sheet sideways to view some images, but you'll get more images on each sheet of paper.

Tip: You can use contact sheets to print multiple copies of one photo. Simply select only one photo before choosing Print.

When iPhoto Balks

You've selected a photo, chosen the Print command, and selected the Standard Prints style. You choose the 4x6 print size, and all seems right with the world.

Then you glance at the little preview area of the Print dialog box where, instead of your photo, you see red text proclaiming, "The selected print size will not fit on the current paper size."

Here are a few remedies to try.

Check print options. Scrutinize the settings you've made in the Print dialog box and make sure that you've chosen your printer and the paper size that corresponds to the desired print size.

Click the One Photo Per Page box. You'll find it under the Size pop-up menu in the Print dialog box.

Give up. When all else fails, give up. Specifically, choose the Full Page print style instead. It's much less finicky.

When Prints Disappoint

When your prints aren't charming, read on.

Verify paper choices. In iPhoto's Print dialog box, be sure to choose the preset that matches the type of paper you're using and the quality you're seeking. It's easy to overlook this step and end up specifying plain paper when you're actually using pricey photo paper.

Check ink. Strange colors? Check your printer's ink supply. Many printers include diagnostic software that reports how much ink remains in each cartridge.

Clean up. The nozzles in an inkjet printer can become clogged, especially if you don't print every day. If you're seeing odd colors or a horizontal banding pattern, use your printer's cleaning mode to cleaning your ink nozzles. Most printers can print a test page designed to show when the nozzles need cleaning. You may have to repeat the cleaning process a few times.

Preserving Your Prints

After all the effort you put into making inkjet prints, it may disappoint you to learn that they may not last long.

Many inkjet prints begin to fade within a year or two—even faster when displayed in direct sunlight. Most printer manufacturers now offer pigment-based inks and archival papers that last for decades, but pigment-based printers are pricier than the more common dye-based printers.

If you have a dye-based printer, consider using a paper rated for longer print life. Epson's ColorLife paper, for example, has a much higher permanence rating than Epson's Premium Glossy Photo Paper.

To prolong the life of any print, don't display it in direct sunlight. Frame it under glass to protect it from humidity and pollutants. (Ozone pollution, common in cities, is poison to an inkjet print.)

Allow prints to dry for at least a few (preferably 24) hours before framing them or stacking them atop each other. For long-term storage, consider using acid-free sleeves designed for archival photo storage.

Finally, avoid bargain-priced paper or ink from the local office superstore. Print preservation guru Henry Wilhelm (www.wilhelm-research.com) recommends using only premium inks and papers manufactured by the same company that made your printer.

Is all this necessary for a print that will be tacked to a refrigerator for a few months and then thrown away? Of course not. But when you want prints to last, these steps can help.

To learn more about digital printing, read Harald Johnson's *Mastering Digital Printing, Second Edition* (Muska & Lipman, 2005).

Ordering Prints

Inkjet photo printers provide immediate gratification, but not without hassles. Paper and ink are expensive. Getting perfectly even borders is next to impossible, and getting borderless prints can be equally frustrating.

There is another path to hard copy: ordering prints through iPhoto. Click the Order Prints button, specify the print sizes you want, and iPhoto transmits your photos over the Internet to Kodak's Ofoto print service. The prints look great, and because they're true photographic prints, they're much more permanent than most inkjet prints.

You can also order prints from other online photofinishers, many of whom also offer free online photo albums and other sharing services. Using these services isn't as straightforward as clicking a button in iPhoto, but it isn't difficult, either. Many services, such as Shutterfly (www.shutterfly.com), offer software that simplifies transferring your shots. And some services offer output options that iPhoto doesn't, such as mouse pads, T-shirts, and even photo cookies. For links to some online photofinishers, see www.macilife.com/iphoto.

To Order Prints

Step 1.

Select the photos you want prints of, then click the Order Prints button or choose Order Prints from the Share menu.

Order Prints

Step 2.

Specify the sizes and quantities you want.

The yellow triangle of doom (⚠) indicates that the photo doesn't have enough resolution for good quality at that size; see the sidebar at right for details.

Want a 4 by 6 of every photo you selected? Specify the quantity here.

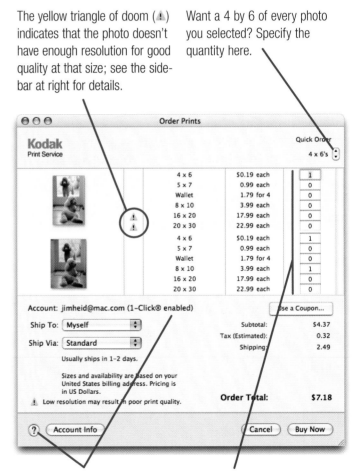

To order prints, you must have an Apple ID account with 1-Click ordering enabled. For help, click the help button.

Specify how many prints you want for each size.

Create a Temporary Album

If you're ordering prints from many different rolls, create an album and use it to hold the photos you want to print. Give the album an obvious name, such as *Pix to Print*. This makes it easier to keep track of which photos you're printing. After you've placed your order, you can delete the album.

Cropping Concerns

The proportions of most standard print sizes don't match the proportions of a typical digital camera image. As a result, Kodak automatically crops a photo to fill the print size you've ordered.

The problem is, automatic cropping may lop off part of the image that's important to you. If you don't want your photos cropped by a machine, do the cropping

yourself, using iPhoto's edit view, before ordering. Use the Constrain pop-up menu to specify the proportions you want.

If you plan to order prints in several sizes, you may have even more work to do. A 5 by 7 print has a different *aspect ratio* than a 4 by 6 or an 8 by 10. If you want to order a 5 by 7 *and* one of these other sizes, you need to create a separate version of each picture—for example, one version cropped for a 5 by 7 and another cropped for an 8 by 10.

To create separate versions of a picture, make a duplicate of the original photo for each size you want (select the photo and press ⌘-D), and then crop each version appropriately.

If you crop a photo to oddball proportions—for example, a narrow rectangle—Kodak's automatic cropping will yield a weird-looking print. If you have

an image-editing program, such as Adobe Photoshop Elements, here's a workaround. In the imaging program, create a blank image at the size you plan to print (for example, 5 by 7 inches). Then open your cropped photo in the imaging program and paste it into this blank image. Save the resulting image as a JPEG file (use the Maximum quality setting), add it to iPhoto, and then order your print.

No Questions, Please

Kodak can't print a photo whose file name contains a question mark (?). No digital camera creates files that are so named, but if you scan and name images yourself, keep this restriction in mind.

Resolution's Relationship to Print Quality

If you're working with low-resolution images—ones that you've cropped heavily or shot at a low resolution, for example—you may see iPhoto's dreaded low-resolution warning icon (⚠) when ordering prints or a book.

This is iPhoto's way of telling you that an image doesn't have enough pixels—enough digital information—to yield a good-quality print at the size that you've chosen.

Don't feel obligated to cancel a print job or an order if you see this warning. But do note that

you may see some fuzziness in your prints.

The table here lists the minimum resolution an image should have to yield a good print at various sizes.

Print Sizes and Resolution

For This Print Size (Inches)	Image Resolution Should be Least (Pixels)
Wallet	640 by 480
4 by 6	768 by 512
5 by 7	1075 by 768
8 by 10	1280 by 1024
16 by 20	2272 by 1704

More Printing Options

If you have a photo-inkjet printer, take advantage of it—don't just restrict yourself to producing ordinary prints. I like to create photo greeting cards with my printer. Yes, I can (and often do) create iPhoto greeting cards, but when I don't want to wait several days for a card to arrive in the mail, I fire up my printer and get out my cutting board.

Here's a step-by-step look at how I do it, along with a few more photo-related gift ideas.

For this example, I scanned an old black-and-white photo of yours truly sitting on Santa's lap.

Trivia tidbit: That isn't really Santa—it's my dad. He was a TV and radio personality in my home town of Pittsburgh, and every year he'd don a Santa suit and play the role at local charity events and children's TV shows. All the other kids were confused and just a little jealous when I told them my dad was Santa.

Step 1. Print the Card

Select your photo (click it once), then choose Print from the File menu. In the Print dialog box, choose Greeting Card from the Style menu, then be sure the Single-Fold button is active.

I like to use heavyweight matte-finish paper for greeting cards. Its reverse side—where you'll write your greeting—accepts ink nicely and doesn't contain any company logos, unlike most plastic resin-coated papers.

Step 2. Fold the Card

Be sure your print is dry and your hands are clean. Then, using a sharp, straight edge, crease the side of the card where you want the fold to be. (For a vertically oriented card like this one, that will be the left edge of the photo.) Carefully fold the card along that crease.

I positioned the edge of the photo on the edge of my cutting board, then created a crease by firmly running my finger along the edge.

Step 3. Trim the Card

With the card folded, cut off the white edges around the photo. A cutting board works best, but a pair of sharp scissors will do.

Picture the Perfect Present

Photos make fabulous gifts. Here are a few of the many ways to give some pixels to someone you love.

Enlargements. Order an enlargement of a favorite photo, and then have it framed. You can use iPhoto to order prints as large as 20 by 30 inches, although you'll need a high-resolution file to get sharp results at large sizes. For even bigger prints, check out JumboGiant (www.jumbogiant.com), which uses special resolution-enhancing software to create spectacularly huge prints.

Books, calendars, and cards. With iPhoto's publishing features, you can create gorgeous photo books, calendars, and yes, greeting cards, all in a variety of sizes and styles. If you're creating a book or calendar for someone, consider including a DVD of it, too. Create a DVD containing a slide show of the same photos you've used in print, and include the DVD along with the hard copy.

Photo gifts. Think beyond paper—have a photo printed on a mug, tote bag, apron, jigsaw puzzle, mousepad, T-shirt, or even a batch of cookies.

You can't order photo gifts like these through iPhoto. But you can order them from Shutterfly (www.shutterfly.com), Club Photo (www.clubphoto.com), and Signature Color (www.signaturecolor.com).

When ordering a photo gift, you'll have to transfer your photo to the online service. Just drag the photo from the iPhoto window out to your desktop; this makes a copy of the photo on your desktop. Upload this copy, then delete it.

Creating Photo Books

Something special happens to photos when they're pasted into the pages of a book. Arranged in a specific order and accompanied by captions, photos form a narrative: they tell a story.

Put away your paste. With iPhoto's book mode, you can create beautiful, full-color books in several sizes and styles. Arrange your photos in the order you want, adding captions and descriptive text if you like. Choose from a gallery of design *themes* to spice up your pages with layouts that complement your subject.

When you're done, iPhoto connects to the Internet and transfers your book to Apple's printing service, where the book is printed on a four-color digital printing press (a Hewlett-Packard Indigo, if you're curious), and then bound and shipped to you.

iPhoto books are great for commemorating a vacation, wedding, or other special event. They're also open for business: architects, artists, photographers, and designers use iPhoto to create spectacular portfolios, proposals, and brochures.

So don't just print those extra-special shots. Publish them.

Creating a Book: The Big Picture

The most efficient way to create a book is to first add photos to an album, and then tell iPhoto to create a book based on that album. Here's an overview of the process.

Step 1.

Create a new album containing the photos you want to publish (page 130). Arrange the photos in approximately the same order that you want them to appear in the book. (You can always change their order later.)

Step 2.

Select the album in the Source list, then choose New Book from the File menu (or click the Book button 🖼 or the Add button ➕).

Step 3.

Choose a book type and a theme, then click Choose Theme. For a summary of the types of books you can order, see the sidebar at right.

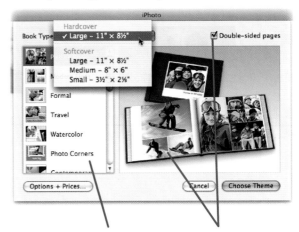

Most book types provide numerous themes. Most themes provide coordinated color schemes and several page designs.

Large hardcover books can have single-sided pages (each left-hand page is blank) or double-sided pages (shown here).

Step 4.

Lay out the book.

You can have iPhoto place the photos for you (the autoflow mode), or you can manually place each photo yourself (see the following pages).

Switch between viewing page thumbnails (shown here) or photos that you haven't yet placed in the book (page 188).

To reposition a photo within its book frame, double-click the photo and drag the size control and/or the photo itself (page 191).

To jump to a page, click its thumbnail. To rearrange pages, drag them left or right (page 188).

Many page designs allow for text, whose type style you can customize (page 190).

For more layout options, Control-click on a photo (page 191).

Move to the previous or next page.

Zoom in on a page for proofreading and fine tuning.

You can view and work with two-page spreads (shown here) or one page at a time (page 189).

Switch themes and page designs and perform other layout and design tasks (pages 188–191).

Display your book's pages as a slide show (page 191).

Step 5.

Click [Buy Book] and pay up using your Apple ID (page 15).

Four Types of Books

Large Hardcover. The classiest book option, and the priciest. The front-cover photo is attached to the linen hardcover.

Large Softcover. A big book on a budget. The white cover contains a cutout revealing the book's first page.

Medium Softcover. Smaller page sizes and a much smaller price. The color-coordinated cover has its own photo.

Small Softcover. Photos to go: up to 100 pages of pictures in your pocket. Small softcover books are sold in packs of three.

Base book: $29.99
Each extra page: $.99–1.49
(See page 187 for details.)

20 pages: $19.99
Each extra page: $.69

20 pages: $9.99
Each extra page: $.49

20 pages: $3.99
Each extra page: $.29

Planning for Publishing

A book project doesn't begin in a page-layout program. It begins with an author who has something to say, and with photo editors and designers who have ideas about the best ways to say it.

When you create a photo book, you wear all of those hats. iPhoto works hard to make you look as fetching as possible in each of them, but you can help by putting some thought into your book before you click the Book button.

What do you want your book to say? Is it commemorating an event? Or is it celebrating a person, place, or thing? Does the book need a story arc—a beginning, a middle, and an ending? Would the book benefit from distinct sections—one for each place you visited, for example, or one for each member of the family?

And no publishing project occurs without a discussion of production expenses. Is money no object? Or are you pinching pennies?

Your answers to these questions will influence the photos you choose, the book designs you use, and the way you organize and present your photos and any accompanying text. The very best time to address these questions isn't before you start your book—it's before you start shooting. If you have a certain kind of book in mind, you can make sure you get the shots you need.

Here's more food for thought.

Questions to Ask

Here's a look at some of the factors that may influence your choice of book sizes and themes.

What Size Book?

The book size you choose will be dictated by your budget and design goals. On a budget? Use the medium-sized or large softcover formats. Want the largest selection of design options? Go large hardcover. Large book sizes are also best when you want to get as many photos as possible on a page.

Your photos may also influence your choice: for example, if you have low-resolution shots and want to present one photo per page, you may need to choose a medium-sized book to get acceptable quality.

How Much Text?

Most photography books contain more than just photos. Will you want text in your book? If so, how much? Some themes provide for more copy than others.

Several of iPhoto's themes can automatically place titles and comments next to each photo. If you've diligently added titles and comments to your photos and want iPhoto to print this information, choose the Portfolio, Yearbook, Classic, or Catalog theme. Note that these themes are available for large hardcover books only; they appear in the Old Themes category.

What Design Options?

Each book size and type provides its own set of themes. Each theme has its own design options, including different color schemes; different ways to arrange photos on each page; and special photo effects, such as collages.

Options to Consider

For this spread in my Paris travel book, the left-hand page shows works from the Museé d'Orsay, shown on the right-hand page.

Think about ways to have the left- and right-hand pages complement each other.

The Baby Boy and Baby Girl (shown here) themes have a page for listing vital statistics.

Don't have high-resolution photos? Consider a medium or small softcover book, or choose page designs with small photo zones or multiple photos per page.

Many themes (including Crayon, shown here) have page designs that allow for text headings and lengthy captions whose formatting you can customize.

In the Portfolio design, photo titles and comments become caption headings and caption text.

One Side Or Two?

When creating a large-sized hardcover book—also called a *Keepsake* book—you can choose between single- or double-sided pages. With double-sided pages, you get two-page *spreads* like those shown at left. With single-sided pages, the left-hand page in each spread is blank.

Given that all commercially published books have double-sided pages, why would you choose a single-sided format? One reason might be if you plan to print the book yourself using iPhoto's Print command (page 192). You can't print on both sides of a sheet of photo paper, so a single-sided scheme makes more sense.

A double-sided layout give you more design options. Large softcover books are always double-sided, as are medium- and small-sized books.

What is a Page, Anyway?

With all book sizes, you pay a per-page fee for each additional page beyond 20 (page 185). A "page" isn't a sheet of paper—it's anything with ink on it. For example, a book containing 20 double-sided pages contains ten sheets of paper.

With large hardcover books, the per-page pricing can seem confusing. If you opt for a single-sided layout, your $29.99 buys you ten pages; each additional page is $1.49. If you go double-sided, you get 20 pages (ten sheets of paper), and each extra page costs $.99.

Got all that? Don't worry. iPhoto calculates your final price when you order your book.

Book Layout Techniques

Automatic or Manual?

When you create a book, you can choose to have iPhoto lay out the book automatically by clicking the Autoflow button, or you can take the wheel and drive yourself by dragging photos onto the book's pages. When you create a new book, iPhoto reminds you of these options.

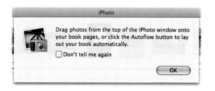

Regardless of the option you choose, iPhoto always creates a book with 20 pages—the minimum a book can contain.

iPhoto also assigns designs to each page. And that's why I prefer to lay out books manually instead of clicking the Autoflow button. I often want to change the designs that iPhoto has chosen, and if I'm going to do that, I might as well start with a blank slate—why have iPhoto position photos that I'm going to be rearranging anyway?

But that's just me. If you'd rather get immediate results and then fine-tune, click Autoflow. Or mix both approaches. If you want to do something fancy at the beginning of your book—maybe have a full-page photo opposite an introduction text page—lay out those first couple of pages. Then click the Autoflow button to have iPhoto do the rest.

Note that the Autoflow feature adds additional pages to your book if necessary to accommodate the rest of your unplaced photos. Those extra pages will cost you, so if you're watching your production budget, keep an eye on your total page count.

Page Type Versus Page Design

It's important to understand the difference between these two similar-sounding terms. In iPhoto's world, *page type* refers to the overall structure of a page: whether it's a text page or, if it's a page with photos, how many photos it displays.

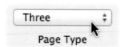

Page design refers to the appearance of a specific page type. Most themes provide a selection of designs for each type of page.

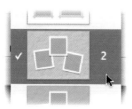

You choose a page *type* first: "iPhoto, give me a page with three photo frames on it." Then, you choose a page *design*: "I want the design with a blue background and overlapping photos."

Adding and Removing Photos

Slinging photos around? Here are some slinging tips.

Adding to a full page. If you drag a photo from the photo browser to a page that already contains photos in each photo frame, iPhoto changes the page type, adding an additional photo frame to accommodate the photo.

With some themes and page designs, iPhoto may add more than one photo frame. For example, in the Picture Book theme, the available page types jump from four photos per page to six. If you add a photo to a fully populated four-photo page, iPhoto switches to the six-photo page type. You can either add a sixth photo or wait until you're finished laying out your book and then use the Clean Up Book command (see page 192).

Incidentally, if a page already has the maximum number of photos supported by that theme, iPhoto won't let you add another one.

Moving to a different page. You can move a photo to a different page. Be sure that your page thumbnails are visible (click the ■ button), then drag the photo to its new page. The same points mentioned previously apply: if the destination page is full, iPhoto may change its page type to accommodate the new photo.

Removing a photo. To remove a photo, select the photo and press the Delete key, or drag the photo up to the photo thumbnails browser. iPhoto moves the photo to the thumbnails area.

You can also remove a photo by Control-clicking on it and choosing Remove Photo from the Shortcut menu.

To remove the photo's frame, switch to a page type that provides fewer photos, or wait until you've finished your book and then use the Clean Up Book command (see page 192).

Swapping photos. To swap two photos on a page or spread, simply drag one photo to the other one.

Editing a photo. Need to edit a photo that you've placed on a page? Control-click on the photo and choose Edit Photo from the shortcut menu.

Adding photos from your library. To add additional photos to a book, drag them from your library to the book's name in the Source list.

Adding and Removing Pages

To add a page, click the Add Page button. If you're viewing two-page spreads, iPhoto adds a full spread, which is two pages. To add just one page, switch to single-page view (click the ▪ View button).

To insert a new spread or page between two existing pages, use the page thumbnails browser to select the page that you want to precede the new page. For example, to add a new page between pages 4 and 5, select page 4, then click Add Page.

When you add a page or spread, iPhoto populates its photo frames with any photos that you have in the book's photo thumbnail browser. You can delete and rearrange these photos as I've already

described. If there aren't any (or enough) photos in the thumbnail browser, iPhoto gives you blank photo frames.

Removing a page. To remove a page, select it in the pages thumbnail browser and press the Delete key. Or, Control-click on a blank area of the doomed page and choose Remove Page from the shortcut menu.

When you delete a page containing photos, iPhoto moves its photos to the photo thumbnail browser so you can use them elsewhere, if you like.

Rearranging Pages

To reorganize your pages, drag their thumbnails left and right in the page thumbnail browser. If you're viewing two-page spreads, you can move spreads back and forth. In the following example, pages 2 and 3 are being moved so they follow pages 4 and 5.

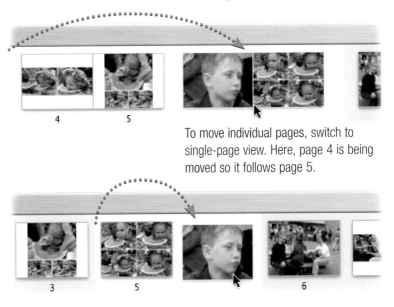

To move individual pages, switch to single-page view. Here, page 4 is being moved so it follows page 5.

Tips for Creating Books

Formatting Text

You can format your book's text in a couple of ways.

Globally: the Settings button. When you want to change the font iPhoto uses for every occurrence of an element in your book (such as its captions), use the Settings button. **Tip:** Each book theme provides its own text elements, and some provide more than others. The Settings dialog box is a convenient way to see what elements a theme provides.

With some themes, such as Contemporary, you'll see elements that are labeled (P) and (L). Those themes provide different default font sizes depending on whether the page contains a portrait-oriented (P) or landscape-oriented (L) photo.

Locally: the Fonts panel. Typographic consistency is important for a book like the one you're reading, but for a photo book that contains only a few text elements, a bit of variety can be fun. You can format individual text elements—indeed, individual letters, if you want to—by using the Fonts panel. Select the text you want to format, and choose Show Fonts from the Edit menu's Font submenu (⌘-T).

The triangle of doom. You've typed some text or changed text formatting, and suddenly the yellow triangle of doom appears in the text box. iPhoto is telling you that the text won't fit with its current type specs. Either change formatting or delete some text.

More Tips for Text

Here are more textual tips.

Low-rent formatting control. All themes provide an Introduction page type. But don't feel obligated to write an introduction. You can adapt the Introduction page to other uses, such as a title page. You can also move items around on the page by using the spacebar or Tab key to bump a line of text to the right, and by pressing Return to move text down. These tricks don't provide page-layout precision, but they work.

Consider a word processor. Planning a lot of text in your book? Consider using your favorite word processor to write and format the text. Then, move the text into iPhoto as needed: select the text you need for a given page, and copy it to the Clipboard. Next, switch to iPhoto, click in the destination text box, and paste. iPhoto even retains your formatting.

This approach lets you take advantage of a word processor's superior editing features, not to mention its Save command—something iPhoto lacks.

Controlling paragraph formatting. iPhoto doesn't provide controls for adjusting the spacing between lines (leading) or paragraph indents. Solution: Use your word processor. Format your text in a word processor, then copy and paste it into the text box on your book page.

Saving custom text styles.

Saving custom text styles. You've pasted in some custom formatting and would like to save it to apply to future books or to other pages in the same book. Here's how.

First, click within the text box that contains the custom text. Then, Control-click and choose Styles from the shortcut menu's Font submenu. In the dialog box that appears, click the Add to Favorites button. In the *next* dialog box, type a name for your custom style, click both check boxes, then click the Add button.

To use that custom style, select the text you want to format, and Control-click on it to summon the shortcut menu. Choose Styles from the Font submenu, then click the Custom Styles button. Locate and choose your style in the pop-up menu, and click Apply.

Fun with glyphs. Some of Mac OS X's fonts contain beautiful alternative characters, such as ornamental swashes and flourishes. To explore and use these alternative glyphs, choose Typography from the [⚙▾] pop-up menu at the bottom of the Fonts panel. Then, explore the options in the Typography panel.

For a good example, choose the Zapfino font, then check out the Stylistic Variants portion of the Typography panel. The Apple Chancery font also has some interesting alternate characters.

Also, many fonts have old-style numerals that lend a classic look, as shown here with the Didot font.

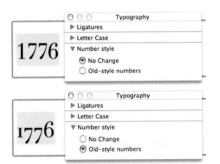

If a font provides old-style numerals, you'll see a Number Style entry in the Typography panel.

Who needs page numbers? Unless you're putting a table of contents or index in your book, you have little reason to print a page number on each page. To remove page numbers, use the Settings dialog box or Control-click on a blank area of a page and make sure that the Show Page Numbers command is unchecked in the shortcut menu.

Positioning Photos in Their Frames

As with the photos in a saved slide show, you can *soft crop* a photo—zoom in and move it around within its frame—by double-clicking the photo. This is a great way to fine-tune composition without having to crop the photo.

If you zoom in too far for a given photo's resolution, iPhoto displays the yellow triangle of doom to let you know that you won't get good quality at that zoom setting.

Changing Stacking Order

When you have multiple items on a page, you can change the way they overlap. For example, some themes position photos so they overlap. To change the way two photos overlap, Control-click on a photo and choose Move to Front or Send to Back.

Printing text on a photo. Want to print text directly on a photo? If you use the Travel theme, there's a way. Choose a two-photo page type and, from the Page Design pop-up menu, choose design 5, 6, 7, or 8. (The number appears to the right of the design thumbnail.) Place the photo so that it fills the page. Don't bother placing a photo in the smaller photo frame—you won't be using it. Type and format your text as desired, and then Control-click on the big photo and choose Move to Front.

Incidentally, you can also print text directly on a photo using the Folio theme. (Choose the one-photo page type.) But the text can't be very large.

Mirroring a Photo

Want to flip a photo so that it appears "backwards"? Select the photo in its book frame, then Control-click on it and choose Mirror Image from the shortcut menu.

Here's a fun and easy design trick: Duplicate a photo, then add it and its twin to the left and right pages of a two-page spread. Then, mirror one of the photos so that the two photos appear to reflect one another.

More Tips for Creating Books

Before You Buy

Before you click the Buy Book button to place your order, do one last proofreading pass of any text in your book. And remember, your Mac can help: select the text in a text box, Control-click, and choose Check Spelling from the shortcut menu's Spelling submenu.

Placeholder text. Also check to see that you haven't left placeholder text on any pages. (This is the stuff iPhoto inserts for you when you choose a page design that supports text. It usually says something profound, such as *Insert a description of your book*.) iPhoto is watching over you in this regard: if your book contains placeholder text and you click Buy Book, iPhoto warns that the placeholder text won't be printed.

Unused photo frames. Don't worry if any pages have unused (gray) photo frames. iPhoto simply ignores them.

Tip: The fact that iPhoto ignores empty photo frames opens up additional design options. For example, say you're creating a book in the Picture Book theme and you want a page with five photos on it—a page type Picture Book doesn't provide. Solution: choose the six-photo page type, but put only five photos on it.

From Book to Slide Show

iPhoto's book editor view provides a Play button that lets you display the pages of your book as a slide show. This opens up some interesting creative possibilities: you can take advantage of iPhoto's book themes and page designs to create "slides" containing multiple images and text. (In the interest of readability, think twice about using a lot of small text.)

You can also send a "book slide show" to iDVD; while in book-edit view, choose Share > Send to iDVD.

Clean Up Your Act

iPhoto provides a somewhat hidden (and completely undocumented) command that helps prepare a book for its voyage to Apple's printing service. The command is called Clean Up Book; to access it, Control-click on the gray area outside of your book's page boundaries to bring up a shortcut menu.

Here's what happens when you choose the Clean Up Book command.

1. iPhoto scans through the book from back to front to find the last-filled photo frame, called the *anchor*.

2. For all pages preceding the anchor, iPhoto removes empty photo frames and changes those pages' page types, if possible.

3. Beginning with the page immediately following the anchor, iPhoto places all unplaced photos by first filling any empty photo frames, then by adding pages.

Because this command can potentially alter your book's formatting (for example, by changing a three-photo page type to a two-photo page type), you might think twice before choosing it. It's better to go through your book yourself for final fine-tuning.

If you do use Clean Up Book and aren't happy with the results, choose Undo before doing anything else to restore your book's design.

Saving Interim Versions

iPhoto doesn't have a Save command, so there's no easy way to save your work as you produce a book (or slide show, for that matter). To commit your work to disk, quit iPhoto and then relaunch it.

Printing Your Book Yourself

iPhoto's Print command is alive and well when you're in book view: you can print some or all of your book for proofreading or to bind it yourself.

Printing a specific page is a bit cumbersome. Here's the easiest way to do it: in iPhoto's Print dialog box, click the Preview button. When Mac OS X's Preview program starts, display its drawer (choose Drawer from the View menu) to find the number of the page you want to print. Then, while still in the Preview program, choose the Print command and specify that page number.

From Book to Poster

How would like to take one page of a particular book and turn it into a 20- by 30-inch poster? If you have Photoshop or Photoshop Elements, you can. The trick involves saving a book design as a PDF, using Photoshop to extract a page from that PDF, saving that page as a JPEG image, then adding it to your iPhoto library.

Here are the details.

Step 1. Create an album containing the photos you want to put on your poster. Depending on the theme you choose, you can have up to 16 photos.

Step 2. Select the album, click the Book button, and choose a theme. Then, position the photos on one page as you want them to appear on your poster.

Step 3. Control-click a blank area of the page or outside the book's page boundaries and choose Save Book as PDF from the shortcut menu. Name the PDF.

Step 4. Switch to Photoshop and open the PDF you just created. The PDF Page Selector dialog box appears. Double click the poster-to-be page.

Step 5. When the Rasterize dialog box appears, specify dimensions of 11 by 8.5 and a resolution of 300 dots per inch. (Feel free to experiment with those values. The idea is to create a file with enough resolution for the print size you plan to order.) From the Mode pop-up menu, choose RGB.

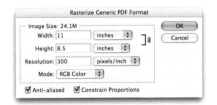

Step 6. After Photoshop opens the poster page, save it as a JPEG image, specifying a maximum quality setting of 12.

Step 7. Drag this JPEG image into your iPhoto window to add it to your library.

Step 8. Use the Order Prints button to order your poster.

Watch your cropping. As described on page 181, Kodak will crop your photo to fill the print size you've selected. To avoid surprises, you might want to crop your poster's JPEG so that its proportions match the print size you're ordering.

Variations on the theme. You can, of course, also use your poster image in a slide show—or even in a book. Indeed, you can use these steps to essentially combine book designs: create pages in one theme, convert them to JPEGs, then use them in a book based on a different theme.

More PDF Fun

Want to email a book to someone? Save the book as a PDF, then email the PDF. You can also post the PDF on a Web site or even store it in your iTunes library, if that's your idea of a good time (see page 78).

Creating a Photo Calendar

Store-bought calendars can be gorgeous, but they lack a certain something: *your* photos. Why build your year around someone else's photos when you can build it around your own?

With the calendar-publishing features in iPhoto, you can create calendars containing as few as 12 months and as many as 24. Choose from numerous design themes, each of which formats your photos and the dates of the month in a different way. Then drag photos into your calendar, fine-tuning their cropping along the way, if you like.

Commercial calendars usually have national holidays printed on them. Yours can, too—and then some. You can add your own milestones to your calendar: birthdays, anniversaries, dentist-appointment reminders. If you use Apple's iCal software (page 106), you can even import events from iCal and have them appear in your calendar.

When you're finished, click the Buy Calendar button. iPhoto transfers your photos and design to Apple's printing service, which prints your calendar and ships it to you. A 12-month calendar costs $19.99. Each additional month is $1.49.

And you don't have to postpone your foray into calendar publishing until next year. You can have your calendar begin with any month you like.

The Big Picture

Step 1. The most efficient way to create a calendar is to first add the photos you want to publish to an album.

Tip: To further streamline your layout work, sequence the photos in the album in the same general order in which you want them to appear in the calendar.

Step 2. Click the Calendar button (📅). The Themes panel appears.

Step 3. Choose a theme (click its name to see a preview of its design), then click Choose Theme.

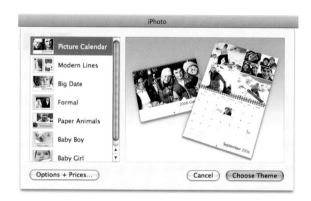

Step 4. Specify calendar details, then click OK. Here's your first big opportunity to customize the calendar so it contains dates that are important to you.

How many months? Type a number between 12 and 24 or click the arrow buttons.

When? Choose a starting month and a year.

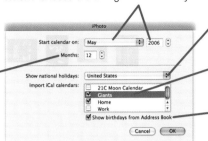

Veterans Day? Deepavali? Queen's Day? Specify your preferred national holiday list, or choose None.

Use iCal? To include iCal dates in your calendar, check the box next to the calendar.

Store birthdays in Mac OS X's Address Book program? You can automatically include them in your calendar.

Step 5. Drag photos into your calendar's pages, or click the Autoflow button ( ).

Switch between viewing calendar thumbnails (shown here) or photos you haven't yet placed in the calendar (page 196).

Switch views and perform various design tasks (page 196).

Layout for the lazy: click Autoflow, and iPhoto adds photos for you (page 196).

To replace this placeholder text with your own, select the text and type.

View the next or previous month.

Zoom in on a page for proofreading and fine tuning.

Step 6. Step through each month of the calendar, fine-tuning designs and adding custom date items as desired (see the following pages for details and tips).

You can adjust a photo's position within its frame.

Each calendar design offers a variety of photo arrangements, some providing space for captions.

To add text to a date, click its name and type the text in the box that appears. As page 197 shows, you can also add photos and captions to specific dates.

Step 7. Click [Buy Calendar] and pay using your Apple ID (page 15).

Tips for Creating Calendars

Choosing Photos

When creating a calendar, try to choose photos that relate to a given month. Use photos of a family member for the month of his or her birthday. If you have some particularly fine holiday shots, use them for the month of December. This sounds obvious, I know, but you'd be surprised how many times I see iPhoto calendars with photos that bear no relationship to the months in which they appear.

Think vivid. I've ordered several calendars, and in my experience, photos with soft, muted colors often print poorly. You're likely to see faint vertical stripes, sometimes called *banding*, in the photos. I get the best results when I use photos that have bright, vivid colors. Black-and-white photos work beautifully, too, provided they have strong contrast.

Layout Techniques

Laying out a calendar involves many of the same techniques behind book creation (pages 184–193). You can add photos by hand, dragging them from the thumbnails area into specific months, or you can click the Autoflow button and have iPhoto sling the photos into your year as it sees fit. As with books, I prefer the manual layout technique for calendars.

How many photos in a month? iPhoto's calendar themes, like its book themes, provide multiple page designs. Some designs provide for just one photo above a given month, while others allow for a half dozen or more.

I like to minimize the number of photos I put on each month. Bigger photos have a more dramatic look, and they're easier to see and appreciate when the calendar is hanging on a wall at the opposite end of a room. For most of my calendars, I put just one photo on each month.

That's a rule that begs to be broken, and I do break it now and then. If I have relatively low-resolution photos and iPhoto displays its yellow warning triangle, I'll switch to a page design that has smaller photo frames. Or if I have a series of photos that tells a story about a particular month, I'll choose a page design that lets me use all of those photos.

Top, bottom, or both? Normally, iPhoto's calendar view displays both halves of a given month—that is, the upper portion, where your photos appear, and the lower portion, where the days and weeks are displayed. Between those two halves is the spiral binding that holds the calendar together.

But when you're fine-tuning a calendar's design, you may find it useful to display only the upper or lower portions. The answer? Tear out the spiral binding. Click the single-pages View button (■), and iPhoto displays only the upper or lower portion of a month.

To switch between viewing the upper or lower portion of a month, display the calendar's page thumbnails (click the ▪ button at the top of the thumbnails area), then click the thumbnail of page you want to view.

Adding Photos to Dates

When creating a calendar, your photo options aren't limited to just the page above each month. You can also add photos to individual dates. To commemorate a birthday, add a photo to the birthday girl's date. To never forget your anniversary, put a wedding photo on the date. (Another good way to never forget an anniversary is to forget it just once, but this method is not recommended.)

To add a photo to a date, drag it from the thumbnails area of the calendar.

To remove a photo from a date, select the date and press the Delete key.

Don't Forget the iCal Angle

When creating a new calendar, you can choose to have iPhoto include event information from iCal (discussed on page 106). You can also add iCal data to an existing calendar by clicking the Settings button and checking the appropriate Use iCal Calendars box.

Don't use iCal to manage your life? As I mentioned on page 107, you can download thousands of calendars from Apple's iCal site as well as iCalShare (www.icalshare.com). Because I like my calendars to include the phases of the moon, I subscribed to a lunar calendar at iCalShare. When I'm creating a new calendar, I simply check the moon-phases calendar and iPhoto does the rest.

Improving Your Calendar Typography

Many of the typographic tips that apply to books (pages 190–191) also apply to calendars.

Global formatting. You can change the fonts that iPhoto uses for various elements of the calendar—its dates and

captions, for example—by clicking the Settings button, then clicking Fonts. Most of the items in the Settings dialog box are self-explanatory. The two that are less than obvious are Page Text and Comments. The Page Text item controls the font in which dates, days of the week, and the month appear. The Comments item controls the formatting of custom text that you add.

Local formatting. As with books, you can also override iPhoto's font settings and apply formatting to individual text items, but within limits: you can't apply local formatting to a specific date. (For example, you can't have February 14 appear in a bold red font.) You can apply local formatting only to comments and photo captions. To do so, display the

item's text box (click on the date, and the text box zooms into view), then select the text and use the Fonts panel as described on pages 190–191.

Curl those quotes. It's common to use apostrophes in calendars: *Sophie's Birthday*, *President's Day*, and so on. But iPhoto commits a cardinal typographic sin by using those heinous "typewriter quotes" instead of true typographer's quotes:

Heinous: Sophie's Birthday

Correct: Sophie's Birthday

Fortunately, it's easy to make your quotes typographically correct. To get a true typographer's apostrophe, press Shift-Option-] (that's the right-bracket key, just above the Return key).

Customizing Photos on Dates

You can customize the way a photo appears on a date.

iPhoto displays the date to which the photo belongs.

To display a text caption adjacent to the photo, check the Caption box. iPhoto uses the photo's title as the caption text, but you can replace that text by selecting it and typing your own. (For details on assigning titles to photos, see page 120.)

As with slide shows and books, you can fine-tune a photo's composition without having to use the Crop tool. Drag the size slider to zoom in, then drag the photo within its frame until it's positioned as desired.

Photo captions appear on an adjacent date, with an arrow pointing to the photo. To choose where the caption appears, click an arrow. In this example, I've clicked the left arrow, telling iPhoto to display the caption on the date to the left of the photo.

Creating Greeting Cards and Postcards

Let us hereby resolve to never buy a greeting card from a store rack again. Okay, maybe that's a bit strong. But with the greeting card and postcard features in iPhoto, you can definitely curtail your contributions to Hallmark's balance sheet.

An iPhoto greeting card measures 5 by 7 inches, and is of the "tent" variety—folded on its top. (Assuming you use a horizontally oriented photo, that is: if you use a vertically oriented photo, the card's fold is on the left side.) In quantities of 1 to 24, cards cost $1.99 each. Order 25 to 49 cards for $1.79 each; 50 or more cards are $1.59.

As for postcards, they measure 4 by 6 inches and cost $1.49 each (1–24), $1.29 (25–49), or $.99 (50 or more). The back of a postcard can contain a full block of text or you can use a standard postcard-mailing format, complete with a "place postage here" box.

Greeting cards and postcards are printed on a heavy card stock and include matching envelopes. Even if you order a postcard with a "place postage here" box, you still get an envelope—complete with an embossed Apple logo on its flap.

So forget this era of email and instant messaging, and use iPhoto to create some old-fashioned correspondence. Your recipients will thank you.

Creating a Greeting Card

Step 1. Select the photo that you want on the greeting card.

Step 2. Click the Card button.

Card

Step 3. Choose Greeting Card from the pop-up menu, choose a theme, then click Choose Theme.

I'm partial to the Picture Card theme, which prints a borderless photo.

Step 4. Replace the card's placeholder text with your own and then fine-tune the design, if desired (opposite page).

Tip: To have the inside of the card appear blank, just leave the placeholder text as is—or, if you're nervous about getting a card that contains the heartwarming message *Insert Title*, delete the placeholder text.

Step 5. Proofread any text you added, then proofread it again. Then, click Buy Card and pay using your Apple ID (page 15).

Creating a Postcard

Step 1. Select the photo you want to include on the postcard.

Step 2. Click the Card button.

Step 3. Choose Postcard from the pop-up menu, choose a theme, then click Choose Theme.

The themes are similar to their greeting-card counterparts.

Step 4. Replace the card's placeholder text and then fine-tune the design, if desired.

Step 5. Do that proofreading thing you do so well, then click Buy Card and pay using your Apple ID.

Card Design Tips

Switching postcard styles. To switch between a self-mailing postcard and one that tucks into an envelope, select the back of the postcard, then use the Design pop-up menu.

Switching designs and backgrounds. All card themes provide more than one design option for the front of the card. Many themes, for example, provide an option that lets you type some text on the front of the card. To access different designs, select the front of the card, then use the Design pop-up menu.

Many theme designs also offer a selection of background colors or textures. You can access them by using the Background pop-up menu.

Fine-tuning photos. As with books, slide shows, and calendars, you can adjust the cropping and positioning of a photo in a card without having to use iPhoto's Crop tool. Simply double-click on the photo, then use the slider to zoom in as desired. To position the photo within its frame, drag it.

Fun with fonts. As with books and calendars, you can customize the font formatting of your card in two ways: by using the Settings button, or by bringing up the Fonts panel (⌘-T). The latter option lets you format text on an individual word (or character, if you want to taunt the design police) basis.

And while you're having fun with fonts, note that the text-formatting tips outlined on pages 190–191 also apply to cards.

Print it yourself. As with books, you can print greeting cards and postcards on your own color inkjet printer. Just choose the Print command while the card editor is visible. Note that if you plan to use both sides of the card, you'll need to use inkjet paper designed for double-sided printing.

Kill the apple. Ever conscious of brand recognition, Apple prints its logo on the back of a greeting card. If you'd rather not provide the free advertising, click the Settings button and uncheck the box labeled *Include Apple logo on back of card.*

Why are these kids smiling?

More Ways to Share Photos

By using the Export command in the File menu, you can turn a photo album—or any set of photos that you've selected—into a portable slide show.

iPhoto can combine a series of photos into a QuickTime movie, complete with a music soundtrack from your iTunes library. You can publish the resulting movie on a Web site, burn it to a CD, or bring it into iDVD and burn it to a DVD. Think of an iPhoto QuickTime movie as a portable slide show. It will play back on any Mac or Windows computer that has QuickTime installed.

As you know, you can create two kinds of slide shows in iPhoto—basic and saved (see pages 160–165). You can export either type as a QuickTime movie. If you export a saved (cinematic) slide show, the resulting movie will have all your Ken Burns moves and custom transition and duration settings. On the other hand, if you simply export an album or selection of photos as a movie, each photo is always separated by a dissolve transition. You can't use the other transitions, such as Cube, that iPhoto's Slideshow dialog box provides, nor will your movie have any automatic Ken Burns moves. When your sweet tooth craves eye candy, you'll want to create a saved slide show and export it.

Looking for still more ways to share? Redecorate your Macintosh desktop with your favorite photo. Or, use a set of photos as a screen saver.

It's obvious: if your digital photos aren't getting seen, it isn't iPhoto's fault.

Exporting a Saved Slide Show Movie

Step 1. In the Source list, select the saved slide show that you want to export. **Note:** If you plan to distribute your slide-show movie, don't use songs from the iTunes Music Store; see page 208.

Step 2. Choose Export from the File menu, and specify export settings.

Name your movie. iPhoto normally stores exported movies in your Movies folder, but you can store them anywhere you like.

Choose a movie size. For a movie destined for email or a Web site, choose the Small or Medium option. If you plan to import your movie into iMovie HD, choose Large.

Portable slide show: An iPhoto-created QuickTime movie playing back in the QuickTime Player program.

Tips

Heading for iDVD? If you want to include a cinematic slide show in an iDVD project, you have an alternative to the Export command: just choose Send to iDVD from the Share menu. iPhoto creates a movie version of your slide show and sends it directly to iDVD.

Heading for iMovie HD? Want to add your exported movie to an iMovie HD project? It's easy: just drag the movie into the iMovie HD window. But take note: because of the way iPhoto prepares movies, the slide show is likely to look a bit fuzzy when you view it on a TV set.

Exporting a Basic Slide Show Movie

Step 1.
Select a set of images or switch to an album, then choose Export from the Photos menu.

Step 2.
To access movie-export options, click QuickTime.

Specify the duration for each image to display.

You can specify that iPhoto add a background color or background image to the movie. The color or image appears whenever the dimensions of the currently displayed photo don't match that of the movie itself. (For example, in a 640 by 480 movie, the background will be visible in photos shot in vertical orientation.) The background will also be visible at the beginning and end of the movie—before the first image fades in and after the last image fades out.

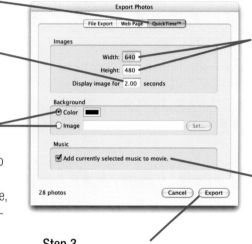

Specify the desired dimensions for the movie, in pixels. The preset values shown here work well, but if you specify smaller dimensions, such as 320 by 240, you'll get a smaller movie file—useful if you plan to distribute the movie over the Internet.

iPhoto uses the song or playlist assigned to your photo library or to the current album (see page 164). To create a silent movie, uncheck this box. **Note:** If you plan to distribute your slide-show movie, don't use songs from the iTunes Music Store; see page 208.

Step 3.
To create the movie, click Export and type a name for the movie.

Using Photos as Desktop Images and Screen Savers

iPhoto's Desktop button lets you share photos with yourself. Select a photo and click Desktop, and iPhoto replaces the Mac's desktop with the photo you selected.

If you select multiple photos or an album, your desktop image will change as you work, complete

with a cross-dissolve effect between images. It's an iPhoto slide show applied to your desktop.

Another way to turn an iPhoto album into a desktop screen saver is to use the Desktop & Screen Saver system preference—choose the album in the Screen Savers list (right).

Warning: Using vacation photos as desktop images has been proven to cause wanderlust.

Burning Photos to CDs and DVDs

The phrase "burning photos" can strike terror into any photographer's heart, but fear not: I'm not talking about open flames here. If your Mac has a CD or DVD burner, you can save, or burn, photos onto CDs or DVDs. You can burn your entire photo library, an album or two, just a few photos, or even just one.

iPhoto's burning features make possible all manner of photo-transportation tasks. Back up your photo library: burn the entire library and then stash the disc in a safe place. Move photos and albums from one Mac to another: burn a selection, then insert the disc in another Mac to work with them there. Or send a few high-resolution photos to a friend who has a slow modem connection: burn the photos and pop the disc into the mail.

iPhoto doesn't just copy photos to a disc. It creates a full-fledged iPhoto library on the disc. That library contains the images' titles and keywords, any albums that you burned, and even original versions of images you've retouched or cropped. Think of an iPhoto-burned disc as a portable iPhoto library.

iPhoto's burning features are compatible with any CD or DVD burner supported by Mac OS X. If you can burn with iTunes, you can burn with iPhoto, too.

Now back away from that fire extinguisher—we've got some burning to do.

Burning Basics

Burning photos involves selecting what you want to burn, then telling iPhoto to light a match.

Step 1. Select items to burn.

Use the selection techniques discussed on page 131 to specify which photos to burn. Remember that you can also select multiple albums by Shift-clicking or ⌘-clicking on each one.

You can also select multiple books, folders, and slide shows—iPhoto can burn them, too. Indeed, burning a disc is the only way to move a book or saved slide show from one Mac to another.

Step 2. Choose Burn Disc from the Share menu.

iPhoto asks you to insert a blank disc.

Tip: If you burn discs frequently, you can have iPhoto display a Burn button in its toolbar. From the View menu's Show in Toolbar submenu, choose Burn.

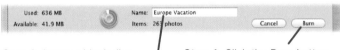

Step 3. Insert a blank disc and click OK.

iPhoto displays information about the pending burn. You can add photos to or remove them from the selection, and iPhoto will update its information area accordingly.

Tip: Give your disc a descriptive name by typing in the Name box.

Step 4. Click the Burn button.

iPhoto displays another dialog box. To cancel the burn, click Cancel. To proceed, click Burn.

iPhoto prepares the images, then burns and verifies the contents of the disc.

Working with Burned Discs

When you insert a disc burned in iPhoto, the disc appears in iPhoto's Source list. To see its photos, select the disc's name. Note that the disc's photos aren't in the iPhoto library on your hard drive— they're in the iPhoto library on the disc.

If the disc contains multiple albums, a small triangle appears next to the disc's name. To view the disc's albums, click the triangle.

You can display photos on a disc using the same techniques that you use to display photos stored in your iPhoto library. You can also display basic slide shows, email photos, and order prints.

However, you can't edit photos stored on a burned disc, nor can you create an iWeb photo album, a saved slide show, a book, a calendar, or a greeting card. To perform these tasks, add the photos to your photo library as described at right.

Copying Items from a Burned Disc

To modify a photo, book, or slide show that's stored on a burned disc, you must copy it to your iPhoto library.

To copy a set of photos, select them and drag them to the Library item in the Source list.

To copy an album, folder, book, or slide show from a burned disc, select it in the Source list and drag it up to the Library item.

Note: When copying a book or saved slide show to a different Mac, be sure that the destination Mac contains the same fonts or music used in the book or slide show.

Burning CDs for Windows Computers

The burning feature in iPhoto creates a disc intended to be used by iPhoto. Among other things, that means that the disc contains a convoluted folder structure that can only be deciphered by iPhoto.

If you want to burn some photos for a friend who uses Windows— or send them to a photofinisher— you need to use a different procedure. You can also use these steps to burn a disc for a fellow Mac user who doesn't use iPhoto.

Step 1. Prepare a disc. Insert a blank CD or DVD in your Mac's optical drive. The dialog box below appears.

Type a name for the CD and click OK. The blank disc's icon appears on your desktop.

Step 2. Copy the photos. Position the iPhoto window so that you can see it and the blank disc's icon. Drag the photos that you want to burn to the icon of the blank disc.

As an alternative to dragging photos, you can also select them and use the File menu's Export command to export copies to the blank disc. This approach gives you the option of resizing the photos and changing their file names.

Step 3. Burn. To burn the disc, drag its icon to the Burn Disc icon in your dock. (The Burn Disc icon replaces the Trash icon when you've selected a blank disc.) In the dialog box that appears next, click the Burn button.

Creating and Managing Photo Libraries

As your photo library grows to encompass thousands of photos, locating specific images can be cumbersome. A huge photo library is also more difficult to back up, since it may not fit on a CD or even a DVD.

One solution: create more photo libraries. iPhoto lets you have multiple photo libraries and switch between them. If your photo library has reached gargantuan proportions, back it up and create a new, empty one.

How often should you create a new library? That depends. You might base your decision on disk space: if you back up your library by burning it to a DVD-R, create a new library each time the size of your current library reaches about 4GB. That way, you can always be sure your library will fit on a DVD. (To see how much space your library uses, select the Library item in the Source list, then look in the Information pane.)

Or, you might prefer a chronological approach. If you take hundreds of photos (or more) every month, consider creating a new library each month. Then again, maybe a subject-oriented approach is best for you. Use one iPhoto library to hold your family shots, and another to hold work-related shots.

The latest iPhoto versions are fast enough to manage thousands of photos, especially if you view your library by roll, and close rolls you don't need to view. But if dividing your photo collection across multiple libraries makes managing and backing up photos easier for you, here's what you need to know.

Creating a New Library

Before creating a new library, you may want to back up your existing library by dragging your iPhoto Library folder to another hard drive or to a blank CD or DVD. For some backup strategies, see the sidebar on the opposite page.

Step 1. Quit iPhoto.

Step 2. Locate your iPhoto Library folder and rename it.

To quickly locate the folder, choose Home from the Finder's Go menu, then double-click the Pictures folder, where you'll find the iPhoto Library folder.

Step 3. Start iPhoto.

iPhoto asks if you want to locate an existing library or create a new one.

Step 4. Click Create Library.

iPhoto proposes the name iPhoto Library, but you can type a different name if you like.

You don't need to store your library in the Pictures folder; see the sidebar below.

Step 5. Click Save, and iPhoto creates the new, empty library.

Switching Between Libraries

There may be times when you want to switch to a different iPhoto library—for example, to access the photos in an older library. Here's how.

Step 1. Quit iPhoto.

Step 2. Locate your current iPhoto library folder and change its name.

Step 3. Start iPhoto.

iPhoto asks if you want to find an existing library or create a new one.

Step 4. Click Find Library. The Open Photo Library dialog box appears.

Step 5. Select the library you want to use and click the Open button.

Managing and Backing Up Your Library

Storing Photos Elsewhere

Normally, iPhoto stores your photo library in the Pictures folder. You might prefer to store your library elsewhere, such as on an external FireWire hard drive.

To store your photo library elsewhere, quit iPhoto, then simply move the iPhoto Library folder wherever you like. If you're copying the library to a different disk, delete the original library folder

after the copy is complete. Restart iPhoto, click the Find Library button, and use the Open Photo Library dialog box to aim iPhoto in the right direction.

Backing Up

In the film days, you had to fall victim to a fire or other disaster in order to lose all your photos. In the digital age, it's much easier to lose photos; all it takes is a hardware failure or software glitch.

Please don't let photo loss happen to you. Take the time to back up your iPhoto libraries.

If your Mac contains a burner and your library will fit on a single blank disc, use iPhoto's burning features to back up.

If you don't have a burner or your library won't fit on a single disc, buy an external FireWire hard drive and drag your iPhoto Library folder over to it. Repeat this procedure every now and then.

Have an iPod with some free disk space? Activate its disk mode (page 98), and copy your iPhoto Library folder to it.

If you don't want to buy a hard drive, use backup software. Apple's own Backup, included with a .Mac membership, can copy photos to CDs, DVDs, or hard drives. Many other backup programs are available, including Dantz Development's powerful Retrospect and Econ Technologies' friendly ChronoSync.

Getting Old Photos into iPhoto

You love your digital camera and the convenience of iPhoto, and it would take an act of Congress to force you to use film again.

And yet the past haunts you. You have boxes of negatives and slides that you haven't seen in years. If you could get them into iPhoto, you could organize them into albums and share them through Web albums, slide shows, prints and books, and even movies and DVDs.

To bridge the gap between pixels and print, you need a scanner. Here's an overview of what to look for, and some strategies for getting those old photos into iPhoto.

Scanning the Options

Before you buy a scanner, take stock of what types of media you'll need to digitize. Do you have negatives, prints, slides, or all three? Not all scanners are ideal for every task.

Flatbed scanners. If you'll be scanning printed photos, a *flatbed scanner* is your best bet. Place a photo face down on the scanner's glass, and a sensor glides beneath it and captures the image.

Repeating this process for hundreds of photos can be tedious. If you have a closet full of photos, you may want to look for a scanner that supports an automatic document feeder so you can scan a stack of photos without having to hand-feed the scanner. Some flatbeds include photo feeders that can handle up to 24 prints in sizes up to 4 by 6 inches. Other scanners accept optional document feeders. Just be sure to verify that the document feeder can handle photos—many can't.

Film scanners. A print is one generation away from the original image, and may have faded with time or been poorly printed to begin with. Worse, many photos are printed on linen-finish paper, whose rough texture blurs image detail when scanned. Bottom line: you'll get better results by scanning the original film.

Many flatbed scanners include a film adaptor for scanning negatives or slides. With some scanners, the adaptor snaps on to the scanner's bed. A more convenient option is a scanner with the adaptor built into the lid, such as Epson's Perfection 4990 Photo. The Perfection 4990 can scan negatives, mounted slides and, unlike many flatbeds, medium-format film, such as the 120 format popular in old cameras.

A flatbed scanner with a film adaptor is a versatile scanning system, but a *film scanner* provides much sharper scans of negatives and slides. Unfortunately, this quality will cost you: film scanners cost more than flatbeds.

Many film scanners provide a dust- and scratch-removal option called Digital ICE (short for *image correction/enhancement*). Developed by Kodak's Austin Development Center (www.asf.com) and licensed to numerous scanner manufacturers, Digital ICE does an astonishingly good job of cleaning up color film. However, it doesn't work with black-and-white negatives.

Scanning Right

Whether you use a flatbed or film scanner, you'll encounter enough jargon to intimidate an astronaut: histograms, tone curves, black points, white points. Don't fret: all scanners include software that provides presets for common scanning scenarios, such as scanning for color inkjet output. Start with these presets. As you learn about scanning, you can customize settings to optimize your exposures.

The right resolution. A critical scanning setting deals with how many dots per inch (dpi) the scanner uses to represent an image. Volumes have been written about scanning resolution, but it boils down to a simple rule of thumb: If you're using a flatbed scanner and you plan to print your scans on a photo inkjet printer, you can get fine results with a resolution of 180 to 240 dpi. If you plan to order photographic prints from your scans, scan at 300 dpi. Scanning at more than 300 dpi will usually not improve quality—but it will definitely use more disk space.

Film scanners are different. A film scanner scans a much smaller original— for example, a 35mm negative instead of a 4 by 6 inch print. To produce enough data for high-quality prints, a film scanner must scan at a much higher resolution than a flatbed. The film scanner I use, Minolta's Scan Elite 5400, scans at up to 5400 dpi.

This difference in approach can make for even more head scratching when it comes time to decide what resolution to use. Just do what I do: use the presets in the scanning software. I typically choose my film scanner's "PhotoCD 2048 by 3072" option, which yields a file roughly equivalent to a six-megapixel image.

Special circumstances. If you plan to apply iPhoto's or iMovie HD's Ken Burns effect to an image, you'll want a high-resolution scan so you can zoom in without encountering jagged pixels. Experiment to find the best resolution for a specific image and zoom setting.

In a related vein, if you plan to crop out unwanted portions of an image, scan at a higher resolution than you might normally use. Cropping discards pixels, so the more data you have to begin with, the more cropping flexibility you have.

Format strategies. Which file format should you use for saving images? iPhoto works best with JPEG images, but the JPEG format is *lossy:* it sacrifices quality slightly in order to save disk space. If this is the last time you plan to scan those old photos, you may not want to save them in a lossy format.

When scanning my old slides and negatives, I save the images as TIFF files. Then, I use Photoshop Elements' Process Multiple Files command to save a second set of photos in JPEG format. This gives me JPEGs that I can use in iPhoto, while my original, uncompressed scans are safely archived.

(If you don't have Photoshop Elements, you can perform this automation chore using a utility such as Yellow Mug Software's EasyBatchPhoto, available at www.yellowmug.com.)

Photos, Meet iPhoto

Once you've scanned and saved your photos, you can import them into iPhoto.

Filing photos. To take advantage of iPhoto's filing features, you may want to have a separate iPhoto roll for each set of related photos. In the Finder, move each set of related photos into its own folder, giving each folder a descriptive name, such as *Vacation 1972.* Next, drag each folder into the iPhoto window. iPhoto gives each roll the same name as its corresponding folder.

You can delete the folders after you've imported their shots, since iPhoto will have created duplicates in its iPhoto Library folder. (If you prefer to retain your existing filing system, you can set up iPhoto to not copy the photos to the iPhoto Library folder; see page 211.)

Turn back the clock. To make your iPhoto library chronologically accurate, change the date of each roll to reflect when its shots were taken, not when you imported them. First, click on the roll's name (if you can't see it, choose Film Rolls from the View menu). Next, type the desired date in the Information pane.

Time for retouching. You can use iPhoto's Retouch tool to fix scratches and dust specks, and its Enhance button and Adjust panel to fix color and exposure problems. For serious retouching, though, use Photoshop Elements or Photoshop. To learn more about digital retouching, I recommend Katrin Eisman's *Photoshop Restoration and Retouching, Third Edition* (New Riders, 2005).

Plug in to photo enhancement. Old photos do fade away, typically acquiring a blue or red tint as their dyes, well, die. If you have patience and a good eye for color, you can improve an old photo's color using iPhoto's Adjust panel or Photoshop.

If you have $49, you can buy a Photoshop plug-in that does the job for you. Digital ROC, from Kodak's Austin Development Center, does an amazing job of improving faded photos. Digital ROC also works in Photoshop Elements. You can download a trial version of it, and more, at www.asf.com.

iPhoto Tips

Red-Eye Removal the Old Way

Apple changed the way red-eye removal works in iPhoto 5 (see page 137). For some cases of red eye, I find the old way works better. Fortunately, it's still available: after opening a photo in edit view, drag across the subject's eyes to enclose them in a rectangle. Then, press the Option key while clicking the Red-Eye button.

If you don't like the results, undo and try the standard technique on page 137.

Entering Custom Crop Proportions

With the Constrain pop-up menu in edit view, you can tell iPhoto to restrict cropping rectangles to standard proportions (page 137). If you want non-standard proportions, choose Custom from the Constrain pop-up menu and enter the proportions in the subsequent dialog box.

Keyword Assistant

Ken Ferry's free Keyword Assistant is an iPhoto plug-in that gives you more ways to assign keywords to photos. You'll find it at VersionTracker and other download sites.

Tinting a Black-and-White Photo

You can use the Adjust panel's color-adjustment sliders to apply a color tint to a black-and-white photo. After converting the photo to black and white (and improving on it using the tip on page 147, if you like), save the photo. Then reopen it in edit view and drag the color sliders.

Purchased Songs and Slide Shows

You can use songs from the iTunes Music Store for slide show soundtracks. But if you plan to export the slide shows as QuickTime movies, note that the songs will play only on computers authorized for your iTunes account. The workaround: burn the songs to an audio CD, then re-rip them into iTunes, and use those unprotected versions for your soundtracks.

Controlling the Camera Connection

You can use the Image Capture program, included with Mac OS X, to control what happens when you connect a digital camera to your Mac. By choosing the Preferences command from the Image Capture menu, you can have the Mac start up iPhoto, start up Image Capture or a different program, or do nothing at all.

Rebuilding Your iPhoto Library

If iPhoto is acting up—for example, taking forever to launch, running unusually slowly, or not displaying photo thumbnails—try rebuilding your iPhoto library. Quit iPhoto, then hold down the ⌘ and Option keys while starting iPhoto. A dialog box appears asking if you're sure you want to rebuild your library and giving you several options for doing so.

If your image thumbnails appear gray or blank, try selecting the first two options. If iPhoto crashes or refuses to load photos when you first launch it, try the third option. If some of your photos seem to have disappeared, try the last option. And if iPhoto is misbehaving in several ways, check all four options.

Important: To avoid the risk of making a bad situation worse, consider backing up your iPhoto Library folder before trying to rebuild your library.

Get links to iPhoto add-ons and
additional online photo services.
www.macilife.com/iphoto

Importing Only Some Images

Speaking of Image Capture, it's the program to use when you want to import only some photos from a camera. Say you've shot twenty photos but you know only five of them are going to be keepers. Rather than import all twenty into iPhoto and then delete fifteen of them, use Image Capture.

After connecting your camera and turning it on, start up Image Capture and click its Download Some button. A window appears containing thumbnail versions of each photo.

Next, you need to tell Image Capture where to store the downloaded photos. I like to store them in a temporary folder

that I create on my desktop. From the Download Folder pop-up menu in Image Capture's toolbar, choose Other. Press ⌘-D to jump to your desktop and then click the New Folder button. Name the folder anything you like—I use the name *Import Me.* Then click the Open button.

Finally, click the Download button to download the photos you selected. Quit Image Capture, drag those photos into your iPhoto window, and delete the temporary folder.

Yes, it's a bit of work, but it's a good technique to use if your camera contains dozens of images and you know you'll only be keeping a small selection of them.

Another way to be selective. Many cameras *mount* on the Mac's desktop as though they were storage devices (which, in a way, they are). If your camera does, you have another way to selectively import photos into iPhoto.

To determine if your camera mounts on the desktop, turn the camera on and connect it. Switch to the Finder and see if a new icon appears on your desktop and in the sidebar area of the Finder's windows. If it does, you can examine the photos on its memory card. Double-click the camera's icon, then double-click the folder named DCIM. Inside *that* folder are one or more folders containing your photos. To preview them, double-click their icons. To copy a photo into iPhoto, drag its icon from the Finder into the iPhoto window.

When your memory card contains many images but you want to copy only a few of them, this method can be faster than the Image Capture technique.

You can even use the Finder to help you determine which images to bring in: choose Show View Options from the Finder's View menu, and check the Show Icon Preview box. Now enlarge the preview icons by dragging the slider at the top of the View Options window.

And by the way, *all* memory readers mount on the desktop, so even if your camera doesn't, you can still use this technique: just pop your memory card into a reader.

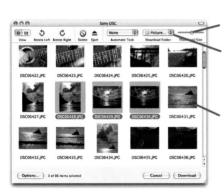

Adjust the size of the thumbnails.

Use the Download Folder pop-up menu to specify where you want downloaded items to be stored.

Select the photos you want to download, remembering to Shift-click to select multiple photos.

More iPhoto Tips

Including Photos in Documents

You may want to include photos in documents that you're creating in Microsoft Word or other programs. It's easy: just drag the image from iPhoto into your document.

If you drag an image to the Finder desktop or to a folder window, iPhoto makes a duplicate copy of the image file. Use this technique when you want to copy a photo out of your library.

Stay Out of the Library

I've mentioned it before, but it bears repeating: *never* add files to or remove them from the folders inside the iPhoto Library folder. Indeed, I recommend that you don't even venture inside this folder. Renaming, moving, or otherwise modifying files inside your iPhoto Library folder is a great way to lose photos. Let iPhoto manage the library for you—add and remove photos only by dragging them into and out of the iPhoto window.

Hacking iPhoto's Book Themes

If you're adventuresome, you can modify iPhoto's book themes to create new themes of your own design. The job isn't for the faint of mouse, and I don't have room to go into all the details here. But if you're already a Mac power user, the following information should be enough to make you dangerous.

Warning: If you delete or alter parts of iPhoto that you shouldn't, you may have to reinstall iPhoto. You might want to duplicate your iPhoto application (select its icon and press ⌘-D), then hack the duplicate.

First, quit iPhoto, and then locate its icon in your Applications folder. Control-click on the icon and choose Show Package Contents from the shortcut menu. In the window that appears, double-click the Contents folder, then double-click the Resources folder. Inside the Resources folder, you'll find a folder named Themes.

Inside *that* folder you'll find a folder for each theme. To modify one, make a duplicate (select and press ⌘-D). Then, double-click the duplicate. Inside, you'll find a folder named Contents. Open it, then open the Resources folder inside. You've reached the treasure.

Of the many files inside a theme's Resources folder, a few are of particular interest. The file named *implementation.strings* contains details about the theme, including its text-color definitions and the default page-layout arrangement that iPhoto uses.

The file named *DesignPrototype.plist* is another key player. It contains information about the theme's page types and designs. Explore this file, and you'll find ways to rotate the text that appears on pages, to create new photo frames, and much more.

And finally, inside the English.lproj folder, you'll find a file named *Localizable.strings*. This file contains the theme's name as it appears in iPhoto's Theme browser.

Also of note is the Shared folder inside the Themes folder. It contains graphic elements that iPhoto places on your book pages, such as the little passport stamps in the Travel theme and the colored backgrounds in the Watercolor theme. By altering these graphics, you can customize your themes.

Just be careful out there.

Make a "Life Poster"

In January 2005, software developer Mike Matas published instructions on how to use iPhoto to create what he called a "life poster"—a large print comprising a collage of 98 smaller images.

It was an exceptionally cool project, but it required quite a few steps, not to mention a trip into Photoshop. Could the process be automated? Could it be automated with Automator, the Mac OS X Tiger technology that puts your Mac on autopilot?

The answers to those questions are yes and yeah, baby.

There's an Automator action that you can download from my Web site that does the job for you. Select 96 photos in your iPhoto library, click a button, then sit back and watch while your Mac does the work of assembling the photos into a spectacular poster. There's no need to manually crop anything, no need for Photoshop or custom paper sizes. When your Mac is done, you can order a 20- by 30-inch poster through iPhoto.

You'll find everything you need to make your own life poster at www.macilife. com/iphoto.

Adding Without Copying

Since the dawn of time—well, since the dawn of version 1.0—iPhoto has always stored images in its iPhoto Library folder. Generally, that's exactly what you want: when you copy photos from a camera or memory card, you want them stashed safely in your iPhoto Library.

But under some circumstances, iPhoto's "do things my way" approach to organization can work against you. As I mention on page 119, when you add photos that are already stored on your hard drive—for example, images that you've scanned and saved—iPhoto makes additional copies in its iPhoto Library folder.

After adding photos to your Library that are already on your hard drive, you need to delete the originals. That isn't exactly a

sweat-breaking chore, but it does take time. And you might prefer to stick with your existing filing system.

Beginning with iPhoto 6, Apple added the option to *not* copy image files to the iPhoto Library folder. If you have a large library of scanned images on your hard drive, you might want to take advantage of this option. You won't have duplicate photos to delete, and you won't have to change the filing system you've developed for your scanned images.

To activate this option, choose Preferences from the iPhoto menu, click the Advanced button, and then uncheck the box labeled *Copy files to iPhoto Library folder when adding to library.*

From this point on, when you copy existing files to your iPhoto library, iPhoto simply creates aliases for each file. (In Mac OS parlance, an *alias* is a small file that simply points to an existing file.) If you edit an image, iPhoto stores the edited version in your iPhoto Library folder, within a folder named Modified.

And by the way, unchecking this option does *not* change how iPhoto stores photos that you're importing from a camera or media reader. Photos that you import from a location other than a hard drive are always stored in your iPhoto Library folder.

Warning: There is one exception to the previous paragraph, and it can cause big trouble if you aren't careful. If you copy photos from a media reader by dragging their icons from the Finder into the iPhoto window, iPhoto creates aliases to the photos on your memory card. If you try to open one of those photos later, an error message warns that the photo can't be found. And, of course, if you've erased your card, the photo is gone for good.

This same problem can occur if you copy files from a camera whose card appears on the Finder's desktop, as described on page 209. Frankly, not-so-little wrinkles like this keep me from unchecking the *Copy files to iPhoto Library* box. I'd rather let iPhoto handle the filing of my photos.

Sharing Your Camera on a Network

When you use the sharing features in iTunes and iPhoto, you're using a Mac OS X networking technology called Bonjour. Bonjour lets devices on a network work together without you having to fuss with networking settings.

The humble Image Capture program also supports Bonjour, and you can use it to share your camera on a network—or even on the Internet. These may not be the most practical tasks in the world, but they're fun geek experiments.

I've written up some tips for using these capabilities; you'll find them at www. macilife.com/iphoto.

Mastering Your Digital Camera

Resolution Matters

Always shoot at your camera's highest resolution. This gives you maximum flexibility for cropping, for making big prints, and for Ken Burns effect in iPhoto and iMovie HD. You can always use iPhoto to make photos smaller (for example, for emailing or Web publishing).

Shutter Lag

Many digital cameras suffer from a curse called *shutter lag*—a delay between the time you press the shutter button and the moment when the shutter actually fires.

Shutter lag occurs because the camera's built-in computer must calculate exposure and focus. If you're shooting fast-moving subjects, it's easy to miss the shot you wanted.

The solution: give your camera a head start. Press and hold the shutter button partway, and the camera calculates focus

and exposure. Now wait until the right moment arrives, then press the button the rest of the way.

ISO Speeds

In the film world, if you want to take low-light shots, you can buy high-speed film—ISO 400 or 800, for example. Fast film allows you to take nighttime or indoor shots without the harsh glare of electronic flash.

Digital cameras allow you to adjust light sensitivity on a shot-by-shot basis. Switch the camera into one of its manual-exposure modes (a common mode is labeled *P*, for *program*), and then use the camera's menus to adjust its ISO speed.

Note that shots photographed at higher ISO speeds—particularly 400 and 800—are likely to have digital *noise*, a slightly grainy appearance. For me, it's a happy trade-off: I'd rather have a sharp, naturally lit photo with some noise than a noise-free but blurry (or flash-lit) photo.

Higher ISO speeds can also help you capture fast-moving action by day. The higher speed forces the camera to use a faster shutter speed, thereby minimizing blur. That shot on this page of Mimi leaping into the air? Shot at ISO 400.

White Balance

Few light sources are pure white; they have a color cast of some kind. Incandescent lamps (light bulbs) cast a yellowish light, while fluorescent light is greenish. Even outdoors, there can be light-source variations—bluish in the morning, reddish in the evening. Each of these light sources has a different *color temperature*.

Our eyes and brains compensate for these variances. Digital cameras try to do so with a feature called *automatic white balance*, but they aren't always as good at it. That's why many cameras have manual white balance adjustments that essentially let you tell the camera, "Hey, I'm shooting under incandescent (or fluorescent) lights now, so make some adjustments in how you record color."

White balance adjustments are usually labeled WB, often with icons representing cloudy skies ☁, incandescent lamps ☀, and fluorescent lighting ☲. You'll probably have to switch to your camera's manual-exposure mode to access its white balance settings.

Sharpness and Color Settings

Digital cameras do more than simply capture a scene. They also manipulate the image they capture by applying sharpening and color correction (including white balance adjustments).

Some photographers don't like the idea of their cameras making manipulations like these. If you're in this group, consider exploring your camera's menus and tweaking any color and sharpness settings you find.

For example, one of my cameras—Sony's 8-megapixel F828—has two color modes: "standard" and "real." The "standard" mode is the default mode, and it punches up the color in a way that I find artificial. One of the first things I did when I got this lovely machine was to switch its color mode to "real."

Another of my cameras (I collect them, or so it sometimes seems) is Canon's 5-megapixel S50. It has several sharpening modes, and the default mode is too sharp for my tastes. I took its sharpening mode down a couple of notches. If I feel that an image needs a bit of sharpening, I'll bring it into Photoshop and sharpen it there.

Custom White Balance

Most cameras also let you create a custom white-balance setting. Generally, the process works like this: put a white sheet of paper in the scene, get up close so the paper fills the viewfinder, and then press a button sequence on the camera. The camera measures the light reflected from the paper, compares it to the camera's built-in definition of *white*, and then adjusts to compensate for the lighting.

If you're a stickler for color and you're shooting under strange lighting conditions, creating a custom white balance setting is a good idea.

Better still, shoot in raw mode if your camera allows it. Then you'll have complete control over color balance.

Stay Sharp

A camera's built-in LCD screen is great for reviewing a shot you just took. But the screen is so tiny that it's often hard to tell whether the photo is in sharp focus.

Most cameras allow you to zoom in on a photo while displaying it. I like to zoom in and verify that my photo isn't blurred—especially if the subject is still in front of me and I have another chance.

If your camera has an electronic viewfinder, it can be a superior alternative to the LCD screen for reviewing your shots, especially in bright light.

Your Camera's Histogram

If you read through pages 144 and 145, you've seen the value that a histogram display can offer for making exposure adjustments.

Many mid-range and all high-end cameras can display a histogram, too, which you can use to adjust exposure settings *before* you take a photo.

With your camera in one of its manual-exposure modes, activate the histogram display. Then adjust your exposure settings—shutter speed, ISO speed, and aperture—so that the histogram's data is as far to the right-hand side of the graph as possible without introducing white clipping. (Remember, white clipping means lost highlight detail.)

Photography gurus call this technique *exposing to the right*, and it ensures that you're getting as much image data as your camera is capable of capturing.

Photographer Michael Reichmann, publisher of the magnificent Luminous Landscape site, has written an excellent tutorial on using histograms when shooting. I've linked to it on www.macilife.com/iphoto.

Learning More

To learn more about digital photography and Photoshop, I heartily recommend *Real World Digital Photography* by Katrin Eisman, Seán Duggan, and Tim Grey (Peachpit Press, 2004).

Tips for Better Digital Photography

Get Up Close

Too many photographers shy away from their subjects. Get close to show detail. If you can't get physically closer, use your camera's zoom feature, if it has one. If your camera has a macro feature, use it to take extreme close-ups of flowers, rocks, seashells, tattoos—you name it. Don't limit yourself to wide shots.

Vary Your Angle

Don't just shoot from a standing position. Get down into a crouch and shoot low— or get up on a chair and shoot down. Vary your angles. The LCD screen on a digital camera makes it easy—you don't press your eye to the camera to compose a shot.

Changing your angle can be a great way to remove a cluttered background. When photographing flowers, for example, I like to position the camera low and aim it upwards, so that the flower is shot against the sky.

Avoid Digital Zooming

Many digital cameras supplement their optical zoom lenses with digital zoom functions that bring your subject even closer. Think twice about using digital zoom—it usually adds undesirable artifacts to an image.

Position the Horizon

In landscape shots, the position of the horizon influences the mood of the photo. To imply a vast, wide open space, put the horizon along the lower third of the frame and show lots of sky. (This obviously works best when the sky is cooperating.) To imply a sense of closeness— or if the sky is a bland shade of gray— put the horizon along the upper third, showing little sky.

This rule, like others, is meant to be broken. For example, if you're shooting a forlorn-looking desert landscape, you might want to have the horizon bisect the image to imply a sense of bleak monotony.

Crop Carefully

You can often use iPhoto's cropping tool to fix composition problems. But note that cropping results in lost pixels, and that may affect your ability to produce high-quality prints. Try to do your cropping in the camera's viewfinder, not iPhoto.

Kill Your Flash

I turn off my camera's built-in flash and rarely turn it on. Existing light provides a much more flattering, natural-looking image, with none of the harshness of electronic flash. Dimly lit indoor shots may have a slight blur to them, but I'll take blur over the radioactive look of flash any day.

Beware of the Background

More accurately, *be aware* of the background. Is a tree growing out of Mary's head? If so, move yourself or Mary. Are there distracting details in the background? Find a simpler setting or get up close. Is your shadow visible in the shot? Change your position. When looking at a scene, our brains tend to ignore irrelevant things. But the camera sees all. As you compose, look at the entire frame, not just your subject.

Embrace Blur

A blurred photo is a ruined photo, right? Not necessarily. Blur conveys motion, something still images don't usually do. A photo with a sharp background but a car that is blurred tells you the car was in motion. To take this kind of shot, keep the camera steady and snap the shutter at the moment the car crosses the frame.

You can also convey motion by turning this formula around: If you pan along with the moving car as you snap, the car will be sharp but the background will be blurred. Here's a canine-oriented example.

Compose Carefully

Following a couple of rules of thumb can help you compose photos that are more visually pleasing.

First, there's the age-old *rule of thirds*, in which you divide the image rectangle into thirds and place your photo's subject at or near one of the intersections of the resulting grid.

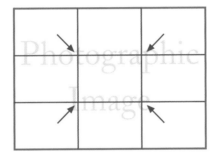

Place your photo's subject at or near these intersections.

This composition technique yields images that are more visually dynamic.

A second technique is to draw the viewer's eyes to your subject and add a sense of dynamism by using diagonal lines, such as a receding fence.

No Tripod?

If you want to take sharp photos in low light, mount your camera on a tripod. If you don't have a tripod handy, here's a workaround: turn on your camera's self-timer mode—the mode you'd usually use when you want to get yourself in the picture—then set the camera on a rigid surface and press the shutter button. Because you won't be holding the camera when the shutter goes off, you won't risk getting a blurred shot.

Go Wide: Shooting Panoramas

A photograph is a keyhole that reveals only a slice of a scene. Back in the film days, I'd capture wide vistas by shooting several pictures, moving the camera between taking each one. Then I'd line up my prints on the dining room table to create a crude panorama.

The digital world is such a better place. Photographing a panorama still involves taking multiple shots, but the similarities end there. After you've transferred the shots to your Mac, you can *stitch* them into a single, seamless image. Then, print your panorama on a photo printer or bring it into iPhoto and order photographic prints.

Making digital panoramas can be a complex process involving specialized stitching software and tripod accessories. But it doesn't have to be. You can get great outdoor panoramas with a hand-held digital camera and the Photomerge feature in Adobe Photoshop Elements.

Shoot. Turn. Repeat.

In a good panorama, the seams where images overlap are invisible. Photoshop's Photomerge feature blends images beautifully, but it helps to shoot with stitching in mind.

Cameras that think wide.

Many cameras have panorama modes: one side of the camera's screen shows a small version of the last shot you took, making it easier to line up the camera for the next slice.

No panorama mode? Just do your best to rotate the same amount between shots. Be sure to include plenty of overlap— 20 to 40 percent—between images.

Consistency counts. Stitching works best when there isn't significant tonal variation from one image to the next. A panorama mode helps here, too—the first shot you take after activating panorama mode determines the exposure and white-balance settings for the remaining shots. If your camera lacks a panorama mode, use one of its manual white-balance settings.

Don't use your zoom lens between shots or change your position significantly. Plant your feet (or your tripod's), and rotate from there.

On the level. Keep your camera level. A tripod helps but isn't essential if you're shooting outdoor panoramas of distant scenes, especially if your camera has a panorama mode. (I hand-held my Canon S-50 for the panorama here.)

Camera positioning is more critical for indoor panoramas or for outdoor scenes with objects close to the camera. To avoid distortion, the camera should rotate over the optical center of its lens. A tripod isn't enough—because your camera's tripod-mounting hole is offset from the center of the lens, the camera won't rotate properly, and the panorama will probably have flaws. For example, the edges of a doorway might appear twice—much as they do on New Year's Eve.

You can retouch some stitching flaws in Photoshop, but you can avoid them to begin with by shooting with a panorama tripod head, such as Kaidan's KiWi (www.kaidan.com). Its adjustable brackets, bubble levels, and calibrated rotation wheel make it easy to follow the rules of panoramic shooting.

Stitching Your Shots

Here's a look at the stitching process in Photoshop Elements.

Step 1: Open Your Originals

In Elements, choose Photomerge Panorama from the File menu's New submenu, then open the images you shot.

Step 2: Refine

Photomerge blends your shots. You can fine-tune overlaps by hand, if necessary. You can often get smoother blends by checking the Advanced Blending box.

Step 3: Crop and Polish

If you hand-held your camera, your panorama is likely to have ragged edges. Use the Crop tool to exclude these ragged edges. Finally, retouch and enhance as needed.

After the Stitch

Into iPhoto. Save your panorama in JPEG format (quality setting of 12), then drag its icon into the iPhoto window. Now you can use iPhoto to print the panorama. Or use the panorama in an iPhoto book or slide show—or in iMovie HD. (Ken Burns *loves* panoramas.)

Printing panoramas. A letter-sized sheet of photo paper doesn't do justice to a wide image, delivering a narrow strip of an image only a few inches high. There are better ways to print panoramas.

Many photo printers can accept roll-fed paper—ideal for dramatic, banner-sized panoramas. In the Print dialog box, be sure to choose the paper size option for roll-fed or panorama paper.

You can also order prints through iPhoto. A 20- by 30-inch print costs $22.99, but you can take advantage of a panorama's narrow orientation to put two panoramas on one photo.

Use Photoshop to combine two panoramas into a single image. Next, bring the combined JPEG into iPhoto and order your print. When it arrives, carefully cut the two panoramas apart. Don't have a steady hand? Have the surgery done at a print shop.

Panoramas in books. iPhoto's double-sided photo book designs make it possible to print a panorama across a two-page spread. After stitching your panorama, use Photoshop to crop and resize it to yield an image 8.5 inches high by 22 inches wide (assuming a large-size book).

Next, use Photoshop's Crop tool to divide the image into two 11-inch-wide slices. Save each as a separate JPEG, import them into iPhoto, then position one slice on the left-hand page and the other on the right. If the images don't align perfectly, zoom and position them within their photo frames until they do (see page 203).

Incidentally, I shot this panorama with a hand-held camera pointed out a restaurant window. There's glare on the glass and the exposure isn't perfect—but it beautifully evokes a sunny lunch overlooking Paris.

Beyond Photoshop. If the panorama bug bites, you might want to explore more-advanced stitching options. Check out the Stitcher family of products from RealViz (www.realviz.com). These programs also enable you to create interactive QuickTime VR panorama movies (you'll find some at www.jimheid.com/fun).

iMovie HD:
Making Movies

iMovie HD at a Glance

Video can be a powerful vehicle for communicating an idea, setting a mood, selling a product, or recalling a memory. It can also be great way to put people to sleep.

Video editing is the process of assembling video clips, still images, and audio into a finished package that gets your message across and keeps your audience's eyes open. Video editing is what iMovie HD is all about.

With iMovie HD, you can import video from a video camera. iMovie HD stashes incoming clips on its Clips pane. If you're using a miniDV or HDV camera, iMovie HD even controls your camera during the importing process.

Then, you edit clips and sequence them by dragging them to the timeline, optionally adding music from your iTunes music library and creating titles, effects, and scene transitions. When you're finished, a few mouse clicks send your efforts back out to tape or to iDVD.

You can use iMovie HD to edit interminable home movies, but you can also use it to assemble montages of photos from iPhoto, promotional videos, and anything else that belongs on the small screen. iMovie HD supports more video formats than did earlier iMovie versions, and that means more options for you.

Quiet on the set.

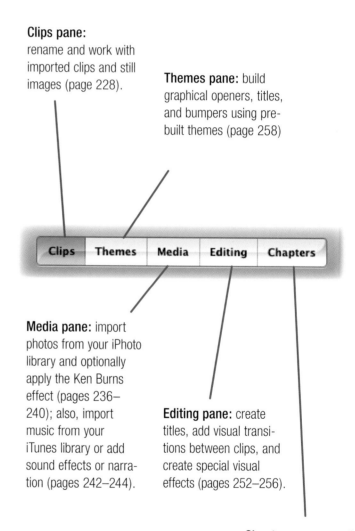

Clips pane: rename and work with imported clips and still images (page 228).

Themes pane: build graphical openers, titles, and bumpers using prebuilt themes (page 258)

Media pane: import photos from your iPhoto library and optionally apply the Ken Burns effect (pages 236–240); also, import music from your iTunes library or add sound effects or narration (pages 242–244).

Editing pane: create titles, add visual transitions between clips, and create special visual effects (pages 252–256).

Chapters pane: create DVD or podcast chapter markers before sending your movie to iDVD, iWeb, or GarageBand (page 266).

The monitor displays video as you import it or play it back.

Switch between the clip viewer and the timeline viewer (page 231).

The scrubber bar lets you move through and crop a clip (page 228).

Your project's video format appears here (page 224).

Adjust the playback volume as you work in iMovie HD.

Video clips and still images that you import are stored in the Clips pane until you add them to the timeline.

The *playhead* indicates the current playback location. Drag it left and right to quickly move backward and forward within your movie or within a single clip.

These buttons switch between iMovie HD's panes, each of which lets you work with a different kind of element.

Create bookmarks to aid in editing and trimming clips (page 232).

You can sequence clips by dragging them from the Clips pane to the timeline (page 230).

Display a track's audio waveform to be able to see changes in the audio (page 246).

Reclaim disk space by emptying the iMovie HD trash (page 229).

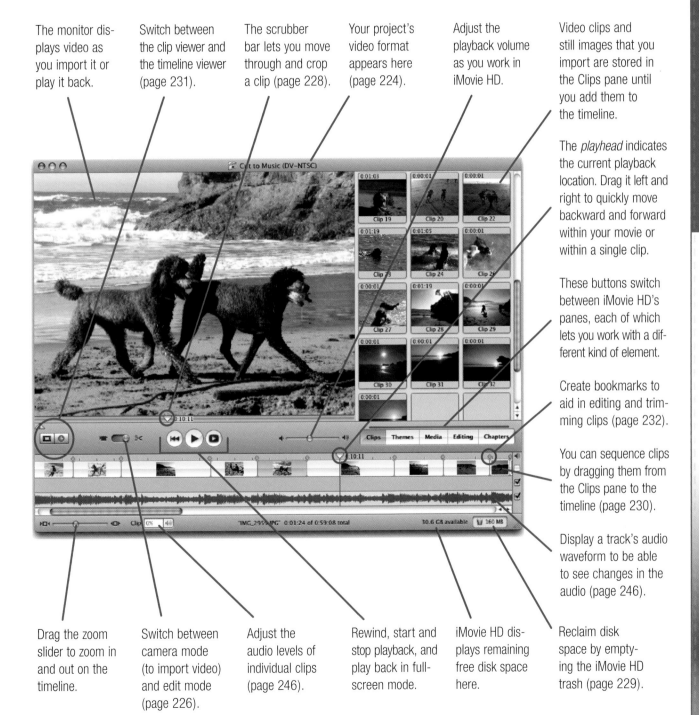

Drag the zoom slider to zoom in and out on the timeline.

Switch between camera mode (to import video) and edit mode (page 226).

Adjust the audio levels of individual clips (page 246).

Rewind, start and stop playback, and play back in full-screen mode.

iMovie HD displays remaining free disk space here.

221

The Essentials of Movie Making

Editing video is one of the most complex tasks you will perform in iLife. Not that it's technically difficult—iMovie HD, FireWire, and the latest video formats have made it easier than ever.

But editing video can be time consuming and labor intensive. Bringing media into iMovie HD, fine-tuning the length of clips, timing shots to match a music track, adding transitions and effects—it all takes time. But as a creative exercise, video editing is hard to beat.

If you're new to video editing, start small. Create a short movie—between 30 and 90 seconds. Try your hand at a simple music video: some video, some still photos from iPhoto, and a music soundtrack from iTunes. Your first effort shouldn't be an epic; it should be a short story, or even a single well-wrought paragraph. That's the best way to learn the art and science of editing—and to appreciate its magic.

Video Editing: The Big Picture

Import Assets

Bring in video from a camcorder and, optionally, add photos and music from iTunes.

Trim the Fat

Use iMovie HD's crop markers and Crop command to discard unwanted portions of clips.

Sequence Clips

Drag clips to the timeline viewer and clip viewer to add them to your final movie. Trim clips as needed to fine-tune their length.

Polish

If you've added music or other audio tracks, you'll want to fine-tune audio levels for each track.

Add Eye Candy

Create transitions between clips, and add titles and any special effects.

Export

Record your movie back to tape, send it to iDVD, GarageBand, or iWeb; or export it as a QuickTime movie for playback on an iPod or other device.

A Short Glossary of Video Terms

aspect ratio The relationship of height to width in an image. A standard-definition TV image has an aspect ratio of 4:3—four units of width for each three units of height.

clip A piece of video footage or a still image. A finished movie generally contains multiple clips, sequenced on the timeline.

FireWire The high-speed interface used to connect video gear, such as a miniDV camcorder, to the Mac. Also used for other devices, including hard drives and, of course, the iPod.

frame A single still image in a movie clip, and the smallest unit of a movie clip you can work with. One second of video contains 30 frames.

HDV Short for high-definition DV, an up-and-coming video format that stores ultra-sharp video on standard miniDV cassettes.

miniDV Often abbreviated DV, a video format that stores high-quality video and stereo audio on a tiny cassette. The miniDV format has been a major factor in the digital-video revolution.

playhead iMovie HD's equivalent to the blinking cursor in a word processor. As a clip plays back, the playhead moves to show where you are in relation to the entire movie or video clip.

rendering The process of creating frames for a transition, title, or effect.

transition A special effect that acts as a segue between two clips.

track An independent stream of audio or video. iMovie HD lets you have one video track and two separate audio tracks.

A Short Lesson in Video Formats

If you have a standard, miniDV camcorder and you're anxious to start making movies, feel free to skip this little lesson and move on to page 226. But if you want to use video from a different kind of device—or you're curious about one of iMovie HD's most intriguing capabilities—read on.

Just as music and photos can be stored in a variety of digital formats, video also comes in several flavors. And, as with music and photos, each video format takes its own approach to organizing the bits and bytes that make up your media.

In early iMovie versions, projects were based on one video format: DV. You could import other formats into iMovie, but iMovie would convert that footage into DV format. DV was iMovie's native tongue, and using other formats meant a translation step that took time, used up disk space, and often compromised video quality.

Times change. New types of video devices have appeared, and iMovie has evolved to keep pace: iMovie HD provides native support for several video formats. iMovie HD is multilingual, and as a result, you have the flexibility to edit video from a wider variety of video devices, ranging from Apple's inexpensive iSight to many digital camera models to the new breed of high-definition HDV cameras from companies such as Sony and JVC.

iMovie HD's basic operation is identical regardless of which video format you use. There are some subtleties to some formats, and I'll share them as we go. But first, let's look at the video languages iMovie HD understands.

How Square Are Your Movies?

Many of the differences among video formats aren't visible at first glance, but one of the differences definitely is: the *aspect ratio* of the video frame.

We encountered the concept of aspect ratio when looking at iPhoto cropping techniques (page 137). The phrase simply describes how square or rectangular an image frame is.

Early iMovie HD versions were limited to one aspect ratio: the standard 4:3 ratio used by most TV sets, DV camcorders, and digital cameras.

Four units of width...

...for every three units of height.

Going wide. iMovie HD adds the ability to work with and create widescreen video in the 16:9 aspect ratio—the format common in high-definition TV sets.

Sixteen units of width...

...for every nine units of height.

The widescreen format provides a more cinematic experience.

Pronunciation guide. Making video small talk at the local coffee shop? The expressions *4:3* and *16:9* are usually pronounced "four by three" and "sixteen by nine." Technically, "four *to* three" and "sixteen *to* nine" are more accurate, since these expressions are ratios. After all, when was the last time you heard a bookie describe "2 by 1" odds on a horse?

Choosing a Video Format

Normally, iMovie HD projects are based on the DV format. If you're using a standard miniDV camcorder with its factory settings, you don't have to bother with choosing a format since iMovie HD is preset to speak its mother tongue.

If you're using a different kind of device or you've set your DV camera to 16:9 mode, you need to tell iMovie HD which format to use. You do that when creating a new project.

To access the Format pop-up menu, click the triangle.

DV. By far the most common format used by digital camcorders, and the format iMovie HD uses for any new project unless you specify otherwise. Now that the era of high-definition TV is upon us, the DV format is often described as a *standard definition* format.

DV Widescreen. Most DV camcorders can shoot in widescreen mode, often by simply cropping the top and bottom of the video frame. (To shoot in this mode, use your camcorder's menus to activate 16:9 mode.) You don't get the picture quality of high-definition TV, but you do get that cinematically wide image.

HDV 1080i and HDV 720p. High definition (HD, for short) TV is gradually gaining momentum, and the new breed of HDV camcorders is helping. The HDV

format brings high-definition videography to advanced amateurs and budget-minded professionals (and, as prices come down, to the rest of us). HDV always uses a 16:9 aspect ratio. For more information on the HDV format, see page 262.

MPEG-4. Many digital cameras shoot their movie clips in this format, as do a growing number of compact video cameras that connect via USB. For tips on importing and working with MPEG-4 clips, see page 263.

iSight. Apple's inexpensive iSight camera, which is built into some current Mac models, is designed for video chatting using iChat AV, but makes a great low-budget TV camera, too. For advice on shooting with an iSight, see page 263.

Mixing Video Formats in a Single Project

Sometimes, you may want to—or *have* to—mix video formats within a single project. Maybe you have a digital camera movie clip that you want to add to a project that's in DV format. Or perhaps you have some 16:9 DV footage that you want to include in a 4:3 DV project. Or maybe you're making a montage of MPEG-4 digital camera movies,

but you're using the DV format so you can output the final montage to a miniDV camcorder.

You can do all of these things and more. If you import a movie clip in which the video format differs from your project's format, iMovie HD converts the clip into whatever format your project uses. This conversion process is called *transcoding*, but you can

also call it *waiting*—it can take a long time. And use a lot of disk space.

Say you import an MPEG-4 digital camera movie clip into a DV project. The movie clip might have a small frame size and use only 20MB of disk space, but in order to make it compatible with your DV-based project, iMovie HD will change its frame size

and other characteristics to conform to the DV standard. The DV version of that movie might take up 120MB.

For these reasons, it's best to stick with one video format within a single project. But when you don't have a choice, iMovie HD is ready—provided you have the time and the disk space.

Importing DV and HDV Video

The first step in an iMovie HD editing project usually involves importing video that you've shot. If you're using a miniDV or HDV camera, you can connect the camera to your Mac's FireWire jack and use iMovie HD's camera mode to bring in your video. (If you're using a different kind of camera, your import procedure will be a bit different; see page 262).

With camera mode, you can control your camera using the transport buttons in iMovie HD's window. There's no need to grope for the tiny buttons on your camera when you need to rewind, fast-forward, stop, or play. Click the on-screen transport buttons, and iMovie HD sends the appropriate signals to your camera through the FireWire cable. Video professionals call this *device control*.

The first step in editing a movie may be importing video, but another step should come first: making sure you have enough free disk space. Digital video eats disk space like I eat Oreos: for miniDV video, you'll need about 200MB of free space for each minute of video. For HDV video, you'll need a few times that amount. Planning to use titles, transitions, and effects? They take up space, too. Bottom line: think about buying an external hard drive and using it for your video endeavors.

Importing from a FireWire Camera

Step 1. Connect your DV or HDV camera to your Mac's FireWire jack.

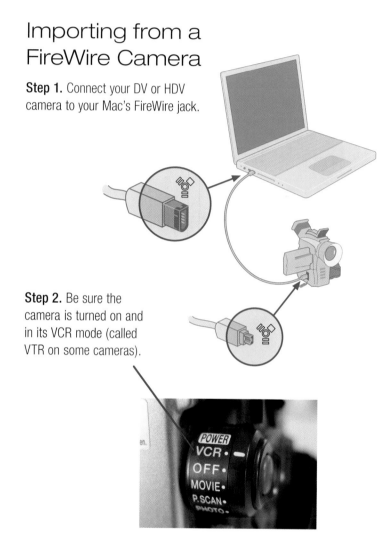

Step 2. Be sure the camera is turned on and in its VCR mode (called VTR on some cameras).

Tip: To store imported video on an external hard drive, simply create your project on the external drive. If you've already started the project and it's on your internal drive, quit iMovie HD, copy the project to the external drive, then open that copy.

Step 3. To start and stop importing, click Import or press the spacebar while the tape is playing back.

When iMovie HD is in camera mode, the playback buttons control your camera.

Click the camera icon and choose your camera from the popup list to put iMovie HD in camera mode.

00:04:24:05

Camera Connected

Import

iMovie HD displays the time code that your camera recorded on the tape. This can help you keep track of where you are on a tape as you fast-forward or rewind.

iMovie HD displays each clip you import on the Clips pane.

Tip: You can also have iMovie HD add imported clips directly to the timeline; in the Import portion of the Preferences dialog box, click the Movie Timeline button.

HD Differences

HD Importing from an HDV camera? With slower Macs, you'll experience an odd delay as the video comes in: the tape may finish playing, but you'll still see video being displayed in iMovie HD's monitor area. The video's motion may also appear jerky.

This occurs because your Mac must transcode (convert) the HD video into a format that allows for fast editing. On the fastest, dual-processor G5 Power Macs and

Intel-based Macs, this process occurs more or less in real time; not so on slower Macs.

One ramification: it's a bit harder to tell when to stop importing, since your Mac may be displaying footage that the camera actually played back seconds or minutes earlier.

To selectively import HDV footage to a slower Mac, view the footage on your camera's LCD screen during the import, and use your camera's buttons to stop and start playback.

Using iMovie HD's Scene-Detection Feature

To make your imported video easy to work with, use iMovie HD's scene-detection feature, which causes iMovie HD to begin a new clip each time it detects a scene break. (Your

camcorder generates a scene break automatically each time you press its Record button.)

To turn on scene detection, choose Preferences from the

iMovie HD menu, then click the Import button in the Preferences dialog box. Next, click the check box labeled *Start a new clip at each scene break.*

Working with Clips

After you import video and other assets, the real work (and fun) of building your movie begins.

All building projects require advance preparation, and video editing is no exception. You might begin by renaming your clips to give them descriptive names. You don't have to rename clips, but doing so can make them easier to sort out and manage.

Next, you might crop a clip to remove footage you don't want. iMovie HD defines cropping differently than imaging programs, such as iPhoto. When you crop a clip in iMovie HD, you change its length, not its dimensions—you remove seconds or minutes, not pixels. After cropping a clip, you might add it to the movie by dragging it to the timeline at the bottom of the screen.

As you perform these tasks, you'll often work with iMovie HD's playhead, moving it to the start of a clip, or dragging it back and forth—a process called *scrubbing*—to find the portion you want to retain.

Naming and cropping—these are the chores that prepare clips for their screen debut. And that debut occurs when you drag the clips to the timeline.

Rename Your Clips

iMovie HD automatically names imported clips, giving them names, such as Clip 01 and Clip 02, that aren't exactly descriptive. Give your clips descriptive titles, such as Bird Close-up or Beach Long Shot, to help you identify them. To rename a clip in the Clips pane, simply click its name and type a new name. Or, double-click on a clip and type a new name in the Clip Info dialog box. You can also rename clips in the clip viewer (described on page 231).

Cropping Clips

Any clip you import may have extraneous junk at its beginning and end. By cropping the clip to remove this excess, you can prepare the clip for its screen debut.

Tip: If you're planning to add a transition before or after a clip, make the clip a bit longer than you otherwise would.

Step 1. Select the clip you want to crop. You can also crop a clip that you've already added to the timeline.

Step 2. Click just below the monitor, then drag the triangular crop markers left and right to mark the footage you want to keep. To review your selection, drag the playhead left and right.

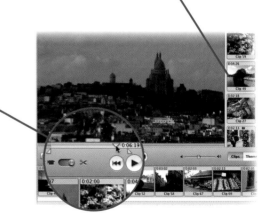

Step 3. To perform the crop, choose Crop from the Edit menu (or press ⌘-K).

As you adjust the crop markers, the bottom of the iMovie HD window (not shown here) tells you how long the cropped clip will be.

Trashing Footage

Chances are your Clips pane will contain clips that you don't end up using. To reclaim disk space, discard those clips: select them and press the Delete key, or drag the clips to the Trash in the lower-right corner of the iMovie HD window.

When you crop a clip, iMovie HD doesn't actually discard any footage. That's great in that it lets you reclaim cropped footage as described at right.

But what if you want to free up disk space by deleting footage you *know* you won't be using? Unlike with previous versions, you're out of luck in iMovie HD 6. Even if you split a clip, throw away one half, and empty the trash, that deleted footage still exists. The upside is that you won't accidentally delete footage you

might want later; the downside is that you're using more hard disk space.

For details on managing iMovie HD's Trash, see page 233.

Reclaiming the Past

You're working on your movie and realize that a shot you cropped really needs to be longer after all. To restore the cropped footage, select the clip, then choose Revert Clip to Original from the Advanced menu.

The Keys to Precision

To fine-tune a crop marker's position, select the crop marker and press the keyboard's left and right arrow keys to move the marker in one-frame increments. To move in 10-frame increments, press Shift along with the arrow key. These keyboard controls work throughout iMovie HD.

Controlling What Plays

You already know that clicking the play button or pressing the spacebar begins playback. You may have noticed that *what* iMovie HD plays back depends on what is selected.

You can choose to play just one item—a clip, a title, a transition, and so on—by selecting that item, then clicking on the play button or pressing the spacebar. This can be a handy way to check out a title or transition you've just added. To play back a portion of your project, select those items by Shift-clicking, then start playback.

To play an entire project, press your keyboard's Home key, then press the space bar.

Trimming Clips (and the Pros and Cons of Jump Cuts)

Trimming is the opposite of cropping. When you crop, you use the crop markers to indicate which portion of a clip you want to keep. When you trim, you use the crop markers to indicate what you want to delete. Drag the crop markers left and right to mark the footage that you want to toss to the cutting room floor. Then, press your keyboard's Delete key or choose Clear from the Edit menu.

It's best to use trimming to remove footage from the very beginning or very end of a clip. If you delete footage from the middle of a video clip, you'll end up with an awkward, visually jarring jump in the action. This kind of sloppy splice is called a *jump cut,* and it's often a sign of shoddy movie-making.

Then again, one director's flaw might be another's effect. Jump

cuts are common special effects in music videos and other "arty" productions.

To avoid a jump cut, put a cutaway or reaction shot at the point where the jump cut would be (see page 234). If you don't have a cutaway or reaction shot, put a three- to five-frame cross-dissolve transition at the jump cut point. This is called a *soft*

cut, and it's common in documentaries and newscasts.

By the way, don't confuse this form of trimming with the direct trimming feature described on page 230. Direct trimming involves changing the start or end point of a clip by dragging its edges in the timeline.

Timeline Techniques: Adding Clips to a Movie

A clip in the Clips pane is like a baseball player on the bench. To put the clip on the playing field, you must add it to the timeline.

Select the clip, then drag it to the timeline.

Tip: Want to insert a clip between two clips that are already on the timeline? Just drag the clip between them, and the two existing clips separate to make room for the addition. (If a transition is between the two clips, you need to delete it first; see page 253.)

Other Ways to Add Clips

Usually, you work with one clip at a time, dragging it to the timeline after you've cropped it as described on the previous pages. But there's more than one way to work with clips.

Drag several at once. You can add multiple clips to the timeline at once. Select each clip by Shift-clicking on it, then drag the clips to the timeline as a group. You can also select multiple clips by dragging a selection rectangle around them; click the narrow gray border between clips to begin drawing the selection.

Drag from another project. If you have more than one iMovie HD project open, you can drag clips from one project to another.

Paste from the Clipboard. You can also add a clip to the timeline using the Paste command. Select a clip in the Clips pane— or a clip that's already in the timeline— and cut or copy, then paste. You can even paste clips from a different iMovie HD project, although if the clips use a different video format, iMovie HD will have to transcode them when you paste. (See the sidebar on page 225.)

Directly from your camera. If you'll be using almost all of the footage you shot— in the order in which you shot it—you might want to have iMovie HD add your clips directly to the timeline when you import your video. In the Import portion of the Preferences dialog box, click the Movie Timeline button.

Timeline Versus Clip: Which Viewer to Use?

You can view your project's march of time in either of two ways: using the timeline viewer or the clip viewer. Each viewer has its strengths, and you're likely to switch between them frequently as you work on a movie. To switch between views, click the clip viewer button or the timeline viewer button, or press ⌘-E.

The Clip Viewer: Basic Sequencing

The clip viewer shows large thumbnail versions of each clip. In this viewer, you can change the order of clips by dragging them left and right. You can also rename clips here. However, this viewer does not show audio tracks or provide audio controls. The clip viewer is ideal when you're first assembling a movie or you want to experiment with different clip sequences. When it's time for audio fine-tuning and other precise work, switch to the timeline viewer.

The Timeline Viewer: Audio, Trimming, and More

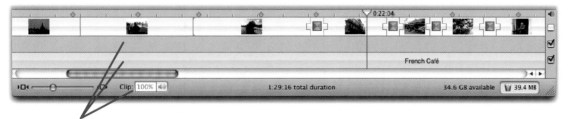

The timeline viewer adds two audio tracks and a control for adjusting audio levels.

Use the timeline viewer to work with sound and trim clips directly as described on the following pages. Unlike earlier iMovie versions, iMovie HD also lets you change the order of clips in the timeline viewer.

Advanced Timeline Techniques

In a well-edited video, the cuts between scenes occur at exactly the right moments. In movies, the action cuts between two actors as they converse, reinforcing both the dialog and the drama. Every moviegoer has experienced this, probably without even thinking about it.

In music videos, scenes change in rhythm with a piece of music, turning the visuals and the soundtrack into a unified performance. Every MTV viewer has seen this, probably without even thinking about anything at all. (I'm kidding, kids—music videos are among the most tightly edited productions on the planet.)

In iMovie HD, several features work together to let you edit with precision. You can set *bookmarks,* visual guideposts that aid in trimming and positioning clips. You can trim clips directly in the timeline, much as you can in high-end programs, such as Apple's Final Cut family. And *timeline snapping* makes it easy to move clips to the desired location as you drag them to and within the timeline viewer.

Setting Bookmarks

A bookmark is a virtual Post-It note that you can tack onto the timeline. Want to go back and refine a section later? Set a bookmark so you don't lose your place. Want to time edits to music? Create bookmarks at each beat, measure, or other musical milestone.

To create a bookmark, position the playhead where you want the bookmark to be, then choose Add Bookmark from the Markers menu or press ⌘-B. A bookmark appears as a small green diamond on the timeline.

Tips: You can set a bookmark while your movie is playing. Press ⌘-B to create a bookmark without halting playback.

You can use the Markers menu or keyboard shortcuts to jump from one bookmark to the next. Press ⌘-[to move to the previous bookmark and ⌘-] to move to the next one.

Trimming Clips in the Timeline

With iMovie HD's direct trimming feature, you can remove footage from a clip after you've added it to the timeline. Video editors often describe this process as changing a clip's *in point* or *out point.*

To trim a clip, move the pointer near one end of the clip and then drag toward the center.

Tips for Trimming

Resurrecting trimmed footage.
Need to bring back some footage that you trimmed away? Just drag the edge of the clip again. For example, to bring back some footage from the end of a clip, drag to the right. To restore the clip to its pre-trimmed state, select the clip and choose Revert Clip to Original from the Advanced menu.

Recognizing trimmed clips. You can tell whether a clip has been trimmed by looking at it. A clip that has been trimmed has square corners.

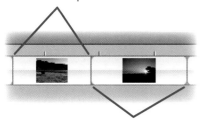

A clip that hasn't been trimmed has slightly rounded corners.

Trimming and adjacent clips. What happens if you trim a clip that already has a clip next to it? It depends.

If you lengthen a clip, the clips to its right move to the right, extending the total length of your project. Videographers call this a *ripple* edit.

What if you don't want to change the position of the remaining clips? For example, maybe you've already timed them to music or narration, and a ripple edit would ruin your work. Easy: just press ⌘ while lengthening the clip. When you ⌘-drag to lengthen a clip, iMovie HD also trims the clip directly next to the clip you're stretching, making it shorter. All other clips stay in place, and the overall length of your project stays the same. This is called a *rolling* edit.

Timeline Snapping

You've probably encountered snapping features in other Mac programs: when you drag one item near another, it snaps toward the second item as though the two share a magnetic attraction.

iMovie HD's timeline-snapping feature brings this magnetism to your movies. Use the Preferences command to turn on time-line snapping, and the playhead snaps to various elements as you drag: to the beginning and end of clips, to bookmarks, to chapter markers, and to silent portions of audio tracks (page 250).

Better still, clips themselves snap to these same elements as you drag them. And so does the mouse pointer when you're using direct trimming. Timeline snapping pairs up beautifully with book-marks and direct trimming.

Tip: You can temporarily activate (or deactivate) timeline snapping: just press the Shift key while dragging an element.

Managing the Trash

As I've mentioned previously, when you delete clips, iMovie HD moves them to its Trash. You can free up disk space by empty-ing the Trash: choose Empty Trash from the File menu.

You can also be selective. Choose Show Trash from the File menu or click the Trash icon, and iMovie HD displays a window showing the contents of the Trash.

What was that clip, anyway? To find out, select it and use the controls below the thumbnail image to play the clip. If you decide you'd rather not trash the clip after all, simply drag it from the Trash window to the Clips pane.

To delete just one clip, select it and click Delete Selected Clip.

To delete all the clips in the Trash, click Empty Trash.

Creating Cutaways

A *cutaway* is a common video-production technique. Think of Barbara Walters nodding solemnly while Fabio describes what kind of tree he'd like to be. Or maybe the video changes to show a close-up of Grandma's garden as she talks about it. To create edits like these, use the Advanced menu's Paste Over at Playhead command.

Try it yourself. Want to experiment with cutaways? Go to www.macilife. com/imovie and download the Cutaway Example Footage archive. Double-click the archive after downloading it, then open the folder named Cutaway Footage and read the instructions inside.

Step 1. Get Your Shots

Begin planning cutaway shots when shooting your video. After Grandma talks about her garden, shoot some close-ups of the plants she talked about. While you're shooting the school play, grab a couple of shots of the audience laughing or clapping. Or after you've shot an interview, move the camera to shoot a few seconds of the interviewer nodding. (In TV news, this kind of shot is called a *noddie*.)

Tip: Still have an old VHS or 8mm camcorder? Dust it off, pop it on a tripod, and use it to shoot short cutaway shots. Dub the footage to your miniDV camcorder, then import it into iMovie HD. The video quality won't match exactly, but your viewers may never notice. And your cutaways will be authentic rather than staged.

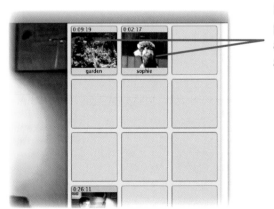

Make sure your primary and cutaway footage exist as separate clips.

Step 2. Set Up for the Edit

With your footage imported, you're ready to set up for the edit. With cutaway shots, you retain the audio from the primary clip and discard the audio from the cutaway shot. iMovie HD does this for you: choose Preferences from the iMovie HD menu, click the General button, and be sure the *Extract Audio When Using "Paste Over at Playhead"* box is checked.

Step 3. Crop the Cutaway.

Using the crop markers as described on page 228, crop the cutaway footage so that it begins at the first frame you want to use as the cutaway. Don't bother specifying the exact end of the cutaway at this point—you'll do that in Step 5.

Step 4. Copy the Cutaway.

In the Clips pane, select the cutaway and choose Copy from the Edit menu (⌘-C).

Another way to cutaway. For those times when you want precise control over the contents of the cutaway clip, use a different technique to insert the cutaway. In Step 3, crop the cutaway clip to the exact length you want it to be. Copy the cropped clip to the Clipboard, then position the playhead at the spot where you want to insert it—don't highlight an area with the crop markers. Now choose Paste Over at Playhead. iMovie HD pastes the entire cutaway clip, replacing an equal amount of footage in the timeline.

Step 5. Mark the Footage You Want to Replace.

With your primary footage in the timeline, navigate to the spot where you want the cutaway to begin (tip: a bookmark can be a handy way to indicate where you plan to insert a cutaway). Select the clip in the timeline, then drag crop markers to indicate the area you want to replace.

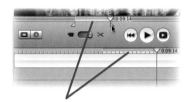

As you drag the crop markers, iMovie HD highlights the region that will be replaced by the cutaway. The cutaway will be inserted where the yellow bar starts, and it will end where the yellow bar ends. iMovie also indicates how long the cutaway will be.

Step 6. Insert the Cutaway.

Choose Paste Over at Playhead from the Advanced menu (Shift-⌘-V).

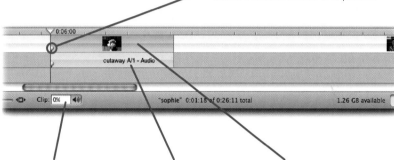

The pushpin icons indicate the audio is locked to the video above it. If you move the video, the audio moves along with it, maintaining synchronization between sound and picture.

iMovie HD mutes the audio of the cutaway clip so you don't hear it.

iMovie HD extracts the audio from the primary clip and puts it in Audio Track 1.

iMovie HD pastes the cutaway footage into the timeline, beginning at the location of the first crop marker.

Cutaway Notes and Tips

When you choose Paste Over at Playhead, iMovie HD uses as much footage from your cutaway clip as is needed to fill the region you highlighted. For example, if the cutaway clip is five seconds long and you highlighted a three-second region with the crop markers, iMovie

HD uses the first three seconds of the cutaway clip.

On the other hand, if the cutaway clip isn't long enough— if you highlight five seconds but your cutaway clip is only three seconds long—you'll have a gap in the timeline. If there's sufficient footage in the cutaway clip,

you can extend the clip to fill the gap by dragging its right edge.

(The one exception to the previous paragraph occurs if your cutaway clip is a still image. In this case, iMovie HD simply extends the length of the still image to fill the region you highlighted.)

Whew. Got all that? It's actually easier than it sounds. Experiment with some spare footage, and you'll be doing cutaways in no time.

Adding Photos to Movies

Photographs are mainstays of many types of movies, especially montages and documentaries. With the photo browser in iMovie HD, you can add photos from your iPhoto library to your movies. You can also add photos that aren't stored in your iPhoto library by dragging them into iMovie HD or by using the File menu's Import command.

When adding photos to movies, consider taking advantage of iMovie HD's *Ken Burns effect* to add a sense of dynamism to your stills. Why name a feature after a filmmaker? Think about Ken Burns' documentaries and how his camera appears to move across still images. For example, a shot might begin with a close-up of a weary face and then zoom out to reveal a Civil War battlefield scene.

That's the Ken Burns effect. Now, Ken Burns himself would probably call it by its traditional filmmaking terms: *pan and scan* or *pan and zoom*. These terms reflect the fact that you can have two different kinds of motion: panning (moving across an image) and zooming (moving in or out).

Whatever the effect's name, its result is the same: it adds motion and life to otherwise static images.

Adding a Photo from Your iPhoto Library

Step 1.

Click the Media button, and then the Photos button.

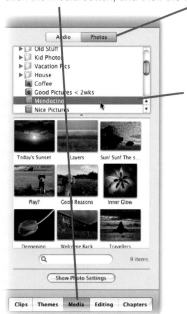

To view a specific album, choose its name from the list.

Step 2.

Select the photo. You can select multiple photos by Shift-clicking or ⌘-clicking on them.

Step 3.

In the Photo Settings panel, adjust the duration and zoom settings, then click ✓.

To pan-zoom a photo, you must specify the start and finish settings for the move: that is, how you want the photo to look when it first appears, and how you want it to look at the end of its duration.

Preview scrubber bar; drag the diamond left and right to "scrub" through the preview.

When zoomed in on a photo, drag the photo using the hand pointer to specify which part of it you want to see.

Cancel and hide the Photo Settings panel.

Apply the settings.

Play or pause the preview.

Loop the preview playback.

Specify the desired start and end zoom settings by dragging the slider or by typing in the box. To change the starting zoom setting, click Start before adjusting the zoom setting. Similarly, to change the ending zoom setting, first click End.

iMovie HD applies the settings and adds the photo or photos to the timeline.

Reverses your settings— for example, turns a zoom in into a zoom out.

To specify the length of time you want the image to appear, drag the slider or type in the box. (Values are in seconds and frames. For example, for a 5½ second duration, type 5:15.)

Note: The Ken Burns effect is sticky. That is, iMovie HD remembers the last set of pan and zoom settings that you used and applies them to future photos.

Photo Tips

Photos from elsewhere. You can also use photos that aren't stored in your iPhoto library. Click the Clips button, then drag the photos into the Clips pane. You can also import photos using the Import command in the File menu. You can even drag a photo's icon directly to the timeline.

When you import a photo using any of these techniques, iMovie HD applies the current Ken Burns effect settings to the photo. To change those settings, see the next page. Alternatively, if you know what Ken Burns settings you want, you can set them up first and then import the photo.

Trimming photo clips. If you've applied the Ken Burns effect to a photo, you can trim its duration in the timeline, but you can't extend it. If you haven't applied Ken Burns, you can trim *and* extend a photo's duration. If you anticipate making significant changes to a photo's duration as you work, wait to apply the Ken Burns effect until *after* you've laid out your clips in the timeline.

Cropping a photo. Want to show just part of a photo, with no motion? Be sure that the Ken Burns Effect box is checked, then select a photo in the Photos pane. Click Start and use the pan and zoom controls to crop the photo. Next, press the Option key and click End. (Pressing Option tells iMovie HD to copy the Start settings to the End settings.) Specify a duration for the clip, then click Apply.

Working with the Ken Burns Effect

Video Formats and Photo Proportions

iMovie HD's support for multiple video formats introduces some special Ken Burns considerations.

4:3 formats. Working in the standard DV, iSight, or MPEG-4 formats? If you plan to show a photo at actual size (that is, a zoom setting of 1.00), be sure your photos' proportions match the 4:3 aspect ratio of these formats. Otherwise, the photos won't completely fill the video frame: they will have black borders.

Most digital camera photos have a 4:3 aspect ratio. If the photos you want to use don't have these proportions, you have two options. The easiest option is to simply use the Ken Burns zoom slider to zoom in just enough that the photos fill the Ken Burns preview box.

The more dramatic option is to crop your photos in iPhoto. From the Constrain pop-up menu in iPhoto's edit view, choose 4 x 3 (DVD). Remember, cropping alters the photo in your library and anywhere else it appears. If you want an uncropped (or differently cropped) version of a photo, duplicate the photo before cropping it.

HD **HD format.** Photos can look beautiful in high-definition format, but in their original form, they will definitely not fill the video frame. Instead, they'll appear *pillarboxed*, with fat black borders on their left and right edges.

To avoid pillarboxing, specify a Ken Burns zoom setting of 1.36.

If you'd prefer to give iMovie HD cropped photos, use iPhoto's Constrain pop-up menu to specify a custom crop proportion of 16 x 9 (HD).

DV Widescreen format. This 16:9 format will also pillarbox a standard digital camera photo. To zoom in just enough to hide the black borders, specify a Ken Burns zoom setting of about 1.36 or 1.40.

For a more drastic fix, crop the photo in iPhoto. You can use the Constrain pop-up menu's 16 x 19 (HD) option, but you may find the resulting photo still has a thin black border. If that's the case, revert to the original version of the photo and crop again, this time specifying a custom crop proportion of 1.818 x 1. It sounds weird, but it works.

Changing Settings

You've applied the Ken Burns effect and now decide that you want to change the clip's pan, zoom, or duration settings. Select the clip in the timeline, click the Media button, then click the Photos button. Now make the desired adjustments in the Photo Settings pane and click Update.

Tip: As an alternative to navigating to the Media pane, you can also Control-click on the clip in the timeline and choose Edit Photo Settings from the shortcut menu.

Note: If there's a transition on either side of the clip, iMovie HD will need to recreate it, since it contains frames that will no longer match the new clip. iMovie HD displays a message warning you that the transition will have to be "re-rendered."

To always have iMovie HD re-render transitions, check this box.

To re-render adjacent transitions, click OK.

To cancel the new Ken Burns settings and keep the old clips, click Cancel.

Image Resolution and Zooming

iMovie HD imports photos at their full resolution. This lets you zoom in on part of a photo and still retain image sharpness.

However, if you zoom in on a low-resolution image or one that you've cropped heavily in iPhoto, you will probably notice some chunky-looking pixelation. So think twice about zooming in on low-resolution images unless you want that pixelated look.

HD If you're working in a high-definition format, you may find that you can't zoom in very far on photos that have relatively low resolution (for example, two megapixels), at least not without seeing ugly visual artifacts.

Searching for Titles

The Photos pane in iMovie HD contains a search box, but it isn't as versatile as its counterpart in iPhoto. You can search for text present in a photo's title only. You can't search for text present in comments, roll names, file names, or keywords.

Zoom to Tell a Story

Creative use of zooming can help tell your story. When you zoom in, you gradually focus the viewer's attention on one portion of the scene. You

tell the viewer, "Now that you have the big picture, this is what you should pay attention to."

When you zoom out, you reveal additional details about the scene, increasing the viewer's sense of context. You tell the viewer, "Now that you've seen that, look at these other things to learn how they relate to each other."

Go Slow

Unless you're after a special effect, avoid very fast pans and zooms. It's better to pan and zoom slowly to allow your viewers to absorb the changes in the scene.

Generally, a zoom speed of 0.05 to 0.1 per second gives a pleasing result. For example, a five-second clip should have a difference between start and finish zoom of about 0.5.

Vary Your Zoom Direction

Variety is the spice of zooming. If you're creating a photo montage and zooming each image, consider alternating between zooming in and zooming out. For example, zoom in on one image, then zoom out on the next.

A fine example of this technique lives elsewhere within iLife: iPhoto's automatic Ken Burns effect alternates

between zooming in and zooming out. So does the screen saver in Mac OS X.

Tip: iMovie HD provides a shortcut that makes it easy to obtain this variety. Select more than one photo in the Photos pane, specify Ken Burns settings, and then press the Option key while clicking the Apply button. iMovie HD adds the photos to the timeline and alternates between zooming in and zooming out.

The Need to Render

When you apply the Ken Burns effect, iMovie HD must create the video frames that represent your efforts. This is called rendering, and is described in more detail on page 253.

You can continue to work in iMovie HD while a clip is rendering, but you may notice that the program's performance is a bit slower.

Advanced Ken Burns Techniques

Ken Burns has some limitations. One is that you can't "hold" on a certain frame. You might want to have a 10-second clip in which the photo zooms for the first eight seconds and then remains static for the last two. Or maybe you want to zoom in part way, freeze for a couple of seconds, and then continue zooming.

Ken can't do that.

Another limitation is that you can't combine multiple moves in a single clip. For example, you might want to pan across a photo and then zoom in on part of it.

Ken can't do that, either.

At least not without a little finessing. It's actually possible to accomplish both of these tasks in iMovie HD. Here's how.

Holding on a Frame

To hold on a frame, save a frame from a Ken Burns-generated clip, then add it to the timeline.

Step 1.

Set up the Ken Burns effect as desired and then apply it, as described on page 237.

Step 2.

Select the clip that iMovie HD has rendered, then move the playhead to its last frame.

Step 3.

Choose Create Still Frame from the Edit menu (Shift-⌘-S).

Step 4.

Locate the still frame in the Clips pane, drag it to the timeline and, if necessary, trim it to the desired length.

Tip: You can also adjust the still frame's duration by double-clicking the clip, then entering a new duration in the Clip Info dialog box.

Variations

You can also start by holding on a frame, and then panning and zooming. First, apply the Ken Burns effect, then navigate to the first frame of the resulting clip and create a still frame from it. Position the still-frame clip before the Ken Burns clip.

Another variation involves inserting a still image in the middle of a Ken Burns move so that panning and zooming stops and then resumes.

For this trick, apply the Ken Burns effect and then split the resulting clip where you want to hold on a frame. (To split a clip, position the playhead at the desired split point and choose Split Video Clip at Playhead from the Edit menu.)

Next, move the playhead to the last frame of the first half of the clip (or to the first frame of the second half). Create a still frame, and drag the resulting clip between the two halves.

Combining Moves

Combining two kinds of moves involves importing the same photo twice and applying different Ken Burns settings each time.

Step 1.

Set up the first Ken Burns move as desired and then apply it.

Step 2.

In the photo browser, select a different photo, and then select the same photo that you selected for Step 1.

This tricks iMovie HD into preparing to create a new clip instead of updating the one you just created.

Step 3.

In the Photo Settings panel, click the Reverse button.

Reverse

This reverses the Ken Burns settings that you set up for Step 1: its end point becomes the new start point.

Step 4.

Specify the End settings for the second Ken Burns move and then apply it.

Beyond Ken Burns: Other Pan-Zoom Tools

Ken Burns isn't the only game in town. Several companies offer pan-zoom tools that work with iMovie HD.

Photo to Movie. Photo to Movie by LQ Graphics (www.lqgraphics.com) makes it very easy to create pan-zoom effects. Create your effect in Photo to Movie, export it as a QuickTime movie, and then bring it into iMovie HD and add it to your project.

Photo to Movie's results are superior to those created by the Ken Burns effect. Photo to Movie does a better job of what animators call *ease in* and *ease out*: rather than motion abruptly starting and ending, the motion starts and ends gradually. The results have a more professional appearance.

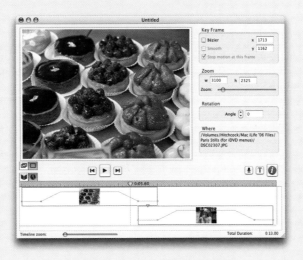

SlickMotion. This simple program is included with GeeThree's Slick Transitions and Effects Volume 4, an extensive library of iMovie effects. SlickMotion also supports ease-in/ease-out, and adds the ability to rotate images.

Motion Pictures. This scaled-down version of Photo to Movie is included with Roxio's Toast.

Adding Audio to Movies

In movie making, sound is at least as important as the picture. An audience will forgive hand-held camera shots and poor lighting—*The Blair Witch Project* proved that. But give them a noisy, inaudible soundtrack, and they'll run for the aspirin.

Poor quality audio is a common flaw of home video and amateur movies. One problem is that most camcorders don't have very good microphones—their built-in mikes are often located on the top of the camera where they pick up sound from the camera's motors. What's more, the microphone is usually far from the subject, resulting in too much background noise. And if you're shooting outdoors on a windy day, your scenes end up sounding like an outtake from *Twister.*

If your camcorder provides a jack for an external microphone, you can get much better sound by using one. On the following pages, you'll find some advice on choosing and using microphones.

If you've already shot your video or you can't use an external mike, there is another solution: don't use the audio you recorded. Instead, create an audio *bed* consisting of music and, if appropriate, narration or sound effects (see page 245).

iMovie HD provides several features that you can use to sweeten your soundtracks. Take advantage of them. And if they don't do the job, consider bringing your movie into GarageBand for additional sonic seasoning (page 362).

Importing Music from Your iTunes Library or GarageBand

Use the media browser to bring in music from your iTunes library or GarageBand.

Step 1.

Position the playhead where you want the music to begin playing.

Step 2.

Click the Media button and then the Audio button.

Step 3.

Select iTunes or GarageBand in the list of audio sources.

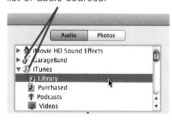

Note: In order to be able to preview a GarageBand project in the media pane, or add the song to the iMovie timeline the project needs to be saved with an iLife preview.

For details, see page 347.

Step 4.

Locate the song you want to import.

You can choose a specific playlist from the list of sources.

You can sort the list of songs by clicking on a column heading. Drag columns left and right to move them. Resize columns by dragging the vertical line between their headings.

Use the Search box to quickly locate a song based on its name or its artist's name.

To play a song, select it and click this button, or simply double-click the song's name.

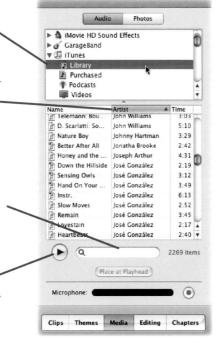

Step 5.

Click the Place at Playhead button.

iMovie HD adds the music to the timeline's second audio track.

Tip: As an alternative to clicking Place at Playhead, you can also click and drag a song to any location on the timeline.

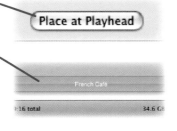

Recording an Audio Narration

If you connect a microphone to your Mac, you can record narration directly within iMovie HD.

To begin recording, click the red button ⊙ next to the volume meter in iMovie HD's Audio pane. To stop recording, click the red button again.

As you record, iMovie HD adds your narration to the first audio track, positioning it at the playhead's location and giving it the name *Voice 01.*

Tip: For the best sound, you want to record loud, but not too loud. At its loudest, your voice should illuminate the yellow portion of iMovie HD's volume meter. If you illuminate the red portions, your sound will be distorted.

Good

Bad

Also, position the mike carefully to avoid the "popping p" syndrome—bursts of breath noise. Record the phrase "pretty poppies" as a test, and back off if the results sound like a hurricane. (Audio trivia: those breathy, percussive consonants are aptly called *plosives.*)

Tips for Recording Better Sound

Upgrade Your Microphone

To get better sound, get a high-quality external microphone and place it close to your subject.

Before you buy an external mike, determine whether your camcorder can accept one. Some inexpensive camcorders don't provide a jack for an external mike; others may require an adapter that connects to the bottom of the camera. Most mid-range and all high-end camcorders have external mike jacks. On most cameras, it's a ⅛-inch stereo minijack.

Clip-on. Microphones come in all sizes and designs. Some are specialized—for example, a *lavaliere* mike, which clips to a lapel or shirt, is great for recording a single voice, such as that of a teacher (or TV host). But a lav mike is unsuitable for recording a musical performance.

Shotgun approach. When you can't get the mike close to your subject but still want to reduce extraneous noise, consider a *shotgun* mike. In a shotgun mike, the microphone capsule is mounted within a long barrel designed to reject sound coming from the side of the mike. Shotgun mikes are popular in TV news and movie making. They're sensitive enough to be located out of the video frame, and their highly directional sensitivity means they won't pick up noise from cameras and crew members.

A shotgun mike works best when mounted on a *boom*, a long pole (often hand-held) that allows the mike to point down at the subject. When you see a video crew with one person who appears to be holding a fishing pole with a long tube on the end of it, you're seeing a shotgun mike (and a sound technician) in action.

Two in one. The most versatile mike you can buy is a *single-point stereo* mike. A stereo mike crams two microphone capsules into a single package. Each capsule is precisely positioned relative to its companion, thus eliminating one of the biggest challenges of stereo recording: getting accurate balance and separation between the left and right channels. I use the AT822 from Audio-Technica (www.audio-technica.com).

With high-quality extension cables, the mike and camera can be up to about 25 feet apart. At greater distances, you risk losing some high frequencies and picking up hum and other electrical noise.

A balanced alternative. When you need to run cables longer than 25 feet or so—or when you want the best possible quality and are prepared to pay for it— consider a *balanced* mike. All of the aforementioned mikes are available in balanced and unbalanced versions. A balanced mike is wired in a way that reduces electrical noise and allows for cable runs of up to 100 feet or so. Balanced mikes cost more than unbalanced ones, but professionals and serious amateurs prefer balanced mikes due to their resistance to electrical noise and their support for longer cable runs.

A balanced mike typically uses an *XLR* connector, and only high-end camcorders have XLR jacks. But there is a way to connect a balanced mike to an unbalanced miniplug jack: the DXA-2 adaptor from BeachTek (www.beachtek.com). A compact metal box that attaches to your camera's tripod mount, the DXA-2 requires no external power supply and has built-in knobs for adjusting volume levels.

Placement is Everything

To do justice to any mike, position it properly. For that school play or recital, use a mike stand and position the mike high, pointing down toward the stage at about a 45-degree angle. If you can't set up your own mike stand, just try to get the mike at least a few feet off the stage and as close to center stage as possible.

How close should the mike be? That depends on what you're recording (see the table at right). The closer the mike is to a sound source, the less room noise and reverberation it picks up.

But if the mike is too close, stereo separation is exaggerated—some sounds come only from the left speaker, others only from the right, and sounds in the center are louder than they should be. Move the mike too far away, and you get a muddy-sounding recording with too much room reverb.

When recording a live performance, try to show up for rehearsals so that you have time to experiment with different mike distances. If your camera has a headphone jack, connect a good pair of headphones—ones whose cups surround your ears and thus block out external sounds. Record a test, play it back, and listen.

For recording narrations, consider assembling a makeshift sound booth that will absorb room echo and block computer and hard drive noise. Glue some sound-absorbing acoustical foam onto two sheets of plywood or foamcore. (See www.soundsuckers.com for a wide selection.) Position the two sheets in front of you in a V shape, with the mike at the narrow end. If you're on a tight budget, use blankets, pillows, carpet remnants, or even a coat closet. The idea is to surround yourself, and the mike, with sound-absorbing material.

Another major microphone manufacturer, Shure, has published some excellent mike-placement tutorials. Download them at www.shure.com/booklets.

A Field Guide to Mike Placement

Scenario	Ideal Mike Position
Solo piano	About a foot from the center of the piano's harp, pointed at the strings (open the piano's recital lid).
Wedding ceremony	As close to the lovebirds as possible. Many wedding videographers attach a wireless lavaliere mike to the groom or the officiator. (Bridal gowns tend to rustle too much.) A mike hidden in a flower arrangement may also work.
Narrator	6 to 9 inches from the speaker's mouth, angled downward. To avoid plosive problems, use a windscreen and position the mike just off to the side, pointing at the mouth. Alternative: a lavaliere mike.
Choral group	1 to 3 feet above and 2 to 4 feet in front of the first row of the choir.
Birthday party around a table	On an extended floor stand, angled downward. Alternative: on a tabletop desk stand, pointing at the birthday kid.

Creating an Audio Bed

If you weren't able to get good audio when you originally shot your video, consider muting your video's audio track and just putting a music bed behind your shots. Create a montage of shots, using bookmarks and direct trimming to help you time your edits to the music.

And finally, a related tip: If you're shooting scenes where the audio is mostly ambient sound—the waves at the beach, the din of a party—shoot a few minutes of uninterrupted video, keeping the camera stationary. After importing the video, delete the video track and keep the audio. (In iMovie HD, drag the video clip to the timeline, then choose Extract Audio from the Advanced menu.) Now you have an audio bed upon which you can put a series of video shots. After you add those shots, mute their audio. This technique eliminates jarring sound changes between shots.

Working with Audio Tracks

Adjusting the volume of an audio track is a common task. And when you combine audio in any way—mixing music, sound effects, dialog, and background sounds— you almost always need to adjust the relative levels of each sound to create a pleasing mix.

iMovie HD provides several ways to work with sound levels. You can reduce the volume of an entire sound clip. You might do this if you're mixing music with the sound of the surf, and don't want the waves to drown out the music.

You can also vary a track's volume level over time. When combining music and narration, you might want the music to start at full volume, fade when the narrator talks, then return to full volume when she stops.

The timeline viewer provides several controls for adjusting volume levels. Many of them are easier to use when you have iMovie HD display audio track *waveforms*. To display waveforms, choose Show Audio Waveforms from the View menu.

A waveform looks a bit like the penmanship of an earthquake seismograph. Back-and-forth lines indicate the intensity of the shaking—in this case, of the sound wave. Being able to see your sound instead of just a horizontal colored bar is a big help when trimming audio tracks, adjusting volume, and creating audio fades.

Adjusting the Volume of a Clip

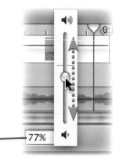

To adjust the volume of an entire audio clip, select the clip and then drag the volume slider located below the timeline.

You can also type a value in the text box.

Fading Out or Fading In

Creating an audio fade involves working with *volume markers* in the timeline.

Step 1.

Choose Show Clip Volume Levels from the View menu.

Step 2.

Click the horizontal line in the audio track to create and adjust volume markers.

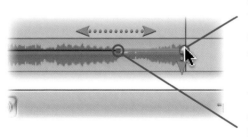

To lower the volume, drag the marker down. To move the marker earlier or later in time, drag it left or right.

To adjust the duration of the fade, drag the beginning point of the marker left or right.

The completed fade.

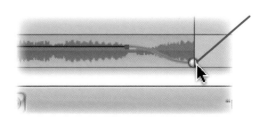

Conversely, to create a fade-in, drag the beginning point of a volume marker all the way down, then drag the end point up.

Adjusting Volume Over Time

Here's how to adjust a track's volume level to accommodate narration or dialog in another track.

Step 1.

Choose Show Clip Volume Levels from the View menu.

When volume levels are visible, iMovie HD displays a volume level bar on each track.

Step 2.

Click on the audio track's volume level bar at the point where you want to adjust the volume. A volume marker appears.

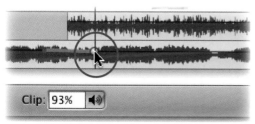

Can't trim clips? Turn off levels. If iMovie HD isn't letting you use direct trimming to adjust the in- and out-points of clips, it's probably because you're viewing clip volume levels—direct trimming isn't available when levels are displayed. Be sure that the Show Clip Volume Levels command in the View menu is unchecked.

Step 3.

To lower the volume, drag the marker down. To increase the volume, drag the marker up. To move the point at which the volume changes, drag the marker left or right.

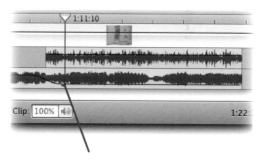

Here, the volume of a music track has been tweaked so that the music gets softer during a narration passage.

To delete a marker, select it and press the Delete key.

Step 4.

When you've finished tweaking volume levels, choose Show Clip Volume Levels from the View menu again so that the command is unchecked.

Applying Audio Filters and Effects

Sound engineers go to great lengths to record high-quality sound during movie making, but what you hear when watching a movie is much different than what you would hear on the set.

A soundtrack is usually sweetened in several ways: speech is given a bit more warmth, background noise is minimized, and so on.

iMovie HD includes several tools for punching up the quality of your movie's audio and sweetening the mix.

Whether you captured audio using a camcorder or imported it from iTunes, it's all digital information—which means it's malleable and ripe for improvement (or just experimentation).

Note: To use audio effects, your Mac must be running Mac OS X 10.4 Tiger or a later version.

To Add an Audio Effect

Step 1.

Select the video or audio clip to which you want to apply an effect.

Step 2.

Click the Editing button and then the Audio FX button.

Step 3.

Select the effect you want to use and change its settings.

Most of the effects offer only one or two sliders that control the degree to which the effect is applied. Some, like Graphic EQ and Reverb, offer convenient presets.

Click the Preview button to hear how the clip will sound. The sound plays over and over until you turn off the preview.

Step 4.

Click the Apply button. iMovie HD extracts the audio (if you applied the effect to a video clip) and renders the new version.

Tip: Pitch Changer can be great for a laugh—or for creating a big, booming Voice of Doom. Applied in small degrees, Pitch Changer can also raise or lower a person's voice slightly to bring out depth or character.

Deleting an Audio Effect

Select the audio clip and press the Delete key to remove the effect.

Updating an Audio Effect

When you apply an audio effect, iMovie HD renders a new audio clip, but doesn't delete the original clip; the effect acts like a layer on top of the original. (Video effects work the same way; see page 256.) The advantage of this approach is that you can "stack" multiple audio effects on a clip and have each effect interact with the layer beneath it.

Unfortunately, you can't pick a layer and change its settings. You must select the audio clip and press the Delete key to remove the effect, and then reapply a new effect with new settings. And if you've applied multiple effects, you need to remove the most recent layers to get to the one you want.

Tip: How many audio effects have you applied? iMovie HD's interface doesn't let on, but there is a way to find out. Select the audio clip and choose Show Info from the File menu. The name of the rendered file indicates how many and what types of audio effects are present.

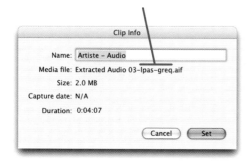

Reduce Background Noise

To minimize the amount of wind or road noise (if the footage was shot in a car, for example), apply the Noise Reducer audio effect. You don't have much control over isolating specific sounds, but this effect does an adequate job of limiting white noise.

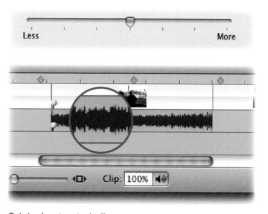

Original extracted clip

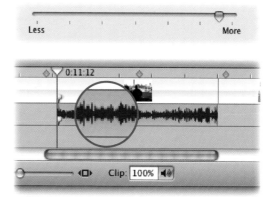

After applying Noise Reducer

Tip: For more information on what effects such as Reverb and Delay actually do, see page 341.

More Sound Advice

Waveform Tips

When you've used the View menu to display audio waveforms, iMovie HD's timeline snapping feature snaps the playhead to silent portions of clips (specifically, when you scroll to within three frames of silence).

To work with more precision when viewing waveforms, zoom in on the timeline. If the audio in a track is on the quiet side, the waveform may be hard to see. Solution: select the audio clip and press the up-arrow key. This accentuates the spikes in the waveform. To make the spikes smaller, press the down-arrow key.

When you import an audio clip or music track, iMovie HD must render the track's waveform—a red progress bar appears at the bottom of the audio track, and the waveform appears a bit blurry until iMovie HD renders it. Because this process takes some time, you may want to leave the waveform display turned off unless you need it for precise editing or volume adjustments.

Trimming Audio

You can trim the start and end of an audio clip using the same direct-trimming techniques described on page 232. As with video clips, you can reclaim audio that's outside of a clip's boundaries by resizing the clip.

Scrubbing Audio

Here's a handy way to locate the exact spot to trim or split an audio clip. Zoom in on the timeline, then press the Option key while slowly dragging the iMovie HD playhead. Your audio plays back, but is slowed down. The sound even plays backwards when you drag the playhead to the left. (Beatles fans: import some *White Album* songs from your iTunes library and have fun.)

Extracting Audio

At times, you may want to use only the audio portion of a clip. For example, you're making a documentary about your grandmother's childhood and you'd like to show old photographs as she talks.

To do this, drag the video clip to the timeline, then select the clip and choose Extract Audio (⌘-J) from the Advanced menu. iMovie HD copies the audio, places it in Audio Track 1, and mutes the audio in the video clip.

Next, select the video clip in the timeline and press the Delete key. The video vanishes but its audio lingers on, and you can now position still images and other clips in the video's place. You can also drag the audio elsewhere in the timeline.

Overlapping Audio in the Timeline

iMovie HD may provide just two audio tracks, but that doesn't mean you're limited to two simultaneous sounds. You can overlap multiple audio clips in the timeline's audio tracks: simply drag one audio clip on top of another.

Repeating Sound Effects

You might want some sound effects to play for a long period of time. For example, iMovie HD's Hard Rain sound effect is less than 10 seconds long, but maybe you need 30 seconds of rain sounds for a particular movie.

For cases like these, simply repeat the sound effect by dragging it from the Audio pane to the timeline as many times as needed. You can also duplicate a sound by Option-dragging it in the timeline. If the sound effect fades out (as Hard Rain does), overlap each copy to hide the fade.

You can build magnificently rich sound effect tracks by overlapping sounds. To create a thunderstorm, for example, drag the Thunder sound effect so that it overlaps Hard Rain. Add the Cold Wind sound while you're at it. And don't forget to use iMovie HD's audio controls to fine-tune the relative levels of each effect.

Get links to sources of sound effects and music.
www.macilife.com/imovie

Camcorder Sound Settings

Most miniDV camcorders provide two sound-recording settings: 12-bit and 16-bit. Always record using the 16-bit setting. If your sound and picture synchronization drift over the course of a long movie, it's probably because you recorded using 12-bit audio.

Muting an Audio Track

You can mute an audio track entirely by unchecking the box to its right in the timeline viewer. If you uncheck the box next to the video track, iMovie HD mutes the video's sound. This can be handy when you're replacing the audio in a series of clips with an audio bed—a segment of background audio that will play across multiple clips.

Splitting Audio Clips

You can divide an audio clip into two or more separate clips whose position and volume you can adjust independently. First, select the audio clip you want to split. Next, position the playhead where you want to split the clip. Finally, choose Split Selected Audio Clip at Playhead from the Edit menu or press ⌘-T.

Sources for Sound Effects and Music

Sound Effects

iMovie HD's library of built-in sound effects, accessed through the audio section of the Media pane, covers a lot of aural ground.

But there's always room for more sound, and the Internet is a rich repository of it. One of your first stops should be FindSounds, a Web search engine that lets you locate and download free sound effects by typing keywords, such as *chickadee*. SoundHunter is another impressive source of free sound effects and provides links to even more audio-related sites.

Most online sound effects are stored as WAV or AIFF files, two

common sound formats. To import a WAV or AIFF file, use the File menu's Import command or simply drag the file directly to the desired location in the timeline viewer.

Managing Sound Effects

If you assemble a large library of sound effects, you might find yourself needing a program to help you keep track of them. You already have such a program: it's called iTunes. Simply drag your sound effects files into the iTunes window. Use the Get Info command to assign descriptive tags to them, and you can use iTunes' Search box to locate effects in a flash. You might

even want to create a separate iTunes music library to store your sound effects.

Music Sources

You'll find a symphony's worth of music on the Internet. For private, non-commercial projects, try Freeplay Music (www.freeplaymusic.com). You can download and use its music clips for, yes, free. For commercial projects, however, be sure to carefully read the company's rate card and licensing requirements.

Plenty of music is also available from sites such as SoundDogs, KillerSound, and Award Winning Music. These sites have powerful

search features that let you locate music based on keywords, such as *acoustic* or *jazz*.

Loopasonic is another cool music site. It offers hundreds of music loops—repeating riffs—that you can assemble into unique music tracks and use in GarageBand (which, of course, you can use to compose your own movie music).

And for building custom-length music tracks, you can't beat SmartSound's Movie Maestro software. Movie Maestro provides an expandable library of songs, each of which is divided into blocks that the Music Maestro software can assemble to an exact length.

Adding Transitions

Visual transitions add a professional touch to your project. Transitions also help tell a story. For example, a cross-dissolve—one clip fading out while another fades in—can imply the passage of time. Imagine slowly dissolving from a nighttime campfire scene to a campsite scene shot the following morning.

Similarly, iMovie HD's Push transition, where one clip pushes another out of the frame, is a visual way of saying "meanwhile..." Imagine using this transition between a scene of an expectant mother in the delivery room and a shot of her husband pacing in the waiting room, chainsmoking nervously. (Okay, so this is an old-fashioned maternity movie.)

iMovie HD's Fade In, Fade Out, and Cross Dissolve transitions are "desert-island" transitions—the ones you'd want when stranded on an island (perhaps while editing an episode of *Survivor*). But unless you are stranded on an island, don't limit yourself—experiment with other types of transitions. To preview any transition, select a clip in the timeline or clip viewer, then click the transition's name in the Transitions pane.

Like effects, transitions are visual spice. Season your video with them, but don't let them overpower the main course: your subject.

Creating a Transition

To add a transition between two clips, first click iMovie HD's Editing button, and then click the Transitions button to display the Transitions pane.

The preview controls (from left) begin playback of the preview, loop playback, cancel the transition, or add it to the timeline.

When you select a transition, a preview appears in the monitor.

If you've selected two or more clips in the timeline, you can apply the transition to all of the clips by clicking Add.

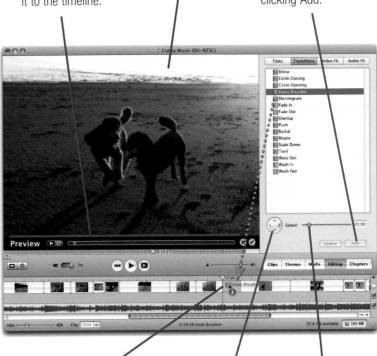

To add the transition, drag it between two clips in the timeline or clip viewer.

Some transitions, such as Push, allow you to specify a direction (for example, to push from left to right or from top to bottom).

To change the transition's duration, drag the Speed slider or type a value in the box.

Testing the Transition

To see the finished transition, select it and press the spacebar.

If you aren't happy with the transition, you can delete it (press the Delete key) or choose Undo.

Inserting a Clip at a Transition

When you create a transition between two clips, you establish a connection between those clips.

If you need to insert a new clip between those two clips, you must first delete the transition: select it and press Delete. Now you can insert the new clip.

Updating a Transition

Change your mind about using a particular transition style? To change an existing transition, first select it in the clip viewer or timeline viewer. Make the desired changes, and click the Update button in the Transitions pane.

Applying a Transition to Multiple Clips

You can apply the same transition to multiple clips in one step: select the clips in the timeline, select a transition, then click the Add button. You can also update multiple transitions at once: select them in the timeline (⌘-click on them or use the Edit menu's Select Similar Clips command), adjust transition settings, then click Update.

Some Background on Rendering

When you create a transition, title, or effect, iMovie HD must create the video frames that represent your efforts. This rendering process takes time; you may notice iMovie HD slows down a bit during rendering.

You can continue to work while rendering takes place. You can even play back your movie, although you may notice stuttering playback when iMovie HD reaches areas it hasn't finished rendering.

Although you can work during rendering, you might want to avoid adding multiple transitions or titles in rapid-fire succession, as doing so can slow iMovie HD to a crawl. To gauge how long rendering will take, look at the transitions, titles, or effects that you've added: a little red progress bar shows how far along rendering is.

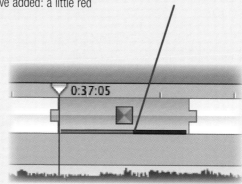

Creating Titles

What's a movie without titles? Incomplete. Almost any movie can benefit from text of some kind: opening and closing credits, the superimposed names of people and places, or simply the words "The End" at, well, the end.

iMovie HD's Titles pane is your ticket to text. You have roughly 50 title styles from which to choose, with customizing opportunities aplenty.

Many of iMovie HD's title styles are animated, and it isn't difficult to transcend the bounds of good taste. Use restraint and lean toward classic title styles, such as Centered and Scrolling. When you want something a bit flashier, consider the Animated Gradient style within the Clip to Characters category.

Regardless of the style you choose, you'll get the best results with sturdy fonts that remain legible despite the limited resolution of television. For example, at small text sizes, Arial Black often works better than Times, which has ornamental serifs that can break up when viewed on a TV set.

You'll also get the best-looking titles if you choose colors conservatively. Avoid highly saturated hues, especially bright red, which can "bloom" when viewed on a standard-definition TV set. High-definition formats are less prone to these problems, but since your video may still end up being viewed on standard-definition TVs, a conservative approach is smart.

Roll the credits.

To Create a Title

Creating a title involves choosing the title style, specifying title settings, and then dragging the completed title to the timeline.

Step 1. Click the Editing button and then the Titles button to display the Titles pane.

Step 2. Choose the title style you want by clicking its name. Some title styles are grouped together in a category; to view them, click the triangle next to the category name.

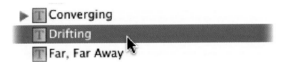

Step 3. Specify the title settings.

See the opposite page for an overview of title settings.

Step 4. Add the title by dragging it to the timeline.

Notes: To add a title to the middle of a clip, position the playhead where you want the title to appear, then click the Add button. To superimpose title text over a specific clip, drag the title to the immediate left of that clip.

Changing a Title

Need to change an existing title? In the timeline, select the title. Next, display the Titles pane and make your changes. Finally, click the Update button in the Titles pane. You can also Control-click on a title and choose Edit Title Settings from the shortcut menu.

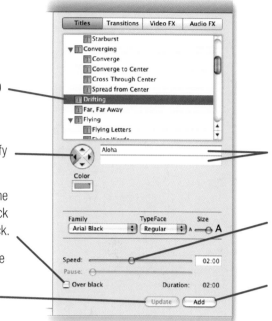

When you click a title style, iMovie HD displays a preview in the monitor (not shown here).

With some title styles, you can specify text position and scrolling direction.

Normally, iMovie HD superimposes the title text over a clip. For a simple black background instead, check Over Black.

To edit an existing title, select it in the timeline, make your changes, and apply the changes by clicking the Update button.

Type or paste the title's text here. In title styles that provide multiple text boxes, you can jump from one box to the next by pressing the Tab key.

Use this slider to adjust the title's duration. For some title styles, this slider adjusts scrolling speed.

To add the title, drag its name to the timeline viewer or clip viewer, or click the Add button.

Tips for Titling

Choosing Colors

To choose a color for title text, click the Color button in the Titles pane. Click on the color palette to choose your hue. To match a color that appears in a clip, click the magnifying glass icon, position the pointer over the color you want to pick up, and then click.

To create a title over a colored background, create a color clip as described on page 274, then add the title to the color clip.

Photoshop Titles

You can use Adobe Photoshop or Photoshop Elements to make gorgeous, full-screen titles. You can add photos, create color gradients, shadow effects, and more.

To create a title in Photoshop, specify an image size appropriate to your project's video format. For DV-format projects, use 720 by 528; for DV Widescreen, use 869 by 480. For iSight and MPEG-4 formats, use 640 by 480. For 720p HD, use 1280 by 720, and for 1080i HD, use 1920 by 1080.

Next, create your title, and avoid putting any text in the outer ten percent of the screen. (It might get cut off when the title appears on a TV set.) And to avoid flicker, make the thickness of any horizontal lines an even number of pixels (for example, 2, 4, 6).

To add the title to your movie, simply drag the Photoshop file's icon into the Clips pane or directly to the timeline. Photoshop gurus: You don't have to flatten a layered file first. iMovie HD accepts layered PSD files. You can even apply the Ken Burns effect to the title if you like.

You can combine Photoshop and iMovie HD's built-in titling to create titles with text superimposed over a moving textured background. Make the background graphic much larger than your movie's frame size so you have room to pan. Import the background graphic and apply a slow pan. Superimpose a title over the resulting clip.

You could also extract a page from an iPhoto book using the technique on page 193 and use it as a title background.

Adding Effects

Special effects are the spice of the movie world. When used sparingly, they enhance a movie and add appeal. When overused, they can make your audience gag.

iMovie HD's Effects pane is the gateway to a full spice rack of special effects. The Aged Film effect makes a clip look like old movie film, complete with scratches and jitter. The Lens Flare effect simulates the glare of bright light entering a camera's lens. Fairy Dust gives you that Tinker Bell look, while Electricity creates *faux* lightning bolts. And the Earthquake effect creates a fast, back-and-forth blur that may tempt you to duck beneath a desk.

iMovie HD introduced a few new effects. The Edges effect creates an edgy, neon-colored look. The Crystallize effect makes a clip looks like it's being viewed through a shower door, while the Edge Work effect creates a pen-and-ink look.

You can also apply speed effects to your clips. Slow a clip down to get slow motion, or speed it up for a chuckle.

You can apply effects to multiple clips at once: Shift-click to select a range of clips, or ⌘-click to select clips that aren't next to each other in the timeline.

Have fun with iMovie HD's effects. But remember: too much spice is worse than none at all.

To Add an Effect

Adding an effect involves selecting one or more clips, specifying effect settings, then applying the effect.

Step 1. Select the clip or clips to which you want to apply an effect.

Step 2. Click the Editing button and then the Video FX button to display the Effects pane.

Step 3. Choose the desired effect by clicking its name. iMovie HD displays a preview of the effect in the monitor.

Step 4. Specify the desired settings for the effect.

iMovie HD can apply or remove an effect over time; see "Effects Over Time" on the opposite page.

Each effect has its own controls; they appear in this area.

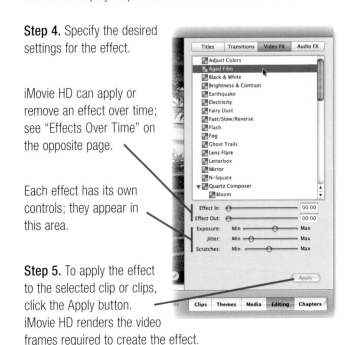

Step 5. To apply the effect to the selected clip or clips, click the Apply button. iMovie HD renders the video frames required to create the effect.

Effects Over Time

Effects aren't an all-or-nothing proposition—iMovie HD can apply or remove an effect gradually. Apply the Black & White effect over time to make a clip start in black and white and turn into Technicolor. Animate the Soft Focus effect to make a clip start out blurry and come into focus, or vice versa.

To animate effects, use the Effects pane's Effect In and Effect Out sliders.

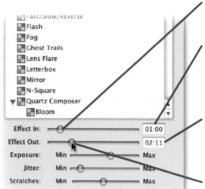

To have the effect appear over time, drag the Effect In slider.

This value indicates how much time will elapse until the effect is fully visible.

This value shows when the effect will start to fade. The time is measured from the end of the clip—in this example, the effect will begin to fade 2 seconds and 11 frames from the end of the clip.

To make an effect go away over time, drag the Effect Out slider.

Effective Tips

Being selective. Another way to control where an effect begins and ends is to apply the effect to only a portion of a clip. To do this, select the clip in the timeline and then drag crop markers to highlight the range of footage to which you want to apply the effect. Now specify the effect settings and click Apply.

Updating effects. To change a clip's effects, Control-click on the clip in the timeline, then choose Edit Effect Settings from the shortcut menu. Make your tweaks, then click Update.

Removing effects. To remove effects from a clip, select the clip and press the Delete key.

Specifying position. Some effects, such as Electricity, can be positioned on the screen. Click in the monitor to set a focus point.

Speed Effects

That video of Junior's winning soccer game could use some slow-motion instant replays. iMovie HD provides them. Select a clip in the timeline, display the Effects pane, and then click on the Fast/Slow/Reverse effect.

Want to see that winning goal in reverse? Click Reverse Direction.

To speed up the clip, drag toward Faster. To slow down the clip, drag toward Slower. When you move the slider, iMovie HD previews your settings in the monitor. To stop the preview, click the preview's Play button. To apply the effect, click the Apply button.

Tips

Silence the sound. Slowing or speeding a clip alters its audio playback, too. You'll probably want to mute the clip's audio: select the clip and type 0 (that's a zero) in the clip volume control below the timeline.

Slow down for smoother motion. Slowing down a clip can also be a nice way to smooth out jerky camera movement. If you had too much coffee before shooting that flower close-up, slow the shot down a bit.

Layer effects. You can apply multiple effects to the same clip, as if they're stacked on top of each other. To remove an effect, select the clip and press the Delete key, as noted at left. To remove *all* effects, choose Revert Clip to Original from the Advanced menu.

Adding Sizzle and Structure with Themes

Watch any TV show, and you'll see that video producers rely on a standard vocabulary of visual building blocks—elements that identify major portions of the show and serve to tie scenes together.

A show opens with a flashy graphic containing text and imagery. The first segment is introduced with another graphic. A city scene appears, and a superimposed *lower-third* graphic identifies the scene. One scene completes, then a short *bumper* appears as a visual separator before the next scene begins. These visual seasonings are sprinkled throughout the rest of the show, and then the credits roll.

These elements of imagery are often called *motion graphics*, and for good reason. Instead of being static text and graphics, they employ slick animation that adds visual appeal. Words don't just fade in and fade out; they glide into view, superimposed over elegant, moving backgrounds.

It's the kind of eye candy we're used to seeing on TV, and now you can serve it up in your productions with the video themes built into iMovie HD 6. Choose a theme, then customize it by adding photos or movies to its drop zones. When you're done, iMovie HD renders the clip and adds it to the timeline.

Themes can do more than just add sizzle to your movies. They can also help you add structure: by employing themes, you can frame the elements of your movie and tell a better story.

Important: To use iMovie HD 6's themes, you must be running Mac OS X 10.4.4 or a later version, if available.

The Elements of a Theme

iMovie HD includes four sets of themes, and many have counterparts in iDVD, iPhoto, and iWeb. Each theme provides one or more drop zones into which you can add photos and video clips. Most theme elements also provide an area where you can type some text.

Each set of themes provides its own mix of visual elements, but all of the sets have some common ground. Here's a look at that common ground from the perspective of the Travel theme.

Opener
Displays a montage of photos or movies, culminating with a title. Use the opener to begin your epic.

Chapter
A shorter motion graphic that's ideal for separating major scenes of a movie. Some themes provide more than one chapter design.

Lower Third
True to its name, a lower third occupies the lower portion of the screen; it's ideal for identifying the people or places in a shot.

Bumper
A bumper is also ideal for separating scenes. In some themes, bumpers display imagery only, with no text. Some themes have multiple bumper designs.

Credits
You know what they are. Some themes provide more than one credits design.

Using Theme Elements

You can add theme elements as you work on a movie, or wait until after you've completed other editing tasks.

Tip: If you're using timeline bookmarks (page 232) to align clips or time them to music or other audio, you might want to add theme elements as you work to avoid disrupting your movie's timing.

To add a theme element, click the Themes button.

Play the preview and control whether the preview plays over and over (loops).

To view specific parts of the theme element, drag the motion playhead left or right.

Step 1. Choose a theme family from the pop-up menu.

Step 2. Click the theme element you want.

Hide (or show) the preview in the monitor.

Hide (or show) the Drop Zones panel.

Step 3. If the element you've chosen provides boxes for title text, type the text.

Step 4. Drag media to the boxes in the Drop Zones panel. To add photos from iPhoto, click the Media button to display the media browser.

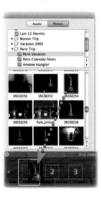

To add a video clip, drag it from the Clips pane or from the timeline. You can also drag it from these locations in other open iMovie projects.

Tip: For best results, be sure that the orientation of a photo or video clip matches that of its drop zone. For example, if the drop zone is vertically oriented, use a vertically oriented photo in it. Otherwise, the photo or clip may appear strangely cropped.

To replace an item in a drop zone, simply drag a new item to the drop zone. To remove a drop zone's item, select the drop zone and press the Delete key.

Step 5. Click ⬭Apply⬭ or the check mark (⊘) in the Preview.

iMovie HD renders the clip and adds it to the timeline. You can work with the clip as you would any other video clip: trim it, add effects, and so on.

Magic iMovie: Editing on Autopilot

With many movie projects, you want control over every step of the editing process: timing cuts to match audio, trimming clips with precision, and fine-tuning your soundtrack until everything sparkles.

But sometimes you just want fast results. It's Sunday afternoon, and your visiting relatives are (finally!) preparing to go home. You shot some video of the kids at the beach earlier that day, and you want to send everyone home with a freshly burned DVD. You can't spend hours in the editing room—you want a movie *now*.

The Magic iMovie feature is for you. Choose a few options, then sit back and watch. iMovie HD imports video from your camera, adds an opening title, tosses a transition between each clip, adds a soundtrack from your iTunes library, and then ships the finished product off to iDVD. It's editing on autopilot.

You can edit a Magic iMovie in any way you want, so you might also use the feature to create a rough cut. After iMovie HD gets you partway there, take the wheel and drive the rest of the way.

Is it magic? Hardly. But Magic iMovie is a fast way to spray some finish on your footage.

Notes: To use Magic iMovie, you must be using a DV or HDV camera; you can't use an iSight or MPEG-4 camera with Magic iMovie. And if you just want to copy a tape to a DVD and don't need transitions, titles, or a music soundtrack, check out the OneStep DVD feature in iDVD (page 299).

Making a Magic iMovie

To make a Magic iMovie, connect and turn on your DV or HDV camcorder (page 226). Then put iMovie HD to work.

Step 1.

Choose Make a Magic iMovie from the File menu, and give your new movie project a name. If necessary, specify the desired video format (see page 224).

Step 2.

Specify Magic iMovie settings.

If you know that the footage you want occupies just a portion of the tape, check this option and specify how many minutes of video to capture. The Magic iMovie feature also stops importing video when it encounters ten seconds of blank tape or when it reaches the very end of the tape.

Turn off this option if you want to start capturing scenes in the middle of your tape.

Your movie's opening title will contain this text, so keep it short.

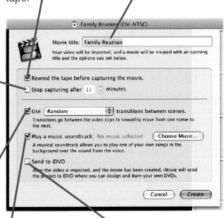

To add a transition between every clip, check this box and choose a transition. **Tip:** Keep it tasteful and avoid the Random option.

To add a music soundtrack, check this box and click Choose Music (see Step 3 opposite page).

If you plan to fine-tune your movie before burning a DVD, uncheck this box.

Step 3 (optional).

Specify music soundtrack settings and click OK.

To see songs from a specific playlist, choose the playlist's name.

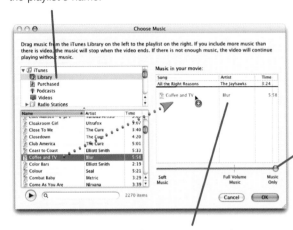

You can rearrange songs after you've added them by dragging them up and down.

To set the volume of your music soundtrack, use the volume slider in the Choose Music dialog box. If your video contains dialog or other important audio, set the level fairly low to keep the music from overwhelming the other audio. Or, if your video contains nothing but wind noise and car horns, set the slider at Music Only to have iMovie HD mute the audio from your footage. As with anything Magic iMovie does, you can change the volume level later if you like. For details on working with audio levels, see page 246.

Step 4.

Click Create.

[Create]

iMovie HD captures your video and prepares the movie.

Tips for Making Magic

Get a Head Start

If you're using Magic iMovie to give you a head start in editing and you plan to trim clips afterwards, consider unchecking the transition option. That way, iMovie HD won't waste time creating transitions that you'll end up deleting anyway.

Tweaking Markers

Normally, the Magic iMovie feature places a DVD chapter marker at the beginning of each clip. If you don't want to divvy up your movie into that many chapters, remove some or all of the markers by using the iDVD pane in iMovie HD (see page 266).

Adding Magic to a Movie

You don't have to use Magic iMovie with a brand-new movie project. If you use the Make a Magic iMovie command when an existing project is open, iMovie HD simply adds the magic movie to the end of the existing project.

Similarly, you can add a Magic iMovie to a different project by copying and pasting its clips. This can be a fast way to put together a montage destined for a different project. Create a new project, then make a Magic iMovie. Then, open a different project, switch to your Magic iMovie project, and choose

Select All from the Edit menu. Finally, drag the clips from the Magic iMovie to the timeline or clips viewer of the new project.

Note: Copying clips from one project to another can take several minutes and devour disk space. After the transfer is complete, consider deleting the original Magic iMovie project file to free up disk space.

Working in Other Video Formats

If you're like the vast majority of iMovie HD users, you shoot and edit in the DV format—the most popular digital video format.

But iMovie HD isn't limited to the DV format. As described on pages 224 and 225, iMovie HD also lets you work in the HDV, iSight, and MPEG-4 formats.

As I mentioned previously, iMovie HD's basic operation is identical regardless of which format you use. But there are some subtle differences between formats. Some formats use more disk space than others—a lot more. Some formats allow for device control—the ability to have iMovie HD operate your camera's mechanism when importing or exporting video—while others require different importing techniques.

Here's a look at the differences you're most likely to encounter as you work with iMovie HD, and some tips for using various formats.

HDV Differences

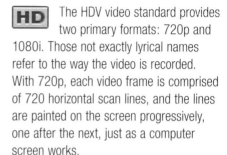 The HDV video standard provides two primary formats: 720p and 1080i. Those not exactly lyrical names refer to the way the video is recorded. With 720p, each video frame is comprised of 720 horizontal scan lines, and the lines are painted on the screen progressively, one after the next, just as a computer screen works.

With 1080i, each frame contains 1,080 horizontal scan lines. The scan lines are drawn in interlaced fashion, like standard-definition TV: first the odd-numbered scan lines, then the even-numbered ones.

The 1080i format provides the best image quality, but its footage uses considerably more disk space than 720p footage. And because each video frame contains more data that iMovie HD must process, transitions, effects, and titles take longer to render with 1080i footage.

MPEG-2 and intermediates. With HDV, video is stored in MPEG-2 format. Because of the way MPEG-2 data is structured, it can't easily be edited on a frame-by-frame basis. (See page 307 for an introduction to how MPEG-2 video is structured.)

In order to make MPEG-2 video editable, iMovie HD converts video into an intermediate format that is easily editable. This conversion process uses a compression scheme called the Apple Intermediate Codec (AIC).

It's this process of converting incoming MPEG-2 that creates the "tape delay" importing effect I described on page 227. Only the fastest Macs are able to transcode MPEG-2 into AIC and display the video in real time. On slower Macs, iMovie HD stashes the MPEG-2 data on your hard drive and transcodes it at whatever pace your Mac is capable of.

A similar but much longer delay occurs when you export HDV video back to a camera, at which time iMovie HD must convert from the Apple Intermediate Codec to MPEG-2 format.

iSight Insights

Apple's inexpensive iSight camera turns your Mac into a hard disk-based camcorder. Connect an iSight to a laptop Mac (or use the iSight built into the MacBook Pro or iMac), and you can shoot video anywhere. Shoot some iSight video, throw in some photos from your iPhoto library if you like, then ship the project off to iDVD.

Recording. To record video and audio with an iSight, first open its shutter and put iMovie HD into camera mode (click ■). Next, click the Record with iSight button to begin recording. To stop recording, click the button again.

Format reminder. You can record with an iSight camera regardless of the video format your project uses. But you'll get the best results and use disk space most efficiently by choosing the iSight format when you create your project. If you

record video into a project containing footage in a different format, iMovie HD will transcode the iSight video you record into your project's format. (See the sidebar on page 225 for more details.)

Speaking of disk space, if your project uses the iSight format, your video will use roughly 65MB per minute.

Weird video? If iMovie HD is displaying a distorted or oddly cropped iSight image, you may have an older camera that needs updating. Get the latest iSight software at www.apple.com/isight/download.

iSight accessories. A couple of inexpensive accessories can make the stand-alone iSight a better iMovie HD companion. For starters, consider a tripod mount. Kaidan (www.kaidan.com) sells an iSight accessory kit that includes an adaptor that lets you mount an iSight on a tripod. Many clever iSight users have also created their own mounts using a few washers and bolts. Do a Google search for *iSight tripod* for some inspiration.

Another accessory you might want is a long FireWire cable to help you to get the camera further from your Mac—particularly handy when you're shooting outdoors with a laptop Mac.

Using MPEG-4 Video

Many cameras can shoot video clips in MPEG-4 format. Gadget gurus are embracing Fisher's FVD-C1 (shown here) and Sanyo's VPC-C4, tiny still/video camera combinations that can shoot up to an hour of video on a memory card—no tape needed. The video quality falls short of what you get from a miniDV camera, but it's surprisingly good—and is far superior to the movie quality most digital cameras provide.

Importing. These cameras don't provide FireWire interfaces and device control. To import their video clips, connect the camera to your Mac's USB jack, then locate the camera's icon on your desktop. Open the icon, locate the video footage, and drag it into the iMovie HD window.

The same format reminder applies: if you import MPEG-4 video into a project that contains footage in a different format, iMovie HD will transcode the footage into the project's format.

It's a Wrap: Exporting to Tape

You've finished your epic—now what? You decide. If you don't have a DVD burner, chances are you'll export many of your movies back to tape. If you're working in the HDV format and you want to view your work in its full, high-definition glory, you'll *have* to export to tape—iDVD doesn't yet support the emerging standards for high-definition video.

Once you export a movie to tape, you can connect your camera to your TV and screen your efforts. Or, connect the camera to a videocassette recorder to make VHS cassette dubs of your movie.

Exporting to a DV Camera

Connect your miniDV camera to your Mac's FireWire jack and put the camcorder in VTR mode. Be sure to put a blank tape in your camcorder, or fast-forward until you're at a blank spot in the tape. Don't make the mistake of recording over your original footage—you may need it again in the future.

Step 1.

Choose Video Camera from the Share menu, or press Shift-⌘-E.

Step 2.

Click the Videocamera button. Adjust settings as desired.

iMovie HD will add some black footage before and after your movie, eliminating the jarring jump from and to the camera's blue standby screen. The preset values of one second probably won't be long enough—add a few seconds of black before the movie, and at least five to 10 seconds of black after it.

Step 3.

Click Share; iMovie HD puts your camera in record mode and plays back your movie, sending its video and audio data over the FireWire cable to the camera.

Exporting to an HDV Camera

HD Exporting high-definition video to an HDV camera involves the same steps listed at left. The one significant difference involves time: as described on page 262, iMovie HD must transcode your finished video from the Apple Intermediate Codec into the MPEG-2 format used by HDV cameras, and mix down and compress the audio. This process can take a long time on slower Macs—several times the length of your movie.

Making VHS Dubs

To make a VHS dub of a movie, connect your camera's video and audio outputs to the video and audio inputs of a video-cassette recorder.

You may have to adjust a setting on the VCR to switch input from its tuner to its video and audio input jacks.

Once you've made the connection, put a blank tape in the VCR, press its Record button, and then play back your movie.

Tip: If you'll be doing a lot of dubbing, look for a VCR that has front-panel audio and video input jacks, which eliminate the need to grope around the VCR's back panel.

If your camcorder and VCR each provide S-video jacks, use them for the video signal. S-video provides a much sharper picture. If you use an S-video cable, use only the audio plugs of the camera's cable; just let the yellow one dangle behind the VCR.

Your camera included a cable that probably has a four-conductor plug on one end, and three RCA phono plugs on the other. Connect the four-conductor plug to the camcorder's output jack (it will be labeled A/V In/Out or something similar). Connect the yellow RCA plug to your VCR's video input jack, the red plug to the audio input jack for the right channel, and the white plug to the audio input jack for the left channel.

Creating Chapter Markers

DVD chapters let you view video on your own terms. Whether you're watching a Hollywood blockbuster or a DVD created by a friend, you can use on-screen menus to instantly access scenes of interest. You can also use the Next and Previous buttons on your DVD player's remote control to jump to the next chapter or to return to the beginning of a chapter and watch it again.

By adding chapter markers to your movies, you give your viewers this same freedom of movement and spare them the tedium of fast-forwarding and rewinding. You can create up to 99 markers in iMovie HD, and iDVD will create menus and buttons for them.

Chapter markers are also instrumental when creating video podcasts (see page 354), letting viewers skip to sections in the video.

Chapter markers can be handy within iMovie, too. You can use them as bookmarks that help you quickly navigate through a lengthy movie: when you click a chapter in the Chapters pane, iMovie HD immediately moves the playhead to that location in the timeline. (You can, of course, also use bookmarks as bookmarks. But iMovie HD doesn't display a list of bookmarks in one place as it does with chapter markers.)

You don't have to create chapter markers in sequential order. If you add a marker to a movie that already contains some markers, iMovie HD automatically renumbers any markers that are located to its right.

Adding Chapter Markers

Step 1.

Position the playhead at the location where you want the chapter marker. Note that you can't have a chapter marker within the first one second of a movie, and that there must be at least one second between chapter markers.

You can drag the playhead there or use the keyboard shortcuts described in "The Keys to Precision" on page 229.

Step 2.
Click the iDVD button.

The Chapters pane appears.

Step 3.
Click the Add Marker button.

Repeat these steps for each chapter marker you want to create.
Tip: You can also create a chapter marker by choosing Add Chapter Marker from the Markers menu or by pressing Shift-⌘-M.

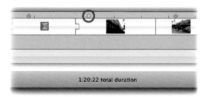

In the timeline viewer, iMovie HD displays a yellow diamond ◈ at each chapter marker's location.

Naming Chapters

For movies containing chapter markers, iDVD creates a "Scene Selection" menu button. When your DVD's viewers choose that button, they get an additional menu or set of menus that enable them to view each scene.

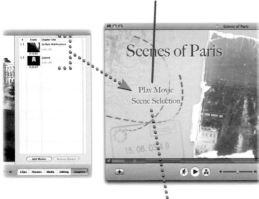

Each marker becomes a button, and each button's name corresponds to the chapter title. Notice that iMovie HD automatically creates a marker for the very beginning of the movie.

Tip: To quickly rename a chapter marker, select it and press Return. You can move from one marker to the next by using the up-arrow and down-arrow keys. By combining the arrow keys with the Return key, you can rename markers without having to reach for the mouse.

When you add a chapter marker, its name appears in the Chapter Title area of the Chapters pane. iMovie HD automatically names a chapter after the clip that appears at the marker's location. When you use that movie in an iDVD project, iDVD names buttons according to the chapter titles.

If you haven't named your clips as I recommend on page 228, you can wind up with meaningless chapter titles and button names, such as *Clip 03* or, for iPhoto images, *Roll 86-2*.

Even if you have named your clips, you might still want different button names. You can always edit button names in iDVD, but you can also edit chapter titles in iMovie HD: simply double-click on the chapter title and then type a new name.

If you're creating a video podcast, you can embed a URL that displays for eight seconds. Double-click the Link URL field, then type a Web address (including the *http://* part). When the viewer clicks that chapter in iTunes, the Web page opens in a new browser window.

Tips for Chapters

How might you use chapters? That depends on what's in your video. Here are some scenarios to give you ideas.

A wedding video

Create chapters for each of the day's main events: the brides-maids beautifying the bride, the groom arriving at the church, the ceremony, the reception.

A kid's birthday party

Create chapters for each phase of the party: the arrival of the guests, the games, the opening of presents, the fighting, the crying.

A vacation video

Create chapters for each day or for each destination you visited.

A documentary

Create chapters for each of the main subjects or periods of time that you're documenting.

A training video

Create chapters for each subject or set of instructions.

A video podcast

Create chapters for each new subject, or when you want a clickable image that leads to a Web page.

Go Small: Internet and iPod Movies

First things first: the Internet isn't the best medium for sharing digital video. The huge size of digital video files means that anything but a very short movie will take a long time to transfer, particularly over a modem line.

But if you have made a very short movie—or you have a fast Internet connection and expect that your viewers will, too—you can use iMovie HD to prepare your work for cyberspace.

With the Share command, you can email a movie, send it to iWeb for viewing on your Web site, or prepare it for a video-capable iPod. iMovie HD compresses the movie heavily to make its file size smaller. In the process, you get an introduction to The Three Musketeers of Internet video: jerky, grainy, and chunky.

A movie compressed for the Internet contains fewer frames per second, so motion may appear jerky. The movie's dimensions are also much smaller—as small as 160 by 120 pixels, or roughly the size of a matchbook. And depending on the options you choose, the sound quality may not be as good as the original.

The best way to watch a movie is on a big screen. But if you're willing to trade some quality for the portability of an iPod or the immediacy of email or the worldwide reach of the World Wide Web, iMovie HD is ready.

To Email a Movie

Step 1.

Choose Email from the Share menu. Specify the settings shown below, then click Share.

Name your shared movie.

Like iPhoto, iMovie HD lets you use any of several popular email programs. Choose yours here.

Read it and weep: iMovie HD tells you just how much your movie will be mangled and how big the mangled version will still be. (Of course, your original movie is still stored in its original format.)

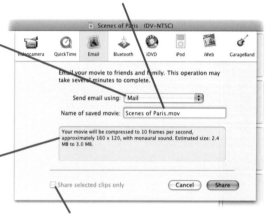

To share only some clips, select them before choosing Share, then check this box.

Step 2.

iMovie HD compresses the movie and attaches it to a new email message. Compose and address the message, then send it on its way.

Tips

If your movie is short and your connection is fast, you might want to email a larger version of the movie than iMovie HD creates. Click QuickTime in the Share dialog box, then choose the Web option from the pop-up menu (see page 270). Export the movie, then attach it to an email message.

Many Internet providers restrict the size of attachments—often to 4MB or thereabouts. If your compressed movie is that large, it's better to share it via iWeb.

To Share to iWeb

In iLife '06, iWeb is the vehicle for publishing your movies to the Web.

Step 1.

Choose iWeb from the Share menu.

Step 2.

Choose to publish the movie on a Web page or as a video podcast as a video podcast. The video podcast option provides higher quality; you can read the specific settings each option uses above the buttons themselves. After you choose the option that's best for your video, click Share or press Return.

After iMovie HD compresses the movie, it switches to iWeb, where you complete the publishing process (see page 382).

To Share to an iPod

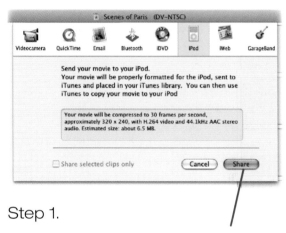

Step 1.

Choose iPod from the Share menu, then click the Share button.

Step 2.

After iMovie HD compresses the movie, it copies the movie to your iTunes library. Use iTunes to copy the movie to your iPod. For details on viewing video on the iPod, see page 96.

HD **Note:** 16:9 movies don't cleanly fit the proportions of the iPod's screen; the movie will be letterboxed with borders above and below the image.

More Ways to Share Movies

Amid the police lineup of the Share dialog box are two buttons that represent iMovie HD's geekier sharing features.

With the QuickTime button, you can export your project as a QuickTime movie. You might export a QuickTime movie in order to publish it on a Web site or burn it on a CD (page 276). Or you might want to email a movie to someone but use your own compression settings instead of those applied by iMovie HD's Email preset.

With the Bluetooth button, you can transfer your movie to a cell phone or other gizmo equipped with Bluetooth wireless technology. An iPod is a better venue for a portable movie, but watching a movie on a phone is great geek fun.

Just remember to switch off your movie theater when the aircraft is not stopped at the gate.

HD **Exporting widescreen.** If you're exporting a 16:9 project, the movie dimensions listed in the Share dialog box are inaccurate—they're for 4:3 movies. Your exported 16:9 movie will have the horizontal dimension listed in the dialog box, but the vertical dimension will be shorter.

If you're using the Expert Settings option described at right, specify a movie dimension of 720 by 405 pixels (or a multiple thereof).

Exporting a QuickTime Movie

To export your project as a QuickTime movie, choose QuickTime from the Share menu, or press Shift-⌘-E, and then click the QuickTime button.

Choose a preset from the pop-up menu.

To specify custom compression settings, choose Expert Settings.

Expert advice. You can often improve on the picture quality provided by iMovie HD's Email, Web, and CD-ROM presets by using the Sorenson Video 3 compression scheme. To access it, hack through the following thicket of dialog boxes. In the Save dialog box that appears after you click Share, choose Movie to QuickTime Movie from the Export pop-up menu, then click the Options button. The Movie Settings dialog box appears; click Settings. In the next dialog box, choose Sorenson Video 3 from the pop-up menu. Now click OK several times to go back to safety. If you like, explore the rest of the Movie Settings dialog box—it's where you can specify the movie's pixel dimensions and sound settings.

To learn about compression, see *iMovie HD 6 & iDVD 6 for Mac OS X Visual Quickstart Guide*, by Jeff Carlson (Peachpit Press, 2006). For more QuickTime resources, see www.macilife.com/imovie.

Exporting to a Bluetooth Device

Bluetooth is a wireless technology that connects devices over distances of up to about 30 feet. You can buy cell phones, printers, palmtop computers, keyboards, and mice that use Bluetooth's radio waves instead of cables to talk to each other and to the Mac.

All current Mac models have built-in Bluetooth. If yours doesn't, you can add Bluetooth using a tiny and inexpensive adapter such as the D-Link Bluetooth USB Adapter, which plugs into any free USB port on your Mac.

Mobile multimedia. Having Bluetooth is just one part of the mobile movie equation. Another part is a multimedia standard called 3GPP, which is supported by a growing number of cell phones and other gadgets. QuickTime supports 3GPP, too, and it's this support, combined with Bluetooth, that makes it possible to play a movie on a phone.

To play a 3GPP movie, you need a 3GPP media player for your device. Two such players are Kinoma Player

(www.kinoma.com) and RealNetworks' free RealPlayer (www.realnetworks.com/mobile).

Making the transfer. Be sure your phone is on, then choose Bluetooth from the Share menu. In the Share dialog box, click the Bluetooth button, then click Share. iMovie HD compresses your movie, then displays a dialog box for transferring it.

To have your Mac search for nearby Bluetooth devices, click Search.

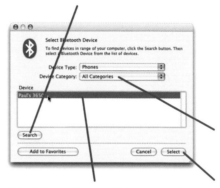

Select the device to which you want to transfer the movie.

Your phone may display a message asking if you want to receive the movie. Choose Yes.

After the transfer is complete, navigate to your phone's messages menu, choose the new message, and watch the show.

Tip: iMovie HD saves the compressed movie on your hard drive; you can use Mac OS X's Bluetooth File Exchange program to transfer the movie again. Inside your movie's package file (see page 274) is a folder named Shared Movies. Inside that folder is a folder named Bluetooth. Your compressed movie is there; its name ends with the file extension .3gp.

If you have numerous Bluetooth devices, you can narrow down the list of devices displayed by choosing the device category.

After choosing a device, click Select.

A Movie In Your Palm

To play a 3GP movie on a Palm OS device, you need player software that supports the 3GP format. Some Palm OS devices, such as the Treo 650 smartphone, can play 3GP movies right out of the box. If your device can't, try Kinoma Player (www.kinoma.com), a versatile

mobile media player that handles 3GP and other formats.

With Kinoma's inexpensive Kinoma Producer, you can compress a movie created in iMovie HD into a variety of mobile formats. To do so, locate the Timeline Movie.mov reference movie for your project using the

instructions on page 276. Drag this icon into Kinoma Producer, choose the desired audio and video settings, and click the Convert Files button. You can use Bluetooth File Exchange to transfer the compressed movie to your Palm.

Fun with Freeze Frames

You see it all the time in movies and TV shows: a scene begins with the action frozen, and suddenly the still image springs to life. The frozen image often has a special effect, too—maybe it's been altered to look like a faded photograph. When what appears to be an old photo suddenly turns Technicolor and starts moving, the effect can be magical.

In Hollywood, they use expensive equipment and expensive artists for cinematic tricks like this. You can do it for free using iMovie HD, and it's a cinch. Simply save a still image from the very beginning of a particular clip, then apply one or more effects to it. Once you've altered the freeze frame, it just takes a few clicks in the iMovie HD timeline to complete the effect.

This effect can be a fun way to introduce an event that just screams nostalgia—a kid opening presents, a family sitting down to a Thanksgiving feast, or some kids hitting a slope for some sloppy sledding. Start your scene with this effect, superimposing some title text if you like, and you've instantly gone beyond a run-of-the-mill home movie.

A still frame always has a duration of five seconds. To change its duration, double-click the clip and specify a new value in the Clip Info dialog box. You can also adjust the duration in the timeline, as described on the opposite page.

Step 1. Trim as Needed

Once you've chosen a video clip for this project, trim its start point so the clip begins at the most appropriate spot. For example, if there are a few seconds of jerky camera movement before Junior starts opening presents, crop or direct-trim the clip to remove the bad footage.

Step 2. Create a Still Frame

Now select the trimmed clip and position iMovie HD's playhead at its very first frame. The easiest way to make sure the playhead is at the very beginning of the clip is to press the Home key.

Next, choose Create Still Frame from the Edit menu. iMovie HD creates a new clip—a still image from the first frame—in the Clips pane.

Play it back if you like: select it and press the spacebar.

Step 3. Add the Still Frame to the Timeline

Before applying the effect, add the freeze-frame clip to the timeline by dragging it from the Clips pane.

Step 4. Add the Effect

Now you're ready to alter the appearance of the freeze frame. If you're after a nostalgic look, try the Aged Film effect—it makes a clip look like a scratched, jittery movie.

Select the freeze-frame clip in the timeline, click the Editing button, then click the Video FX button to bring up iMovie HD's Video FX pane. Click the Aged Film effect.

Adjusting the Effect Out setting. For this project, you want the effect to fade away shortly before the end of the clip; this enables the freeze frame to blend cleanly with the live-action clip that will follow it.

To make this adjustment, drag the Effect Out slider to the right. As you drag, watch the numbers in the slider's text field. This value tells you how much time it will take for the effect to fade away. Try a setting of about one second, or 1:00. You can always adjust this setting later.

After you've adjusted the Effect Out setting, fine-tune any of the effect's other settings if you like. When you're done, click the Apply button. iMovie HD displays a message telling you that the still clip must be converted into a "regular" clip. Click Convert, and iMovie HD renders the frames required to create the effect.

Step 5. Add the Original Clip

If you haven't yet added your original clip—the one from which you extracted the video frame—do so now. Select it in the Clips pane, then drag it to the timeline, positioning it immediately after the freeze-frame clip.

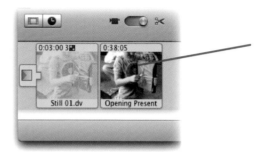

Position the original clip immediately after the modified freeze frame.

Now sit back and admire your work. First, be sure no clips are selected (choose Select None from the Edit menu or just click in a blank area of the timeline). Move the playhead to the beginning of the freeze-frame clip and press the spacebar to begin playback.

Optional steps. Does your freeze-frame clip seem too long? To shorten its duration, trim the clip: in the timeline view, point to the clip's left edge, then drag to the right. For extra precision, use the Zoom slider to zoom in first.

iMovie HD doesn't limit you to just one effect. Maybe you'd like that aged film clip to appear in black and white. It's easy: select the freeze-frame clip in the timeline, return to the Effects pane, and apply the Black & White effect.

To add a title to the freeze-frame clip, use the Titles pane as described on page 254.

Variations on a frozen theme. You can also turn this trick around: have a scene suddenly freeze and then turn into a old movie frame. This can be a fun way to end a scene.

To do it, save a frame from the last frame of a clip. Adjust the Effect In setting of the freeze frame's effect so that the effect appears after a second or so. Then, put the modified freeze frame after the clip from which it came.

iMovie HD Tips

Copying and Pasting Clips

You can make additional copies of a clip by copying it to the Clipboard and pasting it into the Clips pane or the timeline. If you want to experiment with different effects or cropping schemes, select the clip and choose Copy. Next, select another clip on the Clips pane and choose Paste. iMovie HD makes a copy of the clip and puts it on the Clips pane for you. Another way to duplicate a clip is to press the Option key while dragging the clip—either to another box in the Clips pane or in the timeline or clip viewers.

You can even move clips from one project to another by copying and pasting them, though it's often easier to simply open both projects and drag clips between them. If you paste clips into a project that uses a different video format, iMovie HD transcodes the clips into the destination project's format.

Moving Clips Faster

If you need to move a clip a significant distance—say, from the end of a project to the beginning—you could just drag it and let the clip viewer or timeline scroll automatically. But there's a faster way. Drag the clip from the clip viewer or timeline into any empty box on the Clips pane. Scroll to the new destination, and then drag the clip from the Clips pane back into the clip viewer.

Multiple Clips at Once

Remember that iMovie HD lets you select and manipulate multiple clips at once. You can apply the same effect, transition, or Ken Burns settings to several clips in one fell swoop. Just Shift-click to select a continuous range of clips, and ⌘-click to select clips that aren't next to each other. To select a series of similar clips—for example, all transitions—select one clip and then choose Select Similar Clips from the Edit menu.

Creating Color Clips

Want to create a text title with a background other than black? Here's how.

In the timeline viewer, drag any clip to the right to create a gap.

Control-click on this gap and choose Convert Empty Space to Clip from the shortcut menu. iMovie HD turns the gap into a clip whose color is black.

To change the clip's color, double-click the clip, then click the Color swatch in the Clip Info dialog box. (While you're there, consider giving the clip a descriptive name, such as Blue Background.)

Now you can add a title to this clip. You can also use the previous tips to move the color clip to the Clips pane, or make duplicates of it for use elsewhere in your project.

Another Way to Freeze Frames

You can also save a frame as a JPEG or PICT file for use in another program. Position the playhead at the frame you want to save, then choose Save Frame from the File menu (⌘-F). In the Save dialog box, choose the JPEG or PICT format from the pop-up menu.

You can add JPEG frames to your iPhoto library and even make and order prints. However, the images are small, so don't expect to get high-quality prints in large sizes. You can email them, though, and that can be a fun way to share a few particularly good frames.

Combining SFX with FX

In the movie world, SFX are sound effects, while FX are visual effects. As anyone who has watched a Hollywood blockbuster knows, they go together perfectly.

Many of iMovie HD's visual effects are candidates for sound effects, too. Pair the Fairy Dust effect with the Stardust sound effect. Combine the Electricity visual effect with the Electricity sound effect.

And if you're adding a little tectonic action with the Earthquake effect, try using the Suspense sound effect along with it.

You get the idea: think about enhancing your visual effects with complementary sound effects that add impact.

Movies from Your Digital Camera

You can add movie clips taken by a digital camera to your iMovie HD projects. If a movie you want is in your iPhoto library, you can locate it using iMovie HD's photo browser. If the movie isn't in your library, simply locate its icon on your hard drive and drag it into the iMovie HD window.

But let's step back and look at the greater question: why bother? Compared to the quality you get from a real video camera, the movies from most digital cameras look genuinely awful.

And yet there are some good reasons to consider using a digital camera movie in an iMovie HD project.

It's all you have. If you don't have a camcorder but want to include some video in a movie project (as opposed to still photos and Ken Burns clips), use your digital camera. Adjust its menu settings to get the largest frame size and highest quality your camera is capable of. iMovie HD enlarges the video frames to fill the screen, so you'll get better results from larger movies.

For a special effect. Video producers often spend big bucks to get video that looks pixilated and has jerky motion. With digital-camera movies, those

"effects" are standard equipment. Have a video camera? Shoot some footage using it and your digital camera's movie mode. Then cut between the two for a cool effect.

For the sound. When I was in Paris, I wanted to capture the sound of the many street musicians who play in Metro stations. I shot digital camera movies, then brought them into iMovie HD and extracted their audio tracks (see page 250). Then, I added still photos of the street musicians to the timeline and applied the Ken Burns effect to the photos. The result: a montage of still photos with an authentic soundtrack.

Incidentally, if you have a Sony digital camera and you're having trouble importing its MPEG movie clips into iMovie HD, see www.macilife.com/imovie for a workaround.

Navigation Tips

Get Around Faster

Take advantage of iMovie HD's View menu to quickly navigate a large project. If you've scrolled a large distance and want to jump back to the playhead's location, choose Scroll to Playhead

(Option-⌘-P). The Scroll to Selection command (Option-⌘-S) lets you quickly jump back to a selected clip. Zoom to Selection (Option-⌘-Z) zooms in on the selected clip or clips.

And if you're using bookmarks, you can jump to the previous

bookmark by pressing ⌘-[and to the next bookmark by pressing ⌘-].

Control Your Clicks

Remember that you can Control-click on just about anything to

bring up a shortcut menu that lets you perform relevant tasks. Try Control-clicking on a clip in the Clips pane, the playhead, the scrubber bar beneath the iMovie HD monitor, and on audio and video clips in the timeline.

More iMovie HD Tips

Archiving a Project

If you've created a fairly short project, you can archive it on a CD or (more likely) DVD. Choose Burn Project to Disc from the File menu, then insert a blank disc when iMovie HD tells you to. iMovie HD burns your project file to the disc. When it's done, you can free up disk space on your hard drive by deleting the project file.

Unfortunately, if the project is larger than will fit on a single disc, you can't archive it using Burn Project to Disc. Instead, back up the project by copying it to a different hard drive.

Accessing Your Project's Media

In older iMovie versions, a movie project was stored in a folder, and its media assets, reference movies, and shared movies were stored in a folder within it.

iMovie HD works differently. Its project files are *packages*, a special kind of Mac OS X folder. That's good in that it makes it easy to back up a project (just drag its icon to another hard drive) and makes it difficult for iMovie HD newcomers to damage a project by removing or altering files they shouldn't.

But as I've mentioned on previous pages, sometimes you need to get to the innards of a project. You still can: at the Finder, Control-click on a project icon and choose Show Package Contents from the Shortcut menu. The window that appears contains your project's timeline file, source media, and shared movies (ones you created using the Share command).

In the Cache folder is a movie named Timeline Movie.mov. This is your project's *reference movie*—it's a QuickTime movie containing pointers to the media used in your project. You can drag this reference movie into a compression utility such as Kinoma Producer or Sorenson Squeeze.

iSight as Microphone

If you have an iSight camera, you can use it as a microphone to record narration. For the best sound quality, hold the iSight several inches from your mouth and talk to the top of the camera—that's where the microphone is. Put iMovie HD into camera mode as described on page 263, then click Record With iSight.

Add the clip you recorded to the timeline, then Control-click on it and choose Extract Audio. Delete the video portion of the clip, then move the audio to the desired location on the timeline.

Exporting Your Movie's Sound

There may be occasions when you want to export part or all of the audio track of your project. Maybe you want to bring it into an audio-editing program, such as SoundStudio or Amadeus, for fine-tuning. Or maybe you recorded a music recital and you'd like to bring the performance into iTunes or GarageBand.

To export your project's soundtrack, choose QuickTime from the Share menu, choose Expert Settings, and click Share.

In the Save dialog box that appears, choose Sound to AIFF from the Export pop-up menu. Click Options, then choose the desired audio settings.

If you'll be bringing your audio back into iMovie HD, use the default options. If you'll be importing the audio into iTunes or GarageBand, choose 44.100 from the Sample pop-up menu.

Burning Movies to CD and Video CD

If your Mac has a CD burner, you might want to burn your exported movie to a CD so you can share it with others. In the Share dialog box, click QuickTime, then choose the CD-ROM option. Next, insert a blank CD into your Mac's optical drive and copy the movie to the CD. The resulting CD will play on any Mac or Windows computer that has QuickTime installed.

If you have Roxio's Toast software, you can also create a Video CD. This video format is very popular in Asia, and somewhat obscure everywhere else. But most stand-alone DVD players can play Video CDs, as can all current personal computers. (To play Video CDs on a Mac, use Mireth Technology's MacVCD X software, available at www.mireth.com. And if you don't have Toast Titanium, you can also make Video CDs using Mireth Technology's iVCD.)

Video on a Video CD is compressed in MPEG-1 format. The image quality is a far cry from that of the MPEG-2 format used on DVDs; Video CD image quality is more akin to that of VHS videotape. One

Get links to iMovie HD add-ons.
www.macilife.com/imovie

reason is because the video frame size is smaller—352 by 240 pixels, instead of DVD's 720 by 480. Another reason is that the video itself is compressed more heavily—about 90:1, compared to roughly 30:1 for MPEG-2. But on the plus side, a Video CD can shoehorn about an hour of video onto a CD-R disc.

A variation of the Video CD format is called *Super Video CD*, or *SuperVCD.* On a SuperVCD, video is stored in MPEG-2 format, yielding better quality than a Video CD. The SuperVCD format also allows for many DVD-like features, such as alternate language tracks. Its video quality still falls short of a DVD's, however.

Video CD and SuperVCD are second-best alternatives to DVDs, but if you don't have a DVD burner, any alternative is better than none. For background on the Video CD and SuperVCD formats, see www.vcdhelp.com.

Adding On to iMovie HD

Several companies sell inexpensive add-ons that expand iMovie HD's repertoire of effects, titles, and transitions. Companies offering iMovie HD add-ons include Virtix, GeeThree, and Stupendous Software. Each of these companies also offers free iMovie HD effect plug-ins. For links to more plug-ins, see www.macilife.com/imovie.

Editing Like the Pros: Making the TV Connection

The best way to see how your video will look on TV is to watch it on TV while editing it. iMovie HD makes it easy. First, connect your DV camcorder to the Mac with a FireWire cable as usual. (Note: This works with the DV format only, not HD.)

Next, connect your camcorder's video output to the video input of a TV set. If your TV and camcorder each have S-Video connections, you should use them for the best video quality. If your TV lacks S-Video but has a composite video input (an RCA jack), use it. If your TV lacks video inputs, add an RF modulator between the camcorder and the TV set. You can buy the modulator at Radio Shack for about $30.

Once you've made the connections, choose Preferences from the iMovie HD menu, click Playback, and then check the *Play DV Project Video Through to DV Camera* box.

When this option is selected, your project's audio will not play back through your Mac's speakers. You can rely on your camcorder's tiny, built-in speaker for sound playback, but you might want to

connect your camcorder's audio outputs to your TV's audio inputs, if it provides them; to a stereo system; or to a pair of external amplified speakers.

Adjusting playback quality.
While you're setting playback preferences, examine the options iMovie HD provides for optimizing playback. If your Mac is stuttering on a complex project, consider downshifting to the Standard quality setting. Have a fast Mac? Aim high and choose Highest.

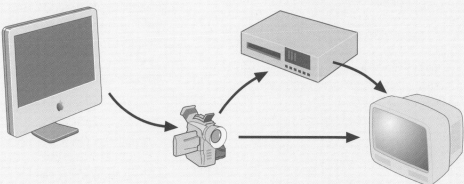

Tips for Making Better Movies

Editing takes more than software. You also need the right raw material. Advance planning will help ensure that you have the shots you need, and following some basic videography techniques will make for better results.

Plan Ahead

Planning a movie involves developing an outline—in Hollywood parlance, a *storyboard*—that lists the shots you'll need to tell your tale. Professional movie makers storyboard every scene and camera angle. You don't have to go that far, but you will tell a better story if you plan at least some shots.

Consider starting with an *establishing shot* that clues viewers in on where your story takes place—for example, the backyard swimming pool. To show the big picture, zoom out to your camcorder's wide-angle setting.

From there, you might cut to a *medium shot* that introduces your movie's subject: little Bobby preparing to belly flop off the diving board. Next, you might cut away to Mary tossing a beach ball. Cut back to Bobby struggling to stay afloat, and then finish with a long shot of the entire scene.

Keep in mind that unless you're planning to use the Magic iMovie feature, you don't have to shoot scenes in chronological order—sequencing your shots is what iMovie HD is for. For example, get the shot of Mary's throw any time you like and edit it into the proper sequence using iMovie HD.

Steady Your Camera

Nausea-inducing camera work is a common flaw of amateur videos. Too many people mistake a video camera for a fire hose: they sweep across a scene, panning left and right and then back again. Or they ceaselessly zoom in and out, making viewers wonder whether they're coming or going.

A better practice is to stop recording, move to a different location or change your zoom setting, and then resume. Varying camera angles and zoom settings makes for a more interesting video. If you must pan—perhaps to capture a dramatic vista—do so slowly and steadily.

And, unless you're making an earthquake epic, hold the camera as steady as you can. If your camera has an image-stabilizing feature, use it. Better still, use a tripod or a monopod, or brace the camera against a rigid surface. Keeping the camera steady is especially critical for movies destined for the Internet—because of the way these videos are compressed, minimizing extraneous motion will yield sharper results.

Compose Carefully

The photographic composition tips on page 214 apply to movie making, too. Compose your shots carefully, paying close attention to the background. Get up close now and then—don't just shoot wide shots.

Record Some Ambient Sound

Try to shoot a couple of minutes of uninterrupted background sound: the waves on a beach, the birds in the forest, the revelers at a party. As I've mentioned previously, you can extract the sound from this footage and use it as an audio bed behind a series of shots. It doesn't matter what the camera is pointing at while you're shooting—you won't use the video anyway.

After importing the footage, use the Extract Audio command, described on page 250, to separate the audio.

Shooting with Compression in Mind

If you know that you'll be distributing your movie via the Internet—either through a Web site or email—there are some steps you can take during the shooting phase to optimize quality. These steps also yield better results when you're compressing a movie for playback on a Bluetooth device, and they even help deliver better quality with iDVD.

First, minimize motion. The more motion you have in your movie, the worse it will look after being heavily compressed. That means using a tripod instead of hand-holding your camera, and minimizing panning and zooming. Also consider your background: a static, unchanging background is better than a busy traffic scene or rustling tree leaves.

Learn more about digitizing old tapes and movies.
www.macilife.com/imovie

Second, light well. If you're shooting indoors, consider investing in a set of video lights. A brighter picture compresses better than a poorly lit scene. To learn about lighting, read Ross Lowell's excellent book, *Matters of Light and Depth* (Lowel Light, 1999).

Vary Shot Lengths

Your movie will be more visually engaging if you vary the length of your shots. Use longer shots for complex scenes, such as a wide shot of a city street, and shorter shots for close-ups or reaction shots.

Be Prepared, Be Careful

Be sure your camcorder's batteries are charged; consider buying a second battery so you'll have a backup, and take along your charger and power adapter, too. Bring plenty of blank tape, and label your tapes immediately after ejecting them. To protect a tape against accidental reuse, slide the little locking tab on its spine.

Don't Skimp on Tape

Don't just get one version of a shot, get several. If you just shot a left-to-right pan across a scene, for example, shoot a right-to-left pan next. The more raw material you have to work with, the better.

Converting Analog Video and Movies

Somewhere in your closet is a full-sized VHS camcorder—the kind that rested on your shoulder like a rocket launcher. You want to get that old VHS video into your Mac.

If you have a DV camera, chances are it has a *passthrough* mode that enables you to use it as an analog-to-digital converter. Connect the video and audio output jacks on the VHS deck to your DV camera's video and audio input jacks. If your VHS deck and camcorder each provide S-video jacks, use them to get the best picture.

Next, put your camera in VCR or VTR mode, and read its manual to see if you have to perform any special steps to use its passthrough mode. With some cameras, you must make a menu adjustment. With others, you simply need to remove the tape.

After you've made the appropriate connections and adjustments, you can play your VHS tape and click iMovie HD's Import button to record the converted footage coming from your camera.

Analog-DV Converter

A faster way to get analog video into your Mac is through a converter, such as those sold by Formac Electronics, DataVideo, Sony, and others. These devices eliminate the time-consuming process of dubbing VHS tapes to DV format. Connect a converter to your Mac's FireWire jack, then connect your old VHS rocket launcher to the converter's video and audio inputs. Then, launch iMovie HD and use its import features to bring in VHS video. Using iMovie HD's Share command, you can also blast edited video through the converter back to the VHS camcorder.

When importing VHS video, you may notice a thin band of flickering pixels at the bottom of the image. Don't worry: these artifacts won't appear when you view your finished video on a TV screen.

Converting Films

As for those old Super 8 film-based flicks, you'll need to send them to a lab that does film-to-video transfers. Many camera stores can handle this for you. The lab will clean your films, fix bad splices, and return them along with videotapes whose contents you can bring into the Mac. If you have a DV camcorder, be sure to use a lab that will supply your converted movies on DV cassettes—you'll get much better image quality than VHS provides. Some labs also offer optional background music and titles, but you can add these yourself once you've brought the converted video into the Mac.

I wrote a feature article on digitizing old tapes and movies for *Macworld* magazine's June 2004 issue. The article is available online; I've linked to it at www.macilife.com/imovie.

Creating Time-lapse Movies and Animation

Our minds are mesmerized by animation, whether it's a time-lapse movie of a brewing storm, some claymation that brings Play-Doh to life, or the hand-drawn artistry of a classic cartoon.

With some inexpensive software and a video camera, you can put your world into motion. The process is simple, if time consuming. For animation, shoot one frame of video at a time, moving objects or changing a drawing between each frame. Time-lapse movies are easier: point your camera at an interesting scene, then go to the mall while your software snaps a frame at whatever interval you like. When you play your final movie, clouds will billow, and flowers will bloom—you get the idea.

A time-lapse or animation project can be a fun school or family endeavor. Here's a look at the tools you'll need, along with some tips and project ideas.

The Tools

To put your world in motion, you need a camera, a tripod, and some software. To get the best video quality, connect a miniDV camcorder to your Mac's FireWire jack. If you don't have a camcorder, an inexpensive Web cam, such as Apple's iSight, will also work.

iMovie HD 6 can create time-lapse movies, as can several other programs. Boinx Software's iStopMotion was designed specifically for the task. It works with DV cameras as well as Web cams.

You can also use Web-cam software, such as Evological's EvoCam or Econ Technologies' ImageCaster. For links to these and other animation tools, see www.macilife.com/imovie.

The Techniques

Prepare your gear. Mount your camera on a tripod and plug the camera's power adapter into a wall outlet—batteries won't last long enough.

Many DV camcorders shut themselves off after a few minutes when you aren't recording to tape. You can usually bypass this auto-shutoff by taking the tape out of the camera. If your camera still insists on slumbering, try leaving its tape door open.

Connect the camcorder to your Mac, launch your software, and you're ready to go. Here are some possible destinations.

Toys in motion. For an easy stop-motion project, put some toys in motion: the Matchbox Car 500. For your animation stage, choose an area where the lighting is going to be fairly consistent over several hours. If you're relying on light from windows, try to shoot on a cloudy day. Dramatic variations in lighting from one frame to the next will ruin the illusion of motion.

For animators, patience isn't a virtue—it's a must. Move objects slowly and gradually—just a fraction of an inch between frames. And whatever you do, don't bump your tripod between frames.

To save time, try shooting two frames, instead of just one, between each move. Animators call this animating *on twos*, and it takes half the time but usually delivers fine results.

Kids in motion. For a variation on the previous theme, animate some kids: point the camera at the backyard, and have the kids take a small step between each frame. In the final movie, they'll appear to move without walking.

Time for time-lapse. Making time-lapse movies is much easier, since your subject does the moving on its own. All you have to do is set up your scene and start capturing.

In iMovie HD, choose Time Lapse from the camera icon's popup menu, choose an interval, and click OK. Then click Import to start recording (see page 226).

What to shoot? A snowstorm, a rose, the clouds, a burning candle, a glass filled with ice, the shadows cast by a fence or set of window blinds. Anything that moves or changes shape slowly in the real world is a great candidate for time-lapse photography.

Sunsets and sunrises make spectacular time-lapse movies. To avoid damaging your camera, don't zoom in on the sun or point the camera directly at a midday sun.

How frequently should you capture a frame? That depends on how quickly your subject is changing and on how long you want your final clip to be. For a time-lapse of a rose blooming, I used a one-minute interval, which turned an hour of real time into one second of video. For some cloud scenes, I used a 15-second interval.

To calculate the ideal frame interval, begin by determining the duration of the real event, the desired duration of your final clip, and the number of frames per second you want the final clip to have (20 frames per second is a good starting point). Say a rose bud takes four hours to blossom, and you want the time-lapse clip to play for nine seconds. Multiplying nine seconds by 20 frames per second yields 180 frames. Finally, divide the duration of the real event by the number of frames you need. In this example, 240 minutes divided by 180 frames equals about 1.3 minutes—or about 80 seconds between frames.

Post-Production

After creating an animation, enhance it.

Make a montage. When researching animation and time-lapse techniques, I shot a variety of time-lapse scenes, then edited them into a montage.

After shooting the clips and importing them into iMovie HD, I added a music track. I've always loved *Koyaanisqatsi,* a film comprised largely of beautiful time-lapse photography; its Philip Glass music score is a perfect complement to time-lapse scenes. A quick search of the iTunes Music Store led to the soundtrack album, and 99 cents later, I had my soundtrack. (Remember, you can't use copyrighted work in commercial projects.)

Next, I imported my time-lapse movies into iMovie HD and added them to the timeline, cropping each clip so that the scenes would change roughly in tempo with the music. Then I added a cross-dissolve transition between the scenes.

Run it backwards. To put a different spin on a time-lapse clip, reverse it: see a rose close itself or a glass of water turn into a glass of ice. After adding the clip to iMovie HD's timeline, select it and use the Fast/Slow/Reverse effect.

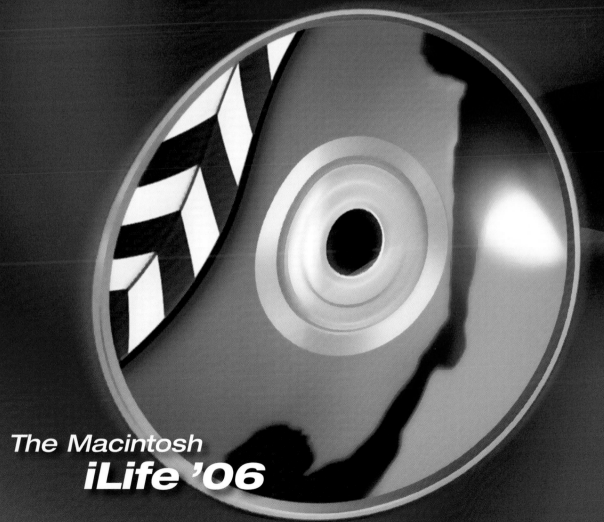

iDVD:
Putting it All
Together

The Macintosh
iLife '06

iDVD at a Glance

iDVD lets you burn movies and photos to DVDs, complete with menus you can fully customize.

Designers and photographers can use iDVD to assemble digital portfolios that they can hand out like brochures. Filmmakers and advertising professionals can distribute rough cuts of movie scenes and commercials to clients and colleagues. Businesspeople can create in-house training discs and video archives of corporate meetings. Videographers can offer DVDs of weddings and other events. And home-movie buffs can preserve and share family videos and photographs.

Creating a DVD involves choosing and customizing a menu design and adding the movies and photos you want to include on the DVD. You can perform these steps in any order and preview your work along the way. When you've finished, you can commit the final product to a shiny platter.

You can narrow down the list of themes displayed (page 286).

iDVD provides numerous pre-designed menu templates, called *themes*, some of which provide motion menus and audio.

Themes with motion menus are indicated by the motion icon.

Some themes share similar designs, ideal for a DVD that contains multiple menus (page 298).

A Short Glossary of DVD Terms

authoring The process of creating menus and adding movies and images to a DVD.

button A clickable area that plays a movie or slide show, or takes the user to another menu.

chapter A video bookmark that you can access from a menu or with a remote control. Creating chapters in a movie lets viewers jump to specific sections.

DVD-R The blank media that you'll use most often when burning DVDs. A DVD-R blank can be burned just once.

DVD-RW A type of DVD media that you can erase and reuse.

menu A screen containing clickable buttons that enable users to access a DVD's contents.

motion menu A menu whose background image is an animation or movie, a menu that plays background audio, or both.

MPEG-2 The compression format used for video on a DVD. MPEG stands for *Moving Picture Experts Group*.

To add a movie to your DVD, drag it into iDVD's window (page 290). iDVD creates a button, whose appearance you can customize (page 301).

Each menu on your DVD has a title, whose position and formatting you can customize (page 301).

Change the volume of the menu playback as you work.

To create a custom menu background, drag an image from iPhoto or another program to the iDVD window (page 301).

Many themes have *drop zones*, special areas into which you can drag photos or a movie (pages 287–289).

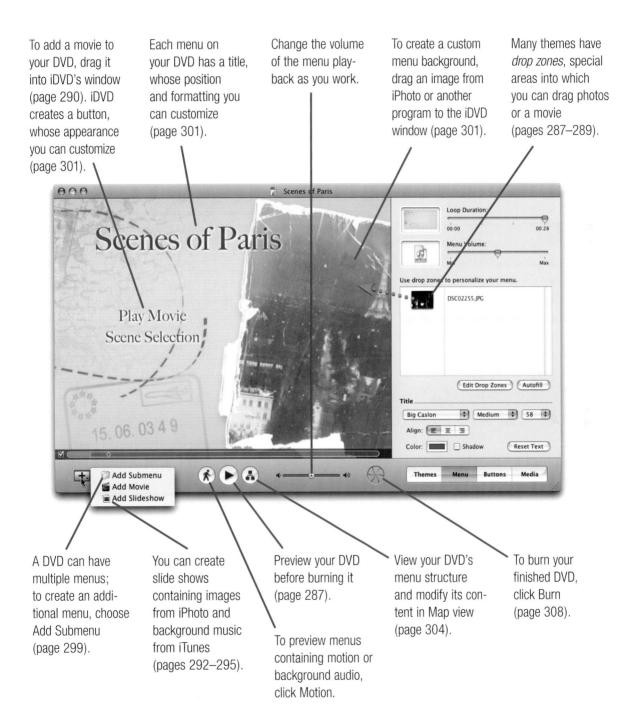

A DVD can have multiple menus; to create an additional menu, choose Add Submenu (page 299).

You can create slide shows containing images from iPhoto and background music from iTunes (pages 292–295).

Preview your DVD before burning it (page 287).

To preview menus containing motion or background audio, click Motion.

View your DVD's menu structure and modify its content in Map view (page 304).

To burn your finished DVD, click Burn (page 308).

Choosing and Customizing Themes

A big part of creating a DVD involves choosing which menu theme you want. iDVD includes menu themes for many types of occasions and subjects: weddings, parties, vacations, kids, and more. Many of these themes have motion menus containing beautiful animations and background music.

In iDVD, all themes are now designed for widescreen presentation. Although iDVD can't yet burn high-definition discs, you can take advantage of the more cinematic 16:9 aspect ratio if you shot widescreen video.

Your design options don't end once you've chosen a theme. Many of iDVD's themes provide *drop zones*, special areas of the menu background into which you can drag photos or movies. Drop zones make it easy to customize a theme with your own imagery.

Most drop zones have special effects that iDVD applies to the photos or movies that you add to them. For example, the Reflection White theme puts your imagery in a set of 3D panels that glide like a moving art gallery. The Road Trip theme puts your imagery in a scrapbook—and if you look closely, you'll see that the pages cast shadows on each other.

Most themes provide "dynamic" drop zones that move around the screen. And as the following pages describe, you have more options for managing the contents of drop zones.

Choosing a Theme

Step 1.

If the list of themes isn't visible, click the Themes button.

Step 2.

Choose the theme you want by clicking it.

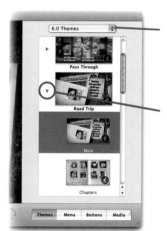

Use the pop-up menu to access themes from older versions of iDVD.

Click the disclosure triangle next to an iDVD 6 theme family to reveal specific menu themes.

Tip: When you select a new theme, iDVD asks if you want to switch between a widescreen or standard-definition aspect ratio. If you get tired of this nagging, click Do Not Ask Me Again before clicking Keep or Change.

Note: In order to see a theme's motion, you must have motion turned on. To turn motion on or off, click the Motion button. As you work on your DVD, you'll probably want to turn motion off since iDVD performs better this way.

Adding Items to a Drop Zone

iDVD provides several ways to add items to drop zones. Here's the technique you're likely to use most often. For details on more drop zone techniques, see the following pages.

Step 1.

Click the Media button. Then, to access photos in your iPhoto library, click the Photos button. To access movies, click Movies.

Step 2.

In the photo or movie media browser, select the item or items you want to add. You can select multiple photos or an entire album. If you add multiple photos to a drop zone, iDVD displays them successively as the menu is displayed. You can add up to 99 items to a drop zone.

Step 3.

Drag the selected items into the drop zone.

As you drag into a drop zone, a dotted line indicates the drop zone's boundaries.

Step 4.

To fine-tune an item's position within the drop zone, drag it using the hand pointer 🖐.

Previewing and Testing Your Work

As you work on a DVD, you'll be anxious to see how the final product will look. To find out, use iDVD's preview mode. Click the Preview button, and iDVD turns itself into a DVD player and starts playing your DVD.

In preview mode, an on-screen remote control lets you navigate—choose menu buttons, jump to chapters, and watch the movies and slide shows you've added to your DVD.

Displays a movie's menu.

Displays the top-most menu on DVDs that contain multiple menus.

Turns preview mode off.

Jumps to the previous or next chapter in a movie, or to the previous or next photo in a slide show.

Click the arrows to navigate. Click Enter to choose the highlighted menu button.

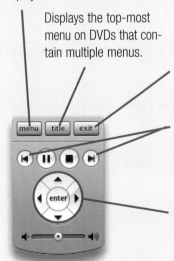

Preview mode plays back whatever is displayed in iDVD's window. If your main menu is visible, that's what plays back. If you're working on a slide show, the slide show begins playing.

Using iDVD's preview mode is a great way to check your work, but you shouldn't rely on it as your only testing tool. As you near the end of your project, create a disc *image* and use Mac OS X's DVD Player program to test it (see page 310). Then burn a disc and test it in your DVD player.

Working with Drop Zones

Here are some tips for working with drop zones.

Drop Zones Versus Menu Buttons

It's important to understand the difference between drop zones and buttons. A drop zone is merely an area of imagery within a DVD menu—it isn't a clickable button that your viewers can use to watch your DVD. A drop zone is a piece of eye candy; a button is a navigation control that plays a movie or slide show, or jumps to another menu.

How to tell the difference. As you drag items into the menu area, how can you tell whether you're dragging into a drop zone or creating a button? Easy: When you're dragging into a drop zone, a dotted-line pattern appears around the edges of the drop zone, as shown on the previous page.

If you don't see this pattern, you aren't in the drop zone, and you'll end up creating a button or changing your DVD's background image. If that happens, head for the Edit menu and choose the Undo command.

Navigating Dynamic Drop Zones

In most themes, drop zones are *dynamic*—they move around on the screen or they appear and disappear as a motion menu plays.

How do you add items to a drop zone that's behind another drop zone or not even visible?

Use the motion playhead. At the bottom of iDVD's menu area is a horizontal motion playhead that lets you scrub through a menu: drag the playhead left and right, and iDVD plays the motion menu, displaying its drop zones. Simply drag the playhead until the drop zone you want is visible.

(If you don't see the motion playhead, choose Show Motion Playhead from the View menu.)

Use the drop zone editor. Double-click on any drop zone, and iDVD displays the drop zone editor. You can add photos and

movies to drop zones by dragging them into the editor.

You can also display the drop zone editor by choosing Edit Drop Zones from the Project menu.

Use the drop zone list. Click the Menu button to view a list of available drop zones. As with the drop zone editor, you can add photos and movies by dragging them to the list. To have iDVD use media you've already added to your DVD, click Autofill.

Older themes. Both the motion playhead and drop zone editor also work with iDVD's older themes.

Introductory Animations

Many iDVD themes provide introductory animations. For example, in the Travel Cards theme, the row of postcards slides into position before the menu buttons become visible.

These animations are cute, but you might not always want to use them. They're fine on a DVD's main menu, but on a submenu (such as a scene selection menu for a movie), they slow down your DVD's users, who must wait for the animation to finish before they can access the menu's buttons.

Solution: Turn off the introductory animations when you don't want them. Just click the little check box at the left edge of the motion playhead.

Other Ways to Add Items

You can also add items to a drop zone by dragging them from the Finder: simply drag the items' icons into the drop zone or drop zone editor. And you can drag photos from iPhoto and other programs directly into a drop zone.

If you don't like dragging and dropping, here's one more way to add items: Control-click within a drop zone, and choose the Import command from the shortcut menu.

Removing and Rearranging Items

To remove the contents of a drop zone, drag the item out of the drop zone. When you release the mouse button, the item disappears in a puff of smoke. As an alternative to dragging, you can also Control-click within the drop zone and choose Clear from the shortcut menu.

What if you have a drop zone containing multiple items and you want to remove a few of the items—or even just one? Here's how. Double-click the drop zone to display the drop zone editor, then double-click the entry for the drop zone that you want to edit. iDVD displays the drop zone photos editor, where you can delete individual items.

You can also use the drop zone photos editor to rearrange the order in which items in a drop zone are displayed: just drag the items around. And you can add items to a drop zone by dragging them into its editor.

Adding Movie Clips from iMovie HD

You can drag movie clips from iMovie HD directly into a drop zone. You can drag from the Clips pane in iMovie HD or even directly from the timeline or clip viewers.

What if you want to use just part of a video clip in a drop zone? You can't use iMovie HD's cropping or direct-trimming features to indicate which portion you want to keep. That's because these features don't actually delete any video; they simply tell iMovie HD which parts you want to use. If you drag a cropped clip into an iDVD drop zone, the entire clip plays in the drop zone.

To control how much of the movie plays in the drop zone, click on the drop zone that contains the movie. iDVD displays a set of crop markers above the movie; drag the markers left and right to specify which portion of the movie should play.

Browsing a Drop Zone

If you have a drop zone that contains multiple items, you can quickly scan through the drop zone's contents without having to open up the drop zone editor. Click on a drop zone, and a small slider pops up; to scan through the drop zone's items, drag the slider back and forth. If, while browsing, you decide to rearrange the drop zone's contents, click the Edit Order button below the slider.

Preview Glitches?

When you've added movies or high-resolution photos to a menu's drop zones, you may see and hear some problems when you preview the menu: the drop zones' motion may appear jerky, and the menu's background audio may break up as it plays.

Not to worry—these problems won't occur on your final DVD. Indeed, the problems often go away once the menu has had a chance to play through once.

Adding Movies to Your DVD

iDVD's job is to integrate and present assets from other programs. The assets you're most likely to add to your DVDs are movies you've created in iMovie HD or another video-editing program, such as Apple's Final Cut Express HD or Final Cut Pro.

You can add movies to your DVDs using a couple of techniques. iDVD can accept movies in just about any QuickTime-compatible format (for some examples of movies you can't use, see page 312). You can also use 16:9 movies in either HDV or DV Widescreen format. If you use high-definition movies, however, note that iDVD will convert them to standard-definition for display—not because it wants to, but because it has to. Today, the high-definition DVD landscape is still in flux, with a couple of standards vying for acceptance.

In the meantime, your high-definition movies will still play in all their widescreen glory if you play your DVD on a wide-screen TV set. On a conventional TV, they'll play in letterboxed format.

To learn more about high-definition DVD standards and working with 16:9 movies in iDVD, see www.macilife.com/iDVD.

Video on a DVD is compressed, or encoded, into a format called MPEG-2. As the sidebar on the opposite page describes, iDVD performs this encoding either as you work or after you click the Burn button.

Adding a Movie Using the Movie Browser

Step 1.

Click the Media button, then click the Movies button.

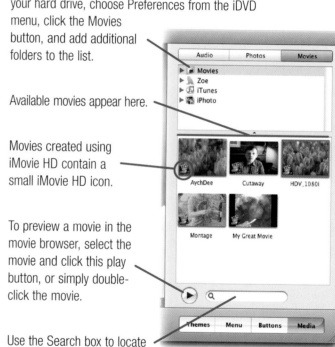

iDVD lists movies contained in your Movies folder. To have iDVD list movies located elsewhere on your hard drive, choose Preferences from the iDVD menu, click the Movies button, and add additional folders to the list.

Available movies appear here.

Movies created using iMovie HD contain a small iMovie HD icon.

To preview a movie in the movie browser, select the movie and click this play button, or simply double-click the movie.

Use the Search box to locate a movie in the browser.

Step 2.

Drag the desired movie into your DVD's menu area.

iDVD adds the movie to your DVD and creates a menu button for it.

If the movie contains DVD chapter markers, iDVD creates two buttons: one named Play Movie and another named Scene Selection. If the movie lacks DVD chapters, iDVD simply creates one button, giving it the same name as the movie itself. To rename any button, select it and edit the name.

Tip: If you don't want iDVD to create a chapter submenu—or if you'd like iDVD to ask if you want one—use the options in the Movies portion of the Preferences dialog box.

Other Ways to Add a Movie

You can also add a movie by dragging its icon from the Finder into the iDVD window, or by choosing the Video command from the File menu's Import submenu. These techniques are convenient if you store your movies on an external hard drive and you don't feel like adding the drive to the movie browser using the Preferences command.

You can also use the media browser to add video clips from your iTunes or iPhoto libraries (although you can't burn your video purchases from the iTunes store). For more details on using digital camera movies in iDVD projects, see page 312.

And finally, you can add a movie by choosing the Video command from the File menu's Import submenu.

Tips for DVD Movies

Encoder Settings

You can have up to two hours of video on a disc—four hours, if you have a dual-layer DVD burner (see page 310). By adjusting iDVD's encoder settings, you can control how much video will fit as well as the quality of the video itself. Choose Preferences from the iDVD menu, click the Projects button, and cast your eyes on the Encoding options. (You can also change encoding settings for an individual project as described on page 313.)

The Very Best

If you have more than one hour of video—or you want the best quality iDVD is capable of—choose Best Quality. In this mode, iDVD puts on its thinking cap and analyzes your video, with the goal of compressing it as little as possible.

You get great quality and two (or four) hours on a disc, but be patient. Encoding upwards of two hours of video may take several hours on slower, single-processor G4 Macs.

The Very Fastest

If you have under an hour of video, consider the Best Performance option. The video still looks great and encoding is much faster. When you choose Best Performance, you have the option of allowing iDVD to encode while you work: click the Enable Background Encoding check box. If iDVD runs sluggishly, uncheck the box, and encoding will take place after you click Burn.

For more encoding insights, see page 311.

Using Movies from Final Cut

iDVD can also encode Final Cut Pro or Final Cut Express movies. Export the movie by choosing QuickTime Movie from the File menu's Export submenu. (In older Final Cut versions, this command is Final Cut Movie or Final Cut Pro Movie.) If the movie has chapter markers, be sure to choose the Chapter Markers option in the Markers pop-up menu of the Save dialog box.

Creating DVD Slide Shows

iDVD slide shows are a great way to share photos. Even low-resolution photos look spectacular on a television screen, and they can't easily be copied and redistributed— a plus for photographers creating portfolio discs. (You can, however, opt to include the originals on the disc, as described in "The DVD-ROM Zone" on page 306.)

iDVD provides a few ways to create a slide show. You can use iDVD's photo browser to drag a few photos or an entire photo album into the iDVD window. You can also use the Send to iDVD command in iPhoto to send an album, a selection of photos, or a saved slide show to iDVD. And you can manually drag photos from iPhoto (or anywhere else) into iDVD's slide show editor.

As the following pages describe, you can give your slide shows background music from your iTunes library and fine-tune other aspects of their appearance. You can also choose to have transitions between images; iDVD gives you twelve transition styles from which to choose (see page 294).

Each image in a slide show can be any size and orientation; however, vertically oriented images will have a black band on their left and right edges.

Creating a Slide Show Using the Photo Browser

Step 1.

In iPhoto, create an album that contains the photos you want in the slide show, sequenced in the order you want them to appear (see page 130).

Step 2.

In iDVD, click the Media button, then click the Photos button.

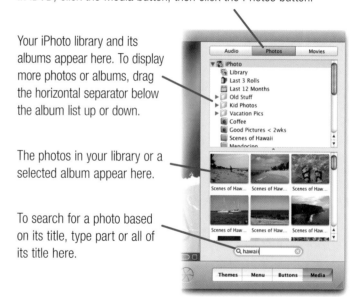

Your iPhoto library and its albums appear here. To display more photos or albums, drag the horizontal separator below the album list up or down.

The photos in your library or a selected album appear here.

To search for a photo based on its title, type part or all of its title here.

Step 3.

Locate the desired album and drag it into the iDVD menu area.

Tip: Be sure you don't drag the album into a drop zone; see "Working with Drop Zones" on page 288.

iDVD creates the slide show and a menu button for displaying it. iDVD gives the button the same name as the album, but you can rename the button to anything you like.

Creating a Slide Show Within iPhoto

You can send photos to iDVD from within iPhoto, and with a couple of different options.

Saved slide show. If you've created a saved (cinematic) slide show, you can add it to iDVD and retain its custom Ken Burns moves and other goodies. In iPhoto, select the saved slide show in your Source list. Then, choose Send to iDVD from the Share menu. iPhoto creates a video version of the slide show and ships it off to iDVD.

If you need to revise the slide show, first delete it from your iDVD project. (Select its button and press Delete.) Then, return to iPhoto, make your changes, and choose Send to iDVD again.

If you create a 16:9 (widescreen) slide show in iPhoto, iDVD displays it in wide-screen format.

Basic slide show. Here's the technique to use if you don't need Ken Burns moves and you'd prefer the advantages of a DVD slide show (for example, more efficient use of disc space and the ability to easily include original images on your disc). In iPhoto, select an album or a series of photos. Then, choose Send to iDVD from the Share menu.

You can revise this type of slide show directly within iDVD using the techniques on the following pages.

Creating a Slide Show from Scratch

You can also create a blank slide show and then manually add photos to it.
You might use this technique to add photos that aren't stored in your iPhoto library.

Step 1.

Choose Add Slideshow from the pop-up menu or choose Project > Add Slideshow (⌘-L).

iDVD adds a button named My Slideshow to the currently displayed menu. Rename this button as desired.

Step 2.

Double-click on the button that iDVD just created. The slide show editor appears.

Step 3.

Drag photos (or a folder containing photos) into the slide show editor. Or, display the photo browser and drag photos from your iPhoto library.

Refining a Slide Show

When you create a DVD slide show, you can fine-tune it using the slide show editor. To display the editor, double-click the slide show's menu button or icon in Map view.

When checked, this box superimposes arrows over the images as a hint to viewers that they can move back and forth in the slide show using their DVD remote controls.

Check this box, and the slide show will repeat until the cows come home—or at least until your DVD's viewer presses the Menu or Title button on his or her remote control.

Switch between list view and thumbnail view.

To display these options, click the Settings button.

To have iDVD store the original images on the DVD, check this box. (For details, see page 306.)

To edit a photo's title or comment, click its text. If Show Titles and Comments is checked, the text appears during the slide show.

To change playback order, drag images. You can select multiple images by Shift-clicking and ⌘-clicking.

You can specify a duration for the images, or have the slide show timed to match its soundtrack. If the slide show has a soundtrack, the Manual option isn't available.

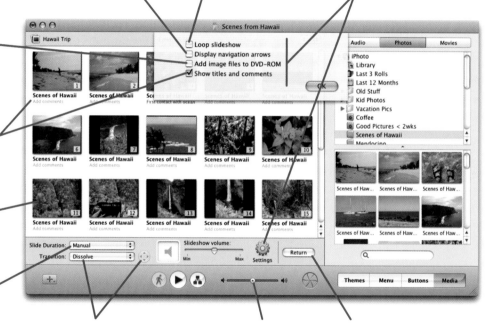

You can have transitions between photos. For some transition styles, you can also specify a direction, such as a left-to-right wipe.

Adjust the volume of the slide show's soundtrack.

Return to the menu that leads to this slide show.

Tip: To delete a photo from the slide show, select it and press the Delete key. This doesn't delete the photo from your hard drive, it just removes it from the slide show.

Adding Music to Slide Shows

You can add a music track to a slide show. One way to add music is by using the iTunes browser in iDVD. Click the Media button, then click the Audio button. Locate the song you want (use the search box if need be), then drag it to the Audio well. To add an entire playlist, drag it to the Audio well.

Don't like to drag? Select the song or playlist you want to add, then click the Apply button in the music browser.

You can also drag a song directly from the iTunes window or, for that matter, from any folder on your hard drive. And you don't even have to drag an *audio* file:

if you drag a QuickTime movie to the Audio well, iDVD will assign its audio to your slide show.

If you create a slide show by dragging an iPhoto album into the iDVD window (or by choosing Send to iDVD while an album is selected in iPhoto), the slide show will retain whatever song was assigned to it in iPhoto. (For details on assigning songs to albums, see page 164.)

Music and timing. How iDVD matches your soundtrack to your slides depends on the option you choose from the Slide Duration pop-up menu. If you choose a specific duration, such as five seconds per slide, iDVD repeats your soundtrack if its duration is shorter than the slide show's total length. If the soundtrack is longer than the slide show, iDVD simply stops playing the soundtrack after the last slide displays. (To have the music fade at the end of the slideshow, use the Slideshow portion of the Preferences dialog box.) And if you choose the Fit to Audio option, iDVD times the interval between image changes to match the soundtrack's duration.

To remove a slide show's background music, drag the icon out of the Audio well. When you release the mouse button, the icon vanishes in a puff of smoke.

Slide Show Tips

TV-Safe Slide Shows

Normally, when you view a slide show on a TV screen, you don't see the outer edges of each photo. This is because TV screens typically crop off the outer edges of an image. If you

want to see your images in their full, uncropped glory, choose iDVD's Preferences command, click the Slideshow button, and check the box labeled Always Scale Slides to TV Safe Area. When this option is active, iDVD sizes images so they don't com-

pletely fill the frame—thus eliminating cropping.

Beyond 99 Slides

The DVD specification limits the number of images in a slide show to 99. Fortunately, iDVD lets you work around this limita-

tion. You can drag more than 99 photos into the slide show editor, and, thanks to some clever technical trickery, iDVD is able to present them as one slide show.

What iDVD can't do is make your viewers patient enough to sit through all those shots.

Making a Magic iDVD

When you want to create a DVD in a hurry, use the Magic iDVD feature that debuted in iDVD 6.

Magic iDVD presents you with a single window containing a list of menu themes, a set of drop boxes for holding movies and photos, and a media browser for accessing your audio, photos, and movies.

Choose a theme, then drag movies into the drop boxes. To create DVD slide shows, drag photos to the drop boxes. Drag an entire album from iPhoto or build a slide show one photo at a time by dragging individual photos into the same box. Want a music soundtrack for a slide show? Drag an audio track into the slide show's drop box.

When you're done, preview your work by clicking the Preview button and using iDVD's standard preview features (page 287). Then click the Burn or Create Project buttons, and iDVD builds your project for you, even creating chapter submenus for movies containing DVD chapters (page 291).

Magic iDVD may be all you need for many projects. And if you need to customize or enhance the DVD it creates, you can bring the rest of iDVD's authoring features to bear. Indeed, Magic iDVD is a great way to rough out a project that you plan to refine later.

Here's how to make DVD magic.

Magic iDVD versus OneStep DVD

iDVD provides two ways to go from zero to DVD with very few steps. Which method should you use, and when?

When to go OneStep. Use OneStep DVD when you want to burn just one movie to a DVD and you don't need navigation menus. When you use OneStep DVD, you don't have the opportunity to customize menu designs—there aren't any. As page 299 describes, OneStep DVD creates an *autoplay*, or *kiosk-mode*, DVD: the disc begins playback as soon as you insert it into a computer or DVD player.

When to go Magic iDVD. Use Magic iDVD when you want navigation menus and more than one piece of content on your DVD—for example, a couple of movies and some slide shows.

To Make a Magic iDVD

Step 1. Choose File > Magic iDVD.

Step 2 (optional). Edit the DVD title.

Step 3. Choose a theme for the DVD by clicking one of the theme thumbnails. (To access additional themes, use the pop-up menu above the row of thumbnails.)

Step 4. To add video to the DVD, click the Movies button in the media browser, then drag one or more movies into the drop boxes.

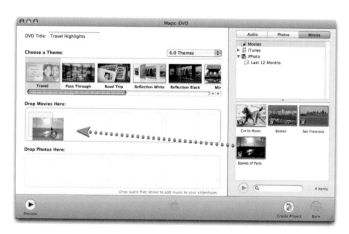

Tips: You can also drag movies directly from folders on your Mac's hard drive. (To have iDVD list movies from other folders in its media browser, use the Preferences command as described on page 290.)

Need to add multiple movies? Simply Shift-click or ⌘-click on each one to select the movies, then drag them as a group, as shown on the opposite page. When you release the mouse button, each movie appears in its own drop box.

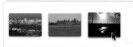

Step 5. To add a slide show to the DVD, drag photos into the photos drop boxes. Each box represents a different slide show.

Tips: You can drag albums from iPhoto, or folders of photos from your hard drive or a CD. If you like to overwork, you can drag individual photos to a drop box, one at a time. You can also combine approaches. For example, you can drag an entire album to create a slide show, then drag individual photos to that slide show's drop box to add them to the show.

And just as you can add multiple movies at once, you can create multiple slide shows at once. Shift-click or ⌘-click on each album in the Photos media browser, then drag the albums as a group. Each album becomes its own slide show.

Step 6 (optional). To add music to a slide show, drag an audio file from the Audio media browser (or elsewhere on your hard drive) to the slide show.

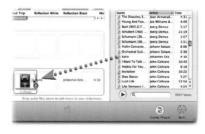

A speaker icon appears on the slide show's thumbnail to indicate that it has a soundtrack.

Step 7. Preview or finish up.

Check your work. To preview the DVD, click the Preview button. When you exit preview mode, you return to the Magic iDVD window.

Ready to bake. If you're happy with the job Magic iDVD has done, click the Burn button. iDVD creates a project containing your content, then immediately switches into burn mode. (For burning details, see pages 308–311.)

Further refinement. If you want to refine the project—for example, to customize some menus or refine your slide shows—click the Create Project button. iDVD creates a project that you can customize using the techniques described throughout this chapter.

Behind the Magic

Here's a look at how Magic iDVD does its design. And remember, you aren't locked into its magical decisions. You can customize anything in the projects that Magic iDVD creates.

Main title. The name you type into the DVD Title box becomes the title of your main menu.

Submenus. Your DVD's main menu will contain buttons that link to submenus for playing the DVD's movies and slide shows.

Chapter menus. Similarly, if you add a movie containing DVD chapter markers, you get a submenu for accessing those chapters. For themes that have separate chapter menu designs (as do all of the new iDVD themes), iDVD uses the chapter menu design for the chapter menu.

Drop zones. iDVD automatically adds movies to the drop zones of whatever menu theme you choose. If your DVD contains only slide shows, iDVD uses photos from the slide shows for the drop zones.

Planning and Creating Menus

When creating a DVD, you're also designing a user interface. If your DVD contains a couple of movies and a slide show, the interface will be simple: just one menu containing a few buttons.

But if your DVD will contain a dozen movies and another half-dozen slide shows, it will need multiple menus. And that means that you'll need to think about how to structure a menu scheme that is logical and easy to navigate.

As you plan a complex DVD, consider how many buttons each menu should have. In iDVD, a menu can have up to 12 buttons. That's a lot—too many choices for a main menu. If you have several movies and slide shows to present, it's better to create a set of *submenus* that logically categorize your content.

It's a balancing act: create too few menus, and you present your viewers with a daunting number of choices. Create too many, and you make them spend time navigating instead of viewing.

All of the new themes in iDVD 6 are designed with submenus in mind. You don't have to use these themes for projects containing submenus, but at least note their underlying philosophy: it's a good idea for a submenu to share some common design traits with the menus that lead to it.

Planning Your DVD

If your DVD will be presenting a large number of movies or slide shows, you need to plan how you will make that content available to the DVD's user. How many menus will you need? How will you categorize the content in each menu? This process is often called *information design*, and it involves mapping out the way you want to categorize and present your content.

A good way to map out a DVD's flow is to create a tree diagram depicting the organization of menus—much as a company's organizational chart depicts the pecking order of its management.

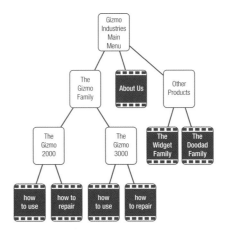

The chart shown here depicts the flow of a DVD a company might create to promote its new Gizmo product line. A main menu contains three buttons: two lead to other submenus, while the third plays a promotional movie about the company.

The submenu "The Gizmo Family" leads to two additional submenus, one for each Gizmo model. The "Other Products" submenu leads to two movies that promote other fine products.

Creating Additional Menus

To create a submenu, choose Add Submenu from the  pop-up menu or choose Project > Add Submenu.

To design the new menu and add content to it, double-click its button. You can customize the look of each sub-menu independently of other menus.

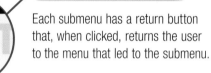

Each submenu has a return button that, when clicked, returns the user to the menu that led to the submenu.

A DVD in OneStep

If you just want to slap some video onto a DVD and you don't want menus, chapters, or slide shows, check out the OneStep DVD feature.

Insert a blank DVD in your Mac's optical drive, connect your DV camera via FireWire, and choose OneStep DVD from the File menu. iDVD rewinds your tape, captures video until it reaches the end of the tape, and then encodes the video into MPEG-2 format and burns it to disc. When you insert the burned disc in a DVD player, the video begins playing back immediately. You can also create a disc from a movie file instead of an attached camcorder; choose File > OneStep DVD from Movie.

OneStep DVD is a fast way to create a DVD, but it isn't a perfect method of backing up a tape—you don't have as much flexibility to edit the video in the future. You can't extract the video from a DVD without some effort (see page 315), and even then, the quality won't be as good as the original, since the video will have been compressed.

OneStep Tips

Controlling the capture.
Normally, OneStep DVD rewinds a tape to the beginning and then begins capturing video. If you begin capturing from the middle of the tape, press your camera's Stop button during the rewind process, then immediately press its Play button. iDVD will begin capturing at that point.

Similarly, to stop the capture before the tape reaches the end, press your camera's Stop button, and iDVD burns what you captured up to that point.

Beware of breaks. If your tape contains a lengthy gap between scenes—a segment of blank tape with no timecode—OneStep DVD will probably stop importing video when it encounters that gap.

Reclaiming disk space.
OneStep DVD stores your captured video in a hidden folder on your hard drive (to see where, choose iDVD > Preferences, then click Advanced). These files are deleted the next time you restart your Mac.

Customizing Menus

The design themes built into iDVD look great and, in some cases, sound great, too. But you might prefer to not use off-the-rack designs for your DVDs.

Maybe you'd like to have a custom background screen containing your company logo or a favorite vacation photo. You might like the background image of a particular iDVD theme, but not its music or its buttons' shape or typeface. Or maybe you'd just like to have the title of the menu at the left of the screen instead of centered.

You can customize nearly every aspect of your DVD's menus and navigation buttons. With the Menu and Buttons panes, you can modify buttons, add and remove background audio, change a menu's background image, and more.

You can also create text labels—for example, some instructions for DVD newbies or a few lines of commentary about the DVD's subject.

iDVD 6 provides more menu customizing options than did earlier versions. You can even have a different shape and style for *each* button on a menu. As with all design tasks, restraint is a virtue. Have fun with your menu designs, but don't lose sight of the menu's main purpose: to provide convenient access to your DVD's contents.

Moving Items Around

Normally, iDVD positions buttons on a fixed grid. This keeps them lined up nicely, but (a little smoother read) to manually specify a button's location—perhaps to line it up with a custom background image.

To manually control button position, select the Free Positioning option in the Buttons pane. Now you can drag buttons wherever you like.

You can change the position of a menu's title text by simply dragging it anywhere on the menu.

Changing Menu Durations

You like a particular motion menu but you don't want to use all of it. Maybe you don't need all eight drop zones in the Reflections themes. Just shorten the menu's duration. Go to the Menu pane, then drag the Loop Duration slider until the menu is the desired length.

This technique works best with themes that don't have background music, so either choose a theme that lacks music or delete the music (see page 302).

Adding Text

To add descriptive text, captions, or instructions to a menu, choose Add Text from the Project menu (⌘-K). A text area appears; drag it to the desired location, then click within that text area, and type. To start another line, press Return.

To format the text, use the Text area of the Menu pane; see the opposite page.

Kill the Watermark

iDVD displays the Apple logo watermark on each menu screen. To get rid of it, choose Preferences from the iDVD menu, click the General button, and then uncheck the Show Apple Logo Watermark box.

Staying TV Safe

TV sets omit the outer edges of a video frame—a phenomenon called *overscan*. To make sure buttons and other menu elements will be visible on TV sets, choose the Show TV Safe Area command in the View menu, and avoid putting buttons or other elements in the shaded area.

Changing the Background Image

To change the background image of an iDVD menu, simply drag an image into the menu area. For the best results, be sure to use a photo with proportions that match your project's aspect ratio: 4:3 for standard television or 16:9 for widescreen or HD television. You can ensure these proportions when cropping in iPhoto: from the Constrain pop-up menu, choose 4 x 3 (DVD) or 16 x 9 (HD).

Tips: Some photos make better backgrounds if you reduce their brightness and contrast so the image doesn't overwhelm the buttons. In iPhoto, duplicate the image and then adjust the brightness and contrast of the duplicate.

If you replace the background on a theme that has a drop zone, the drop zone remains. To remove a drop zone when replacing a background, press ⌘ while dragging the image into the menu.

Want a plain white background? You can download one from www.macilife.com/idvd. You can also make your own patterned or solid-colored backgrounds in a program like Photoshop Elements. Create a graphic with dimensions that are 640 by 480 pixels (854 by 480 pixels for widescreen), save it as a JPEG image, and then drag it into iDVD.

If your project contains several menus, you can apply one menu's custom design to other menus in the project; see page 303.

And, if you decide you'd rather just have the theme's original background, simply drag the custom background's image thumbnail out of the Background well (next to the Loop Duration slider) in the Menu pane.

Customizing Button Shapes

To change a button's shape, select it and choose a shape in the Button Shapes area of the Buttons pane. To change the shape of every button in a menu, select them all before choosing a shape: choose Edit > Select All Buttons (⌘-A).

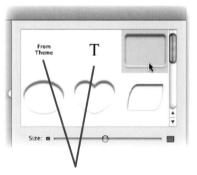

To use the button shape from the current theme, choose From Theme. For a text-only button, choose the T option.

Each button style has its own style of highlight, which appears when a user selects the button. To change the highlight color, click the Highlight Color well.

You can also control the size of the buttons by dragging the Size slider.

Changing Button Text Labels

When you choose a button shape, your buttons consist of text labels and little thumbnail images or movies. With the Label area of the Buttons pane, you can change where a button's text labels appear in relation to the button's thumbnail image.

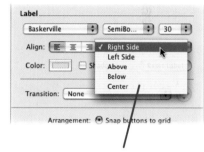

To customize button labels, choose an option from the pop-up menu.

To add a soft shadow to some text, select the button or label and click the Shadow box.

You can also change the font, font color, and type size for button text and for the menu's title and any text you've added. If you don't like the results, choose the Undo command as many times as needed to get back to where you started.

Tip: To format all of a menu's buttons at once, select them all first: click on one button, then press ⌘-A. Similarly, to select every text item you've added, click one item and then press ⌘-A.

More Design Tips

Adding Transitions

You can have a transition between menus. For example, when your DVD's viewers choose a button to go to a movie, you can have the menu appear to peel away to reveal the movie.

You can choose from a dozen different transition styles. For menu transitions, I'm partial to cube, page flip, or wipe—each conveys the notion of moving from one area to another.

You create menu transitions by assigning them to buttons. You can assign a different transition to every button in a menu, but in the interest of good taste, it's better to stick with just one or two different transition styles. For example, you might choose the cube transition for buttons that go from one menu to another, and the fade through black transition for buttons that lead directly to movies and slide shows.

To assign a transition to a button, select the button and then choose the desired transition from the Transition pop-up menu in the Buttons pane. Some transitions, such as cube, also allow you to specify a direction—set this by clicking the little arrows next to the pop-up.

Varying the direction of transitions can be a nice way to add variety without resorting to using a lot of different transition styles. For example, when a viewer chooses a button to go to a slide show, you might have a cube that rotates to the left. For a different button that leads to another menu, you might have a cube transition that rotates downward.

Tip: If you've mixed and matched transitions and decide you'd prefer to use just one transition style, you don't have to change the transitions one button at a time. Just use iDVD's map view to change the transitions in one fell swoop; see page 305.

Note: A menu transition is, unfortunately, a one-way street. That is, a transition appears only as you drill *down* into a DVD's menu structure. If you navigate from a submenu back to a main menu, you don't see a transition.

Moving Buttons Between Menus

To move a button from one menu to another, select the button and choose Cut. Next, move to a different menu (use map view to get there in a hurry), then paste.

You can also *copy* a button instead of pasting it. You might do this to provide access to a piece of content from several different menus.

For example, say you've created a series of online help screens in the form of a slide show. To make the online help available from every menu in your DVD, copy its button and then paste it into each menu.

New Menu from Selection

After adding numerous items to a DVD, you realize that a particular menu has too many buttons. The solution: move some of those buttons to a new menu. But don't wear out your wrists cutting and pasting. Just select the buttons you want to move (Shift-click on them), then sprint up to the Project menu and choose New Menu from Selection. iDVD removes the selected buttons and stashes them in a new menu.

Silencing Motion Menus

You might like the look of a motion menu, but maybe you don't want any music or sound effects to play. To silence a motion menu, go to the Menu pane and drag the Menu Volume slider to its leftmost position. If you change your mind, raise the volume level. To silence the menu for good, drag the icon out of the Audio well, and it disappears in an animated puff of smoke.

Audio-Only Menus

Conversely, maybe you would like some background audio to play, but you don't want motion in your menus. First, choose a theme that lacks motion, or replace an existing motion theme's background with a static image. Next, drag an audio file, iTunes playlist, or QuickTime movie into the Menu pane's Audio well. To hear the audio, click the Motion button. A menu can play for up to 15 minutes before it loops.

Motion Buttons

In many themes and button styles, iDVD also applies motion to your movie buttons: small, thumbnail versions of the movies play back when the menu is displayed.

You can even specify which portion of the movie plays: just select its button and then drag the slider that appears above the movie.

To specify how much of a movie plays in a motion button, drag the Loop Duration slider in the Menu pane.

There are times when you might not want a movie's button to be a thumbnail movie. Maybe the movie thumbnail distracts from the motion menu's background. In any case, simply select the movie's button and then uncheck the Movie checkbox that appears above it. Now use the slider to choose a static thumbnail image for the movie.

If you're using a theme that has text-only buttons, you can add motion or thumbnail buttons by choosing a different button style in the Buttons pane.

Copying Custom Menus

Your project contains several menus and you've customized one of them. Now you decide you'd like to apply your design to all the menus in your project. Easy: choose Apply Theme to Submenus from the Advanced menu.

Conversely, if you've customized a submenu and want to apply that design to the project's other menus, choose Apply Theme to Project.

Copying Button Styles

You've changed a button's text and color, and would like to apply that formatting to other buttons. Easy: select the formatted button and choose Edit > Copy Style. Then select one or more other buttons and choose Edit > Paste Style.

Saving a Theme Design

Happy with the results of a menu-design session? Save your customized theme as a "favorite," and you can apply it to future projects with one mouse click.

Choose Save Theme as Favorite from the File menu. If you have multiple user accounts on your computer, you can make the custom theme available to all users: check the Shared For All Users box.

The new theme appears in the Themes pane. To see it, choose Favorites or All from the themes pop-up menu. On your hard drive, saved themes are stored in your home directory in the following path: Library > Application Support > iDVD > Favorites. Shared themes are stored in the same path at the root level of the drive.

Fading Menu Audio

To have a menu's audio fade out at the end of the menu loop, use the General portion of the Preferences dialog box.

More Themes

Want to go beyond the themes that are built into iDVD? Try out some of the themes from DVDThemePak (www.DVDthemepak.com). Other sources for iDVD themes include iDVDThemes (www.iDVDthemes.com), and KeynotePro (www.keynotepro.com).

Navigating and Authoring with Map View

iDVD's map view lets you see the organization of your DVD project using a display that looks a lot like the organizational chart depicted on page 298.

In map view, you can see at a glance how your project is organized. More to the point, you can get around quickly. By double-clicking the icons in map view, you can jump to a specific menu or preview a slide show or movie. Need to drill down into a deeply nested submenu to do some design work? Display the map, then double-click the submenu's icon.

Map view is about more than just seeing the big picture. You can use it to rearrange submenus, change menu themes, create menu transitions, and add content to your DVD. You can also use map view to loop a slide show or movie so that it plays over and over again. And you can use map view to have a movie or slide show start automatically when your DVD is played.

To switch to map view, click the Map button. To exit map view, click the Map button again, double-click an icon in the map, or click the Return button in the lower-right corner of the map.

Customizing Your View

When you're on the road, sometimes you need the big picture and sometimes you need street-by-street details. Map view provides this flexibility, and then some.

Switch between left-to-right (shown here) and top-to-bottom views.

To scroll quickly, press the Option key and drag within the map.

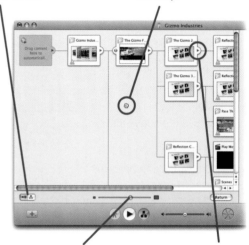

To zoom in and out on the map, drag the size slider. When zoomed out, you see only icons representing folders, slide shows, and movies.

When you zoom in, iDVD displays small thumbnail images as well as names of menus and other content.

If you don't need to see a particular set of icons, click the right-pointing triangle to hide them and free up viewing space.

See a warning triangle? Point to it, and iDVD displays details about the problem.

Authoring in Map View

Customizing Menus

To customize a menu in map view, select the menu by clicking it once. To change the menu's theme, use the Themes panel. To change the menu's background, audio, drop zones, or text formatting, use the Menu pane. To change the appearance of all buttons on a menu and set a transition, use the Buttons pane.

Here's the best part: you can customize multiple menus at once. Just Shift-click on each menu you want to change, and then use the panes to make your changes.

Note: When you use map view to specify a transition for a menu, every button on that menu will use the same transition. If you want a different transition for some of the menu's buttons, assign a transition to each button individually as described on page 302.

Rearranging Your Project

Want to move a slide show or other item to a different menu? Simply drag the item's icon to another menu.

Checking Transitions

To see which transitions a menu uses, point to the menu's icon, and a description of the transition appears.

Adding Content to a Menu

To add content to an existing menu, drag it from the media browser or the Finder to the menu's icon.

If you drag a movie or iPhoto album to an existing menu, iDVD creates a button for that item.

You can also change a menu's background image using the map: just drag a single image to the menu's icon. (For more details on customizing menu backgrounds, see page 301.)

Looping a Movie or Slide Show

To have a movie or slide show *loop* (play over and over), select its icon and choose Loop Slideshow from the Advanced menu.

(When you aren't in map view, you can specify looping by selecting a movie's or slide show's menu button and choosing Loop.)

Adding AutoPlay Content

On many DVDs, a movie appears when the DVD begins playing—an FBI warning, for example, or a movie-studio logo.

You can use map view to add this *AutoPlay* content to your DVD. Simply drag a movie, a photo, a set of photos, or an entire iPhoto album to the project icon.

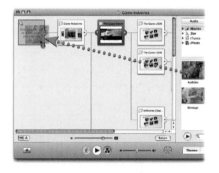

If you drag photos to the project icon, you can double-click the project icon to open the slide show editor where you can specify transitions and add background music (page 294).

Don't want an AutoPlay item after all? Just drag it out of the project icon, and it disappears in a puff of pixel smoke.

Creating a Kiosk DVD

Want a movie or slide show to play automatically and continuously? Drag it to the project icon and then, with the project icon still selected, choose Loop from the Advanced menu.

Adding DVD-ROM Content

One of the reasons why the DVD format is so versatile is that it can accommodate not only video, sound, and pictures, but also any disk files that you may want to distribute.

Here's the scoop on this aspect of DVD authoring, along with a peek under the hood to see how MPEG-2 compression manages to squeeze up to two hours of video onto a 4.7GB DVD.

The DVD-ROM Zone

A DVD can hold more than video and slide shows; it can also hold "computer files"—Microsoft Word documents, PDF files, JPEG images, and so on. You might take advantage of this to distribute files that are related to your DVD's content.

If you've created an in-house training DVD for new employees, you might want to include a PDF of the employee handbook. If you've created a DVD containing a couple of rough edits of a TV commercial, you might also include some PDFs that show the print versions of your ad campaign. If you've created a DVD promoting your band, you might include some audio files of your tunes.

When a DVD-Video disc also contains files intended to be used by a computer, it's said to have a *DVD-ROM* portion. If users play the DVD in a living-room DVD player, those files are invisible. However, if they use that same DVD with a personal computer, they can access the files.

Including Photos

As described on page 294, when creating DVDs containing slide shows, you can have iDVD copy the original images to the DVD-ROM portion. In the slide show editor, click Settings, then check the box labeled Add Image Files to DVD-ROM.

This option is ideal for photographers who want to distribute high-resolution versions of their images along with slide shows. You might also find it a useful way to back up a set of digital photos. The slide shows serve as a handy way of viewing the images, while the original, high-resolution files are archived in the DVD-ROM portion of the disc.

Note: If your slide show includes raw-format photos from iPhoto, iDVD includes both the raw-format originals and the JPEG stand-ins that iPhoto created. If you'd rather not include the raw originals (or the JPEGs), save your DVD as a disc image and edit the contents of the disc image as described on page 311.

Tip: If you *always* want to include a slide show's original images on your DVD, choose Preferences from the iDVD menu, click the Slideshow button, then check the box labeled Always Add Original Photos to DVD-ROM Contents.

Managing DVD-ROM Content

To add other types of files to your DVD, choose Edit DVD-ROM Contents from the Advanced menu. Use the DVD-ROM Contents window to manage and organize the contents of the DVD-ROM folder.

Your DVD will contain a folder with the name of your project plus *DVD-ROM Contents*.

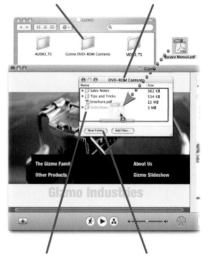

To add files to the DVD-ROM area, drag them into the DVD-ROM Contents window, or use the Add Files button. To delete a file from the DVD-ROM area, select it and press the Delete key.

If you've added photos from one or more slide shows to the DVD-ROM area, they appear in a folder named Slideshows. You can't rename this folder or move it to another folder. To delete it, return to the slide show editor and uncheck its DVD-ROM box.

You can create additional folders within the DVD-ROM folder, and you can drag files or other folders into it.

MPEG: Compressing Space and Time

One of the jobs iDVD performs is to compress your movies into MPEG format, the standard method of storing video on DVD-Video discs. Like image and audio compression,

MPEG is a *lossy* format: the final product lacks some of the quality of the original. But as with image and audio compression, the amount of quality loss depends on the degree to

which the original material is compressed.

Like JPEG, MPEG performs spatial compression that reduces the storage requirements of

individual images. But video adds the dimension of time, and MPEG takes this into account by also performing *temporal compression*.

The key to temporal compression is to describe only those details that have changed since the previous video frame. In an MPEG video stream, some video frames contain the entire image; these are called *I-frames*. There are usually two I-frames per second.

An I-frame describes an entire scene: "There's a basketball on a concrete driveway."

Sandwiched between those I-frames are much smaller frames that don't contain the entire image, but rather only those pixels that have changed since the previous frame.

"It's rolling toward the street."

To perform temporal compression, the video frame is divided into a grid of blocks, and each square is examined to see if anything has changed. Areas that haven't changed—such as the stationary background in this example— are simply repeated in the next frame.

This is why video with relatively little motion often tends to look better than video that contains a great deal of motion. When little changes from one frame to the next, the quality of each frame can be higher.

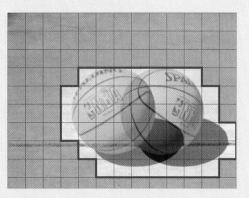

Burning Your DVD

You've massaged your media and made your menus. What's next? Burning the final product onto a blank DVD. Simply click iDVD's Burn button and insert a blank disc. But before you burn, read the following tips.

Preview First

Before you insert that pricey blank DVD, preview your work by clicking iDVD's Preview button. Use the iDVD remote control to step through your menus and spot-check your video, slide shows, and any menu transitions you've added. And don't forget to proofread your menu titles and button text.

Consider a Disc Image

Before you burn, consider creating a *disc image*, a kind of virtual disk that can be extremely useful for testing and burning. You'll find full details on working with disc images on page 310.

If your DVD has a lot of menus, transitions, and content, consider creating a disc image and using Mac OS X's DVD Player program to test it. And if you have a slower Mac—or just seem to have trouble burning reliably—creating and burning a disc image can be a great way to increase your success rate.

Note: If you will be burning a dual-layer DVD, do not try to burn it from a disc image. For details, see page 310.

Run Lean

When burning a DVD, avoid running complex programs that put a lot of demands on your system. Recording a track in GarageBand while also burning a DVD is not a good idea, for example. Also, consider turning off file sharing and quitting any disk-intensive programs.

What Kind of Media?

Several types of writable DVD media exist: DVD-R, DVD-RW, DVD+R, and DVD+RW. Previous versions of iDVD could handle the DVD-R format only, but iDVD is now much more versatile. It can burn any of the aforementioned formats, assuming your DVD burner supports them. Most of the SuperDrives in today's Macs can; older SuperDrives support the DVD-R and DVD-RW formats only.

The differences between the "minus" and "plus" camps are technical ones and don't have much bearing on your burning endeavors. The more important difference deals with R and RW: an RW disc can be erased and reused roughly 1,000 times. If you insert an RW disc that already contains data, iDVD even offers to erase it for you.

RW discs are great for testing, although as the following page describes, you're more likely to encounter playback problems on some DVD players. Also, RW discs are more sensitive to damage and aging than write-once discs.

If you're interested in the technical details between the minus and plus formats, read Jim Taylor's superb DVD FAQ at www.DVDdemystified.com.

Dual-Layer Differences

Many of today's Macs include SuperDrives capable of burning on dual-layer DVD+R media. With a dual-layer drive, you can burn nearly 8GB, or about four hours' worth of video.

To see if your Mac is capable of dual-layer burning, choose Project > Project Info, and click on the DVD Type pop-up menu. If you have a dual-layer drive, you'll have the option of specifying dual-layer media.

Incidentally, if you have a single-layer SuperDrive but would like to double your pleasure, you can buy external dual-layer burners that work just fine with iDVD. But note that more is not always better. Dual-layer burned discs often do not play in standalone DVD players, and may lack the longevity of single-layer discs.

Will It Play?

You've burned a disc and are ready to show it off to your boss. You pop the disc into the conference room DVD player and proudly press the play button—and nothing happens.

Welcome to The Incompatibility Zone. The sad fact is, some DVD players and personal computer DVD drives are unable to read burned DVD media. Generally, older DVD players and drives are most likely to have this problem, but you may encounter it in newer players, too.

Roughly 85 percent of DVD players can read DVD-R and DVD+R discs, and about 80 percent can read DVD-RW and DVD+RW discs. Those are good num-bers, although they won't be of much solace if your player—or your boss's—is in the minority.

The picture is much more bleak when it comes to dual-layer DVD burning: a large percentage of DVD players have trouble playing dual-layer burned DVDs. If you're shopping for a new DVD player, be sure to verify compatibility with the type of media you plan to burn. And diplomatically inform your friends, family, and colleagues that if they have problems playing your DVD, the fault probably lies with their players.

Making More

You can burn multiple copies of a DVD using iDVD, but you might find the job easier with Roxio's Toast or Popcorn software, both of which provide copying features. Or, make a disc image and use Mac OS X's Disk Utility program to burn multiple copies (see page 310).

If you need to have more than a few copies of a disc—for example, 2,000 training DVDs for a large company—you'll want to work with a replicator. Most replicators will accept a burned DVD as a master.

One excellent source for low-volume repli-cation is CustomFlix (www.customflix.com), which also provides e-commerce and shipping services.

Archiving Projects for Burning Elsewhere

iDVD provides an archiving feature that saves a project and all of its assets in one self-contained file.

Archiving enables you to author on one Mac, then burn on another. This is great for anyone who has multiple Macs but not multiple DVD burners. If you have a PowerBook without a SuperDrive and a desktop Mac with one, you can still work on a DVD on a cross-country flight. Just archive and transfer your project when you land.

To archive a project, choose Archive Project from the File menu.

If you created customized themes for the DVD—or if you want to be certain that your themes will be available in a future version of iDVD—check the Include Themes box. If you're using standard themes and aren't obsessed about future compatibility, you can uncheck this box and your archive file will be a bit smaller.

If iDVD has already encoded the DVD's content, you can include those encoded files in the archive by checking the Include Encoded Files box. Doing so will make your archive file quite a bit larger, however.

After you specify archive settings and click Save, iDVD goes to work, copying everything in your project into a file. You can trans-fer this file to another Mac using a fast network, a FireWire hard drive, or the Fire Wire disk mode that laptop Macs provide.

Burning Tips

For many projects, one click of the Burn button is all it takes to commit your work to plastic. But sometimes it's better to take the roundabout route: creating a *disc image* and then using it as the basis for your burns.

If you've downloaded software from the Internet, you're probably already familiar with the concept of disc images. But if you haven't heard the term before, it can seem confusing.

And for good reason: a disc image isn't a disc or an image. It's a file on your hard drive. The bits and bytes in this file are organized in the same way that they would be on a disc. If you double-click a disc image file, the Mac's Finder reads the disc image and creates an icon on your desktop—as if you'd inserted a disc.

iDVD lets you create a disc image for a DVD project. When you do, iDVD performs the same steps that it performs when you click the Burn button, with one exception: After iDVD finishes preparing your DVD's assets, it doesn't fire up your DVD burner. Instead, it simply saves the data in a file on your hard drive—as a disc image.

Important: If you plan to burn a dual-layer disc, note that Apple recommends burning the disc directly from iDVD, rather than creating a disc image and then burning from that image. To quote from iDVD's online help, "double-layer discs burned from a disc image may cause playback issues in some DVD players, such as freezing during playback."

Creating a Disc Image

Step 1.

Choose Save as Disc Image from the File menu (Shift-⌘-R).

Step 2.

Give your disc image a name and click Save.

iDVD compresses your video, encodes your menus, and then saves the resulting data in the disc image file. The file's name ends in .img.

Testing a Disc Image

To test your DVD using Mac OS X's DVD Player program, begin by double-clicking the disc image file to create an icon on your desktop.

If you double-click this icon to examine its contents, you'll see two folders: AUDIO_TS and VIDEO_TS. (If you added DVD-ROM content to the DVD, you'll see a third folder.) Those awkward names are required by the DVD standard, as are the even more awkward names of the files inside the VIDEO_TS folder.

(The AUDIO_TS folder will always be empty, but don't try to create a DVD that lacks one; the DVD may not play in some players. And if it ever comes up in a trivia contest, TS stands for transport stream.)

To test your disc image, start DVD Player and choose File > Open DVD Media. (In pre-Tiger Mac OS X versions, choose File > Open VIDEO_TS Folder.) Navigate to your disc image, select its VIDEO_TS folder, and click Choose or press Return. Now press the spacebar or click DVD Player's Play button, and your faux DVD will begin playing back.

Burning a Disc Image

If you found a problem when testing your disc image—a typo, for example, or a missing piece of content—you haven't wasted a blank DVD. Simply trash the disc image, make your revisions in iDVD, then create and test another disc image.

And if you're ready to burn? If you're burning a single-layer DVD, don't bother with iDVD's Burn button—use the disc image instead.

First, start up Mac OS X's Disk Utility program. (It's located in the Utilities folder within your Applications folder.) Next, click the Burn button in the upper-left corner of Disk Utility's window. In the dialog box that appears, locate and double-click the disc image file. Disk Utility displays another dialog box. Before you click its Burn button, click the little down-pointing arrow to expand the dialog box.

What's the hurry? You can get more reliable burns—and increase the chances that your DVD will play in other players—by burning at your drive's slowest speed.

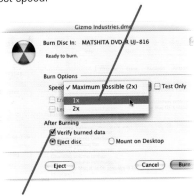

In a hurry? If you uncheck Verify Burn, your disc will be ready sooner. On the downside, you won't know if data was written inaccurately until you try to play the disc.

Other Ways to Burn

If you have Roxio's Toast Titanium software, you can drag your disc image's AUDIO_TS and VIDEO_TS folders into Toast and burn your disc there. If you've installed Toast's Toast It shortcut menu, the job is even easier: Control-click on your disc image icon and choose Toast It from the shortcut menu. (Use Toast's Preferences command to install the Toast It shortcut menu plug-in.)

You can also use Toast to fine-tune any DVD-ROM content you've added—for example, removing the raw versions of the photos that you've included in a slide show (see page 306).

Toast also gives you a choice of burning speeds. For critical projects where you need the broadest compatibility, burn at 1x speed.

Encoding Insights and Tips

You don't have to know how iDVD encodes MPEG-2 video, but if you're curious, here are the details.

Best Quality. When you choose Best Quality in the Encoder Settings area of the Preferences dialog box, the bit rate depends in part on how much media is in your project. Data rates will vary from a low of 3.5 megabits per second (Mbps) to 7 Mbps. With best-quality encoding, iDVD uses variable bit rate (VBR) encoding: the bit rate of a video stream changes according to the complexity of the scene. Motion-intensive scenes get a higher bit rate, while scenes containing little motion get a lower rate.

(For you compression gurus, iDVD uses single-pass variable bit rate encoding. Thus, iDVD still can't quite deliver the degree of quality you can get from Apple's Compressor program, which supports two-pass VBR and provides additional quality-optimization settings.)

Best Performance. When you choose Best Performance, iDVD encodes at a fixed bit rate of 8 Mbps.

Tip: If you've burned a DVD using best-quality encoding and you delete some content from the project, you may be able to improve the video quality of the remaining content by having iDVD encode it all over again. Choose Delete Encoded Assets from the Advanced menu, then burn the project again.

iDVD Tips

Make It Last

Burned discs don't last forever. To improve their reliability and longevity, don't use peel-and-stick labels. If a label isn't perfectly centered, the DVD will be off-balance when it spins, and that could cause playback problems. If you want to label your DVDs, use an ink-jet printer that can print on DVD media.

Label discs with a Sharpie or other permanent marker. Write small and be brief—the solvents in permanent ink can damage a DVD's substrate over time.

Keep burned DVDs in jewel cases, and store them in a cool, dark place. Be careful to never flex the disc—a DVD is comprised of several different layers, and flexing a disc can cause the layers to separate. To remove a disc from a jewel case, press the center button of the case, then lift the disc out—don't simply pull the disc by its edges. (This advice applies to all optical media, by the way.)

The National Institute of Standards and Technology has published an excellent guide to improving the longevity of optical discs of all kinds. You can download the guide from the Web; I've linked to it at www.macilife.com/iDVD.

Which Movie Formats Work with iDVD?

You can include digital camera movies in an iDVD project—just drag them into the iDVD window. If the movies are in your iPhoto library, you can use iDVD's photo browser to access them.

Indeed, you can burn nearly any kind of QuickTime movie onto a DVD, including movies you've downloaded from the Web or copied from an old CD-ROM.

If a movie is smaller than the DVD standard of 720 by 480 pixels, iDVD enlarges it to fill the screen. This results in a loss of sharpness, but enlarged movies can still look good when viewed on a TV. It's better to have shared a blurry movie than never to have shared at all.

You can't use movies stored in MPEG-1 or MPEG-2 formats. Sony digital cameras use the MPEG format for their movies, and many of the movies that have been posted on file-sharing networks are in MPEG format.

There are free or cheap utilities that enable you to convert MPEG movies into a format that iDVD (and iMovie HD) can use. I've written up instructions on my site; see www.macilife.com/imovie. You can also use Toast Titanium's Export Video command, as described at right.

Incidentally, this MPEG prohibition does not apply to MPEG-4 movies created by digital cameras or to iMovie HD projects created in MPEG-4 format. Those movies work just fine in iDVD.

Reverting Your Project

You've made some modifications that you don't like. Many programs, including iMovie HD and GarageBand, have a Revert command that lets you get back to the last version you saved. iDVD lacks a Revert command, but you can simulate one: just reopen the project by choosing its name from the Open Recent submenu in the File menu. Click Don't Save when iDVD asks you if you want to save changes before reopening the project.

Extracting Video

You burned some cherished video to a DVD, then lost the original tape—and now you want to edit it in iMovie HD.

You can extract video from a DVD and convert it into DV format, but you will lose some quality in the process. If you have Toast Titanium, click its Video tab and drag your DVD's VIDEO_TS folder into the Toast window. Locate the clip you want to extract, select it, and choose Export Video from the Disc menu.

You can also extract video using any of several free or cheap utilities. Video guru Matti Haveri has published a fine tutorial on his Web site; I've linked to it at www.macilife.com/iDVD.

Project Management Tips

When you add a movie or set of images to iDVD, the program doesn't actually add those files to your project file. Rather, iDVD simply links to the existing files on your hard drive.

If you need to move a project from one Mac to another, create an archive of the project using the Archive Project command in the File menu. As described on page 309, this command copies all of the project's assets into one file.

If you copy just the project file—or if you delete an asset that you added to the project—iDVD displays broken-link icons for buttons whose assets are missing.

When you open a project containing broken links, iDVD displays an error message.

If you've moved a file to a different folder or drive, you can aim iDVD in the right direction: click Find File, then locate and double-click the file.

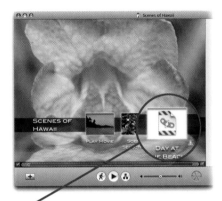

You can avoid the hassle by not moving assets once you add them to a project, or by creating an archive of the project to gather all its assets in one place.

To get the big picture of a project, choose Project Info from the Project menu.

Use these options to change a project's video format and encoding settings.

To reconnect to a missing file, double-click its entry, then locate the file and double-click its name.

You can change the DVD's name here. This doesn't change the name of your project file; rather, it changes the name of the final DVD. The DVD specification doesn't permit a disc name to have spaces in it; iDVD replaces any spaces with underscores, as in HAWAII_SCENES.

The Project Info window displays a list of the project's assets; its Status column indicates if any assets are missing (Ø).

More iDVD Tips

Painless Pane Switching

You want to drag a movie, audio file, or image into the Menu pane, but the Media pane is currently visible. How do you get your media from here to there? Easy: just drag the media's icon *over* the Menu button and pause there for a moment—iDVD switches to the Menu pane. Now continue dragging into the Background or Audio well.

Browsing Other Folders

You can use the Preferences command to tell iDVD to search other folders and hard drives when displaying its movie browser (page 290). You can expand your browsing options for audio and photos, too. Just drag a folder from the Finder into the appropriate media browser.

This also works for the movie browser—and it's a handy alternative to the Preferences dialog box.

Hacking iDVD Themes

Previous versions of iDVD stored the themes within the application itself, but for iDVD 6, Apple moved them to a more sensible location: Computer > Library > Application Support > iDVD > Themes.

Each theme (which ends with the text .theme) is also a *package*—to explore it, Control-click on its icon and choose Show Package Contents from the shortcut menu. Double-click the Contents folder and then the Resources folder, and you'll find background movies and audio

loops. To extract an item—for example, to grab the background audio from the Drive In One theme—press Option while dragging the item's icon out to the desktop. This makes a duplicate of the item, leaving the original theme unchanged.

Take care to not throw away or alter any resources whose purpose you don't understand, lest you have to reinstall the iDVD application.

From PDF to DVD

An iDVD slide show isn't restricted to the JPEG image format. A slide show can display numerous graphics formats, including PDF.

iDVD's PDF support means that you can display just about any document in a slide show. Want to put a Microsoft Word document or a Web page in a slide show? Create a PDF version of the document: choose Print from the File menu, then click the Save as PDF button. Drag the PDF into the iDVD slide show editor, and iDVD creates a slide containing the contents of the PDF's first page. (If you have a multi-page document, save each page as a separate PDF or use the Preview application to extract specific pages, as described in the following tip.)

Before making a PDF of a document, you might want to choose the Page Setup command and click the landscape-orientation button. That way, your PDF will have the same horizontal orientation as a slide. If you make the PDF in

portrait orientation, your slide will have black borders on either side of the page.

Think twice about using a PDF that contains lots of text, especially in font sizes below 14 point. Small text looks fuzzy on a TV screen.

From iPhoto Book to Slide Show

On page 193, I discussed a method for saving an iPhoto book as a PDF and then extracting pages for printing. Here's a variation of that technique that lets you include iPhoto book pages in iDVD slide shows.

After saving your book as a PDF, open the PDF in Mac OS X's Preview program. Next, open Preview's drawer (choose Drawer from the View menu). In the drawer, locate the page that you want to turn into a slide. Select the page and choose Copy from the Edit menu.

Next, choose the New from Clipboard command from the File menu. The Preview program creates a new document and pastes the page you copied into it.

Now add that page to your slide show. Position the iDVD and Preview windows so you can see them both. Then, drag the thumbnail from the new Preview document you created into the iDVD window.

You don't have to save the Preview documents—you're simply using Preview as a tool for extracting individual pages from your book's PDF.

By the way, if you've tried the technique on page 193, you may be wondering why you can't use Preview to extract a PDF for poster printing. The reason is that Preview generates a low-resolution (72 dots per inch) PDF. That's too low for good-quality printing but fine for a TV-bound slide show.

Making Custom Motion Menus

You aren't limited to the motion menus that accompany iDVD. You can make any QuickTime movie a motion menu background: just drag the movie to the Background well in the Menu pane.

If your motion menu movie is smaller than full-screen, iDVD enlarges it to fit. For the best video quality, use a movie whose dimensions are 640 by 480 pixels or 720 by 480 pixels.

As for what to put in your own custom menu, that's up to you. If the star of your DVD is an iMovie production, you might use a two- or three-minute excerpt of your movie. (Select a few clips in the timeline, then click the Share Selected Clips Only option in iMovie's Share dialog box.) Open a new iMovie project, bring that footage in, then use iMovie's Brightness & Contrast effect to make the footage appear faint. That way, buttons and text labels will still be easy to read. Save your work, then drag the movie to the Background well in iDVD's Menu pane.

Smooth looping. A motion menu loops until a user chooses a menu option. To avoid a visually jarring loop point, try this: In iMovie, create a still frame of the very first frame of your menu movie. Add this still frame to the very end of the movie, and put a fairly lengthy (say, two-second) dissolve between the end of the movie and the still frame. Finally, use direct trimming to make the remainder of the still frame as short as possible. (Drag its right edge to the left until it's right next to the dissolve in the timeline.) Now, when your movie loops, its last frame will appear to gradually dissolve into its first frame.

If you're after something more abstract, you can buy royalty-free libraries of animated backgrounds that you can use as motion menus. Two sources are ArtBeats (www.artbeats.com) and Digital Juice (www.digitaljuice.com). If you have Final Cut Pro, you can use its LiveType program to create rich animated textures.

A motion menu in iDVD can be up to 15 minutes long. But keep in mind that menu video uses disc space just like any other video clip.

Automating iDVD

iDVD provides thorough support for AppleScript, the automation technology that's built into Mac OS X. iDVD's AppleScript support enables you to create scripts that automate the creation and layout of DVDs.

The ultimate example of iDVD's autopilot features is a free utility that Apple has created called iDVD Companion. iDVD Companion is a program that runs alongside iDVD, adding a window containing three tabs that let you nudge buttons in single-pixel increments, align multiple buttons, and specify the exact pixel location of a menu's title—all things that iDVD alone can't do.

To download iDVD Companion and other iDVD scripts, visit www.apple.com/applescript/iDVD. At this writing, the scripts hadn't been updated since iDVD 2.1 came out in 2002. Test the scripts before running them while working on a critical project. Or just use them as a source of iDVD automation ideas.

Back to the Top

If you have a DVD containing several levels of submenus, you might want to offer your viewers a button that lets them get back to the uppermost, or title, menu. To do so, choose Project > Add Title Menu Button.

GarageBand:
Music, Podcasts,
and More

The Macintosh
iLife '06

GarageBand at a Glance

GarageBand turns your Mac into a musical instrument and a multitrack recording studio. Even if you aren't a musician, you can use GarageBand to create original songs.

If you've never played a note, start by exploring GarageBand's library of pre-recorded musical phrases, called *loops*. Assemble the loops you like into a tune. For extra credit, change the pitch of some loops by *transposing* them.

If you play the piano, plug a music keyboard into your Mac and go to town— GarageBand's *software instruments* enable your Mac to mimic instruments ranging from pianos to guitars to drums and beyond. Use loops to create a rhythm section, and then play along. Record your performances, then use GarageBand's editing features to make yourself sound better.

If you sing or play an instrument, connect a microphone, electric guitar, or other audio input to your Mac and hit the Record button. Create a three-part harmony by laying down vocal tracks one at a time. Or record multiple tracks at once.

As you compose, you may want to enhance certain tracks with *effects*. Add reverberation to create a concert hall sound, simulate old guitar amplifiers, or modify a software instrument to create a unique sound. Refine your mix as you go along by adjusting volume levels and stereo *panning*. When you're finished, export your song to your iTunes music library.

Here's how to become a one-Mac band.

The Loop Browser

To locate and audition loops, use the loop browser. Find loops by clicking buttons or typing search terms, such as *conga* (page 325). To hear a loop, click its name.

The Track Editor

Refine your performance using the track editor.

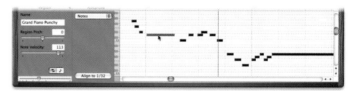

Editing notes. With the track editor for software instruments, you can edit individual notes, either in piano-roll format (above) or in standard music notation (below); see page 332.

Editing audio. With the track editor for real instruments, you can modify recordings (page 339).

Each track is a member of your virtual ensemble (page 322). Each track has controls for muting, adjusting volume, and more.

Use the track mixer to adjust a track's overall volume and left-right stereo position (page 342).

By repeating and modifying loops in the *timeline*, you can assemble everything from rhythm sections to entire arrangements (page 324).

The moving playhead shows the current playback location; drag the playhead to move around within a song.

The *beat ruler* shows beats and measures. To move the playhead to a specific spot, click the ruler.

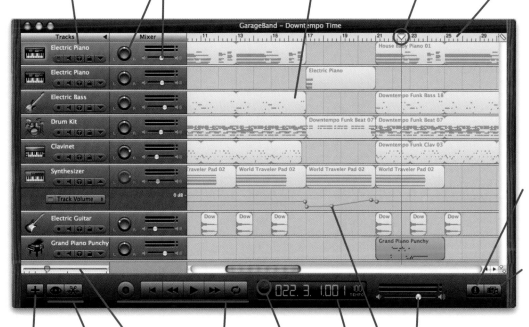

Podcasts, too.
You can also use GarageBand to produce podcasts (see page 354).

Display the Track Info pane (pages 330 and 336).

Display the media browser, for accessing your other iLife media (pages 356 and 362).

Create a new track (pages 324, 330, and 336).

Display the loop browser and the track editor (opposite page).

Drag the zoom slider to zoom in and out on the timeline.

Transport controls: record, play, rewind, and cycle playback (page 327).

Tune up with the instrument tuner (page 337).

The time display shows the playhead's exact position and the song's tempo. Drag the numbers to move the playhead and change the tempo.

Monitor and adjust the overall song volume.

To control volume and panning over time, create volume and pan curves (page 342).

How to Be a Songwriter

How you use GarageBand depends on your musical experience and your musical tastes. Here's a look at a few different paths you may take. And note that you aren't restricted to just one route—you might move from path to path as a song comes together.

Composing with Loops

Use the loop browser to locate a loop that sounds interesting (page 324).

Playing a Keyboard

Create a software instrument track and choose the desired software instrument (page 330).

If you like, customize the instrument to create a unique sound (pages 340 and 350).

Start a New Project

Specify the key, tempo, and time signature for your song. You can change any of these details later. You can even adjust tempo while your song is playing back.

Recording Audio

Create a real instrument track and choose the desired effect settings (page 336).

Adjust volume levels to get a loud, but not distorted, signal (page 336).

Use the Instrument tuner to get in tune (page 337).

Drag the loop into the timeline to add it to your song; drag the loop pointer to repeat the loop as desired (page 325).

Refine as desired: split and transpose regions (page 328), edit them (pages 332–335), and change the track's effects (page 340).

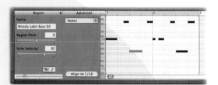

Record your performance, using GarageBand's Count In command and metronome to keep you in tempo (page 330).

Refine and arrange: modify and move regions (page 326), apply effects (page 340), and fix mistakes (pages 332–335).

Mix

Adjust each track's volume levels and panning, optionally adding a set of final-mastering effects and a fade-out (page 344). When you're finished, export the song to your iTunes music library.

Record your performance, laying down multiple takes if you like (page 336).

Edit your recording—rearrange it, change its effects, enhance its tuning or timing, or combine the best parts of several takes into a single track (page 339).

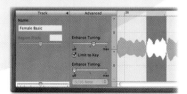

Two Types of Tracks

When you compose in GarageBand, you work with two very different types of tracks: *real instrument* tracks and *software instrument* tracks. The loops that GarageBand provides also fall into these two broad categories: loops with a blue icon are real instrument loops, and loops with a green icon are software instrument loops.

But what's the difference between a real instrument and a software instrument? The answer lies in the fact that today's Macs are powerful enough to generate sound using more than one technique. In fact, GarageBand is able to generate sound using multiple techniques *at once*.

Here's a look a how GarageBand makes its noise—and at what it all means to you.

Real Instruments: Recorded Sound

A real instrument track holds a digital audio recording—a riff played by a bass player, some strumming on an acoustic guitar, a phrase played by a string section, or a vocal that you record.

A real instrument track is blue, and a real instrument loop has a blue icon ▦. Notice that the track and the icon depict a waveform—a graphical picture of sound, similar to what we saw back on pages 26 and 246.

Variations. When you record an audio source, its regions are purple. If you import an audio file, its region is orange. See page 339 for all the colorful details.

Software Instruments: Sound on the Fly

A software instrument track doesn't hold actual sound. Instead, it holds only *data* that says what notes to play and how to play them. The sounds you hear when you play a software instrument track are being generated by your Mac as the song plays back.

A software instrument track is a bit like the music rolls that a player piano uses—just as the holes in the music roll tell the piano which notes to play, the bits of data in a software instrument track tell your Mac which notes to generate.

A software instrument track is green, and a software instrument loop has a green icon ♪. Instead of depicting a waveform, a software instrument region shows individual notes—why, it even looks a bit like an antique player piano roll (see photo, left).

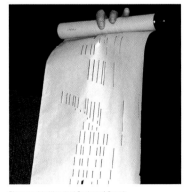

Photographic Historical Society of Canada

Comparing Approaches

Each type of track has advantages and capabilities that the other lacks.

The real advantage. When it comes to realism, you can't beat real instrument tracks. Listen to the Orchestra Strings loops that come with GarageBand. They don't just sound like a string section— they *are* a string section. Compare their sound to that of the software instrument loop named 70s Ballad Strings 02.

Another advantage of real instrument tracks is that they can hold *your* digital audio. When you plug a microphone into your Mac and belt out *My Way,* your voice is stored in a real instrument track.

The software advantage. The primary advantage of software instrument tracks is versatility. Because software instrument tracks store individual note data, you can edit them in almost any way imaginable. You can even change the instrument entirely. Want to hear how your bass line would sound when played by a synthesizer instead of an electric bass? Just double-click on the software instrument track's header and choose a synth.

On the down side, software instrument tracks make your Mac work harder than real instrument tracks—it's harder to generate sound on the fly than it is to play back a recording.

Common ground. Although real instruments and software instruments work differently, you can do many of the same things with both types of tracks. You can repeat loops within both types of tracks, and you can apply effects to both types. You can even transpose both types of tracks, including audio that you've recorded. However, you can't transpose audio regions across as wide a range as you can software instruments—they'd sound too artificial.

By supporting audio recordings (real instruments) and also being able to generate sound on the fly (software instruments), GarageBand gives you the best of both worlds.

How Apple Loops Work

The loops that come with GarageBand are stored in *Apple Loop* format. If you've played with GarageBand, you've experienced the program's ability to adjust the pitch and tempo of loops to fit your song. Here's how that works.

Apple Loops contain more than just sound. They also contain *tags*—tidbits of data—that describe the sound, starting with

the key and the tempo in which the loop was originally recorded. The tags also contain information about the *transients* in the recording. A transient is a spike in volume—such as occurs when a drumstick slaps a drumhead. Transients denote where beats occur, and GarageBand uses this information when changing the playback tempo of an Apple Loop.

When GarageBand transposes an Apple Loop to a different key, it's performing a process called *pitch shifting*. When GarageBand changes a loop's tempo, it's *time stretching*.

Apple Loops also contain descriptive tags, such as *Guitar* and *Jazz*. These tags are what you use to sift through loops by clicking on the buttons in the loop browser.

The green loop difference. Finally, it's important to know that software instrument loops (the green ones) contain more than just "piano roll" note data. They also contain audio, just as real instrument loops do. This lets you use them in real instrument tracks—and thus lighten the load on your Mac; see pages 345 and 352.

Working with Loops

For many GarageBand musicians (including yours truly), a song begins with some loops: a bass line, some percussion, a repeating synthesizer riff, or maybe all three.

The gateway to GarageBand's library of loops is the loop browser, whose buttons and search box let you quickly home in on loops of specific instruments or specific styles.

Once you find a loop that sounds interesting, you can add it to your song by dragging it into GarageBand's timeline. Once that's done, you can repeat the loop over and over, edit it, and transpose it.

GarageBand lets you audition loops even as your song is playing back—simply click on a loop in the loop browser. This is a great way to hear how a particular loop will fit into the arrangement you're building.

Working with loops is as easy as clicking and dragging. But as you master GarageBand, there's a powerful subtlety behind loops that you may want to take advantage of. Specifically, you can use software instrument loops in real instrument tracks in order to lighten the load on your Mac's processor.

If that makes no sense to you now, don't worry. When your arrangements become complex and you want to wring every bit of performance out of your Mac, you'll find all the details on pages 345 and 352.

Adding a Loop to a Song

To display the loop browser, click ⊙ or use the ⌘-L keyboard shortcut. To add a loop to a song, drag the loop into the timeline.

Creating a new track. When you drag a loop into an empty area of the timeline where there is no existing track, GarageBand creates a new track for the loop. The vertical bar indicates where the loop will begin playing. To move the loop after you've added it, drag it left or right (if the loop is too tiny to drag, zoom in).

Adding to an existing track. You can add a loop to an existing track. Mixing loops within a track is one way to add variety to a song.

Tip: You can drag a software instrument loop into a real instrument track, but not vice-versa. For more details, see page 345.

Looping a Region

When you add a loop to a track, you create a *region* that you can modify without changing the original loop. The most common kind of modification you'll perform is to loop a region so that it plays repeatedly.

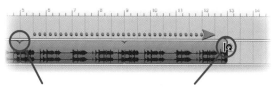

The notches show the beginning and end of each repetition of the loop.

To loop a region, point to its upper-right corner and drag it to the right.

Using the Loop Browser

Resets the loop browser, clearing any search text and deactivating any keyword buttons you've clicked.

Have lots of loops? Use the Loops pop-up menu to focus on specific collections (page 349).

To view more loop keywords, enlarge the loop browser by clicking here and dragging upward.

Tip: You can customize the loop browser buttons. To reorganize buttons, drag them around. To change a button's keyword, Control-click on the button and choose a keyword from the pop-up menu. To restore the original buttons, use the Preferences command.

To sort the loop list, click any column heading.

Love that loop? Click the Fav check box to add it to your Favorites list. To display your favorites, click the Favorites button (it's under the Reset button).

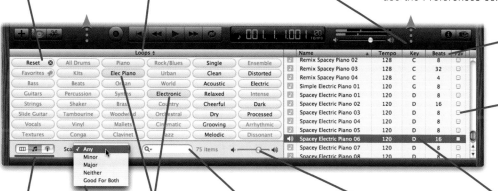

Switch between column view, music loop view (shown here), and podcast sounds view (page 356).

Click the keyword buttons to home in on specific instruments or styles.

Many loops use major or minor scales. You can use this menu to filter the list of loops to only those that complement your song.

To search by keyword, type some text and press Return. You can search for instruments (for example, *piano* or *guitar*) or styles (*jazz*, *funk*).

If you're auditioning a particular loop and it's overwhelming the rest of your arrangement, use this slider to turn down the loop browser's volume.

To audition a loop, click it. To hear how the loop sounds with the rest of your song, begin playing the song before you click the loop.

Working with Tracks and Regions

Tracks can be a lot easier to work with than musicians. Tracks never show up late for a gig, they always play in tune, their sense of timing is impeccable, and they never trash the hotel room.

Nonetheless, there are some important points to know about working with tracks and the regions that they hold. (A *region* is a set of notes or a snippet of sound. When you drag a loop into the timeline, the timeline or record a performance, you create a region.) For starters, when creating multitrack arrangements, you should rename tracks so you can tell at a glance which parts they hold: the melody, a solo, an alternate take of a solo.

As you compose, you may want to silence, or *mute*, certain tracks. Maybe you've recorded several versions of a solo, each on its own track, and you want to audition each one to hear which sounds best.

On the other hand, there may be times when you want to *solo* a track—to mute all the other tracks and hear only one track. Soloing a track can be useful when you're fine-tuning a track's effects settings or editing a region in the track.

A big part of creating an arrangement involves copying regions within a track or from one track to another. And as you move regions around, you often have to work with the beat ruler at the top of GarageBand's timeline. By fine-tuning the ruler's *snapping* feature, you can have your regions snap into place on exactly the right beat.

Here's how to get along with the members of the band.

Renaming a Track

Normally, GarageBand names a track after the instrument you've assigned to it. When you have multiple tracks that use the same instrument, it's hard to tell the tracks apart. Give your tracks descriptive names, such as *Vocal (Second Take)* or *Third Verse Strings.* To rename a track, click its name in the track header, then type a new name.

Soloing, Muting, and More

Your turn: enable the track for recording (pages 330 and 336).

Lock up: prevent changes and help performance (page 352).

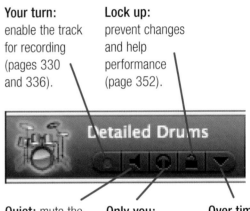

Quiet: mute the track. Keyboard shortcut: M.

Only you: solo the track. Keyboard shortcut: S.

Over time: create volume and pan curves (page 342). Keyboard shortcut: A.

Track Tips

You can move tracks up and down by dragging their headers. Consider grouping related tracks together—put all your rhythm section tracks together, then all your solo tracks, and so on.

When a track header is selected, you can use your keyboard's up- or down-arrow keys to select the track above or below the current track. This shortcut teams up nicely with those described above.

Play It Again: Cycling

When you're rehearsing, mixing, or recording, it's often useful to have part of a song play over and over. To do this, click the Cycle button (🔁) and then drag in the area just below the beat ruler to indicate the region that you want to repeat.

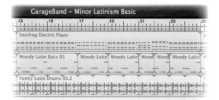

The yellow region repeats until time comes to an end or your parents pull the plug, whichever comes first. To resize the region, drag its left or right edge. To move the region, drag it left or right.

When cycling is on, playback always begins at the start of the cycle region.

Duplicating a Track

You can make a duplicate of a track: a new, blank track with the same instrument and effect settings as the original. Select the track's header, then choose Duplicate from the Track menu (⌘-D).

Use the Duplicate command when you want to record multiple takes of a part, each in its own track. After you've laid down 12 takes, copy and paste the best parts into a single track.

Copying Regions

Copying a region is a common task, and GarageBand provides a couple of ways to accomplish it. You can copy and paste: select a region, choose Copy, move the playhead to the destination, and paste. You can also press the Option key while dragging the region you want to copy.

Note: If you want to copy a region to a different track, the tracks must be of the same type. You can't copy a software instrument region to a real instrument track, or vice-versa.

Zooming tip: When you're moving regions over a large distance, use GarageBand's zoom slider to zoom out for a big-picture view. And use the keyboard shortcuts: Control-left arrow zooms out, while Control-right arrow zooms in.

Copying Versus Looping

You can repeat a region by either looping it or copying it. So which technique should you use? Looping is the fastest way to repeat a region over and over again: just drag the loop pointer as described on page 325.

The advantage of copying a region is that each copy becomes an independent region that you can edit without affecting other copies. With a repeating loop, if you edit one note in the loop, that edit is present in each repetition.

Snap to the Beat

When moving a region, you almost always want to move it to the exact beginning of a particular measure or beat. GarageBand's *timeline grid* supplies this precision: when the grid's snapping feature is active, GarageBand automatically snaps to beats and measures as you drag regions, move the playhead, drag loops to the timeline, and perform other tasks.

Normally, GarageBand adjusts the sensitivity of its grid to match the way you're viewing your song. If you're zoomed all the way out, GarageBand assumes you're performing fairly coarse adjustments, such as dragging a region from one part of a song to another. In this case, GarageBand's grid will snap to the start of each measure.

If you're zoomed all the way in, GarageBand figures you must be making precise adjustments, so it adjusts its grid to snap in sixty-fourth-note increments.

You can override GarageBand's automatic grid sensitivity: just choose the desired value from the grid menu.

Click the timeline grid button (▦) to display the grid menu.

The "swing" options delay every other grid point. This lets you maintain a swing feel when dragging regions. The amount of delay is greater with the "Heavy" options.

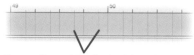

Every other grid point is delayed slightly.

Transposing and Creating Chord Changes

Unless they're from the soundtrack of *Wayne's World*, most songs aren't built around just one chord. Most songs contain chord *changes* or *progressions*—variations in key that add harmonic interest. Chord changes can be simple, such as those of a 12-bar blues, or they can be complex, such as those of Billy Strayhorn's jazz classic, *Lush Life*.

You can build chord changes in a couple of ways. For fast results, use the master track to create a *pitch curve* that transposes every track in your song (with two exceptions, noted at right).

When you want more control, transpose individual regions as described on the opposite page. This approach lets you be selective about what you transpose. For example, you can transpose some piano or guitar chords while keeping your bass track at the root key of your song. You can also edit individual regions to better fit your song's chord changes.

Transposing with the Master Track

Creating a pitch curve in the master track is the fastest way to "program" chord changes.

Step 1. Choose Show Master Track from the Track menu (⌘-B).

Step 2. In the master track header, choose Master Pitch from the pop-up menu.

Step 3. In the timeline, click at the point where you want to create a chord change—for example, at the beginning of a measure.

Step 4. Drag the control point up or down to transpose in increments of one *semitone* (one half-step). For example, to program the first chord change in a blues, drag up five semitones.

Notes and Tips

Audio limitations. A pitch curve will *not* transpose any audio regions that you recorded (purple regions) or imported (orange ones). To transpose purple regions, see the opposite page. To transpose orange regions, convert them into purple ones first; see page 339.

Changing a change. To remove a control point, select it and press the Delete key. To change its pitch, drag the control point up or down. To change the point when the chord change occurs, drag the control point left or right.

Adjusting precision. The point in time when GarageBand places control points is determined by the current timeline grid setting (see the previous page). If you want more precision in placing or adjusting a control point's position in time, zoom in or choose a smaller note value from the timeline grid button.

Unlock first. If you've locked any tracks (page 352), you can't adjust the pitch curve. If you try, GarageBand displays a dialog box that lets you unlock all locked tracks.

Transposing Individual Regions

This method is more work than creating a pitch curve, but as I noted on the opposite page, it offers more options and creative control.

The fastest way to use this technique is to repeat a loop for the entire duration of a verse (for example, 12 measures), split the loop at each point where you need a chord change, and then transpose the appropriate regions. This is a quick way to lay down a bass track.

If you'd like to follow along with the steps below, create a new song in GarageBand and add the loop named Woody Latin Bass 01 to it.

Step 1. Drag a loop into the timeline and use the loop pointer to drag it out to the desired length.

Step 2. Split the loop at the start of the change.

Drag the playhead to the beginning of the measure that needs to be transposed, then choose Split from the Edit menu (⌘-T).

Step 3. Split the loop at the end of the change.

Drag the playhead to the *end* of the measure that needs transposing, and choose

Split again. You now have an independent region that you can transpose.

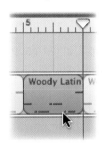

Step 4. Prepare to transpose.

Select the region you just created and open the track editor by clicking the track editor button (▨). Shortcut: Double-click the region to open it in the track editor.

Step 5. In the track editor, drag the Region Pitch slider or type a value in the box.

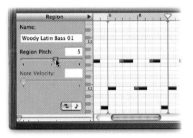

You can transpose in one-semitone increments. In the timeline, GarageBand indicates how far you've transposed a region.

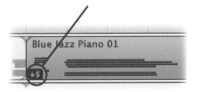

Notes and Tips

Editing a region to fit the changes.
Building a bass line from software instrument loops? You can build a better bass line by editing regions so that they complement your chord changes. For example, if you're going from F to C, you might make the last note of the F measure a C# or a B. That way, the bass will "lead in" to the new chord change. Edits like these can also take some of the repetitiveness out of tracks built from loops.

First, double-click the region you want to edit. Then, in the track editor, drag the last note of the region up or down to the desired note. GarageBand plays the note as you drag it, making it easy to determine where the note should be.

For details on editing software instrument tracks, see pages 332–335.

Transposing real instrument regions.
You can also transpose regions in real instrument tracks, but within a narrower range: one octave in either direction, as opposed to three octaves for software instrument tracks. And although you can't change individual notes as you can with software instrument tracks, you *can* perform some edits to regions in real instrument tracks; see page 339.

Recording Software Instruments

When you connect a music keyboard to your Mac, you unlock a symphony's worth of software instruments that you can play and record. There are pianos and keyboards and guitars of all kinds. There are synthesizers, strings, a flute, and some horns. And there are some drums you just can't beat.

As the following pages describe, you can edit your recordings and use effects to refine your tracks. You can even create completely new instruments of your own design.

If you don't have a music keyboard and don't want to spend a fortune on one, check out the offerings from M-Audio (www.m-audio.com). Its Keystation 61es is a 61-key (five octave) keyboard that sells for under $200. Its "semi-weighted" action gives it a piano-like feel, and its keyboard is *velocity sensitive:* it measures how hard each key is pressed. Most of GarageBand's software instruments respond to this velocity information, changing their loudness and other characteristics to allow you to play (and record) with expression.

You can also use a costlier keyboard that requires a separate MIDI interface. (MIDI stands for *Musical Instrument Digital Interface*, and is a standard for interconnecting electronic instruments and computers. Think of it as USB with a music degree.) Pricier keyboards often provide *weighted action*—their keys respond like a piano's instead of like an organ's, and thus feel more natural to experienced pianists. You'll also find more keys—up to 88 of them.

Recording a Software Instrument

Step 1. Create a new track. Click the New Track button (![+]) or choose New Track from the Track menu (Option-⌘-N).

Step 2. In the New Track dialog box, click Software Instrument, then click OK or press Return.

Step 3. Select a category, and then select an instrument.

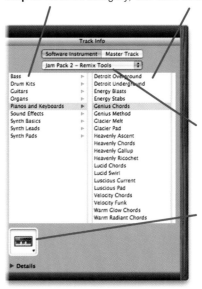

Tip: You can use the up arrow and down arrow keys to move from one instrument to the next.

You can use the pop-up menu to choose from a specific instrument collection (see page 349).

Optional: choose an icon to appear in the track header.

Tip: You can try out the selected instrument by playing keys on your music keyboard or by clicking the on-screen keys in GarageBand's Keyboard or Musical Typing windows (see page 333).

Step 4. Get ready. Position the playhead a few measures before where you want to begin recording. To give yourself time to get ready, choose Count In from the Control menu.

Step 5. Hit it. Click the Record button (●) or press the R key. To stop recording, press the spacebar or click the Play button (▶).

Notes and Tips

Watch your playing. As you record, GarageBand displays the new region (and its notes, in piano-roll style) in the timeline. Display the track editor for the current track, and your performance appears as you play—even in music notation.

Recording in an existing track. The instructions at left assume you're starting a brand-new track. You can, of course, also record in an existing software instrument track. Just select the track's header to enable it for recording. To change the track's instrument—before or after you record—double-click the track header to display the Track Info pane.

Multitrack recording. You can record one software instrument track and some real instrument tracks at the same time: record a vocal while you play, or record a couple of acoustic instrumentalists. For details, see page 338.

Anatomy of a Music Keyboard

Like many keyboards, M-Audio's Keystation 61es contains no sound-generating circuitry. When you play, the keyboard transmits MIDI data that describes which keys you pressed, how hard, and for how long. Keyboards that lack sound-generating circuitry are often called *controllers*.

Most keyboards can accept an optional foot pedal that plugs into the back of the keyboard and acts like a piano's sustain pedal. If you frequently play piano software instruments, you'll want a pedal. Some keyboards also accept a volume pedal that many software instruments respond to, giving you more expressive options.

On the Keystation 61es, the volume slider controls the volume of the currently selected software instrument track.

All music keyboards provide two controls that allow for more creative expression when you play.

A *pitch bend wheel* lets you do something no acoustic piano permits: bend notes the way guitar players do. The pitch bend wheel pairs up well with guitar and synthesizer instruments.

A *modulation wheel*, or *mod wheel*, lets you vary the sound of an instrument, usually by adding a vibrato-type effect. In Apple's Symphony Orchestra Jam Pack, the mod wheel also lets you obtain different articulations (see page 349).

Adjust Your Sensitivity

If your keyboard seems overly sensitive—even a relatively light touch triggers a software instrument's louder sounds—use the Audio/MIDI portion of the Preferences dialog box to turn down the sensitivity. Conversely, if you have to really pound to get louder sounds, increase the sensitivity.

Keyboard Sensitivity:
Less   Neutral   More

Editing Software Instrument Regions

Editing Software Instrument Regions

We've already encountered one form of software instrument region editing: transposition (page 329). That's just the beginning. There's almost no end to the ways you can edit MIDI data, and unlike when you're onstage, you can always undo any disasters.

You can edit regions you record or regions that you create by dragging loops from the loop browser. And you can edit in either of two views: the piano roll-style *graphic* view or music-notation view. In either view, you can change notes, modify their duration, change their velocity values, draw new notes, and more.

To switch views, click the button in the lower-left corner of the track editor.

Selecting Multiple Notes

You often need to select multiple notes—for example, prior to duplicating them or adjusting their velocity. To select more than one note, Shift-click on the notes or drag a selection rectangle around them.

Editing in Graphic View

Editing is easy in the graphic view's piano-roll display.

Fixing wrong notes. To fix a wrong note, drag it up or down until it becomes the right note. If the note is very high or low, scroll the track editor or make it taller by dragging the area to the left of the Record button.

If you fumbled and accidentally hit two keys when you meant to hit just one, delete the extra wrong note: select it and press the Delete key.

Notes and Tips

Improving expression. By editing the velocity values of some notes, you can improve expression and realism. This is especially true for software instruments, such as Classical Acoustic, that change dramatically depending on how hard you play a note.

To edit a note's velocity, select it and then specify the desired velocity in the Note Velocity box. To change the velocity of a range of notes, select the notes first.

Velocity values can range from 1 (quiet as a hoarse mouse) to 127 (way loud). To give you a visual hint at a note's velocity, GarageBand uses shading:

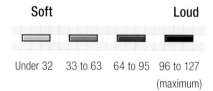

Soft			**Loud**
Under 32	33 to 63	64 to 95	96 to 127
			(maximum)

Moving a note in time. To move a note backward or forward, drag it left or right. To zoom in for more precision, drag the track editor's zoom slider to the right. You may also want to adjust the track editor's grid sensitivity by using its grid ruler button. Or turn the grid off entirely (⌘-G).

Changing a note's duration. To make a note longer or shorter, drag its right edge to the right or to the left.

Drawing a new note. To draw a new note, press ⌘ and then drag within the track, using the little vertical piano key legend (and your ears) as guides.

Chords in a hurry. You can create chords by duplicating notes: press the Option key, click on a note, and then drag up or down by the desired note interval. This also works on a range of notes: select the notes, then Option-drag them.

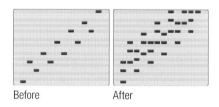

Before　　　　　After

Tip: Want to create a cinematic string section? Record a series of single notes, then duplicate them and drag the duplicate up seven semitones (a musical fifth). For some heavy metal action, try this with the Big Electric Lead guitar instrument. Just warn me first.

Editing in Notation View

Read music? Want to learn? Notation view is for you. It's also an ideal place to draw new notes and edit or create sustain-pedal information.

The techniques on the opposite page also apply to notation view, with the following differences.

Adjusting grid precision. When working in notation view, you'll want to use the grid ruler pop-up menu in the track editor to specify the degree of precision you want. For example, to move a note in quarter-note increments, choose 1/4 note. If you choose a small grid increment, you may see a lot of strange and small note or rest values, such as sixty-fourth notes.

Using the arrow keys. You can move notes by selecting them and pressing the arrow keys on your keyboard. You can also drag notes with the mouse.

Changing a note's duration. To change a note's duration, select the note, then drag the green duration bar left or right.

Drawing new notes. To draw a new note, first click the note value button in the Advanced area of the track editor, and choose the note value you want.

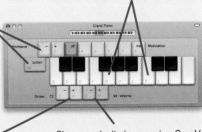

Then, press ⌘ and click within the staff to create the note.

Enlarging the notes. To make the notation view larger, make the track editor taller: drag the area to the left of the Record button upwards. Similarly, to increase the horizontal spacing between notes, drag the track editor's zoom slider.

Playing GarageBand's Keyboards

GarageBand provides two onscreen keyboards that let you audition (and even record) software instruments without having to reach for (or even have) a music keyboard.

Keyboard window. To view this simulated piano keyboard, choose Keyboard from the View menu (⌘-K).

The current track's instrument appears here.

Musical Typing window. This window lets you play by pressing keys on your Mac's keyboard. Choose Musical Typing from the Window menu (Shift-⌘-K).

Note: When the Musical Typing window is visible, some of GarageBand's keyboard shortcuts—such as pressing Home to move to the beginning of the song—aren't available.

Play chords by pressing more than one key at once.

Add pitch bend, modulation, or sustain by pressing the number keys or Tab key.

Change the octave range by pressing Z or X or by clicking the little keyboard at the top of the window.

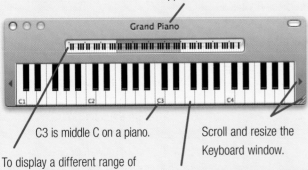

C3 is middle C on a piano.

To display a different range of notes, click the little keyboard.

Scroll and resize the Keyboard window.

The keyboard is velocity sensitive: the closer you click to the bottom edge of a key, the louder the note.

Change velocity by pressing C or V.

More Region Editing Techniques

More Controller Editing Options

Modulation and sustain are just two forms of MIDI controller data that you can edit. Here's a look at more controller editing options.

Pitch bend. A music keyboard generates pitch bend data when you move its pitch bend wheel. You can edit this data or draw your own.

Expression. True to its name, expression data lets you increase or decrease the loudness of a region. You might draw in expression data to create a crescendo or decrescendo. Try recording a chord with a horn section instrument, then adding an expression curve to it.

With Apple's Symphony Orchestra Jam Pack, moving the pitch bend wheel generates expression data.

Tip: If you have a volume (expression) pedal connected to your music keyboard, you can have GarageBand respond to and record the data it transmits. Be sure your keyboard is transmitting the pedal's data as expression data (MIDI controller #11), not volume data (MIDI controller #7).

Foot control. Apple's Symphony Orchestra Jam Pack uses foot control data to control articulation for some of the orchestral instruments, such as strings.

Doubling a Track

You can create a duet by duplicating a region in a different track. Create another track of the same type (software instrument or real instrument), then Option-drag the region into that track. (You can also copy and paste.) To start with the same instrument and effect settings, duplicate a track: select it and press ⌘-D.

Next, refine your duet. If it's a software instrument track, experiment with different instruments. You might also transpose one of the tracks to create a harmony or put each part an octave apart. You might also experiment with different effects, panning, and volume settings.

Tip: One way to add richness to a duet is by very slightly offsetting the second track's region. Turn grid snapping off (⌘-G), zoom in on the region, then nudge it ever so slightly to the left or right. This way, the regions won't play back at exactly the same time, strengthening the illusion of multiple musicians.

Importing MIDI Files

GarageBand can also import files created in standard MIDI format. Most sequencers can create MIDI files, and thousands of them are available on the Internet. (Jazz lovers: check out www.thejazzpage.de. Classical buffs: go to www.classicalarchives.com, especially if you have Apple's Symphony Orchestra Jam Pack. Downloading a MIDI file usually involves Control-clicking on it and choosing Download Linked File from the shortcut menu.)

A standard MIDI file's name ends with *.mid*. To import the file into GarageBand, simply drag it into the timeline. GarageBand reads the file, creates tracks, and assigns instruments to them.

You may have to fine-tune the results of an importing session. I often have to transpose the bass track up by one octave and reassign software instruments.

Still, importing a MIDI file is a great way to move a song created in a different sequencer into GarageBand. It's also a fun way to practice and create songs: download a MIDI file, drag it into GarageBand, then remix it, change its tempo, or play along.

Fixing Timing Problems

You can have GarageBand *quantize* a region—move its notes so that they fall exactly on the beats in the beat ruler.

Before quantizing a region, use the track editor's beat ruler menu to choose the desired grid resolution. If you're quantizing a walking bass line in 4/4 time, use the quarter-note (1/4) resolution. If you're quantizing a more nuanced performance, use a higher resolution. For jazz or other syncopated styles, try one of the swing settings.

After you've chosen a resolution, select the region you want to quantize and then click the Align button in the Advanced area of the track editor. Play back the results and undo if necessary.

You can also quantize individual notes within a region: just select the notes, then click the Align button.

Quantizing can be a mixed bag; it works well with extremely mechanistic music styles (such as dance and even some classical), but expect disappointing results when quantizing a jazz piano solo or any musical form that plays somewhat fast and loose with beats. Fortunately, the Undo command will get you out of any quantizing quagmires.

Editing Controller Information

Not all MIDI data deals with notes. A keyboard's pitch and modulation wheels also generate data, as does a sustain pedal. You can edit and create this *controller data* in the track editor's graphic view.

Editing controller data involves working with *control points* similar to those of pitch, volume, and panning curves. By adjusting this data, you can change the expressiveness applied by a pitch or mod wheel, adjust your pedal work, and more.

Say you have a software instrument whose sound timbre "sweeps" when you move the modulation wheel (examples include Star Sweeper, Aquatic Sunbeam, Cloud Break, and Falling Star). If you want that sweep to change over a specific number of measures, create a *modulation curve*.

To create controller data from scratch, choose the controller type from the pop-up menu in the Advanced area of the track editor. ⌘-click to create control points, then drag them as needed.

You'll find an example of this on my Web site, at www.macilife.com/gbandexamples.zip. Expand the archive by double-clicking it, then open the folder. Check out the GarageBand project named Modulate Me. It contains two regions, each playing the identical note. But in the second region, I drew a modulation curve to create a precisely timed sweep.

As for editing sustain data, you can clean up sloppy pedal work by fine-tuning the position of the control points that represent each pedal push: just drag the control points left or right.

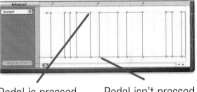

Pedal is pressed (sustain is on).   Pedal isn't pressed (sustain is off).

And if you don't have a sustain pedal, you can draw your own sustain data. Check out the project named Add Sustain in the aforementioned examples folder. I recorded the first region without using my sustain pedal. Then I duplicated the region and added sustain data to the duplicate.

Press the pedal: ⌘-click to create a control point.

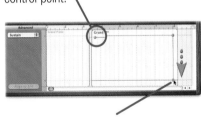

Release: ⌘-click where you want the pedal release, then drag down to the bottom of the grid. Drag control points left and right as needed to fine-tune timing.

I wouldn't want to draw in sustain data for a Billy Joel ballad, but for the occasional sustained arpeggio, it works.

Recording an Audio Source

If you sing or play an instrument—sax, guitar, kazoo—GarageBand provides yet another dimension to explore. Connect a microphone or other sound source to your Mac, and you can record a performance in a real instrument track.

If your Mac has an audio input jack, you can plug a microphone, guitar, or bass into it and start making noise. Note that the Mac's audio input jack works best with mikes that produce a fairly loud, *line-level* signal. Many mikes do not, and if yours is among them, you won't get a loud enough signal for the Mac. No problem—products aplenty await your wallet. M-Audio, MOTU, and Digidesign are a few of the companies that sell first-rate audio interfaces for the Mac. For links, visit www.macilife.com/garageband.

GarageBand lets you apply effects to audio that you record. You can even have GarageBand simulate the sound of a vintage guitar amplifier. But your audio is always recorded and saved with no effects—unprocessed, or *dry*. GarageBand applies its effects as your music plays back, so you can experiment with effects settings.

Before recording a real instrument track, be sure your audio hardware is properly configured. You may need to visit the Sound system preference and GarageBand's Preferences dialog box to ensure that the audio input is set to the hardware you plan to use. And be sure you have plenty of free disk space before you start—your recording will use 10MB per minute for a stereo track.

Recording to a New Track

Step 1. Create a new track. Click the New Track button (+) or choose New Track from the Track menu (Option-⌘-N).

Step 2. Click the Real Instrument button and click Create or press Return.

Step 3. Choose an instrument.

When you select an instrument, you're choosing a set of effects that GarageBand will apply when playing back the track. You can change this setting later if you like: double-click the track header and choose a different setting in the Track Info pane.

Select a category, then select an instrument within the category.

Don't want to apply any effects to the track? Select No Effects.

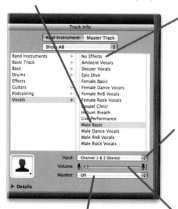

If you've connected a stereo microphone or device, choose Channel 1 & 2 (Stereo). Otherwise, choose the channel that your sound source is connected to (see page 338).

When monitoring is on, you can hear your instrument or microphone. This can be great with a guitar or bass, but with a mike, you're likely to get loud feedback when monitoring is on. This is why monitoring is turned off by default. If you're using a mike, you might want to plug headphones into your Mac when monitoring.

To adjust recording levels, use the Volume slider (see opposite page).

Tip: To quickly create a real instrument track with no effects, choose New Basic Track from the Track menu. A basic track is set to record in stereo; double-click the track's header to change audio settings.

Step 4. Adjust recording levels.

Sing or play some notes, and watch the level meters in the track's header. If the clipping indicators light (see below), ugly distortion looms. Lower the volume of your input source—for example, lower the Input Volume slider of the Mac's Sound system preference, or, if you're using a mixer or audio interface, adjust its volume controls.

Step 5. Get ready.

Move the playhead a few measures before where you want to start recording, or use the Count In command in the Control menu to give yourself time to get ready.

Step 6. Press Record (●) and make us proud.

The meters should illuminate fully during loud passages, but the two clipping indicators (the tiny circles) shouldn't light up. If they do, lower the input volume as described above.

Tip: When the clipping indicators light, they stay lit until you click them. This is GarageBand's way of telling you that clipping occurred while your eyes were closed as you belted out *My Way*.

When you're setting levels, this *isn't* the volume control to use. This slider adjusts the track's playback volume, not its recording input level. See for yourself: turn down the track volume while singing or playing, and you'll see that the meters still move. Here's the rule: To adjust *playback* volume, use the track mixer. To adjust *record* volume (technically, input gain), follow the instructions in Step 4, above.

Get In Tune with the Instrument Tuner

Is your axe in tune? GarageBand can help. Its instrument tuner listens to the audio coming into a real instrument track and displays its note value. (This works with single notes only, not with chords.)

To use the instrument tuner, select the track for the instrument you want to tune and make sure that its Record button is enabled. Then, click the tuning fork icon at the left of the time display or choose Show Instrument Tuner from the Control menu (⌘-F).

The tuner displays the note you're playing.

If the note is flat, the indicator moves to the left of center. If the note is sharp, the indicator moves to the right. When you're in tune, the indicator is centered, as shown here.

More Audio Techniques

Multitrack Recording

GarageBand is a great tool for musicians who labor alone. But what if you want to record a couple of musicians simultaneously and put each performer on a different track? Or what if you'd like to record yourself singing a vocal while strumming a guitar or playing a MIDI keyboard?

If your Mac has a basic stereo input, you can record two real instrument tracks simultaneously, *plus* one software instrument track: two singers and some GarageBand piano, for example. Connect multichannel audio hardware, and you can record up to eight real instrument tracks and one software instrument track: a real garage band.

Here's how to record two simultaneous audio tracks using your Mac's built-in audio input or a basic adaptor, such as Griffin's iMic. These basic steps apply to more ambitious multitracking tasks, too.

Get jacked up. Your Mac's built-in audio input can accommodate two signals: left channel and right channel. When multitrack recording, forget left and right: you're using one channel for one audio source (say, a mike), and the other channel for another source (for example, an electric guitar).

Use a splitter cable or Y-adaptor that has a ⅛-inch stereo miniplug on one end and two audio jacks on the other. Those two audio jacks can be RCA phono jacks, ¼-inch mike jacks—whatever meshes with the gear you plan to connect.

Connect each audio source to one of the splitter's input jacks.

Assign channels. Next, assign one input channel to one track and the other channel to a different track. Double-click a real instrument track's header (or create a brand-new track), and use the Input pop-up menu in the Track Info panel to assign the input to Channel 1. Adjust your audio device's level to get a good input level as described on the previous page.

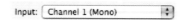

Next, repeat this process for the other track, assigning it to Channel 2.

Arm the tracks. Make sure that the two tracks are enabled for recording: click the red Record button in their track headers. If you want to record a software instrument along with the two real instrument tracks, now's the time to create that track and enable it for recording, too.

Get down. Set up the metronome and count-in as desired, and record.

Notes and Tips

Panning your tracks. The technique I've described here creates two mono audio channels. And yet when you play your recording, you'll hear each channel coming from *both* speakers. To control each track's position in the stereo field, use the track's panning knob in the track mixer. For panning advice, see page 343.

Hard drive labor. Recording two simultaneous audio tracks puts your Mac's hard drive to work, especially if you're also playing back some existing real instrument tracks. If you have a slower Mac—or a laptop Mac or Mac mini, all of which have slower hard drives—you might need to mute some existing real instrument tracks to lighten the load on your hard drive and to avoid an error message.

The same applies to software instrument tracks that you've locked (see page 352): if GarageBand displays an error message while recording, try muting those tracks.

Working with Real Instrument Regions

You can modify real instrument regions —either ones you've recorded or those you created by dragging blue loops into the timeline—in several ways.

Copy, paste, and dupe. You can duplicate a region by copying and pasting or by simply Option-dragging it. Duplicating a lengthy region doesn't use any additional disk space.

Digital splicing. You can also do some basic editing. Maybe you belted out a *yeah* that sounded more like Howard Dean than James Brown. Double-click on the region to open it in the track editor.

Drag across the offending utterance (zoom in and turn off grid snapping for more precision), then choose Delete from the Edit menu.

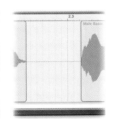

You can also copy and paste part of a region: select it in the track editor, then choose Copy. Now paste it at a different position or in a different real instrument track.

Tip: To "double" a vocal and add a richer sound, offset the duplicate slightly using the technique on page 335. And pan each member of your chorus to a different position (see page 343).

Enhancing tuning and tempo. Singer sour? Drummer dragging? Use the track editor's Enhance Tuning or Enhance Timing slider. Every track is different, so drag the slider until things sound good.

When adjusting pitch, you can have GarageBand limit enhancement to the song's key (check the Limit to Key box) or to the chromatic scale (uncheck the box). And to try your hand at an effect first popularized by Cher back in the last century, crank Enhance Tuning all the way up.

Track editor tips. Want to turn a selection into an independent region? Just click within the selection.

And with some strategic mouse positioning, you can move, resize, and loop regions directly within the track editor— no need to journey up into the timeline. To move a region, position the pointer near its upper-left corner. When the mouse pointer changes to a ◀▶, drag left or right.

To resize a region within the track editor, point to its lower-left corner and drag. To loop a region, point to its upper-right corner and drag.

Orange Loops: Imported Audio and More

You can import audio from iTunes and the Finder: just drag the audio file into the timeline. GarageBand accepts AIFF, WAV, Apple Lossless, MP3, and AAC formats.

(You can't import a song purchased from the iTunes Music Store. The workaround: burn the song to a CD, then rip it back into iTunes and import that version.)

GarageBand displays imported audio regions in orange.

You can't shift the tempo of orange audio regions, nor can you transpose them—at least not without a little trickery. If you know that your song's tempo and key match those of the

orange region (or if you don't care—maybe you just want to slow down a solo to figure it out), here's the secret: select the orange region, press Control-Option-G, and then click elsewhere in the timeline. GarageBand "stamps" the region with your project's key and tempo settings and turns the orange region into a purple one. Now you can transpose it and

stretch its tempo. This is great for doing remixes of iTunes tracks.

Incidentally, if you open a project created in GarageBand 1.x, its once-purple regions will be orange. Use the Control-Option-G trick to convert them.

Tip: To calculate a song's tempo, try iTunes-BPM Inspector; it's free and available from download sites.

Refining Your Sound with Effects

Effects can be just as important to your final arrangement as the notes you play. With effects, you can add richness to a track—or brain-liquefying distortion, if that's your idea of fun. You can add some spice to a track, or change it beyond recognition.

Effects alter the "color" of sound. Some effects simulate real-world phenomena, such as reverberation and echo. Other effects let you sculpt your sound to enhance certain frequencies, much like the equalizer in iTunes. Still other effects process (and sometimes mangle) audio in ways that could only exist in the digital world.

Recording studios have racks of hardware effects boxes. GarageBand's effects exist in software: by applying complex math to your sound, GarageBand can simulate the reverb of a concert hall, the characteristics of an old guitar amplifier, and much more. Best of all, you can customize GarageBand's effects in a limitless number of ways to create sounds that are yours alone.

You can apply GarageBand's effects to software and real instrument tracks alike. And as I've said previously, GarageBand never alters your original audio; effects are applied as your song plays. This lets you experiment with effects until you arrive at just the right amount of sonic seasoning.

Here's a look at how GarageBand applies its effects and how you can customize them.

Effects Basics

All of GarageBand's software instruments employ effects to some degree. Similarly, when you create a real instrument track and choose an instrument, GarageBand assigns a collection of effects to that track (page 336). And as I describe on page 344, a song's master track can apply effects to your entire song.

To examine and change a track's effects settings, double-click the track header, then click the Details button in the Track Info pane.

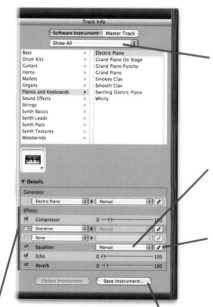

If you create your own presets (opposite page), you can view them by choosing My Settings from the pop-up menu.

Choose effect presets from these pop-up menus.

To create your own settings for an effect, click the pencil (see opposite page).

For software instruments, standard effects include Compressor, Equalizer, Echo, and Reverb. (Real instrument tracks provide these same effects, and they add a *noise gate* effect, which removes noise from silent portions of a recording.) You can choose two additional effects by using the two pop-up menus.

Like what you've come up with? You can save the customized version of the instrument and use it again in future songs (see opposite page).

The Fab Four

Compressor, Equalizer, Echo, and Reverb are mainstay effects, the salt and pepper of sonic seasoning.

Compressor. A compressor is a kind of automatic volume control that adjusts volume thousands of times per second. Most popular music is heavily compressed, and FM radio stations often compress it even more. Compression can add punch to drum tracks and vocals, but too much compression can add an annoying "pumping" quality to sound.

Equalizer. As an iTunes veteran, you know all about EQ—it's a fancy set of bass and treble controls. GarageBand provides 16 EQ *presets*—factory settings—that you can apply and customize. Want to beef up that drum track? Try the Big Drum preset.

Echo. Also called *delay,* the echo effect simulates evenly timed sound reflections.
Tip: GarageBand's echo repeats at a rate that matches your song's tempo. Try applying echo to vocal or synthesizer "stabs" in a dance, electronica, or hip-hop tune. To have different echo

rhythms on each track, use the Track Echo effect.

Reverb. A distant cousin to echo, reverb consists of thousands of randomly timed sound reflections. Reverb simulates the sound of an acoustic space: a concert hall, a small lounge, a stadium. In GarageBand, reverb is controlled in part by the song's master track (page 344).

Customizing Effects

You can customize effects in several ways.

Turn them off. Maybe you love GarageBand's Arena Run synth, but you don't like the way it echoes every note. Just turn off the Echo effect by unchecking its box.

Turn them on. GarageBand's most intriguing effects lurk within the two pop-up menus in the Effects area. Want to add a rich, swirling texture to a track? Try Flanger, Phaser, or both. Want to liquefy your listeners? Unleash Distortion, Bitcrusher, or Amp Simulation. Want a track to continuously pan between the left and right channel? Try the tremolo effect's Circular Structure setting. Want to turn a male singer into a female—or a

chipmunk? Try the amazing Vocal Transformer.

Important: Some settings can produce speaker-damaging volume levels. Lower the volume when experimenting. This is particularly prudent if you're experimenting with the Distortion, Bitcrusher, and Amp Simulation effects, or adjusting the Resonance slider in effects that provide one.

Try different presets. Many of GarageBand's effects have an assortment of presets that you can apply with a click.

Create your own presets. Click the little pencil () next to an effect's Preset pop-up menu, and a dialog box appears where you can adjust the effect's parameters.

To create a new preset containing the current settings, open the pop-up menu and choose New Preset.

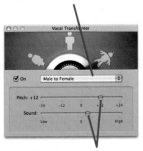

Each effect has a unique set of parameters that you can adjust.

Saving Instruments

When you change a track's effects, you're customizing the way GarageBand has defined that software or real instrument. If you switch to a different instrument or effect preset, GarageBand asks if you want to save the changed instrument before switching.

If you click Discard (or just press Return), GarageBand discards your settings. If you think you'll want to use them again, click Save before switching to a different instrument or effect setting.

If you like tinkering with effect settings and you don't want GarageBand pestering you about saving them all the time, check the Do Not Ask Me Again box. You can also use GarageBand's Preferences command to control this paranoia mode.

For more details on creating instruments, see page 350.

Refining the Mix: Volume and Panning

A good song has a pleasing mix of melody, chord changes, and maybe lyrics. A good *recording* of a song has a pleasing mix between instruments. It's possible to have a poorly mixed version of a great song, and as a spin of the radio dial will confirm, it's also possible to have a well-mixed version of a lousy song.

As a GarageBand-based recording engineer, the job of mixing is yours. Adjust each track's volume so all the tracks mesh—no single instrument should overwhelm the others, but important instruments or voices should be louder than less important ones.

And to create a rich stereo field, pan some instruments toward the left channel and others toward the right. You'll find some tips for panning on the opposite page.

To adjust a track's playback volume level and panning position, use the Mixer area of GarageBand's window. If the Mixer isn't visible, display it by clicking the little triangle at the top of the Tracks area or by choosing Show Track Mixer from the Track menu (⌘-Y).

To have a track's volume or panning change as the song plays, create a *volume curve* or *panning curve*—a set of control points that tell GarageBand how to change volume or panning over time.

Note: If you've edited a track's volume or panning curve, you can't drag the volume slider or turn the panning knob. Instead, make volume or panning adjustments to the curve.

Adjusting Volume

To adjust a track's playback volume, drag the slider.

To avoid distortion, lower the volume if the clipping indicators light.

Editing a Volume Curve

To create fades, add expression, or mute a track for part of a song, edit the track's volume curve.

Step 1. Click the triangle next to the track's Lock button or select the track header and press the A key.

Step 2. Choose Track Volume from the pop-up menu and click the little box at the left edge of the pop-up menu to turn on the curve for editing.

Step 3. The horizontal line represents the track's volume. Click the line to create a control point where you want the volume change to begin.

Step 4. Click at a different point on the line to create a second control point, then drag it down to lower the volume, or up to raise it.

To turn off a volume or pan curve without deleting its control points, click the little blue indicator.

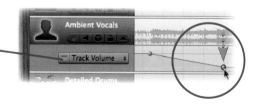

Adjusting Panning

To pan a track, drag its pan knob to turn it clockwise (toward the right speaker) or counterclockwise (toward the left). To return to dead center, Option-click the knob.

Editing a Pan Curve

To pan a track from one channel to the other as the song plays, edit the track's pan curve. Display the track's curve by clicking its triangle or pressing A. Then, choose Track Panning from the pop-up menu and click the little box at the left edge of the pop-up menu to turn on the curve for editing.

Next, create control points and drag them. To pan toward the left channel, drag a control point up. To pan toward the right, drag a control point down.

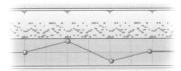

Tips for curves. To adjust a control point's location in time, drag it left or right. To delete a control point, click it and press the Delete key. To delete or move multiple control points at once, select them by Shift-clicking or dragging across them.

If you move regions within your song, any curves you created for them don't move along with the regions. To move the curves, select their control points and then drag them left or right as a group to reunite them with the regions they're supposed to affect.

Mixing Tips: Panning

By sweating the details of your stereo mix, you can make your song more aurally interesting. Two ears, two speakers—take advantage of them.

Sit right. Your position relative to your speakers will affect how you hear a stereo mix. When refining your track panning, sit directly between your speakers. Test your mix with headphones if you like, but don't rely exclusively on them—your listeners won't.

Panning hard. Think twice about panning tracks *completely* to the left or right. In the real world, sound reaches both ears even when a musician is at the far side of the stage. Of course, some songs have little to do with the real world, so feel free to bend this rule.

Panning for realism. If you're after a realistic stereo mix, visualize your ensemble and pan accordingly. In a jazz combo, the drums might be slightly to the left, bass in the middle, piano slightly to the right, and sax further right.

Panning a duet. If your song contains a vocal duet or two instruments that trade solos, pan one of the vocalists or instruments somewhat left (about 10 o'clock on the pan wheel) and the other somewhat right.

To simulate backup singers, record each part on a separate track and pan the tracks near each other on one side of the stage—for example, one track at 9 o'clock and the other at 10 o'clock.

Panning similar instruments. If your song contains multiple instruments that have a similar frequency range—for example, a solo guitar and a rhythm guitar—pan each instrument to the opposite side of center. The 10 o'clock and 2 o'clock positions are good starting points.

Consider your effects. If you've applied an effect that enhances a track's stereo—for example, Chorus, Flanger, or Tremolo—think twice about panning that track heavily to one channel. You'll lose many of the benefits of the effect.

Panning percussion. If you've built up a drum kit by recording different drums and cymbals on different tracks, pan the tracks to increase realism. Put the snare and kick drum dead center. Pan the hi-hat slightly right, and the ride and crash cymbals slightly left. If you're using tom-toms, pan them according to their pitch: high-pitched toms slightly right, low-pitched toms slightly left. This layout mirrors the typical layout of a drum kit: the hi-hat is on the drummer's left and the floor tom is on his or her right.

Creating the Final Mix

When you've refined each track, turn your attention to the big picture: display the song's Master Track to apply final-mastering effects and optionally to create a fade-out at the end of the tune.

Once you've polished your song until it glitters like a platinum record, you can export it to your iTunes music library, where you can burn it to an audio CD, transfer it to your iPod, and use it in the other iLife programs.

Working with the Master Track

GarageBand's *master track* is a special kind of track that doesn't hold notes or regions, but instead controls certain aspects of your entire mix. Specifically, you can transpose the entire song (page 328) and you can apply effects to the master track and create a volume curve to have your song fade in or fade out.

To show the master track, choose Show Master Track from the Track menu (⌘-B).

Applying effects. Apple has created dozens of final-mastering effects settings for common musical genres. Explore and apply them by double-clicking the master track's header. And, of course, you can customize them and create your own final-mix effects using the techniques I've described on previous pages.

Creating a fade. To fade a song, create a volume curve for it in the master track. **Tip:** To create a musically appealing fade, edit the volume curve so that the fade *ends* at the very beginning of a verse or measure. Don't have a fade end in the middle of a measure— it feels abrupt.

Customizing reverb and echo. In GarageBand, reverb and echo effects are controlled by the master track. As described on page 340, you can adjust *how much* echo and reverb you want on a specific track, but to adjust the actual echo and reverb parameters that GarageBand uses, use the master track's Track Info pane.

Echo Presets

Reverb Presets

GarageBand's dozens of reverb and echo settings (shown at left) are worth exploring. The reverb presets are spectacular—everything from a living room to a large cathedral, with some offbeat stops in between. Explore them to add just the right sonic ambience to your track. And if you're into dance and electronic music, you can while away a weekend trying out and customizing GarageBand's echo presets.

Exporting to iTunes

When you've polished your song to perfection, add it to your iTunes music library by choosing Send Song to iTunes from the Share menu. GarageBand mixes your tracks down to two stereo channels and saves the song as an AIFF file.

GarageBand saves files in full CD-quality form: 44KHz, 16-bit. To convert a song into AAC, MP3, or Apple Lossless format, configure iTunes for the format you want to use (page 22), then select your song and choose Convert from the Advanced menu. iTunes won't replace the AIFF version of

your song, so if you want to free up space in your iTunes library (and iPod), use the Show Song File command to move the AIFF file out of your music library.

Exporting an excerpt. At times, you may want to export only part of a song. Maybe you want to email it to a collaborator or mix it down in order to bring it back into GarageBand (see page 353). To export a portion of a song, turn on cycling and then resize the yellow cycling region in the beat ruler to indicate the portion you want to export.

Preserving effect tails. If your song has reverb or echo effects that last well beyond the last note, you may find that these *effect tails* are cut off after you export to iTunes. To fix this, turn cycling on and then resize the yellow cycling region so that it extends beyond the point where the effects die off. Now export the song again.

Customizing tags. To customize how your song is categorized in iTunes—artist name, album name, and so on—use the General portion of GarageBand's Preferences dialog box.

A Closer Look at Software Instrument Loops

On page 327, I mentioned that software instrument loops contain more than just piano-roll MIDI notes—they also contain audio. To see this for yourself, drag a green loop into a real instrument track—instead of the usual piano-roll notation within a green region, you'll see a waveform display within a blue region.

Two in one. How does this work? A software instrument loop is really two loops in one. It contains not only the MIDI note data that can be used by a software instrument track, but also a *rendered* version of the loop—an actual audio recording, complete with effects.

Here's another way to see this for yourself. Use the Finder's Find command to locate a software instrument loop, such as Southern Rock Guitar 01. You'll notice the loop's file name ends in .AIF—it's an audio file in AIFF format. You can open and play this file using QuickTime Player or iTunes. You can even drag it into iMovie or iDVD. But embedded within the AIFF file is MIDI note data that GarageBand can use.

The fact that software instrument loops also contain audio data has an important ramification: As I mention on page 352, if you plan to use a software

instrument loop as is, you can lighten the load on your Mac's processor by using the loop in a real instrument track.

If you haven't yet created the track for the loop, take advantage of the following shortcut: press the Option key while dragging a green loop into the timeline, and GarageBand creates a real instrument track for it.

If you frequently use software instrument loops without changing them, you can use the Loops portion of the Preferences dialog box to have GarageBand *always* create real instrument

tracks when you drag green loops into the timeline.

The downsides. There are some downsides to using a green loop in a real instrument track. You can't edit individual notes or change instrument or effect assignments, since all these things are part of the audio recording. Also, you can't transpose an audio region over as large a range. But for those times when you want to use a green loop as is, adding it to a real instrument track is a great way to improve GarageBand's performance.

Arranging Tips

More Ways to Work with Regions

I've already discussed the most common tasks you're likely to perform with regions: looping them, moving and copying them, splitting them, transposing them, and editing them.

There's more. Here are a few additional ways you might work with regions.

Resizing a region. To extend a region—make it longer—point to its lower-right corner and drag to the right.

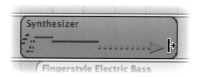

Why extend a region? Say you recorded a riff that you want to loop. If your recorded region doesn't end at the proper measure boundary, the region won't loop properly. By extending the region, you can have it loop.

Another reason to extend a region is to be able to draw in additional notes or controller data using the track editor. Yet another is to add some silence before a region's content repeats.

To make the region shorter, drag its lower-right corner to the left. You might shorten a region in order to "crop out" some unwanted notes—possibly as a prelude to rerecording them. When you shorten a region, you don't delete the notes in the hidden portion of the region. To restore the notes, lengthen the region.

You can also resize a region from its beginning by dragging its lower *left* corner. This enables you to add silence to the beginning of a region (drag to the left) or to crop out audio from the beginning of a real instrument recording (drag to the right).

Joining regions. You've transposed a set of loops using the Split technique from page 329, and now you want to transpose the entire verse to a different key. Select all the loops and choose Join from the Edit menu (⌘-J). GarageBand turns all the regions into one region that you can transpose.

Note: When you join real instrument regions that you've recorded, GarageBand combines those regions into a single audio file. GarageBand asks if you want to create a new audio file. Click Create, and GarageBand merges the real instrument regions into a new audio file.

Adding Variety

When you're working with loops, it's easy to create overly repetitious arrangements. Fortunately, it's also easy to add variety and make your loop-based songs sound less repetitious.

Vary loops. Many of the bass and drum loops that come with GarageBand and Apple's GarageBand Jam Packs have variations that sound similar but not identical. Rather than relying on just one loop for a bass or drum track, switch between some different but similar-sounding ones.

Edit some loops. Make your own loop variations. Make a copy of a software instrument loop and edit it—delete a few notes or transpose others. For real instrument loops, select part of the loop, copy it, and then paste it elsewhere.

Another way to edit loops is to change the instrument played by a software instrument loop. Try assigning an electric piano or clavinet to a bass loop.

Record your own bass track. Use bass loops to sketch out an arrangement and choose instruments, then replace the loops with your own bass line.

Take breaks. Add a *drum break* now and then—silence your drums for the last beat or two of a measure or for an entire measure. You can split the region and then delete part of it. Or you can edit the region if it's a software instrument drum track. Or leave the region alone and create a volume curve that plunges the track's volume down all the way, then brings it back up.

Add fills. Don't want to edit a drum loop? Create a new track that uses a software instrument drum kit. Use this track to hold drum fills, such as an occasional cymbal crash or tom-tom fill. Want a kick drum to mark the beat during a drum break? Put it in this track.

Vary the percussion. Add one or more percussion tracks to some verses—shakers, tambourines, claves, congas, bongos. Click the loop browser's Percussion button to explore.

Add a pad. A *pad* is a note, a series of notes, or a chord that forms a sonic background for a song. It's often a lush string section or an atmospheric synthesizer that plays the root note or a fifth (for example, G in a song written in C). One way to add variety to an arrangement is to have a pad play throughout one verse. Stop the pad at the start of the next verse, or add another track with a pad that uses a different instrument.

Changing Effects

Want to apply an effect, such as echo, to only part of a track? You can use the hijacking technique, but here's an easier method. Duplicate the track, then move the region to which you want to apply the new effect to the duplicate track. Now apply the effect to the duplicate track. To create a smooth transition between the two tracks, create volume curves for each track.

Saving an iLife Preview

A new feature in GarageBand 3 lets you save an audio "preview" along with a project. A preview is simply a stereo mix of the song, stashed inside the project file.

Saving a project with a preview makes possible a couple of tricks. For one thing, you can access the project using the media browsers in the other iLife programs—use a song in an iPhoto slide show or in an iMovie HD project, for example.

Another benefit to saving a preview along with the project is that you can import one song into another, as described below.

To have GarageBand create a preview when you save a project, choose Preferences from the GarageBand menu, click General, and check the box labeled Render a Preview When Saving.

The next time you save the project, you'll encounter the biggest drawback of this feature: it greatly increases the time required to save a project, since GarageBand must create a stereo mix of your song. For this reason, you might want to leave this feature turned off as you're working on a song—a time when you are (or should be) using the Save command all the time. Then, when you've finished the tune, turn on the preview feature and save the project again.

Importing Songs into Songs

If you save your GarageBand projects with an iLife preview as described above, you can import one song into another. This makes possible some versatile composition options: create each verse of a song (or each movement of a symphony) separately, then combine them into a finished project.

Importing one song into another can also be useful for working around a performance problem caused by a slower Mac, or a very complex song: complete as many tracks as your Mac can handle,

then import that song into a new project and continue adding tracks.

To add one song to another, open the media browser by clicking the ![] button, then locate the GarageBand song you want to import and drag it to the timeline. It appears as an orange region, like any other audio file that you import (page 339).

When you import one project into another, GarageBand maintains a link to the original project, enabling you to go back and make changes, then have those changes reflected in the second project.

To open the original version of a project that you've imported, double-click on the orange region. In the Advanced area of the track editor, click the Open Original button. GarageBand opens the original project, where you can make changes. When you save those changes and close the project file, GarageBand reopens the second project and asks if you'd like to update it to reflect your changes.

Expanding Your Loop Library

For a GarageBand musician, loops are like groupies: you can't have too many. A large loop library is a source of creative inspiration. A few minutes of clicking in the loop browser is often all it takes to get the songwriting juices flowing.

A large loop library is also a great source of variety—something that's missing from many loop-based compositions.

There's no shortage of loop collections for GarageBand. Apple offers several great collections of its own: the GarageBand Jam Pack series includes not only thousands of loops, but some ear-stunning software instruments and effects, too (see the opposite page).

Many other companies have also created loop packages for GarageBand; you can sample many of them through GarageBand community sites, such as iCompositions (www.icompositions.com).

GarageBand can also work directly with loops in the ACID format. (ACID is a pioneering loop-based music program that debuted on Windows computers back in 1998.) There are more ACID loops available than you can fit on your hard drive.

GarageBand also lets you create your own loops. Record a riff or edit an existing loop, then—with a few mouse clicks—turn it into a new loop. Your own loops show up in the loop browser and will work like any other Apple Loops: you can shift their pitch and tempo, search for them using the loop browser's buttons and search box, and more.

Creating Your Own Apple Loops

You can turn any region into a loop with a few mouse clicks.

Step 1. If necessary, resize or split a region to make it the proper length of your custom loop.

Step 2. Drag the region to the loop browser or select it and choose Add to Loop Library from the Edit menu.

Step 3. Specify information about the loop, then click Create.

For rhythmic regions, choose Loop; this enables GarageBand to shift the loop's tempo to match the song in which it's used. If the region won't require tempo shifting—maybe it's a recording of a single dog bark— choose One-shot.

Type a name for the loop.

Assign as much information to the new loop as you like. The more information you specify, the easier it will be to locate the loop in future searches.

Narrowing Down Your Choices

If you've installed multiple Jam Packs and other loop collections, there may be times when you want to browse for loops from one specific collection.

To focus on a specific loop collection in the loop browser, point to the word Loops (Loops ⬍), hold down the mouse button, and then choose a collection.

To switch back to browsing your entire loop library, choose Show All. To view GarageBand's original, factory-installed loops, choose GarageBand.

As I've described previously, GarageBand provides a similar feature when you're assigning an instrument to a track.

Importing ACID Loops

To add ACID loops to your loop library, simply drag a folder containing the loops into the loop browser. The loops remain in ACID format, but GarageBand indexes them in a way that lets you search using the loop browser's buttons and search box.

Jam Packs: More than Just Loops

If you're looking to expand your sonic options, Apple's series of GarageBand Jam Packs should be one of your first stops. Each Jam Pack provides not only thousands of meticulously recorded loops, but also a large assortment of additional software instruments and effects. Here's an overview of each Jam Pack; you can learn more and audition each one at www.apple.com/garageband/jampacks.

Remix Tools. If the turntable on the box doesn't give it away, the sounds will: this Jam Pack is aimed at dance, hip-hop, and electronica composers. Its loops lean toward drum beats and bass lines, synthesizer patterns, and special effects (including, of course, vinyl scratches). Several

vintage drum machine software instruments and a sizzling assortment of synthesizers round out the collection.

Rhythm Section. Let the beating begin: this two-DVD set contains roughly 1,000 drum loops in a variety of styles, as well as another 1,000 bass lines and guitar and keyboard loops. Software instruments include drum sets ranging from jazzy brushes to steel drums, as well as basses and guitars of all kinds—from acoustic to electric, and from Dobro to banjo.

Symphony Orchestra. iPhoto and iMovie HD have the Ken Burns effect; Symphony Orchestra gives you the John Williams effect. It's a jaw-drop-

ping collection of symphonic orchestra loops and software instruments—the most ambitious Jam Pack of them all. (And the most demanding: to take full advantage of its software instruments, you'll need at least 512MB of memory, preferably 1GB or more.)

Its beautifully recorded symphonic loops are an aural feast, but what really sets this Jam Pack apart are its software instruments. By moving the modulation and pitch-bend wheels of your music keyboard—or by creating controller data in the track editor—you can vary the way an instrument plays to obtain amazing realism. To create crescendos and decrescendos of a sustained

note or chord, move the pitch bend wheel. To obtain different articulations, such as staccato or legato, adjust the modulation wheel. And don't miss the accompanying PDF documentation, which includes interesting backgrounders on orchestral history and arranging.

World Music. Go global: this Jam Pack includes a collection of ethnic percussion, wind, and string instruments—from tabla drums to bagpipes to Native American flutes, Peruvian pan-pipes, Persian santoors, Spanish Flamenco guitars, and much more. Completing your travels are over 3,000 loops recorded by pros from around the planet.

Creating Your Own Instruments

In GarageBand, a software instrument is based on a foundation called a *generator*, and every generator has settings that you can tweak. You can create your own software instrument by picking a generator and then adjusting its settings.

For example, say you want to create an instrument that has a funky electronic synthesizer sound. Here's one way you might approach the task.

Step 1. Create a new software instrument track, and pick an instrument—any instrument.

Step 2. Double-click the track's header and examine the Generator pop-up menu.

Some generators are based on short recorded *samples* of actual instruments, such as piano and guitar. Other generators create their sound "from scratch," based on sound synthesis techniques.

Step 3. Choose a generator.

Step 4. Examine the generator's presets. Try them out—you might find one you like.

Step 5. Click the pencil to the right of the generator's preset pop-up menu. This displays the settings that apply to the generator you chose.

Many generators let you customize what's often called the *ADSR envelope*. You can dramatically change a sound's percussive qualities by changing its envelope.

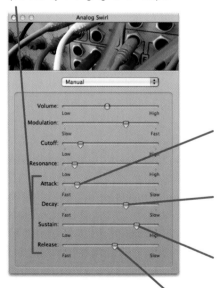

Tip: To get a feel for the kinds of settings each generator provides, drag the settings window so that you can see it and the Track Info pane at the same time. Then paw through the generators and their presets, and watch the settings window change.

Step 6. Play with the settings until you arrive at a sound you like. While you're at it, adjust effects as desired—they're stored along with the generator settings.

Step 7. Click the Save Instrument button in the Track Info pane and type a name for the new instrument. GarageBand saves the instrument settings on your hard drive (see the sidebar on the opposite page).

How quickly should the note sound when a key is pressed? A piano has a fast, or *sharp*, attack (as the hammers hit the strings). A flute has a slower attack.

How quickly should the sound volume fade or drop to the sustain level?

Should the sound sustain when a note is pressed and held down? A piano note decays over time; an organ note doesn't.

What happens when the key is released? With a fast release, the sound ends immediately. With a slower release, the sound fades gradually after the key is released.

Adding Audio Unit Instruments

You can expand GarageBand's sound-generating and effects capabilities with software plug-ins called *Audio Units.* Some absolutely stunning software instruments are available in Audio Unit format. My favorite is Native Instruments' B4, which mimics the legendary Hammond B3 organ with frightening realism. And yes, it runs within GarageBand.

I'm also a big fan of Pluggo from Cycling '74 (www.cycling74.com).

Pluggo is a collection of more than 100 synthesizers and effects, and it lets you run software instruments that use other plug-in formats, such as the popular VST format.

High-end software instruments like B4 cost several times what iLife '06 costs. If you don't want to spend that much, there are some great-sounding Audio Unit instruments and effects that don't cost a dime. To explore what's available, go to www.icompositions.com or do a Google search for *audio units.* Don't expect to get any work done for a while.

Where they live. Commercial Audio Unit plug-ins usually include an installer program that puts things where they belong, but some free Audio Units don't have these installers. So for the record, Audio Units are stored in Library > Audio > Plug-Ins > Components. They can also reside in your home directory, in the same path.

Adding Effects

There's also a large selection of Audio Unit effects, and the aforementioned sites are great places to find them.

You might also explore ChannelStrip from Metric Halo (www.mhlabs.com). This legendary set of mastering effects has long been popular among recording professionals, and now it's available for GarageBand.

And while most people think of Apple's Jam Packs as being primarily a source of loops and software instruments, they're also a source of effects.

If you have a Jam Pack and would like to see what additional effects it provides, double-click any track's header, then choose the Jam Pack's name from the pop-up menu at the top of the Track Info pane. Next, choose an effect and explore its pop-up menu of presets.

How GarageBand Stores Instruments

GarageBand stores a software instrument as a file with a name that ends with .cst—for example, if you named your instrument *Wacko*, its file will be Wacko.cst. GarageBand stores its instrument files deep inside your hard drive's Library folder.

Tip: To put your custom instrument in a different category in GarageBand's Track Info pane, move its file into the appropriate category folder. For example, to move an instrument from the Synth Leads category to the Bass category, move its file from the Synth Leads folder to the Bass folder.

- Bass
- Choir
- Drum Kits
- Guitars
- Horns
- Mallets
- Organs
- Pianos and Keyboards
- Strings
- Synth Basics
- Synth Leads
- Synth Pads
- Woodwinds

Optimizing GarageBand's Performance

With apologies to the great James Brown, GarageBand is the hardest-working program in show business. It synthesizes sound, plays back audio tracks, generates effects—and never skips a beat.

Of course, this assumes that your Mac is fast enough. On slower Macs—for example, older G4 iMacs or iBooks—GarageBand can stumble and display an error message if it isn't able to perform its duties. GarageBand works hard to avoid stopping the music. For instance, if your Mac starts working up a sweat during playback, GarageBand defers scrolling the screen and updating its time readout.

To let you know how hard it's working, GarageBand changes the color of its playhead: from white (don't worry, be happy) to yellow (I will survive) to orange (the thrill is gone) to red (the sound of silence). If you see the red playhead, anticipate an error message—GarageBand is on the verge of maxing out your Mac.

But as I tell my guitar player friends, don't fret. You can do a lot to bring the music back—besides buying a faster Mac.

Performance Tips

Lock tracks. If your song has numerous software instrument tracks or real instrument tracks that use a lot of effects, locking some tracks should be your first step. For details, see the opposite page.

Add memory. A memory upgrade will improve your Mac's overall performance.

Quit other programs. Let your Mac devote all its attention to GarageBand.

Quit and relaunch. Clear GarageBand's head: quit the program and then launch it again.

Use the audio in software instrument loops. If you plan to use a software instrument loop as is (that is, you aren't going to edit the loop or change its instrument or effects assignments), you can lighten the load on your Mac by dragging the loop into a real instrument track. For more details, see the sidebar on page 345.

Tweak preferences. Choose GarageBand's Preferences command and click the Advanced button. There you can examine and change settings that GarageBand normally makes automatically. Try reducing the number of voices per instrument. Note that this restricts the number of simultaneous notes you can play.

Simplify your song. Mute some tracks and turn off some effects. The Amp Simulation effects are particularly power hungry. You *can* greatly lighten GarageBand's burden by unchecking Reverb and Echo in the Master Track's Track Info pane, but doing so will eliminate the ability to use these effects in your song. Still, you might find this a worthwhile price to pay for extra tracks. You can always transfer your song to a faster Mac to get the polish that good reverb provides.

Use an external drive. A high-performance external FireWire hard drive may be able to keep up with multiple real instrument tracks better than your Mac's built-in drive, especially if you have a laptop Mac or Mac mini.

Optimize laptop performance. If you're using a laptop Mac, open the Energy Saver system preference and choose Highest Performance from the Optimize Energy Settings pop-up menu.

Turn off FileVault. Mac OS X's FileVault feature can dramatically slow the reading of data from the Home directory of your hard drive. Turn off FileVault using the Security system preference, or store your songs outside your Home directory.

Bouncing to Disk

If the measures I've described here don't do it for you, there's still hope: an update of a technique that us old fogies—people who grew up with analog multitrack recording—know about all too well.

Back in the analog multitrack days, when you approached the limit of your four-track cassette deck, you would mix down the three tracks you had already recorded and put them on the fourth track. After the mix-down, you could erase and re-use the original three tracks.

This technique was often called *bouncing*, and it's alive and well in GarageBand. Say you've laid down a sweet rhythm section groove—some drums, some bass, and maybe a keyboard or synthesizer pad.

You want to play a synth solo over this, but your PowerBook doesn't have the power.

Solution: save your project with an iLife preview (page 347), then add the project to a new GarageBand project.

Fine-tune your mix. Adjust every setting—panning, volume, effects, everything—until your mix sounds exactly as you want it.

Save with preview. Use the Preferences command to activate the save-with-preview feature, as described on page 346. Then, save the project. GarageBand creates a stereo mixdown of your tune and saves it along with the project.

Start over. Start a new GarageBand project. Be sure to set the key signature and tempo to match your song's settings. Locate your song in the GarageBand media browser, then drag it into the new project.

Add tracks and have fun. Because your rhythm groove is now one audio track—not a whole bunch of different, system-taxing tracks—your Mac can devote its energy to the new tracks.

Making changes. If you decide to change your rhythm groove, just open up your original project, make your changes, and save again. Because GarageBand maintains a link between the two projects, your changes will be incorporated in the second project when you reopen it.

The Key to Locking Tracks

If your Mac is choking during playback, try locking one or more tracks. To lock a track, click the padlock button in the track's header. Then, play the song from the beginning. GarageBand renders the locked track to disk: it creates an audio file containing the track's audio.

When the song begins playing, GarageBand plays back that audio file instead of making your Mac's processor do the heavy lifting involved in generating sounds and effects in real time.

Locking candidates. The best candidates for locking are software instrument tracks (particularly ones that use the Symphony Orchestra Jam Pack) and real instrument tracks containing complex effects, such as the guitar amp simulators.

Harder on the hard drive. Alas, locking tracks makes your hard drive work harder. If you have a laptop Mac or a Mac mini—computers that have slower hard drives than other Macs—you may find that locking a lot of

tracks causes playback problems. When you lock tracks, your project also uses more disk space.

Extracting a locked track. You can use the Finder to extract the audio from a locked track. Control-click on your project's icon and choose Show Package Contents from the shortcut menu. In the window that appears, open the Freeze Files folder: it will contain the audio files that GarageBand has rendered. You can open these files

in other programs (including iTunes), but you can't import them into GarageBand.

To avoid corrupting a project, don't rename or delete any files in the project's Freeze Files folder.

Unlocking a track. You can't edit a locked track or change its instrument or effects settings. (You can make volume and panning adjustments, however.) To change a locked track, unlock it by clicking the padlock button again.

Creating a Podcast at a Glance

I've already described how you can use iTunes and your iPod to listen to podcasts of all kinds (pages 36–37). With GarageBand 3, you can go from listener to producer.

GarageBand 3 turns your Mac into a radio studio—with broadcast engineer. Connect a microphone to your Mac or use the built-in mike that some Macs provide. You can also use the microphone built into Apple's iSight video camera. GarageBand 3 contains audio filters that optimize the sound produced by an iSight or built-in Mac mike.

Record your rants, vacation dispatches, family interviews—whatever you like. You can even record remote interviews with iChat users. Your audio is recorded into real-instrument tracks, so you can edit it using the same techniques described earlier.

Need theme music? Compose your own or use one of the many royalty-free music jingles included with iLife '06. Use the *ducking* feature to have GarageBand automatically lower and raise the music volume when you start and stop talking—just like the radio.

But don't stop there. Consider creating an *enhanced podcast*. Add chapter markers that enable listeners to conveniently jump around through your show. Add artwork that appears during playback in iTunes and on any iPod that can display photos. And add Web URLs that let iTunes users jump to specific Web pages as your show plays.

When you're finished, send your completed production to iWeb for publishing on the Internet. Here's how to become a podcaster.

Pick a Background

Use the loop browser to explore and choose from more than 100 jingles, including many sets that provide the same song in lengths of 7, 15, and 30 seconds. You can also choose from hundreds of sound effects and music *stingers*—and even use the Musical Typing window to play them as you do your show (page 333).

Add Visuals

Use the media browser to add photos (page 358) or movies (page 362). Use the search box to quickly locate what you need.

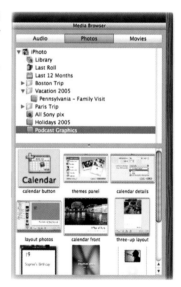

Add Web Connections

Want your listeners to be able to jump to Web pages that relate to your subject? Add Web addresses (URLs) to your markers (page 359).

When you create a new podcast, GarageBand gives you a standard set of tracks for common elements. You can customize these tracks and add more.

Use the *podcast track* to view and edit marker regions—for example, to synchronize a piece of artwork with a specific section of your show (pages 358 and 359).

Control how a track's volume is affected by the ducking feature. Click the down-pointing arrow for a background music track (page 357).

Preview the appearance of your enhanced podcast as it plays back (page 357).

Drag an image here to add *episode artwork* to your podcast (opposite page and page 359).

Create, edit, and manage the markers in your enhanced podcast (page 359).

Switch between displaying the Media browser (opposite page) and Track Info pane, where you can refine your sound.

Specify episode information, which appears in iTunes and iWeb.

Podcast Production Techniques

Plan

There are as many types of podcasts as there are types of songs. But no matter what topic you cover, you have a common set of planning and production options to consider.

Script (or at least sketch). You don't have to script every word of your podcast, but at least sketch out the structure of your show. And because they're the critical bookends for your barking, consider scripting your introduction and conclusion.

How long? Around 20 to 30 minutes is a good balance between depth and reasonable download times, not to mention listener attention span.

How much? You can record one non-stop rant, but I'm unlikely to listen to it. Consider covering several topics, limiting each to five minutes or so.

What's the theme? Start your podcast with an introductory music jingle. Compose your own or use the ones that come with GarageBand. To explore them, display the loop browser, then click the 🎙 button.

GarageBand's jingles come in several durations. Consider using a 30-second version for your intro and a seven-second version as a separator, called a *bumper*, between topic segments.

Tip: Don't waste time by letting your intro music play and play. Your listeners want to hear *you*, so let the music play for just a few seconds, then start your intro. Use GarageBand's automatic ducking feature to lower the music's volume when you start talking.

Who else? Will you have guests? A variety of voices makes for more interesting listening. You can record guests via phone (page 360), via iChat AV (page 362) or, ideally, in person, with a second microphone.

Produce

Get started. As shown on the previous pages, when you click New Podcast Episode while creating a new GarageBand project, you get a set of tracks for male and female voices. You also get jingles and radio sounds, such as sound effects and *stingers*, which are short, sonic spices of the kind you hear on the radio before traffic and weather reports.

If you'll need additional tracks—perhaps to record a guest with a second microphone, or some music using a software instrument and your music keyboard—add the tracks using the techniques described earlier in this chapter.

Prepare for recording. Record in a quiet location and with the best microphone you can use. (For advice on obtaining good sound, see pages 243–245.) If you're using multiple mikes or audio sources, assign inputs to each track (page 338). Adjust your recording levels (page 337).

Cue the band. When should you add music to your podcast? I recommend waiting until after you've recorded and refined the core content of your podcast. Save the music for the post-production phase. The way GarageBand lets you drag audio regions around makes it easy to time where you want the music to come in.

On the air. To begin recording, click the Record button or press the R key. Make a mistake? Pause for a second or two, then pick up at a point before your blunder. You can edit out the flub later using the techniques on page 339.

Polish

Optional: Adjust effects. The male and female tracks that GarageBand provides in a new podcast project are fine for most efforts. But you might want to open the Track Info pane and explore some of GarageBand's effects and audio-enhancement options. Double-click on the track header for the track you want to tweak, then click the Details button in the Track Info pane.

The Speech Enhancer effect can sweeten a voice in several ways. Explore the presets in the pop-up menu, then click the pencil button to view all your options. If you're using an iSight camera's mike or the mike built

into your Mac, you can choose options that will optimize sound quality. You can also apply a noise-reduction filter.

To add punch to a spoken voice, apply the Compressor effect, but don't go overboard.

Add music and refine timing. Now's the time when I like to add theme and bumper jingles and refine the timing of my podcasts. To take advantage of GarageBand's volume-ducking feature, be sure the down-pointing arrow is active in the Jingles track (or other music tracks you may have added) and the up-pointing arrow is active in your primary voice track or tracks.

Optional: Enhance your podcast. If you're creating an enhanced podcast—one with artwork, chapter markers, URL markers, or any combination thereof—add those items now. See the following pages.

Publish

Preview and proofread. Before exporting the final podcast, play it all the way through. If you've added artwork, chapter, or URL markers, use the Podcast Preview pane to verify that they appear when they should. Click any URL markers to ensure that they go to the proper Web address. (If the Podcast Preview pane isn't visible, double-click on the track header for the Podcast track.)

Make sure there are no odd audio glitches caused by editing. Adjust volume levels as necessary to deliver a strong signal with no clipping. If the automatic ducking feature didn't bring down music levels sufficiently, add volume curves to perfect your mix (page 340).

Optional: Adjust export settings. With the Export portion of the Preferences dialog box, you can fine-tune how GarageBand saves your podcast to balance file size against sound quality. You can also specify how GarageBand saves the final mix of your podcast: by sending it directly to iWeb or by simply saving it to disk (page 359).

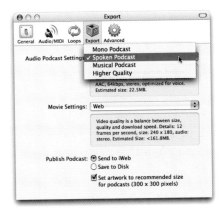

Export your podcast. Use the Share menu to send your podcast to iWeb (pages 359 and 380) or save it to disk for uploading to a different Web server.

Enhancing Your Podcast

With enhanced podcasts, your options go beyond sound to include photos, chapter markers, and URL markers. You can use just one of these enhancements in your podcasts, or you can use all three.

By adding images to the podcast track, you can add photography and artwork that appears in the iTunes window or on photo-capable iPods. Create a training podcast that illustrates the steps involved in performing a task. Or an art history podcast that shows famous works as you talk about them. Or a vacation travelogue that shows your stops.

With chapter markers, you can add convenient navigation to your podcast. When your podcast is played in iTunes, a chapter menu appears that allows listeners (and viewers) to jump to sections of interest. When playing your podcast on an iPod, your audience can navigate the chapters using their click wheels.

With URL markers, you can add the immediacy of the Internet. Create links to pages that relate to your subject. The link appears in the iTunes window, and your podcast's audience can jump to the link's URL by clicking it.

The one downside to an enhanced podcast is that you must deliver it in the AAC audio format, which means that the podcast will play only in iTunes and on iPods. If you're planning to deliver your podcast in MP3 format to reach the broadest possible audience, keep your podcasts unenhanced.

Adding Artwork

Step 1. Display the media browser by clicking the ▣ button.

Step 2. In the media browser, click the Photos button, then locate the photo you want to add.

Step 3. Drag the photo to a location in the podcast track.

Step 4. To fine-tune the amount of time the artwork appears, drag the edges of its region left or right.

You can also drag the entire artwork region left and right, just as you can other GarageBand regions.

Notes and Tips

Editing art. You can adjust the zooming and cropping of an art item much as you can in iPhoto. In the podcast track editor, double-click the artwork's thumbnail in the Artwork column. Use the Artwork Editor to zoom in and adjust which part of the art is visible, then click Set.

You can also replace an image by dragging a new image to the editor.

Art from elsewhere. You can also add an image to the podcast track by dragging it from the Finder. You can even add an image from a Web page by dragging it from the Safari window.

More than just art. An artwork region can also represent a chapter marker and a URL marker. For example, maybe you'd like a chapter to begin when a particular image appears. In the podcast track, select the image. Next, in the podcast track editor, click in the Chapter Title box and type a name for the chapter. For more details, see the opposite page.

Adding Chapter Markers

Step 1. Position the GarageBand playhead at the point where you want the marker to appear, then click the Add Marker button in the podcast track editor.

Tip: You can click Add Markers to add markers as your podcast plays back.

Step 2. In the podcast track editor, select the marker's *Chapter Title* placeholder text in the Chapter Title column, then type a title.

In iTunes, chapter markers appear in a menu, indicated by a ▣ icon, to the left of the iTunes search box.

Tip: As noted on the opposite page, you can use an artwork region as a chapter marker by simply typing a title in the region's Chapter Title box.

Adding URL Markers

As with chapter markers, you can assign a URL to a region that contains artwork; just skip to Step 2 below.

Step 1. Position the playhead at the point where you want the marker, then click the Add Marker button in the podcast track editor.

Step 2. In the podcast track editor, type the URL title and address.

Type the address of the Web page here. You can also copy an address from the Safari location bar and paste it here.

The URL title is displayed in the artwork area of the iTunes window.

Adding Episode Artwork

Episode artwork is a single image that appears in iTunes while your podcast is playing. iWeb also uses episode artwork when you add a podcast to a Web page (page 380). You might use episode artwork to display your company logo, a favorite photo from your vacation podcast, or a graphic created in Photoshop or Photoshop Elements that contains a few words about the podcast's topic.

If your podcast also contains artwork regions as described on the opposite page, the regions replace the episode artwork. When those artwork regions end, the episode artwork reappears.

To add episode artwork, drag an image from the media browser (or elsewhere) to the Episode Artwork well at the left edge of the podcast track editor. To tweak the cropping of the artwork, double-click it in the Episode Artwork well, then use the Artwork Editor as described on the opposite page.

Podcasting Tips

Stamp Your Podcast

Many podcasters like to begin each episode with a very brief announcement of the podcast's name and date: *This is The Digital Hub, Episode 3, for August 17, 2006.* This little "stamp" is handy for listeners who are using iPods. It lets them immediately verify that they're listening to the right episode—without having to take their eyes off the road.

Recording iChat Interviews

If you use Mac OS X 10.4 Tiger or a later version, you can use Apple's iChat conferencing software to record audio interviews with distant guests. GarageBand stores each participant's voice in its own track. And if you're conducting a video conference, GarageBand grabs a still shot of each participant when he or she begins speaking and adds that image to the podcast track.

To record iChat interviews, you must initiate the audio or video conference—that is, *you* must be the one to invite the other guests to the conference. Do that, and then chat with your guests for a minute or two to make sure that your Internet connection, and the Internet as a whole, are behaving themselves. I've had best-laid interview plans shattered by Internet difficulties that were out of my control. Use this testing time to remind your guests that you'll be recording them.

When you're ready to begin recording, click GarageBand's Record button or press the R key. GarageBand asks if you want to record the chat.

Click Yes, and GarageBand begins recording. Now grill your guests and grill them hard.

In my experience, you need a fairly fast Mac to get good results when recording iChat conferences. My 1.67GHz PowerBook G4 sometimes stumbles, but a G5 or Intel Duo system does a good job. And needless to say, a fast Internet connection is a must, particularly for multi-guest interviews.

Recording Phone Interviews

iChat interviews can be fun, but you might prefer to back away from the cutting edge and conduct your interviews the way many radio stations do: via telephone.

You have a few options for recording a telephone call. Radio Shack sells several phone-recording adaptors for under $30. Connect the adaptor to your phone and attach it to your Mac's microphone jack, and you're underway.

The problem with inexpensive recording devices, though, is that *your* voice also sounds like it's coming over the phone (which, from your Mac's standpoint, it is). What you want is for your voice to be recorded by that high-quality microphone that you were smart enough to buy. For this, you need a specialized piece of hardware called a *telephone hybrid.*

A telephone hybrid is a box that contains jacks for the telephone line and your microphone. Connect your mike and your phone to the hybrid, then connect the audio output of the hybrid to your Mac's microphone jack. Some hybrids also have volume knobs that let you adjust the mix between your mike and your guest's phone.

A good source for telephone hybrids is JK Audio (www.jkaudio.com). The company's least expensive device, the AutoHybrid, sells for under $200. A Google search for *telephone hybrid* will yield more sources.

Adjusting Export Settings

As I mentioned on page 357, you can use the Export portion of GarageBand's Preferences dialog box to specify audio quality settings for your final podcast. For talk show-style podcasts, GarageBand's standard settings are fine. If you play a lot of music in your podcast, though, you may want to choose the Musical Podcast option.

Music Rights and Wrongs

Speaking of music podcasts, it's important to note that you can't legally publish a podcast containing commercial recordings—at least not without paying for the rights to do so.

To learn the latest about the frequently changing world of digital music licensing, do some Google searches for *podcast music licensing* and *podcast music rights*.

Tune Into Magnatune

You might also investigate music sources that permit rebroadcasting and podcast use. A great stop is Magnatune (www.magnatune.com), which has refreshingly simple policies for podcasters: "Magnatune is one of the only record labels on the planet whose music you can legally use in your podcast, without paying for a licensing agreement. Because we work directly with artists, we can legally do this."

And you have to love a record label whose corporate slogan is "We are not evil."

Saving Your Podcast

Normally, GarageBand is set up to send your final podcast to iWeb for subsequent publishing on the Internet (page 380). But as I mentioned on page 357, you can also use the Export portion of the Preferences dialog box to have

GarageBand simply save your podcast's final mix on your hard drive. In the Publish Podcast area of the dialog box, click the button labeled Save to Disk.

When you activate this option, the Share menu contains a command named Export as Podcast. Choose that command, and you get a standard Save dialog box that lets you name your final podcast file. Avoid using any spaces or special characters in the name; they're likely to cause problems when you upload the podcast to a Web server.

After GarageBand has mixed down your podcast and exported it, you can play the exported podcast in iTunes or upload it to a Web server.

Delivering in MP3

Whether you send your podcast directly to iWeb or export it to disk, GarageBand saves the podcast in AAC format. Given the dominance of iTunes and the iPod in the digital audio scene, that may not bother you.

But what if you want to deliver your podcast in MP3 format to reach the largest possible audience? Use iTunes to convert the podcast.

First, use the Advanced portion of the iTunes Preferences dialog box to specify your desired MP3 encoding settings (see page 24). For a voice podcast, consider a bitrate of 64 kbps or 80 kbps.

Second, use the Export portion of GarageBand's Preferences dialog box to specify the Higher Quality export setting. This minimizes the amount of lossy compression GarageBand applies. Export your production as a podcast.

Next, in iTunes, press the Option key and choose Convert to MP3 from the Advanced menu. In the subsequent dialog box, locate and double-click the podcast's file. iTunes converts the podcast to MP3 format.

Finally, select the converted podcast in iTunes and choose Show Song File from the File menu. There's your MP3, ready for uploading. (Again, avoid using any spaces or unusual characters in the MP3's name.)

Scoring Movies with GarageBand

iMovie HD's audio features are adequate for many projects, especially given the new effects and filters built into iMovie HD 6 (page 248).

But your soundtrack options don't end with iMovie HD. You can bring video into GarageBand and apply GarageBand's audio and music-making features to the movie's soundtrack.

GarageBand's video features aren't for editing the picture; that's a job for iMovie HD. Rather, you bring a finished edit into GarageBand for additional sonic seasoning. Punch up the sound with GarageBand's effects. Record and edit narration with more precision than iMovie HD provides. Or compose your own music soundtracks by using loops and by recording your own performances. When you're finished, send the final movie to iDVD for burning or export it as a QuickTime movie.

You might also use GarageBand's video features to create a *video podcast*: a podcast that adds the dimension of motion. As with GarageBand's audio podcasting features, you can add chapter and URL markers to the video. When you're done, you can send your final product to iWeb or save it for manual uploading to a Web server.

You'll need a fast Mac with a fast hard drive for movie scoring. If you have playback problems, consult the advice on pages 152 and 153 to optimize GarageBand's performance. And make sure you're using GarageBand 3.0.2 or a later version, if available.

Refining an iMovie HD Soundtrack

Step 1. In iMovie HD, finish your edit.

Step 2. In iMovie HD, choose GarageBand from the Share menu, then click the Share button in the dialog box that appears.

iMovie HD sends the movie to GarageBand, which displays it in the video track (see opposite page).

Step 3. Enhance to your ears' content: add tracks, record narration, apply effects, or add chapter and URL markers for a video podcast.

Step 4. Use the commands in the Share menu to send your finished movie to iWeb or iDVD, or to export the movie as a QuickTime movie (opposite page).

Note: If you reopen an iMovie HD project that you've enhanced in GarageBand, you won't see (or hear) any new tracks that you've added. It's best to think of the iMovie HD/GarageBand connection as a one-way street: you can go from iMovie HD to GarageBand, but if you return to iMovie HD to do more work on your project, you won't hear all your sonic enhancements.

Other Ways to Add Movies

There are other ways to open a movie in GarageBand and enhance its soundtrack.

The media browser. GarageBand's media browser gives you convenient access to movies in your Movies folder, iTunes library, and iPhoto library. Click the ▦ button, then click Movies. As in the other iLife programs, you can preview a movie in the media browser by double-clicking its thumbnail.

Drag and drop. Simply drag a movie's icon from any location on your hard drive into the GarageBand window.

Working with Movies

When you've brought a movie into GarageBand, here's what you see—and what you can do.

Your movie's video frames appear in the video track. The more you zoom in on the timeline, the more sequential frames you see. When you want to position a region (for example, a sound effect) so that it begins when a specific frame appears, zoom in until you see that frame.

The video track editor works much like the podcast track editor: you can add chapter markers and URL markers. If you send the completed project to iDVD, the chapter markers become DVD chapter markers. (If you created markers in iMovie HD, they appear here, too.)

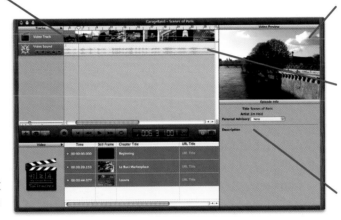

When you play the project, the movie plays here.

Your movie's soundtrack appears as an imported audio region. You can add filters or effects to this track using the techniques described earlier in this chapter.

Creating a video podcast? Use this area to type a description for the podcast.

Tips for Video

Second tracks. If you added a second audio track to an iMovie HD project, both audio tracks are mixed into one sound track in GarageBand. If that second track contains background music or sound effects, you'll want to use iMovie HD's audio controls to fine-tune the mix between the two tracks *before* sending the project to GarageBand.

Enhancing narration. If you've recorded a voice-over or other narration in GarageBand (or, for that matter, in iMovie HD), consider applying GarageBand's audio effects to it. For example, use the Compressor effect to add punch to a narration. Use the Speech Enhancer filter to reduce noise and optimize male or female voices.

Exporting your final effort. When you've finished refining a movie's soundtrack, you can use the Share menu to send your final effort to iWeb or to iDVD.

You can also export the project as a QuickTime movie, and you have several export options that balance file size against quality. To adjust movie-export settings, choose Preferences from the GarageBand menu, then click Export.

To use the exact format of the original video, use the Full Quality setting.

As with audio podcasts, you can set up GarageBand's export preferences to either send a video podcast directly to iWeb or save it to disk save it to disk (see page 361).

iWeb:
Your World
on the Web

The Macintosh
iLife '06

iWeb at a Glance

With iWeb, you can put your world on the Web. You can create Web sites containing text, photos, movies, podcasts, and more. iWeb insulates you from Web publishing technicalities, such as markup languages and servers.

Start by choosing one of the site design *templates* that are built into iWeb. Many of those designs have counterparts in other iLife '06 programs. For example, the Travel template in iWeb resembles the Travel theme in iPhoto, iDVD, and iMovie HD. Thus, you can create a Web site about your vacation and have it match your iPhoto books and calendars, your iMovie video travelogue, and the DVD containing your video and travel slide shows—a consistent visual identity, as the marketers would say.

Each iWeb template provides several types of pages, as shown at right. As you create a site, you simply add new pages as needed to accommodate what you want to publish.

Decided on a design? Just add content. Replace the placeholder photos and text with your own. Use the page design as is, or use iWeb's formatting tools to customize it to your own liking. If you've used Apple's Pages or Keynote software, you'll feel at home with iWeb's formatting features.

iWeb also simplifies creating blogs and podcasts. Creating a new blog or podcast entry is as easy as creating a new email message. iWeb also manages the chores of creating archive pages and RSS feeds.

When you're finished, one click sends your site to Apple's .Mac service—and to the world.

A Gallery of Web Pages

Each iWeb template provides six page styles, each aimed at a specific type of content. Each design has placeholders for text and graphics; you can also add additional graphics and text boxes.

Welcome

An introductory home page, ideal for welcoming visitors and stating the purpose of your site.

About

A good place to describe yourself, your business, your organization—whatever your site is about.

Photos

A photo album, with small photo thumbnails and a button for displaying photos as a slide show. You can also create a photo page from within iPhoto (page 378).

Movie

A page designed to present a QuickTime movie. You can also create a movie page from within iMovie HD (pages 269 and 384).

Blog

A page that holds a single blog entry—for example, one dispatch from your vacation. You can also create a blog entry from within iPhoto (page 380).

Podcast

A page designed to present a podcast episode. You can also create a podcast entry from within GarageBand (page 361) and a video podcast entry from within iMovie HD (page 269).

The *Site Organizer* lists the sites you create and their pages. You can create multiple sites with iWeb, and even move pages between sites.

As you create pages, iWeb creates a *navigation menu* that your site's visitors will use to get around. iWeb updates your navigation menu as you rearrange and expand your site.

Create your pages on the *webpage canvas*. Drag text and graphics around, add and remove text boxes and photos, type and format text, add shapes, and more.

Add photos from your iPhoto library or another source (page 378).

Open the Media browser (right) for accessing photos, movies, and music.

Open the Adjust panel (right) for image tweaking, such as in iPhoto (page 375).

Add a new Web page (page 369).

Send the site to .Mac for all—or only some —to see (page 382).

Add text boxes (page 372) and shapes (page 375) and refine layouts (page 374).

Open the published version of the site in your Web browser.

Add a *hit counter* to count the visitors to your site, and an email link to allow visitors to contact you (page 384).

Open the Inspector (right) for precise formatting, linking, and more.

Creating a Web Site

What do you want to publish? A few iPhoto albums? The occasional movie? A podcast? Or a full Web site containing numerous pages as well as photo albums, a blog, and a podcast?

iWeb can handle any of these tasks. If you're planning an ambitious site, though, consider sketching out the site's structure on paper before you start. You might want to draw an organizational chart, with the home page at the top and other pages beneath it—much like the DVD menu diagram on page 298. This kind of advance planning can help you map out your site and organize your thoughts.

After you've planned your attack, perform it. Start by creating a new site and choosing a page template for its design. Then replace the placeholder content with your own text and graphics. Tweak the text formatting if you like, but be careful—the "wrong" kinds of formatting can cause iWeb to create large pages that load slowly (page 373).

As your site comes together, you'll add additional pages and create links to connect them. You might also create links to other sites on the World Wide Web. You'll add graphics and adjust their appearance. And then you'll publish your site on Apple's .Mac service.

I cover each of these phases and more in the pages that follow. Here's how to get started.

Creating a New Site

First Time Here?

The first time you start iWeb, it presents its list of templates and page styles.

Step 1. Choose the template that best matches what you have in mind for your site. Remember, you can customize your pages.

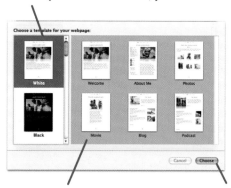

Step 2. Choose a page style. The Welcome and About Me styles are good starting points for general-purpose pages, while the remaining styles are tailored for specific tasks (page 366).

Step 3. Click Choose or press Return.

Repeat Customer?

You can create multiple Web sites and switch between them with the click of a mouse. When you want to create a new site, choose New Site from the File menu (Shift-⌘-N), then choose a template and page style as described above.

Renaming Sites and Pages

To change the name of a site or page, double-click it in the Site Organizer, then type a new name.

Brevity rules. Unless you specify otherwise (page 371), iWeb adds a navigation menu link for a new page. If you use a wordy page name, the link may not display correctly—and it will definitely look hokey.

Note that if you use spaces in page names (as in *Main Menu*), iWeb will translate them into codes (for example, *Main%20Menu*) when you publish your site. The links will still work, but they'll look unwieldy and will be hard to recite over the phone. For the tidiest page addresses, avoid spaces.

Case counts. When naming sites, don't use names that are the same except for their case. For example, don't have one site named *HomePage* and another named *Homepage*. The sites won't publish properly.

Creating a Page: The Basics

After you choose a page style, iWeb gives you a page filled with placeholder graphics and text. By replacing this placeholder content with your own, you can create an attractive Web page.

Here's a look at the basic techniques behind iWeb page design. In the following pages, I describe how you can tailor a page design to your tastes.

Replacing placeholder text. To replace a section of placeholder text, select it and begin typing.

Adventures in Paris

Replace placeholder photos. To replace a placeholder photo with one of your own, drag the photo from the media browser or from any folder on your hard drive to the placeholder folder.

Kill the advertising. To remove the "Made on a Mac" graphic, select it and press the Delete key.

Creating Additional Pages

To add a new page to a site, choose New Page from the File menu or click the ⊞ button. Choose a template and page style as described on the opposite page.

Off the menu. Normally, iWeb includes a new page in your site's navigation menu. In some cases, you may not want this—maybe you plan to use a text link or other button to provide access to that page. Use the Inspector to remove a page from the navigation menu; see page 371.

Where iWeb Stores Your Sites

iWeb stores all of your sites and their pages in one place: a file named *Domain* tucked deep within your hard drive. Specifically, the Domain file lives in your home directory, within Library > Application Support > iWeb.

Get in the habit of backing up the Domain file now and then. If you use Apple's Backup 3, included with a .Mac subscription, you can have this done automatically.

Page Design Basics

If you aren't a tailor, it's better to buy off the rack than to try to make your own suit. And if you aren't a Web designer, it's a good idea to stick with the built-in page styles that each iWeb template provides.

But the temptation to tinker may beckon. Maybe a certain page style requires a few more graphics to meet your needs, and maybe one of those graphics could use some work. Maybe you'd like to use a different type font, or adjust the line spacing of some text. Maybe a page needs another block of text, or a different background color.

You can perform many design tweaks directly on the webpage canvas. Click and drag blocks of text or graphics to move them around. Resize an item by selecting it and then dragging one of its selection handles.

For other design tasks, you'll turn to iWeb's Inspector. Its numerous controls allow you specify paragraph formatting, add and remove page backgrounds, create special graphics effects, and more.

For still other tasks, you'll use menu commands and the tools at the bottom of the iWeb window. Add additional text boxes to a page. Add shapes, such as lines and boxes. Control how objects overlap, specify colors and fonts, modify images, and more.

Here's a tour of your design studio.

Moving an Object

To move an object (for example, a text box or a graphic), click and drag it to the desired location.

iWeb displays *alignment guides* when an object you're dragging is centered on the page or aligned with another object on the page. To customize the alignment guides, use the Preferences command (page 384).

As you drag an item, iWeb displays its location on the page, in pixels. Here, the photo is 91 pixels from the left edge of the page and 203 pixels from the top.

Notes and Tips

Go straight. If you press the Shift key while dragging, iWeb constrains the item's movement to horizontal, vertical, or a 45-degree angle.

Keyboard control. To nudge an item in one-pixel increments, select the item and then press one of the arrow keys on your keyboard. To nudge in 10-pixel increments, press Shift along with an arrow key.

Have another. To duplicate an item, press the Option key while dragging the item.

Resizing an Object

To resize an object, select it and drag one of its selection handles. If you resize a text box, its text reflows to fit the new size.

To resize an item in just one direction, drag a side handle.

Tip: To avoid changing the proportions of a text box or shape when resizing it, press the Shift key while dragging.

Anatomy of a Page

Each page style in an iWeb template has four regions. Each region serves its own purpose, and by changing the dimensions of the regions, you can change the appearance and dimensions of a Web page.

To see each of the four regions, choose Show Layout from the View menu (Shift-⌘-L). iWeb displays faint gray lines between each region.

Some page styles use some regions, but not others. For example, the page styles in the Travel template lack header regions. You can add those regions, however, by using the Page Inspector as described at right.

The *header* appears at the very top of the page.

The *navigation bar* contains the menu for moving from page to page.

The *body* holds the main page content.

All page styles contain *text boxes* with placeholder text that you can replace or delete. You can also add additional text boxes.

The *footer* is at the very bottom of the page and typically holds the "Made on a Mac" graphic along with other optional elements, such as page counters and "email me" buttons (page 384).

Introducing the Inspector

The Inspector is the gateway to many design and formatting tasks in iWeb. This small floating window is actually seven control panels in one; you display the inspector you need by clicking a button at the top of the Inspector window.

To display the Inspector, click the ![Inspector icon] button near the lower-right corner of the iWeb window, or choose Show Inspector from the View menu (Option-⌘-I).

If you don't want a page to appear in your site's navigation menu, uncheck this box.

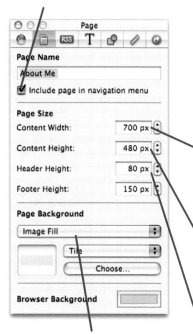

With many page styles, you can customize the page background here (see page 376).

Changing Pages: The Page Inspector

One design change you may want to make is to change the dimensions of a page: to make it longer, for example, so it can hold more content.

iWeb's page styles tend to have short pages that your site's visitors can scroll through with just a click or two. That's convenient, but maybe you have more content than will fit within a page's confines. As long as your design is uncluttered (and your content interesting), there's nothing wrong with having a longer Web page.

To change a page's dimensions, use the Page Inspector. Display the Inspector, then click ![icon] to display the Page Inspector.

The Page Size values determine the dimensions of a page and each of its regions.

You can make a page wider by increasing the value in the Content Width box, but don't go overboard: you don't want your site's visitors to have to scroll horizontally to read the entire page.

To make a page longer, increase the Content Height value by clicking the arrows or typing a new value. (The values are in pixels.)

Want to add a header region to a page style that lacks one? Specify a value here.

Working with Text

To state the obvious, text plays a large role on Web sites. iWeb gives you plenty of text control. You can use the fonts that Apple has used for page templates, or you can summon the Fonts panel and format as you prefer.

But there's a peril to this typographic freedom. If you use fonts that aren't commonly available on Macs and Windows PCs, or if you perform some non-standard formatting (as I describe on the opposite page), iWeb renders that text as a graphic. Instead of getting a full page of fast-loading text, you get a large "picture of text" that makes your Web page load slowly. And because the text won't *really* be text, if your site's visitors try to print the page, they'll get poor-quality hard copy.

The best way to avoid this problem is to format large passages of text conservatively: stick with the fonts in iWeb's templates, or with fonts that are common on Macs and Windows PCs, such as Verdana. If you want a headline in a fancy font, create a separate text box for it.

Finally, because Web sites aren't Web sites without hyperlinks, you can turn a word or series of words into a link that whisks your visitors off to another page—elsewhere on your site or elsewhere in the world.

Text Basics

Mind your placeholder. As you delve into iWeb, you'll quickly notice something about the placeholder text in iWeb's templates: you can't delete its text boxes. You can delete the text *inside* a placeholder text box—just drag across the text and press the Delete key—but you can't delete the box itself.

You can always recognize a text box that iWeb won't let you delete: when you select it, its selection handles are gray. On objects that you *can* delete, selection handles are white.

Adding a text box. iWeb's built-in templates have text boxes that you can move and resize. You can also add a new text box to a page by clicking the Text button (**T**) or choosing Insert > Text.

Linking to another page. It's easy to turn a word or phrase into a hyperlink that connects to another Web page. Select the word or phrase, then turn to the Link Inspector. Click the ⓘ button, then, in the Inspector, click 🔘.

Check the box. (To turn a hyperlink into ordinary text, uncheck the box.)

You can link to another page on your site, a page elsewhere on the Web, a file, or an email message (page 384).

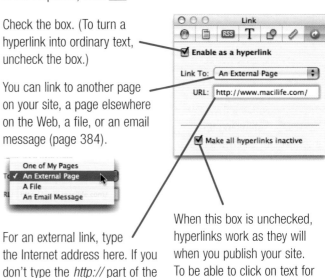

For an external link, type the Internet address here. If you don't type the *http://* part of the address, iWeb adds it for you.

When this box is unchecked, hyperlinks work as they will when you publish your site. To be able to click on text for editing, check this box.

Text Formatting Techniques

Formatting characters. To change your text's font, size, and style, use the Fonts panel. To display the panel, click the  button or choose Format > Font > Show Fonts (⌘-T). Select the text you want to format, then use the Fonts panel to do the job. **Important:** Avoid using the drop shadow feature available in the Fonts panel. Adding a drop shadow to even one character causes iWeb to render the entire text box as a graphic.

Formatting paragraphs. You can also apply paragraph-level formatting: line spacing, alignment, and so on. For these tasks, use the Text Inspector. Click the 🛈 button, then, in the Inspector, click ⊤.

Copying and pasting style. To copy one text box's formatting to another, select the formatted text and choose Format > Copy Text Style. Then select the text you want to format and choose Format > Paste Text Style.

Lose the text, keep the style. You may prefer to write your text in a word processor, then paste it into iWeb when you're done. At the same time, though, you may want to retain the existing font formatting of some placeholder text. No problem. After copying your text to the Clipboard, switch back to iWeb, select the text box where you want your new text to reside, then choose Edit > Paste and Match Style. iWeb pastes the new text but gives it the formatting of the old.

More Text Tricks

Resizing and rotating. You can resize text boxes using the mouse or the Metrics Inspector. You can also use the Metrics Inspector to rotate text, but note that iWeb will turn the text into a graphic.

Opacity and more. To change the opacity of text—for example, to make it appear faint—use the Graphics Inspector (page 374). You can also add a solid or dotted border around a text box.

iWeb can automatically flow text around another shape, such as a photo or graphic (page 375).

You can format a series of paragraphs as a bulleted or numbered list.

Control whether the text is positioned at the top of its box, centered within the box, or positioned at the bottom.

Specify margin alignments. Think twice about using justified text (even left and right margins); it's difficult to read on screen.

Add a background color to a text box.

Control the spacing between characters. Tightening up large text can improve its appearance, provided characters don't actually touch.

Control line spacing. The values are in points, of which there are 72 in an inch.

Control how much space is around the text.

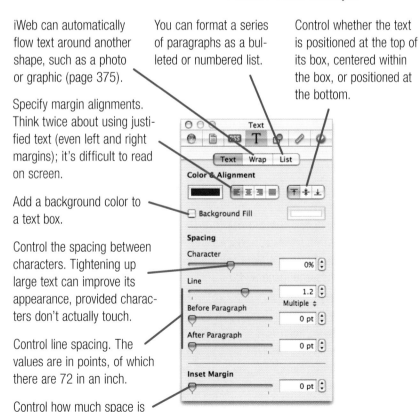

Working with Graphics

Essential Photo Techniques

Words are important, but a picture can be worth at least few of them. iWeb makes it easy to add images to your pages. Just drag them from the media browser (or from any location on your hard drive) to the webpage canvas.

Then, you can modify the photos—make them larger or smaller, crop them, and more. You can also use iWeb's layering controls to change how the photos stack with other objects on the page.

Chances are most of the images you'll be adding will be photos, but you might also add non-photo graphics: your company's logo, an elaborate headline created in Photoshop, and so on.

Basic formatting. You can resize an image by dragging its selection handles (see page 370). For more precision, click the Inspector's ✐ button. This summons the Metrics Inspector, where you can specify exact pixel dimensions. (To squish or squeeze a photo, uncheck the Constrain Proportions box.)

You can also use the Metrics Inspector to rotate images and specify their exact location on the page. And you can use the Graphics Inspector to add shadows, reflections, borders, and more. To make the image faint so you can superimpose text over it, use the Graphic Inspector's Opacity slider.

Fixed versus inline. When you add a photo to a page, its location is fixed at the point where you drag it. However, you can also insert a photo *inside* a text box. That's called an *inline graphic*, and because it lives among the letters, it moves when you move them. It also moves within the text box as you edit and format.

Use inline graphics for images that need to stay close to specific pieces of text—a photo of a business executive next to her biography; or the photos or illustrations in a report, an educational page, or a lengthy travelogue.

To add a photo as an inline graphic, press the ⌘ key while dragging the

photo into a text box. As you drag, position the vertical insertion point where you want the graphic to appear—for example, just before the first letter in a paragraph. When you release the mouse button, iWeb inserts the photo, which you can resize as needed.

You can also use the Text Inspector to have iWeb wrap the text around the graphic (see the opposite page).

Replacing a placeholder image. iWeb's placeholder images remind me of those photos of strangers that are tucked inside new wallets. To replace an iWeb stranger, drag a photo to the placeholder photo. When the placeholder photo's frame highlights, release the mouse button.

Make it link. You can turn a graphic into a button that, when clicked, takes your site's visitors to another Web page. Select the graphic, display the Link Inspector, and specify the link details (see page 372).

Forward and Backward: Layering Controls

As you add items to a page, you may have objects that overlap each other. For example, in the Travel template's Welcome page, two photos overlap each other, and the photos themselves overlap a

couple of design elements (the passport stamps).

When you add a new object to a page, it appears at the top of the "stack." You can control how objects overlap by using the Forward and Backward

buttons at the bottom of the iWeb window, or the commands in the Arrange menu.

For example, to change the layering order so that a dog photo appears atop a cat photo, select the dog photo

and click Forward, or select the cat photo and click Backward.

Forward   Backward

I guess you can tell: I'm a dog person.

A Gallery of Image Techniques

Cropping a Photo

In iWeb's world, cropping is called *masking*. To crop out part of an image, you must adjust the size of the image's mask.

Step 1. Select the image.

Step 2. Click the toolbar's Mask button (🔲) or choose Format > Mask.

iWeb displays a mask rectangle in the middle of the image.

Drag the mask and its selection handles to indicate the part of the image you want to retain. You can also nudge the mask using the keyboard's arrow keys.

Step 3. Click outside of the image or press the Return key.

iWeb hides the portion that was outside of the mask. To remove the cropping, click the Unmask button in the toolbar or choose Format > Unmask.

Adjusting a Photo

iWeb's Adjust panel works much like its counterpart in iPhoto, with one big exception: your original photo isn't altered. iWeb simply applies your adjustments to the copy of the photo that you add to the page.

The Adjust panel in iWeb lacks a Straighten slider, but provides an option iPhoto lacks: an Auto Levels button. Clicking the button is roughly the same as dragging the black-point and white-point sliders to the shoulders of the histogram (pages 142–149).

Note: You can't use iWeb's Adjust panel to adjust the thumbnail images on a photo album page (page 378).

Wrapping Text Around a Photo

For inline graphics, you can set up a *text wrap* so that text flows around vertical and horizontal boundaries of the photo.

After adding a photo as an inline graphic as described on the opposite page, select the photo and open the Text Inspector. Click its Wrap button, and check the Object Causes Wrap box.

The object can appear at the left or right edge of a paragraph.

You can add extra space around the image.

Reflections, If You Must

In some of iWeb's page styles, photos have a reflection effect, as though they're suspended over a piece of frosted glass.

You can apply the reflection effect to photos that you add, too—but don't overdo it.

Select the photo, then display the Graphic Inspector (🔲). Check the Reflection box. To adjust the intensity of the reflection, drag the slider.

To remove the reflection in an iWeb template that uses it, select the graphic and uncheck the Reflection box.

Adding Shapes

With the Shapes pop-up menu you can endow a page with anything from straight lines to comic book speech bubbles.

You can turn a shape into a hyperlink, and you can resize and modify shapes using the Graphic Inspector, the Color window, and the techniques discussed throughout this chapter. Some shapes have settings panels for specifying details like the number of points in a star.

Tip: To insert a shape as an inline graphic, first click within a text box at the spot where you want the shape to live.

Customizing Page Backgrounds

Many of iWeb's page templates have background images or patterns. By using the Page Inspector, you can customize the backgrounds of Web pages in several ways. Open the page that has the background you want to customize, then display the Page Inspector. Choose one of the following options from the pop-up menu in the Page Background area.

Color Fill. Give the page a solid background color. After choosing Color Fill, click the color well (located below the pop-up menu) to display the same Colors window used by other Mac programs, including iMovie HD, iDVD, and iPhoto.

Gradient Fill. Add a *gradient* (a gradual shift from one color to another). After choosing this option, use the controls below the pop-up menu to fine-tune the gradient.

Specify the start and end colors of the gradient. To swap the two colors, click the double-headed arrow.

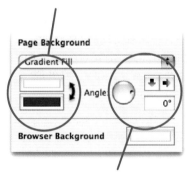

Control the angle of the gradient by dragging the Angle dial, by clicking the arrows, or by typing a value.

Image Fill. Add a photo or other graphic to the background. Use the controls below the pop-up menu to fine-tune the fill (see "Using Background Images," at right).

Tinted Image Fill. Similar to Image Fill, this option lets you add a color tint to the background image. To make the color more or less transparent, use the Opacity slider in the Colors window.

Changing the Browser Background Color

At the bottom of the Page Inspector is a color well for customizing the background color of the browser window. This is the area outside the dimensions of your Web page: if you imagine your Web page as a sheet of paper, the browser background color is the color of the desk on which the paper rests.

Visitors to your site who have relatively small displays may not even see the browser background color, but those lucky folks with 30-inch Apple Cinema Displays are quite likely to.

Normally, the browser background color is white, but you can change the color by clicking the Browser Background color well and then specifying a new color. Note that you won't see the new color in iWeb—you'll need to publish your site and view it in a browser in order to see the color.

Tip: To pick up a color that is present elsewhere on your Web page, click the magnifying glass in the Colors window, and then click on the color you want to

match. This trick works in any Mac program that uses the Colors window.

Creating Background Textures

Web browsers have a cool capability: they can repeat, or *tile*, a small image so that it completely fills the background of the Web page.

Web designers take advantage of tiles to create page backgrounds that have interesting textures or patterns. Because a Web browser can tile a small image, the Web designer doesn't have to worry about creating a massive background graphic that's big enough to accommodate any size of browser window.

You can download an astronomical quantity of free page-background textures from a variety of Web sites. Do a Google search for *web page backgrounds*, and prepare to spend a lot of time exploring.

Once you've found a pattern you like, drag it to your desktop. Then drag that icon into the image well of the Page Inspector, (see the opposite page) and choose the Tile option from the pop-up menu.

You'll find a lot of garish, busy background patterns out there. Avoid them—they'll make your page look amateurish and will impair the legibility of your text.

Using Background Images

Adding a background image or texture to a Web page can be a nice way to dress it up—provided that the image or texture doesn't impair the legibility of the page's text.

To add a background image to a page, choose Image Fill from the Page Background pop-up menu in the Page Inspector. Then add the image and specify how you want iWeb to display it on the background of the Web page.

Add an image to the image well. Here, I'm dragging a photo from the media browser, but you can also drag an image from any location on your hard drive. You can also click the Choose button and locate the image in the subsequent dialog box.

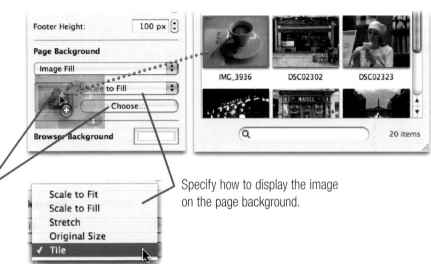

Specify how to display the image on the page background.

Here's a look at each image-fill option.

Scale to Fill. iWeb enlarges the image to fill the page dimensions; the outer portions of the image are cropped off. This is the most useful option when you want an image to fill a page.

For this example, I added a solid white shape to the navigation bar so that its text didn't appear superimposed over the image.

Scale to Fit. iWeb displays the entire image, with no cropping. With horizontally oriented images, this option is likely to leave large borders above and below the image.

Stretch. iWeb fills the page with the image, altering the image's proportions to avoid any cropping. The image is likely to have a squished or stretched appearance.

Original Size. iWeb displays the image at its original size. For large images, such as digital camera photos, you're likely to see only a small part of the image on the page.

Tile. iWeb repeats the image across the background. Use this option to create background textures, as described on the opposite page.

Creating a Photo Album

With iWeb photo pages, you can create online photo albums with a few mouse clicks. The album pages contain rows of small thumbnail images that your visitors can click to see larger versions. They can also view a slide show.

Thanks to the way the iLife programs work together, you can start your foray into photo albums in either iPhoto or iWeb. In iPhoto, stash some photos in an album and then sequence them in the order you want them to appear. Then use the Share menu or iWeb button to send the photos to iWeb.

Prefer to start in iWeb? Create a new page and choose a Photos page style. Then drag photos into the placeholder area, or better yet, drag an entire roll or album from the media browser.

iWeb places a caption beneath each thumbnail image. And here's another good reason to use iPhoto to assign titles to your photos (page 120): iWeb uses a photo's title as its caption.

A photo page in iWeb can contain up to 99 photos. You can customize numerous aspects of a photo page: whether to display two or three columns of thumbnail images; how much room to leave for text captions; the kind of frame you want to appear around each thumbnail; and more. And you can apply all the other design techniques described earlier in this chapter: add text, change backgrounds, and tweak formatting.

Creating a Photo Page within iPhoto

Step 1. Stash the photos you want to publish in an album. If you're lazy, you can also simply select a series of photos in your library.

Step 2. Choose Share > Send to iWeb > Photo Page or, from the iWeb button at the bottom of the iPhoto window, choose Photo Page.

Step 3. In iWeb, choose a template, then click Choose or press Return.

Creating a Photo Page within iWeb

Step 1. Choose File > New Page or click the ⊞ button in the lower-left corner of the iWeb window.

Step 2. Choose a template, then select its Photos page style, and then click Choose or press Return.

Step 3. Drag photos into the thumbnails placeholder area. Here, I'm using the media browser to add an entire iPhoto album.

Notes and Tips

Mix and match. You can mix and match approaches: create a photo page using iPhoto, then switch to iWeb to add additional photos to the existing page. You can't take the opposite route, however—when you send photos from iPhoto to iWeb, the photos are always added to a *new* photo page.

Rearrange and refine. To change the order of the photos in a photo page, simply drag the photos. To remove a photo, select it and press the Delete key. To change a photo's caption, click it and start typing.

Learn how to customize iWeb slide shows.
www.macilife.com/iweb

Photo Page Tips and Techniques

Customizing the Photo Grid

To customize the grid of thumbnail photos that iWeb displays, select any thumbnail in the grid and then display the Graphic Inspector.

You can add a frame to the thumbnail images. Scroll through the list to find one you like, then click it to apply.

I like a two-column grid: its thumbnails are larger.

Want lengthy captions? Increase the caption height by dragging the slider.

To add a drop shadow to each thumbnail, check the Shadow box, then adjust the settings.

To have a box appear around each thumbnail, choose a line style from the Stroke pop-up menu, then specify a color and line width.

You can reduce the opacity of the photo thumbnails to make them appear faint, and I'd like to hear a good reason why you'd want to.

Moving the Grid

You can move the photo thumbnail grid by dragging it elsewhere on the webpage canvas. You can also resize the grid, although not by dragging its selection handles; instead, use the Metrics Inspector.

Customizing Captions

You can use the Text Inspector and the Fonts panel to customize your thumbnail captions. You might want the captions to be left-aligned, instead of centered, below each thumbnail. Or you might want to use a different font for the captions.

You can change these attributes for individual thumbnail captions, but for the sake of good taste, it's best to use the same formatting for all captions on a page.

To apply formatting changes to every caption, you need to select the thumbnail grid, but *without* selecting any thumbnails. Click near one of the edges of the grid. If you also end up selecting a thumbnail, click closer to one of the grid's edges.

Publishing a Photocast

If you drag a photocast album into a photo page, iWeb adds its photos as it would with an ordinary album. This works whether you drag a photocast album that you created or one that you've subscribed to.

You can also create a button that will allow your site's visitors to subscribe to the photocast. To do so, drag the photocast album to a spot on the page *other than* the thumbnail grid. When you release the mouse button, iWeb adds the button.

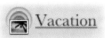

For the lowdown on photocasts, see pages 168–171.

Slide Shows

When a visitor to your site clicks the Start Slideshow button on a photo page, Apple's .Mac service creates a glitzy display: each photo is on a black background with that ubiquitous reflection effect, and a row of thumbnail images appears when you move the mouse toward the top of the window.

Some intrepid iWeb users have figured out ways to customize the slide show display to remove that reflection effect. You'll find links to instructions on my Web site.

Creating a Blog

The term *blog* sounds like something that would make you reach for the stain remover, but it's actually a corrupt contraction of the words *Web log*.

My *Webster's* defines *blog* thusly: "A personal Web site that provides updated headlines and news articles of other sites that are of interest to the user; also may include journal entries, commentaries and recommendations compiled by the user."

I'll build on that definition to add that a blog's contents, called *postings* or *entries*, are generally presented in reverse chronological order: the most recent entry appears first. I'll also add that blogs almost always use RSS to let readers subscribe and have new postings delivered to their RSS newsreaders.

And I'll amend the definition to remove the word *personal*. It's true that blogs are often personal journals. But businesses of all kinds have embraced blogging, too, relying on blogs to conduct conversations with their customers and engage in a dialog that's often more honest than the public relations people would like (see *Publish & Prosper: Blogging for Your Business*, by DL Byron and Steve Broback, New Riders, 2006).

iWeb makes it easy to create a basic blog. Apple's .Mac service even handles the technicalities behind creating RSS feeds.

The process of publishing podcasts is nearly identical to that of publishing blogs; simply choose the Podcast page style instead of Blog. For details on podcast production, see the previous chapter.

Creating a New Blog

Step 1. Choose File > New Page or click the ⊞ button.

Step 2. Choose a template, click its Blog page style, then click Choose or press Return.

The Entries page appears.

To add a new blog entry, click Add Entry. iWeb creates a new page, which appears below the list of entries.

Each blog entry appears here. To edit an entry, select it. To change an entry's title, double-click it.

Take it back: to delete a blog entry, select the entry and then click Delete Entry. Change your mind? Choose Undo to resurrect it.

Create your blog entry here. You can replace placeholder text and graphics and perform all the other design tasks described earlier in this chapter.

To resize the list of entries, drag the horizontal separator up or down.

Notes and Tips

Today's the day. It's common for each entry in a blog to be stamped with the day of its posting. When you create a new blog entry, iWeb gives it the current date.

Room for everyone. You can have as many blogs and podcasts within a Web site as you like. Have several family members (or colleagues) with something to say? Each one can have his or her own blog.

The Elements of a Blog

In the course of managing a blog, iWeb creates and manages three types of pages.

Blog Page

The blog page is the main lobby for your blog. Visitors see excerpts of up to 50 of your most recent entries, and each excerpt has a link that lets them read the full entry. (You can customize the number and size of excerpts as described below.)

In the Site Organizer pane, the main blog page has the name *Blog*, although you can rename it as you can any iWeb page.

Entry Pages

An *entry page* contains one blog posting: your rant of the day (or the hour). Each entry page also contains links, labeled *Previous* and *Next*, that allow your site's visitors to step through each of your blog entries. You can delete these links if you'd prefer that your visitors use your blog and archive pages to navigate.

Archive Page

The *archive page* is the dusty newspaper morgue where old back issues live; that is, it's where visitors can access all of your blog posts, not just recent ones.

Customizing the Main Page

You can use the Blog & Podcast Inspector to specify how many excerpts appear on your blog's main page as well as the length of each excerpt.

In the Site Organizer pane, select the blog's main page, then display the Inspector and click its [RSS] button.

You can show as few as one excerpt or as many as 50. To avoid creating a huge, slow-loading page, think twice about showing more than five or 10 excerpts.

Control how much of each entry iWeb excerpts. If you drag the slider all the way to the left, your visitors will see only the entry title and the *Read More* link.

Tip: Want to reduce the amount of clicking your visitors must do to read your latest dispatch? Show only one excerpt, and drag the Excerpt Length slider all the way to the right. Your latest entry will

appear by itself, in its entirety, on the blog's main page.

The RSS Angle

Normally, iWeb adds a Subscribe button to your blog's main page. Visitors to your site can use this button to subscribe to the RSS feed that Apple's .Mac service creates for your blog. If you don't want to offer an RSS subscription option, delete the Subscribe button.

Excerpts and RSS. The excerpts that iWeb creates for each entry are also what subscribers see when they update your subscription. If you want to deliver the entire blog post to your subscribers—a nicety that many newsreader users appreciate—drag the Excerpt Length slider all the way to the right.

Publishing Your Site

When your site is ready for its debut, you'll *publish* it on Apple's .Mac service. Click iWeb's Publish button, and iWeb translates your designs into *HTML* (Hypertext Markup Language, the coding language used to describe the appearance of Web pages). iWeb also prepares your graphics, and then transfers everything to Apple's servers, which dish it out the world.

Similarly, when you change your site—create a new blog entry, fix a typo, or add an entire set of pages—you must publish it in order for your changes to become available. When you publish a site that you've updated, iWeb transfers only those pages that changed since the last time you published the site.

Normally, the sites you publish are available for anyone to see. But you can also post a guard at the door: using the Site Inspector, you can specify a user name and password that visitors must specify before they can see your site.

iWeb meshes best with .Mac, but you can also publish your sites to a folder on your hard drive. You might take this path if you plan to modify iWeb's pages yourself, distribute a site on a CD or DVD-ROM, or transfer your site to a different Internet provider.

To Publish on .Mac

Before publishing your work, be sure that you've signed up for a .Mac account and entered your user name and password in the .Mac system preference.

Then, choose File > Publish to .Mac or click the [Publish] button.

A dialog box lectures you to verify that you have the rights to publish your material. To avoid this legal nag in the future, check the *Don't show this again* box, then click Continue.

After iWeb publishes the site, it displays a dialog box that lets you visit the site or send an announcement email containing the site's address.

Notes and Tips

Join the group. On .Mac, *groups* are private areas that only members can visit. You can publish your iWeb site to a group, allowing only group members to see the site. In the Site Organizer, select the site that you want to publish to a group. Then, use the Site Inspector to assign a group to that site. You'll find more details in iWeb's help screens.

Assigning a password. To protect a site with a password, select the site in the Site Organizer, open the Inspector, click the [●] button, then click the Password button.

Use the Site panel to publish a site to a group, change a site's name, and monitor your iDisk usage.

Hire the guard: check the box.

Train him: specify the user name and password that visitors must enter. Every visitor will have the same user name; you can't specify different names for different visitors.

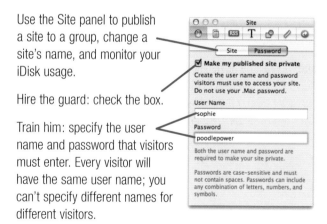

Get more tips for iWeb publishing.
www.macilife.com/iweb

Publishing Tips

Where Your Sites Live

iWeb stores your sites on your iDisk, the virtual storage locker that is included with your .Mac subscription. To view your iDisk, switch to the Finder, then choose Go > iDisk > My iDisk.

Within your iDisk is a folder named Web. Your iWeb-created sites are therein.

Publish Everything

When you publish to .Mac, iWeb transfers only those pages that changed since you last published. However, you can force iWeb to transfer everything: press the Option key, then choose File > Publish All to .Mac.

If you notice that links between your iWeb sites aren't working, try this technique to fix the problem.

Publishing to a Folder

To have iWeb publish your site on your hard drive, choose File > Publish to a Folder. A dialog box appears that lets you specify a location for the published site. Normally, when you publish to a folder, iWeb saves the site in the Sites folder within your home folder.

Note: If you'll be uploading the site to a Web server and your site contains RSS links, be sure to enter your site's URL in the Publish to a Folder dialog box. iWeb uses this URL to build the RSS feed to your site.

Each time you publish a site to a folder, iWeb generates every page in the site, whether the page changed or not. That can make it tricky to figure out which pages you need to upload to a Web server. Some iWeb users have developed cumbersome but serviceable workarounds for this; for links to them, see my Web site.

Clear Your Cache

You've changed a page and published it, but the page looks the same when you visit your site. That's probably because your Web browser has retained the previous version of the page in its *cache*. A browser keeps recently loaded graphics in its cache to avoid having to load them again should you revisit a page.

If you're using the Safari browser, you can empty the browser cache by choosing Safari > Empty Cache. If you'd rather not empty the entire cache, you can force Safari to reload the entire page by pressing the Shift key while clicking Safari's `c` button.

iWeb Tips

Adding Goodies

You can add several kinds of goodies to your pages.

It's a hit. A *hit counter* is a Web odometer that displays how many times a particular page has been viewed. To add a counter to a page, choose Insert > Button > Hit Counter. iWeb inserts the hit counter.

You can position the hit counter wherever you like, but be sure it fits entirely within the webpage canvas.

Notes: A hit counter works only if you serve your site through Apple's .Mac service. To reset the hit counter to zero, delete the hit counter, publish the page, then add a new hit counter and publish the page once more.

Keep in touch. Want to provide a convenient way for your site's visitors to email you? Add an Email Me button: choose Insert > Button > Email Me. When a visitor clicks that button, his or her email program will open a new message addressed to you.

If your site is served by .Mac, the message will be addressed to your .Mac mail account. If you use a different

server, the message will be addressed to whatever email address you have listed in the Me card of Mac OS X's address book program.

If you want incoming email messages to go to a different address, create a text or graphic hyperlink and, in the Link Inspector, choose An Email Message from the Link To pop-up menu. Specify the address and subject for the email in the boxes that appear.

Date and time. It's common for a Web page to contain a date listing when the page was last modified. When you want to date-stamp your pages, don't look at your calendar—let iWeb do the work. Click within a text box to create a blinking insertion point, then choose Insert > Date & Time. A dialog box appears giving you a choice of date and time formats. Select the one you want, then click Insert or press Return.

If you've worked on a page and would like to update its date or time stamp, Control-click on the page and choose Update Date & Time Now from the shortcut menu.

Playlists. Want to share a list of your favorite tunes with your site's visitors? Drag an iTunes playlist from the media browser into the webpage canvas. iWeb creates a set of links for each song.

When a visitor clicks a song's link (or link arrow), he or she will be taken to that song in the iTunes Music Store. You can reformat and resize the playlist, but avoid making it so narrow that a song's title takes more than one line to display. If a song's title spills over to a second line, the link may not work properly.

By the way, you can also link to any item on the iTunes Music Store by simply dragging the item from iTunes into the webpage canvas.

More goodies. With Chad Brantly's iWeb Enhancer, you can add other kinds of goodies to your iWeb sites: photos from Flickr, Google AdSense advertising, and more. With iComment, you can give your blog's visitors the opportunity to leave comments on your postings.

Get links to iWeb resources and templates.
www.macilife.com/iweb

GO TO WEB

Beyond Apple's Templates

Want to go beyond the templates that are built into iWeb? Go visit Suzanne Boben. A graphic designer who's apparently also a glutton for punishment, she hacked her way through iWeb's templates to figure out how they work. Then she wrote documentation describing how to modify them, and came up with her own line of templates—some of which are free.

Check out her amazing contributions to the iWeb world at www.11mystics.com.

Customize Your Guides

With the Preferences command, you can customize the alignment guides that iWeb displays as you drag items on the webpage canvas. You can change the color of the guides and you can have iWeb display guides at the edges of an object as well as at its center.

Activating this second option can make it easier to align items. (Apple's iWork '06 programs provide a similar convenience.)

From iWork to iWeb

Speaking of iWork, it's worth noting that you can paste elements created in Keynote or Pages into iWeb. Need a chart or a price list table on your Web page? Create it in Pages or Keynote, then select it, copy it, and paste it into iWeb.

Adding QuickTime Movies

Each iWeb template provides a page style designed specifically for holding a QuickTime movie. But you aren't restricted to just that page style. You can add a QuickTime movie to any iWeb page: simply drag it from the media browser or any location on your hard drive. If the movie is larger than 10MB, iWeb warns you that it may take a lifetime to download on slower connections.

As with graphics, movies can stand alone on a page or they can be in line with text. You might format a movie as an inline object if you want to have text wrap around it. For details on working with inline objects, see page 374.

If you drag a movie to the image placeholder in a blog entry, the movie becomes a video podcast.

Resizing a movie. After adding a movie to a page, you can resize it by dragging its selection handles. Making a movie appear smaller will *not* make it download any faster, so there's little point in shrinking your flicks. But making a movie appear larger can make up for the fact that movies compressed for the Web tend to have a small frame size. When you enlarge a movie, you'll notice some visual distortion, but depending on your movie's contents, you may find that to be a worthwhile tradeoff.

Audio only. You can also add an audio file to a Web page by dragging it from the media browser or any location on your hard drive.

Dealing with Blog URLs

When iWeb creates a blog entry page, it gives the page a ridiculously long URL. If you try to email that URL to a friend so he or she can read a specific entry, the link may not work—email programs are notorious for breaking links that take up more than one line.

The solution? TinyURL. Go to www.tinyurl.com, where you can paste a lengthy link and have it turned into a small one that you can email.

Index

Index

Index

390

Index

Index

Index

Reviewers and readers rave—
praise for previous editions of
The Macintosh iLife.

The book you're holding is the fifth edition of the original Macintosh digital hub book. Since its debut, *The Macintosh iLife* has become the top-selling book on iLife. Wonder why? Here's a sampling of what reviewers and readers have said about previous editions.

"The book is attractively laid out with plenty of pictures, sidebars and glossaries."

—*Leander Kahney, Wired News and author,* The Cult of Mac

"Jim Heid has created the best 'how to' book I have seen."

—*Arthur Arnold, Alaskan Apple Users Group*

"Jim Heid has been writing and teaching about the iLife applications for quite a while, and his expertise is visible on every page. If you want a great book that splendidly covers all the iLife applications, don't ask questions, just buy this book."

—*Tim Robertson, MyMac.com*

"The beautiful color illustrations jump out at you, making this book so enjoyable to read and so easy to follow at your computer."

—*Maria Arguello, Main Line Macintosh User Group*

"The layout of the book is highly accessible. Rather than imposing pages of unrelenting text, the book is filled with screenshots, diagrams and all sorts of helpful, easy-to-follow instructions. Even with all the pictures, this book is no lightweight. There is a wealth of information on all the iLife products."

—*R.C., on Amazon.com*

"Jim has done a great job distilling these feature rich applications down to their essence."

—*J.H., on Amazon.com*

"What a refreshing style of presentation!"

—*E.B.*

"This book is incredibly helpful for people just beginning on the Mac. It sets up each program separately and also shows you how to get the best use of all of them together."

—*A.P., on Amazon.com*